The Why of Consumption

CW01497528

This unique volume brings together contributions from leading scholars who have extended our knowledge of the "why" of consumption, in a world where consumption itself has become the defining phenomenon of human life and society. The authors draw from branches of psychology, decision theory, sociology, and cultural anthropology to present a diverse selection of new and critical perspectives on consumer motivation. Motivational factors implicated in a variety of consumption behaviors are discussed, including consumer decisions on brands and products; consumption of products, services, and time; compulsive buying; recycling behavior; and mutual influences between consumers and the mass media.

This multifaceted collection provides many penetrating insights for both expert and novice consumer researchers, from both academic and practitioner backgrounds.

S. Ratneshwar is Professor of Marketing and Ackerman Scholar at the School of Business, University of Connecticut. His articles have been widely published in major scholarly journals. He serves on the editorial boards of the *Journal of Consumer Research*, *Journal of the Academy of Marketing Science*, and *Journal of Interactive Marketing*.

David Glen Mick is the Robert Hill Carter Professor of Marketing at the McIntire School of Commerce, University of Virginia. His research has been widely published and has received best-article awards in leading journals such as the *Journal of Consumer Research* and the *Journal of Marketing*. He has also served as associate editor and then editor of the *Journal of Consumer Research*.

Cynthia Huffman teaches at the Wharton School of the University of Pennsylvania. She has published articles in several leading journals including the *Journal of Consumer Research* and the *Journal of Consumer Psychology*.

Routledge Interpretive Marketing Research
Edited by Stephen Brown
University of Ulster, Northern Ireland
and Barbara B. Stern
Rutgers, the State University of New Jersey, USA

Recent years have witnessed an 'interpretative turn' in marketing and consumer research. Methodologists from the humanities are taking their place alongside those drawn from the traditional social sciences.

Qualitative and literary modes of marketing discourse are growing in popularity. Art and aesthetics are increasingly firing the marketing imagination.

This series brings together the most innovative work in the burgeoning interpretative marketing research tradition. It ranges across the methodological spectrum from grounded theory to personal introspection, covers all aspects of the postmodern marketing 'mix', from advertising to product development, and embraces marketing's principal sub-disciplines.

The Why of Consumption

Contemporary perspectives on
consumer motives, goals, and desires

Edited by
**S. Ratneshwar, David Glen Mick, and
Cynthia Huffman**

 Routledge
Taylor & Francis Group

LONDON AND NEW YORK

First published 2000
by Routledge
2 Park Square, Milton Park, Abingdon, Oxon, OX14 4RN

Simultaneously published in the USA and Canada
by Routledge
711 Third Avenue, New York, NY 10017, USA

First published in paperback 2003

Routledge is an imprint of the Taylor & Francis Group, an informa business

British Library Cataloguing in Publication Data
A catalogue record for this book is available from the British Library

ISBN 0–415–31617–0

For Shuba, Cindy, and Doug –
the why of our lives

Contents

Figures and tables

Figures

Tables

Contributors

Eric Arnould is Professor of Marketing and Interim Director of the Agribusiness Program at the University of Nebraska-Lincoln despite the fact that he holds a PhD in Social Anthropology from the University of Arizona. He spent ten years trying to do less harm than good working on economic development problems in more than a dozen West African nations. Since 1990, he has been a full-time academic teaching about consumer behavior, marketing and globalization, and research employing qualitative data. His research interests include: market organization and development policy in West Africa, household forms and activities, consumption rituals, and service relationships. To his enduring surprise, Arnould's work appears in the three major US marketing journals and many other social science periodicals and books. Arnould is beginning a second term as associate editor of the *Journal of Consumer Research*. He has presented his research in numerous professional forums around the world.

Søren Askegaard was born in 1961. He is Professor of Marketing at SDU Odense University, Denmark. He has a Masters Degree in Social Sciences from Odense University, a post-graduate Diploma in Communication Studies from the Sorbonne University, Paris and a PhD in Business Studies from Odense University. Before his academic career, he was a life style analyst in Paris. His research interests are generally stuck in the field of consumer behavior analysis from a cultural perspective, globalization and branding processes, although he finds it difficult to concentrate very long on one particular topic. He has received two well-deserved (if you ask his wife) Danish research awards. His work does not appear in most major journals, but he once contributed to "The Flag Bulletin."

Richard P. Bagozzi is the J. Hugh Liedtke Professor of Management and Professor of Psychology at Rice University. He earned his PhD from Northwestern University. He has published numerous articles in marketing, psychology, organization behavior, and health journals. He has written several books including *Principles of Marketing Management, Marketing Management, Basic Principles of Marketing Research, Advanced Methods of*

Marketing Research, and the *Social Psychology of Consumer Behavior*. His awards include the O'Dell Award for the best article in the *Journal of Marketing Research*, the Maynard Award for best article on Marketing Theory in the *Journal of Marketing*, the Paul D. Converse Award, a lifetime award for contributions to marketing science by the American Marketing Association, the Fellow in Consumer Behavior award by the Association for Consumer Research, the Distinguished Educator Award by the AMA and Richard D. Irwin Co., and an Honorary Doctorate from the University of Lausanne.

Hans Baumgartner is Professor of Marketing in the Smeal College of Business at the Pennsylvania State University. He received his PhD in marketing from Stanford University and has been a visiting professor at K.U. Leuven in Belgium and the University of Innsbruck in Austria. At Penn State he teaches courses in consumer behavior and research methodology. His research focuses on affective and motivational influences on consumer behavior, but he is also interested in methodological issues, particularly structural equation modeling, cross-cultural measurement problems, and citation analysis. He has published articles on these topics in the *Journal of Consumer Research*, *Journal of Marketing Research*, *Journal of Marketing*, *Journal of Consumer Psychology*, *International Journal of Research in Marketing*, *Marketing Letters*, *Psychology & Marketing*, *Journal of Business Research*, *Journal of Economic Psychology*, *Sociological Methods & Research*, *Organizational Behavior and Human Decision Processes*, *Educational and Psychological Measurement*, *European Journal of Social Psychology*, *Cognition and Emotion*, and *Journal of Economic Literature*. Between 1997 and 1999 he was associate editor of the *Journal of Consumer Research*, and he currently serves on the editorial boards of the *Journal of Consumer Research* and *International Journal of Research in Marketing*.

Russell Belk is N. Eldon Tanner Professor in the David Eccles School of Business at the University of Utah. He has taught there since 1979 and has had previous appointments at the University of Illinois; Temple University; the University of British Columbia; the University of Craiova, Romania; Africa University, Mutare, Zimbabwe; and Edith Cowan University, Perth, Australia. His PhD is from the University of Minnesota. He is president of the International Society of Marketing and Development, past president of the Association for Consumer Research, and a fellow in the American Psychological Association, and the Association for Consumer Research. He is past recipient of the University of Utah Distinguished Research Professorship and two Fulbright Fellowships. He currently edits *Research in Consumer Behavior*, has been an advisory editor for the *Journal of Consumer Research* and an associate editor for the *Journal of Economic Psychology* and *Visual Sociology*. He is currently associate editor of the *Journal of Consumer Culture*. He has also served on the editorial review boards of 25 journals, has written or edited 18 books or monographs, and has published over 300 articles, papers, and videotapes. His research primarily involves the meanings of possessions, materialism, collecting, non-First World consumer culture, and gift-giving. Since the mid-1980s much of his research and writing has been qualitative and cross-cultural.

James R. Bettman is Burlington Industries Professor of Business Administration at the Fuqua School of Business, Duke University. His BA in Mathematics-Economics and PhD in Administrative Sciences are from Yale University. Consumer decision-making has been his research focus, with recent emphases on constructive choice processes and the effect of emotion on choice. He has published three books, *An Information Processing Theory of Consumer Choice, The Adaptive Decision Maker,* and *Emotional Decisions: Tradeoff Difficulty and Coping in Consumer Choice.* Bettman's articles have appeared in the *Journal of Consumer Research, Journal of Marketing Research, Journal of Marketing, Management Science, Journal of Experimental Psychology: Learning, Memory, and Cognition, Journal of Risk and Uncertainty, Organizational Behavior and Human Decision Processes,* and *Administrative Science Quarterly,* among others. He has served as co-editor of the *Journal of Consumer Research* and is the current editor of *Monographs of the Journal of Consumer Research.*

Steven Brownstein is Assistant Professor of Marketing at Pace University's Lubin School of Business. He holds a BS in Microbiology from the University of Florida, a MS in Mathematics from Lehigh University, and a MBA from Baruch College, City University of New York. Steven is currently completing his PhD in Business Administration from Arizona State University. His research centers upon the lattice-theoretical and topological representation of cognitive systems of object-attribute relationships and the embedding of these structures within a formal mathematical logic. Steven has been a Kenneth A. Coney Memorial Scholar and Southwest Doctoral Consortium Fellow, and a recipient of the Center for Services Marketing Research grant from Arizona State University.

June Cotte is Assistant Professor of Marketing at the Ivey School of Business, University of Western Ontario. Cotte received her PhD in Marketing from the University of Connecticut in 1998. Her current work deals with two main areas: how perceptions of time influence consumption and work behavior, and emotional appeals in advertising. Cotte's articles have appeared, or will appear, in the *Journal of Managerial Psychology, Journal of Business Research, Journal of Strategic Marketing, Journal of Leisure Research* and various conference proceedings. In 1999, Cotte's dissertation received an Honorable Mention in the AMA/John A. Howard Dissertation competition.

Robin Coulter is Associate Professor of Marketing at the University of Connecticut. Coulter received her MBA and PhD in Marketing from the

University of Pittsburgh. Her research interests span a variety of areas, including advertising effects and effectiveness, customer responses to dissatisfaction in service relationships, cross-cultural consumer behavior, and the use of metaphor to better understand the meanings associated with consumer behavior and marketing phenomena, including goal setting and new product concepts. Her articles have appeared in the *Journal of Applied Psychology*, *Journal of Advertising*, *International Journal of Research in Marketing*, and elsewhere.

Maria L. Cronley is Assistant Professor of Marketing at Miami University (Ohio). She earned her PhD in Marketing from the University of Cincinnati in 2000. Her primary research interests include selective processing in consumer decision-making and persuasion processes. Her research has appeared in the *Journal of Consumer Psychology* and *Advances in Consumer Research*.

Jennifer Edson Escalas is Assistant Professor of Marketing at the University of Arizona. She earned her PhD in Business Administration from Duke University in 1996. Her research focuses on the use of narrative processing to create brand meaning and the effects of advertising narratives. She has published articles in the *Journal of Consumer Research*, *Journal of Consumer Psychology*, and *Journal of Public Policy and Marketing*.

Ronald J. Faber is Professor of Mass Communication and Co-Director of the Communication Research Division in the School of Journalism and Mass Communication at the University of Minnesota. He is also the editor of the *Journal of Advertising* and serves on the Editorial Boards of the *Journal of Consumer Research*, the *Journal of Consumer*, *Journal of Current Issues and Research in Advertising* and the *Interactive Journal of Advertising*. He received his PhD from the University of Wisconsin in Mass Communication. His current research focuses on compulsive buying and other forms of compulsive consumption, impulse buying and self-control, political advertising and third-person effect. His research has appeared in a wide variety of journals including the *Journal of Consumer Research*, *Journal of Clinical Psychiatry*, *Journal of Marketing*, *Journal of Advertising*, *Communication Research*, and the *American Behavioral Scientist*. Stories regarding his research have appeared in the New York Times, Washington Post, Wall Street Journal, Psychology Today, and American Demographics as well as on several television and radio programs.

Güliz Ger is Professor of Marketing at Bilkent University (Turkey). Ger received a MBA from Middle East Technical University in Turkey and a PhD in Marketing from Northwestern University. Her articles have appeared in *California Management Review*, *Journal of Material Culture*, *Journal of Economic Psychology*, *Journal of Consumer Policy*, *Journal of Public Policy and Marketing*, *International Journal of Research in Marketing*, and elsewhere. She co-edited *Consumption in Marketizing Economies*. Ger's recent work investigates consumption in transitional societies and among transitional groups (e.g. immigrants), Islamic consumption, consumption desires across cultures, cultural products and globalization, and product-country images. She is a member of the Board of Directors of the International Society of Marketing and Development, and departmental editor for the *Journal of International Business Studies*; she also serves on the editorial boards of various journals.

Elizabeth C. Hirschman is Professor II, Department of Marketing, School of Business, Rutgers University. Her primary research interests include semiotics, phenomenology, feminism, and popular culture. She has published articles in the *Journal of Consumer Research, Journal of Marketing Research, Journal of Marketing, Journal of Advertising, Journal of Advertising Research, Journal of Retailing, Harvard Business Review, American Journal of Semiotics, Semiotica* and the *Journal of Communications*, among others. Hirschman is a past President of the Association for Consumer Research and a Fellow of the Association for Consumer Research. This chapter is based on her recently published book, *Heroes, Monsters, and Messiahs*.

Cynthia Huffman teaches at the Wharton School of the University of Pennsylvania. She received her PhD in Marketing in 1991 at the University of Minnesota. Her research focuses on goals, their influence on learning and cognitive structure, and their relationships to various marketing applications. Her projects include researching methods to improve both product organization and the process of preference elicitation under high variety and mass customization strategies, understanding how consumer goals shift and change over time under various circumstances, and the effects of providing different types of information to aid in salesperson performance evaluation. Huffman has published articles in various journals including the *Journal of Consumer Research*, the *Journal of Retailing*, the *Journal of Consumer Psychology*, and *Psychology & Marketing*.

Frank R. Kardes is a Professor of Marketing at the University of Cincinnati. He received his PhD in Psychology from Indiana University and is a former faculty member of the Sloan School of Management at M.I.T. His research focuses on consumer judgment and inference processes, persuasion and advertising, the pioneering brand advantage, and consumer and managerial judgments based on limited evidence. His research has appeared in many leading journals and he serves on the editorial boards of the *Journal of Consumer Research*, the *Journal of Consumer Psychology*, the *International Journal of Marketing Research*, and *Marketing Letters*. He is a former co-editor of *Advances in Consumer Research* and the *Journal of Consumer Psychology*, and a former associate editor of the *Journal of Consumer Research*. Kardes is a Fellow of the American Psychological Association, the American Psychological Society, the Society for Consumer Psychology, and the Society for Personality and Social Psychology.

Jerome B. Kernan (PhD, University of Illinois) is an emeritus professor at George Mason University.

Mary Frances Luce is an Associate Professor of Marketing at the University of Pennsylvania's Wharton School. She earned a PhD degree from Duke University in 1994, and her chapter co-authors were her dissertation advisors. Her primary research interest involves how individuals cope when they have to make decisions that are inherently, negatively emotion-laden content. Her articles have appeared in the *Journal of Consumer Research*, the *Journal of Marketing Research*, *Marketing Science*, the *Journal of Experimental Psychology: Learning, Memory and Cognition*, *Organizational Behavioral and Human Decision Processes*, and *Management Science*.

David Glen Mick is the Robert Hill Carter Professor of Marketing, at the McIntire School of Commerce, University of Virginia. He has held previous faculty positions at the University of Wisconsin, University of Florida, Indiana University, Dublin City University, and the Copenhagen Business School. His research has primarily centered on the nature and role of meaning in consumer behavior, particularly in the domains of advertising processing, self-gifts, and the consumption of technological products. His research has appeared in the *Journal of Consumer Research*, *Journal of Marketing*, *Harvard Business Review*, *International Journal of Research in Marketing*, *Journal of Retailing*, and *Semiotica*, among other outlets. He has also published an array of book chapters and conference papers. His publications have received a Best Article award in the *Journal of Consumer Research*, an Honorable Mention award in the Robert Ferber Competition for dissertation-based research in the *Journal of Consumer Research*, and the Maynard Award for best article on Marketing Theory in the *Journal of Marketing*. He is a member of the editorial review boards of the *Journal of Consumer Research* and the *Journal of Marketing Research*, and he has served previously as associate editor and then editor of the *Journal of Consumer Research*.

John W. Payne is the Joseph J. Ruvane, Jr. Professor of Business Administration at the Fuqua School of Business, Duke University. Payne received a PhD in Psychology from the University of California, Irvine. His main area of study is individual decision behavior. He has studied consumer choice, risk taking, stress effects on decision-making, contingent valuation of natural resources, jury decision making, and probabilistic judgments.

Rik Pieters is Professor of Marketing in the department of Marketing at Tilburg University (the Netherlands). He holds a PhD in Psychology from Leiden University. Rik has been a visiting professor at the Universities of Florida, Missouri, Innsbruck, and Pennsylvania State University. His research interests focus on attention processes and satisfaction formation, as well as on attitude-behavior relationships. His publications appear among others in *Journal of Marketing Research, Journal of Consumer Research, International Journal of Research in Marketing,* and *Organizational Behavior and Human Decision Processes.*

Linda L. Price (PhD University of Texas, Austin) is the E.J. Faulkner Professor of Agribusiness and Marketing and Marketing Department Chair at University of Nebraska-Lincoln. Her research interests focus on the social context of marketplace behaviors and consumers as emotional, imaginative and creative agents. Her research appears in the leading journals in marketing and consumer behavior including *Journal of Consumer Research* and *Journal of Marketing.* She is co-author of *Consumers,* a text exploring worldwide consumer behavior patterns. Over the past several years she has served on the editorial boards of *Journal of Consumer Research, Journal of Marketing* and *Journal of Public Policy and Marketing.*

S. Ratneshwar is Professor of Marketing and Ackerman Scholar at the School of Business, University of Connecticut. He received his PhD from Vanderbilt University. His research interests include consumer goals and motivation, judgment and decision-making, categorization and memory processes, time consumption, persuasion and advertising, and interactive marketing. His articles have appeared in *Journal of Consumer Research, Journal of Marketing Research, Journal of Marketing, International Journal of Research in Marketing, Journal of Consumer Psychology, Journal of the Academy of Marketing Science,* and *Marketing Letters,* among others. He serves on the editorial boards of the *Journal of Consumer Research, Journal of the Academy of Marketing Science,* and *Journal of Interactive Marketing.*

Peter H. Reingen is the Davis Distinguished Research Professor of Marketing at Arizona State University. He received his PhD in Business from the University of Cincinnati in 1974. Prior to his current appointment, he served on the faculties of the University of Houston, University of South Carolina, and Iona College. Reingen's current research interests center on interdisciplinary, multi-method approaches to the study of consumer behavior and marketing strategy. His work has appeared in the *Journal of Marketing Research, Journal of Consumer Research, Journal of Marketing, Journal of Consumer Psychology,* and *Journal of Applied Psychology.* Reingen is the co-author of two Ferber Award articles and an article that received the 1999 Best Paper Award of papers published in the *Journal of Consumer Research* in 1996. He currently serves on the editorial review boards of the *Journal of Consumer Research* and the *Journal of Consumer Psychology.*

Dennis W. Rook is Professor of Clinical Marketing in the Marshall School of Business, University of Southern California. Rook received his PhD in Marketing from Northwestern University's Kellogg Graduate School of Management in 1983, where he concentrated in studying consumer behavior through uses of qualitative research methods. His published research has appeared in the *Journal of Consumer Research, Research in*

Consumer Behavior, and Advances in Consumer Research. He has served on the editorial board of the Journal of Consumer Research since 1988.

Ajay K. Sirsi (PhD in Marketing, Arizona State University, 1994) is Associate Professor of Marketing at the Schulich School of Business, York University, where he teaches Marketing Research, Consumer Behaviour, Business-to-Business Marketing, Marketing Management, Retail Marketing Strategies, and Services Marketing. Sirsi has published his work in the *Journal of Consumer Research*, *Canadian Journal of Marketing Research*, the *Journal of Health Care Marketing*, the *Journal of Hospital Marketing*, and the *Journal of Professional Services Marketing*. His 1996 paper in the *Journal of Consumer Research* won both the Ferber Award and the Best Paper Award.

Dirk Smeesters is Assistant Professor at Tilburg University (the Netherlands). He received his training in Psychology (Licentiate, PhD) at K.U. Leuven (Belgium). His research interests are in the fields of social psychology and consumer behavior, and more specifically in the field of automatic processes, social cognition, social dilemmas, judgment and decision-making, and consumer motivation. His research is to appear in the *Journal of Personality* and *Social Psychology* and other journals.

Barbara B. Stern is Professor II and Chair of the Marketing Department at Rutgers, The State University of New Jersey, Faculty of Management, Newark. She has published articles in the *Journal of Marketing*, *Journal of Consumer Research*, *Journal of Advertising*, and other publications. She is on the editorial boards of the *Journal of Marketing*, *Journal of Consumer Research*, *Journal of Advertising*, and other publications, and is the editor of Marketing Theory. Her research has introduced principles of literary criticism into the study of marketing, consumer behavior, and advertising. Additionally, she has focused on gender issues from the perspective of feminist literary criticism, using feminist deconstruction to analyze values encoded in advertising text.

Craig J. Thompson is Churchill Professor of Marketing at the University of Wisconsin - Madison. He joined the UW - Madison faculty in 1991 after completing his doctoral work at the University of Tennessee. His research focuses on the phenomenology of consumption, the construction of identity though consumption with a particular emphasis on gender, and postmodern trends in consumer culture. His research has been published in the *Journal of Consumer Research*, *Journal of Marketing Research*, *Consumption, Markets, & Culture*, *Journal of Public Policy and Marketing*, *Journal of Advertising*, *International Journal of Research in Marketing*, *European Journal of Marketing*, *Psychology & Marketing*, *Advances in Consumer Research*, and he has contributed chapters to several edited books on consumption. He has co-authored a book entitled *The Phenomenology of Everyday Life*. He is on the editorial boards of the *Journal of Consumer Research*, *Journal of Public Policy & Marketing*, and *Consumption, Markets, & Culture*. Thompson is associate editor of the *Journal of Consumer Research*.

Pierre (Piet) Vanden Abeele is Professor of Marketing at the Faculty of Economics and Applied Economics, and Professor of Economic Psychology at the Department of Psychology, at the Katholieke Universiteit Leuven in Belgium. He is Dean of the Faculty of Economics and Applied Economics at K.U. Leuven. He received his training in Applied Economics and in Psychology at Leuven, and holds an MS in Statistics and a PhD in Business Administration from Stanford University. His research has been published in *Marketing Science, Journal of Marketing Research, Journal of Consumer Research, International Journal of Research in Marketing, Journal of Retailing,* and *Journal of Economic Psychology*. He is a former editor of *IJRM* and currently chairs the Commission for Advertising Ethics of the Belgian Advertising Council.

James C. Ward is Professor of Marketing at Arizona State University, Tempe, Arizona. He received his doctoral degree from the University of Minnesota. His research interests include the relations between social and psychological processes in consumer decision processes, consumer reasoning and categorization processes, and environmental psychology. He has published in the *Journal of Consumer Research, Journal of Marketing Research,* and *Journal of Marketing* as well as other outlets.

Luk Warlop is Associate Professor of Marketing at the K.U. Leuven, Belgium. He received a Licentiate degree in Psychology and a MBA from K.U. Leuven, and a PhD in Marketing from the University of Florida. His research interests are in the areas of consumer decision-making, learning, and persuasion. His research has been published in the *International Journal of Research in Marketing, Journal of Consumer Research, Journal of Consumer Psychology, Marketing Letters, Management Science, Journal of Personality and Social Psychology,* and *Accounting Organizations and Society*. He serves on the editorial board of the *International Journal of Research in Marketing*.

Gerald Zaltman is the Joseph C. Wilson Professor of Business Administration at the Harvard Business School. He is a member of Harvard University's interdisciplinary initiative, "Mind, Brain, and Behavior," and Co-Director of the Harvard Business School's Mind of the Market Laboratory. Zaltman developed the patented research tool known as ZMET (Zaltman Metaphor Elicitation Technique) being used by major corporations to understand the mental models underlying customer and manager thinking and behavior. He is author or co-author of fourteen books including, most recently, *How Customers Think: Essential Insights into the Mind of the Market*. He has also edited or co-edited twelve other books and has published extensively in major academic journals. Zaltman has served as President of the Association for Consumer Research, and serves on the editorial boards of numerous journals in marketing and the social sciences. He is widely recognized for his contributions to both research and teaching and received the American Marketing Association's Richard D. Irwin Distinguished Marketing Educator Award in 1989, the Association for

Consumer Research Distinguished Fellow Award in 1990, and the Knowledge Utilization Society's Thomas J. Kiresuk Award for Excellence in Scientific Research in 1992. Zaltman earned his PhD in Sociology from John Hopkins University and his MBA and Bachelor's degree from the University of Chicago.

Marcel Zeelenberg (PhD in Psychology, University of Amsterdam) is Professor of Social Psychology at Tilburg University (the Netherlands). He previously held positions at Eindhoven University of Technology (the Netherlands), at Sussex University (the United Kingdom) and at the Marketing Department of Tilburg University. His research interests are in anticipated emotions and actual emotional experiences and their interaction with consumer behavior. His publications appear in the *Journal of Personality and Social Psychology*, *Journal of Consumer Research*, *Cognition and Emotion* and elsewhere.

Acknowledgments

We gratefully acknowledge the help of the numerous individuals whose dedicated efforts and strong enthusiasm made this book possible. We thank Stephen Brown and Barbara Stern, who encouraged us to pursue this project with Routledge. We are also very grateful to the following chapter reviewers who offered timely, astute, and highly constructive comments: Eric Arnould, Søren Askegaard, Rajeev Batra, April Benson, Steve Brown, Fuat Firat, Eileen Fischer, Susan Fournier, Curt Haugtvedt, Beth Hirschman, Morris Holbrook, Doug Holt, Carol Kaufman, John Mowen, Rebecca Ratner, Sharon Shavitt, Jonathan Schroeder, Barbara Stern, Craig Thompson, and George Zinkhan. We thank Jane Scott for her patient and painstaking efforts in getting the manuscript ready for publication. Thanks also to Lisa Ricci for her help in this project. We are also grateful to the entire staff at Routledge and Swales & Willis for their help and support. Finally, we are deeply indebted to the many accomplished scholars who agreed to write the chapters in this volume.

S.R.
D.G.M.
C.H.

1 Introduction

The "why" of consumption

S. Ratneshwar, David Glen Mick, and Cynthia Huffman

What is the nature of motives, goals, and desires that prompt consumption behaviors? Why do consumers buy and consume particular products, brands, and services from the multitude of alternatives afforded by their environments? How do consumers think and feel about their strivings and cravings and how do they translate these pursuits into actions? And what explanations might we offer for differences in consumer motives and goals across individuals and situations? These are central questions in any theory of consumer behavior, and this book attempts to provide a few answers.

Considering our topic, it seems appropriate to first say a little more about the "why" of this project. The three of us were drawn together by our complementary research perspectives and the shared perception that there was a strong need for a volume that would do justice to the truly multifaceted nature of consumer motivation. We were aware that consumer researchers employing many different theories and methodologies were addressing this area. We felt the field needed a collection of articles that would provide perspective, take stock of recent findings, offer appropriate theoretical frameworks, and suggest future research directions. We wanted to put together a volume that included many of the leading voices that are extending knowledge of the why of consumption in a world where consumption itself has become – according to many observers – the central and defining phenomena of human life and societies. With these objectives in mind, we approached some of the best-known scholars in consumer behavior. Our targets were people we respected and people who reflected the plurality of perspectives and methods we desired. We were delighted by the uniformly favorable and enthusiastic responses we obtained.

The resulting collection of chapters in this book presents many diverse ideas about consumer motivation and how it might be studied. Our authors draw on multiple literatures including cognitive, social, clinical, and humanistic psychology; behavioral decision-making theory; economics; communication science; sociology; and cultural anthropology. They build on the work of pioneers such as Alderson (1957), Dichter (1964), Freud (1923/1957), Howard and Sheth (1969), Levy (1981), Lewin (1936), Maslow

(1970), Miller, Gallanter, and Pribram (1960), Newell and Simon (1972), and Veblen (1899).

We asked our authors to stake out bold and interesting positions and to avoid mechanical literature reviews. The book has no pretensions of being a comprehensive "Handbook of Consumer Motivation" – some important aspects of this area such as variety-seeking behavior, impulse buying, and personality trait theory are either missing or accorded less priority. Nevertheless, the chapters presented here provide an up-to-date snapshot of the current state of knowledge concerning numerous key issues on the why of consumption. More importantly, perhaps, *our* motives and goals for this project will have been fulfilled if this volume stimulates further penetrating insights in future research on this fascinating and elemental topic.

Organization of the book

A general organizing framework for the book is shown in Figure 1.1. The central concern of all of the chapters in this book is the *why* of consumption behaviors. Concepts such as motives, goals, and desires are employed for describing the *why*. The reader might wonder, the why of *what?* Our authors discuss and explain motivational factors implicated in a variety of consumption phenomena including consumer decision-making; consumption of products, services, and time; compulsive buying; disposition of the remains of consumption; and mutual influences between consumers and marketing institutions such as the mass media.

Several of the chapters also address linkages between the *why* and the *how,* and the *what* and the *how,* by inquiring into cognitive and affective processes which have a symbiotic relationship with consumer motives, goals, desires, and actions. An important premise in many of the chapters is also that to get at the *why* question we need to examine the *who:* differences among individuals, households, social groups, genders, religions, nations, and cultures. Finally, some of the chapters stress that consumption motives and behaviors are located in time and space, both physical and psychological. Therefore, the authors of these chapters emphasize the *when* and the *where* in their explanations by invoking situational and contextual factors.

Chapters Two to Nine offer specific theoretical frameworks, perspectives, and points of view. They also often summarize relevant empirical findings. Collectively, these chapters provide diverse perspectives and approaches for getting at the central *why* question. Chapters Ten to Twelve extend our domain beyond the usual buying and consuming of goods and services, and they do so in three different directions. Chapters Thirteen to Fifteen mainly offer innovative methodological tools for the study of consumer motives and goals. They also offer valuable conceptual and substantive insights that complement the previous chapters. Chapters Sixteen and Seventeen provide commentaries on the preceding chapters.

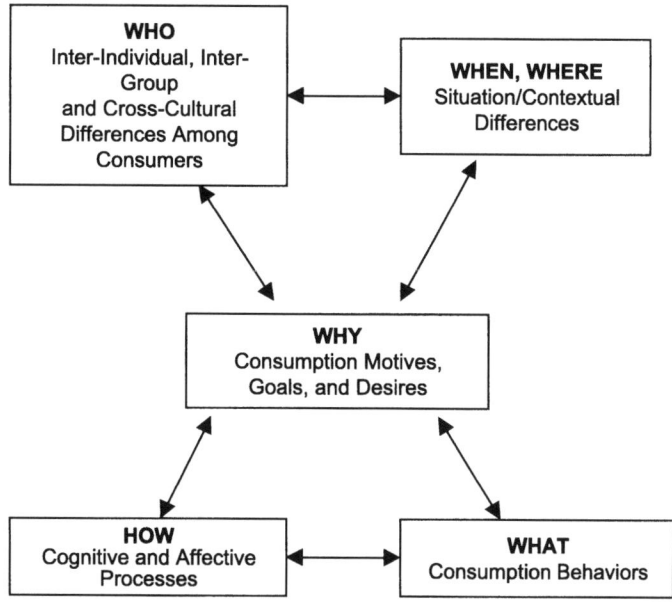

Figure 1.1 The "why" of consumption.

A preview of what follows

In Chapter Two, Huffman, Ratneshwar, and Mick put forward an integrative framework that addresses the hierarchical structure of consumer goals as well as the processes by which goals are determined. Their six-level model of consumer goal structure spans the realms of being, doing, and having. Goal determination processes include top-down ("incorporation") and bottom-up ("abstraction") influences among goals at different levels, as well as the influence of contextual factors on goals ("adaptation"). Huffman *et al.* also discuss the dynamics of goal change and how consumers might deal with goal conflict. Their framework, when considered as a whole, focuses on the *why* and *how* of consumption decisions and actions, but also links these factors to *who* (especially the self), *when*, and *where* (situation/context).

In Chapter Three, Bagozzi, Baumgartner, Pieters, and Zeelenberg examine the linkages between emotions and goal-directed behavior. In contrast to the cognitive, problem-solving perspective found in Chapter Two, Bagozzi *et al.* emphasize the multi-faceted role of affect and emotions in explaining *why* and *how* people strive to achieve goals. They offer an innovative taxonomy for research in this area wherein (1) emotions are conceptualized in terms of either underlying dimensions or discrete categories, and (2) behavioral effects deal with either currently experienced emotions or anticipated future emotions. They then discuss unresolved issues and a research agenda for the field to move toward an integrated conceptualization of the role of emotions in a theory of goal-directed behavior.

In Chapter Four, Luce, Bettman, and Payne offer a different viewpoint on the relationship between affect and goals by examining *how* the minimizing of negative emotions in decision-making can be an important meta-goal in and of itself. With this meta-goal in mind, they discuss necessary modifications in the standard effort-accuracy paradigm for studying decision trade-offs. Luce *et al.* first summarize the antecedents of emotional trade-off difficulty. Next, they discuss how decision-makers cope with emotion-laden trade-offs. The consequences of such coping implicate dependent variables such as information-processing effort, processing patterns, decision rules, and decision outcomes. Luce *et al.* suggest several intriguing propositions for both the antecedents and the consequences of trade-offs involving negative emotions. They also conclude with a discussion of future research directions and methodological issues.

In Chapter Five, Kardes and Cronley explore further the *how* and the relationship between *how* and *why*. They proceed from the theoretical position that beliefs are "possessions" that people are quite reluctant to give up – a simple proposition, but one that leads to interesting consequences for the study of consumer motivation and persuasion. Kardes and Cronley first build on Katz (1960) and relate different belief functions to approach versus avoid tendencies; for doing so, they employ theories of self-regulation. They then discuss the manner in which chronic, self-related factors as well as situational influences affect why people approach and avoid particular end-states. Using this theoretical foundation, they offer a contingency model for predicting the types of persuasion appeals most likely to succeed in changing consumers' beliefs.

In Chapter Six, Belk, Ger, and Askegaard not only dig deep into the *why* but also take a dig at a rational, "passionless" view of needs and goals. Instead, they emphasize *desire* as a powerful motivational force, unleashed by external objects and the human body rather than the mind, fueled by imagination and fantasy, and characterized by a complete domination of one's thoughts, feelings, and actions. Belk *et al.* trace how Freud's psychoanalytic legacy evolved into Lacan's (1970) influential work on the nature of desire. They discuss how social and cultural forces shape desire in individuals. They then link desire to notions of pleasure, joy, control, and transgression in the context of Western and Eastern religion and moral philosophy. Belk *et al.* also discuss the emotional and behavioral correlates of desire and the future role of this construct in consumer research.

In Chapter Seven, Thompson examines the postmodern ("pomo") movement in consumer research and its implications for the *why* of consumption. He describes the historical background and origins of postmodern theorizing and discusses the relationship between postmodernism and popular culture. Thompson then offers us "the absolute, scientific truth" about pomo consumer goals and actions with concepts such as nostalgia and re-enchantment, communal consumption, and bricolage and identity-creation. He also discusses why and how postmodern consumers choose to engage in acts of flexible and ironic consumption. He concludes by reflecting on the challenges and rewards of studying the why of postmodern consumers.

In Chapter Eight, Arnould and Price make a strong case for tying the *why* (motives) and *what* (consumption behaviors) to *who* (self and community). They do so by suggesting that people's strivings toward self-authentication and sense of community drive many consumption behaviors. They first provide an overview of postmodern issues and trends (e.g. globalization and deterritorialization), both in an individual's construction of the self and in the social dynamic of communities. Next, they discuss how people respond to these trends via self-authenticating acts and authoritative performances that reaffirm a collective sense of identity. Arnould and Price then illustrate how consumption objects and experiences play a key role in constructing a sense of self and community. They also identify and discuss important obstacles to self-authenticating acts and authoritative performances.

In Chapter Nine, Hirschman and Stern give us a different perspective on the *who* by examining images and representations of women in film and television over the last several decades. Beginning with the depictions of women in ancient cultures, they suggest how these have been carried forward into today's mass media. Their analysis focuses on the content of top movies and television shows since the late 1930s and up to present times. Hirschman and Stern highlight the core meanings and subtle messages in media representations of female roles and identities (e.g. as "Nurturant and Destructive Goddesses" and "Passive Princesses"). They also link popular media images of women to sociocultural themes such as androgyny and the American Dream. They suggest how media depictions of female roles, goals, and identities are constantly evolving and yet, in many ways, are always reminiscent of the ancient.

In Chapter Ten, Faber examines the *why* of compulsive buying and the diverse motives and reasons underlying this abnormal consumer behavior. He first provides a broad overview of research on compulsive buying. Faber then introduces and applies a uses and gratifications framework for understanding the phenomena. He suggests that motives for compulsive buying fall in the categories of surveillance (e.g. a desire to experience new products), enhancement of personal identity, construction of personal relationships, and diversion. He also discusses the role of factors such as gender, social systems, and cultural characteristics in compulsive buying. Overall, Faber's framework not only links the *why* and *what* of compulsive consumption to *who* (i.e. one's culture and self-identity) but also implicates the *how* by suggesting that compulsive buying can be used in the service of affect (mood) management.

In Chapter Eleven, Warlop, Smeesters, and Vanden Abeele examine the *why* and *what* of garbage disposition behavior from a social marketing perspective. They discuss the potential trade-offs and goal conflicts faced by consumers when it comes to sorting and recycling household waste. Warlop *et al.* argue that many social marketing programs aimed at promoting recycling behavior assume unreasonable amounts of consumer involvement and mental control in day-to-day matters. They suggest that social marketers instead might adopt a low-involvement model of the consumer. In this vein, social marketers could implement tactics similar to the marketers of consumer packaged-goods and just prime their target consumers with simple, frequent, and to-the-point messages. Warlop *et al.* thus emphasize that successful communication strategies involve a solid understanding of the relationship between the *why* (goals and motives for particular behaviors) and the *how* (cognitive decision processes).

In Chapter Twelve, Cotte and Ratneshwar address time consumption by delving into *why* people do whatever it is that they do with their discretionary time. They argue that decisions to engage in particular activities are often related to an individual's timestyle, i.e. how a person perceives, plans, and thinks about time. Cotte and Ratneshwar put forward a four-dimensional, integrative framework for timestyle. They then suggest a variety of factors that can shape timestyle, ranging from factors such as culture and family socialization to individual-difference factors such as life themes and values. They also discuss situational influences such as a person's work versus home environment. Cotte and Ratneshwar then suggest how timestyle could be related to leisure consumption decisions and discuss future research directions.

In Chapter Thirteen, Escalas and Bettman examine how narratives help us understand consumption motives. They first provide a conceptual overview of narrative structure, quality, and processing. They then discuss in detail the functional aspects of narratives, especially in the construction and maintenance of one's self-identity. Escalas and Bettman subsequently illustrate how narratives provide insights into consumer motives and goals. They focus their discussion on the structural analysis of narratives and contrast it against content analysis. They propose three general propositions regarding relationships between consumer goals and narrative quality, narrative genre, and narrative elements. In each case, they address relevant methodological issues and provide empirical support. As part of their chapter, Escalas and Bettman also provide useful scale items for coding narrative structure.

In Chapter Fourteen, Coulter and Zaltman argue for the power of metaphor in uncovering consumer goals and motives. Their position is that much thought is unconscious and that metaphors and idiomatic expressions serve as handy vehicles for transporting less-than-conscious thoughts into consciousness. Coulter and Zaltman discuss different types of metaphors and how they help us understand a variety of consumer goals and motives. They then suggest how a specific metaphor-based method, the Zaltman Metaphor Elicitation Technique (ZMET), provides significant insights into consumer motives. Using ZMET data on people's ideas and perspectives regarding good oral hygiene and visits to the dentist, Coulter and Zaltman illustrate the role of various metaphors in fathoming the why of consumer behaviors.

In Chapter Fifteen, Brownstein, Sirsi, Ward, and Reingen discuss the use of lattice analysis for exploring the interfaces between cognitive and social phenomena in consumer motivation. They point out that consumption beliefs are typically influenced by others in one's social environment. Hence, we need to understand how people's belief structures and social structures interact in jointly determining consumption behaviors. Towards this end, Brownstein *et al.* discuss the analysis of dual-mode data involving groups of respondents and their consumption beliefs. Using several illustrative examples, they show how the Galois lattice technique enables meaningful graphic representation of such data. For instance, lattice diagrams can depict the ideological structure that motivates some consumers to consume or avoid particular foods. Simultaneously, such lattices can also reveal relationships between individuals' beliefs and social structure and important differences between expert and novice consumers.

Finally, in Chapters Sixteen and Seventeen, Kernan and Rook round out our collection by providing insightful and witty commentaries on the previous fifteen chapters and the research area more generally. Kernan argues that the "why" of consumption represents not one, but three very different kinds of questions, depending on the metaphoric model assumed. Rook comments on theory and method in motivation research and points out four key issues that need resolution.

References

Alderson, W. (1957) *Marketing Behavior and Executive Action*, Homewood, IL: Richard D. Irwin.

Dichter, E. (1964) *The Handbook of Consumer Motivations*, New York: McGraw-Hill.

Freud, S. (1957) *The Ego and the Id*, in J. Strachey (ed. and trans.) *Standard Edition of the Complete Psychological Works of Sigmund Freud* (pp. 85–132), London: Hogarth Press. (Original work published 1923.)

Howard, J.A. and Sheth, J.N. (1969) *The Theory of Buyer Behavior*, New York: Wiley.

Katz, D. (1960) "The functional approach to the study of attitudes," *Public Opinion Quarterly* 24 (2): 163–204.

Lacan J. (1970) "Of structure as an inmixing of an otherness prerequisite to any subject whatever," in R. Macksey and E. Donato (eds) *The Languages of Criticism and the Sciences of Man*, Baltimore: Johns Hopkins University Press.

Levy, S.J. (1981) "Interpreting consumer mythology: a structural approach to consumer behavior," *Journal of Marketing* 45 (Summer): 49–61.

Lewin, K. (1936) *Principles of Topological Psychology*, New York: McGraw-Hill.

Maslow, A.H. (1970) *Motivation and Personality*, 2nd edition, New York: Harper & Row.

Miller, G.A., Galanter, E., and Pribram, K.H. (1960) *Plans and the Structure of Behavior*, New York: Holt.

Newell, A. and Simon, H.A. (1972) *Human Problem Solving*, Englewood Cliffs, NJ: Prentice-Hall.

Veblen, T. (1899) *The Theory of the Leisure Class*, reprinted in 1973 with an introduction by J.K. Galbraith, Boston: Houghton Mifflin.

2 Consumer goal structures and goal-determination processes

An integrative framework

Cynthia Huffman, S. Ratneshwar, and David Glen Mick

Over a half-century ago, Alderson (1957) argued that consumer behavior is best understood as problem-solving behavior. His functionalist approach was fundamentally concerned with the goals toward which consumers strive and the processes through which they seek to attain these goals. Unfortunately, attention to the nature and role of consumer goals waned afterward, due in large part to the information-processing revolution that swept both psychology (see, e.g., Sorrentino and Higgins 1986) and consumer research (e.g. Alba and Hutchinson 1987).

In the last decade or so, however, psychology has witnessed a renaissance of interest in goal-directed behavior (e.g. Bandura 1989; Cantor 1990; Cantor *et al.* 1987; Carver and Scheier 1996; Markus and Ruvolo 1989), most impressively evinced in Austin and Vancouver's (1996) comprehensive review and in books edited by Gollwitzer and Bargh (1996), Pervin (1989), and Higgins and Sorrentino (1990). So too, research on goals in consumer behavior is now receiving vigorous attention (e.g. Bagozzi and Dholakia 1999; Bettman *et al.* 1998; Huffman and Houston 1993; Kleine *et al.* 1993; Park and Smith 1989; Pieters *et al.* 1995; Ratneshwar *et al.* 1996; Walker and Olson 1997; Reynolds and Gutman 1988; Sirsi *et al.* 1996).

Not surprisingly, the rapid growth and eclecticism of recent research in consumer goals has led to valuable but highly fragmented insights as each researcher has invariably emphasized different issues. For instance, some researchers have focused mainly on the structural relations between different goal levels, particularly those who have worked within the means-end paradigm (see, e.g., Pieters *et al.* 1995; Reynolds and Gutman 1988; see also Kleine *et al.* 1993; McCracken 1986; and Walker and Olson 1997 for alternative paradigms with a structural emphasis). Most often these studies have directly connected the *being* side of life (e.g. an individual's values or social identity) with its *having* side (preferred products and their features), typically via hierarchies in which consumers' values drive the desired psychosocial consequences of product consumption, and the latter, in turn, influence product preferences. As yet, however, consumer researchers have not effectively bridged higher and lower goals with the types of mid-level goals (e.g. life projects, current concerns) that psychologists have recently explored to account for the *doing* side of life (see, e.g., Cantor 1990; Cantor *et al.* 1987; Emmons 1986; Gollwitzer 1996; Little 1989). In addition, the structural approaches have mostly adopted a macro-motivational perspective and, therefore, have rarely considered process issues regarding *how* goals at different levels impact on each other.

Although other researchers have eschewed structural concerns and addressed goal-determination processes, they have restricted themselves to micro-motivational perspectives (e.g. how consumers adapt lower-level goals such as product-feature preferences to proximal task and contextual factors; see Bettman *et al.* 1998). In general, researchers have yet to meld the macro and micro approaches to consumer goals (see, however, Bagozzi and Dholakia 1999 for a recent effort in this direction). Moreover, although a handful of researchers have argued persuasively for the inescapable role of situational influences on consumer goals – such as the social, cultural, physical, and temporal contexts of consumption (e.g. Belk 1975; Ratneshwar and Shocker 1991; Sherry 1983; Brownstein *et al.*, this volume) – most have simply ignored such factors and their relations to consumer goals.

For advancing theory and directing future research, there is a substantial need for a framework that addresses the hierarchical structure of consumer goals as well as the specific processes by which consumer goals are determined. We propose here such a framework in the context of consumer behavior that is assumed to be pragmatic, purposive, and problem-solving oriented (see Alderson 1957; Howard and Sheth 1969). We assume that goals are cognitive representations of desired end-states and these representations serve as standards in the control of behavior (Austin and Vancouver 1996; Carver and Scheier 1996). Hence, as presently developed, our framework does not explicitly address consumer behavior based on purely experiential or hedonic motives (see, e.g., Holbrook and Hirschman 1982; Holt 1995); we also exclude from our scope unconscious and perhaps uncontrollable urges (see Faber, this volume; Rook 1987); finally, we do not examine here the role of emotions in goal formation, goal striving, and goal attainment (instead, see Bagozzi *et al.* and Luce *et al.*, this volume).

A brief review of prior research on consumer goals

Research on consumer values and means-end chains

Higher-order goals such as a person's terminal values have often been stressed in explanations of individual differences in buyer behavior and media exposure (e.g. Kahle *et al.* 1986; Kamakura and Novak 1992; Richins 1994). Indeed, the most important forerunners of the structural component of our framework are means-end chain models that seek to connect product-feature preferences to a consumer's values (e.g. Pieters *et al.* 1995;

Reynolds and Gutman 1988). Although means-end chains are not intended to be a theory of individual goal-directed behavior *per se*, they clearly presume a hierarchy of goal levels at which a product's concrete attributes might be interpreted and preferred by the consumer. Means-end chains do not usually consider situational influences on consumer goals or person-situation interactions (cf. Ratneshwar *et al.* 1996). Further, research on means-end chains has generally assumed static goal structures, with little discussion of how goals might evolve. Neither do means-end researchers inquire into the cognitive processes associated with goal formation and goal change. Finally, means-end theory does not offer middle-level goal constructs for bridging the large gap between higher-level, abstract goals at the being or self level with lower-level, concrete goals at the having level of preferred product features and benefits.

Social identity theory

Social identity theory in consumer behavior is largely based on two key notions. First, people are posited to take actions and consume products (at least in part) to enact identities consistent with their ideal self-images (see Kleine *et al.* 1993; Sirgy 1982). This notion is related to the work of Markus and her colleagues in social psychology which posits that individuals strive and act to create ideal selves (see, e.g., Markus and Ruvolo 1989). Similarly, recent research by Fournier (1994) has focused on the idea that consumers' relationships with brands may be based on meanings that are central to the individual's self-concept. Second, social identity theory asserts that there is not just one global identity that a person enacts, but multiple identities (e.g. mother, professor, volunteer), triggered or activated as a function of the different social contexts in which the person moves (Kleine *et al.* 1993). Our multiple selves are thus assumed to be more or less salient in different contexts; the self or selves that are currently active are then the drivers of actions designed to establish and reinforce those selves. Social identity theory does not offer a precise formulation for how lower-order consumer goals are linked to the ideal self in a hierarchical goal structure, nor does it examine the specific processes by which goals at lower levels are formed and modified.

Behavioral decision theory

Behavioral decision theory is currently a major paradigm for investigating consumer choice processes. A dominant theme in this paradigm is that choice processes and outcomes are contingent on a number of contextual factors such as the set of available alternatives or their attribute values, and task factors such as time pressure (see, e.g., Bettman 1979; Bettman *et al.* 1998). Further, decision-makers are thought to adapt to such variables in a dynamic fashion such that feature preferences are often constructed – not merely revealed – in judgment and choice tasks. Clearly, behavioral decision theory has produced an impressive body of knowledge on process issues, and it has contributed the view that consumers adapt in a dynamic fashion to their choice environments. Nonetheless, work in this genre has usually ignored macro motivational factors such as an individual's values. Also, the effects of many situational variables (e.g. social surroundings, physical environment) on consumers' goals, and the effects of different types and levels of goals on each other, have rarely been considered.

Attitude theory

Attitude theory (e.g. Fishbein and Ajzen 1975) can explain at least part of the cognition-motivation interface associated with goals (see, e.g., Bagozzi and Warshaw 1990). Consumer research based on attitude theory mainly emphasizes how preferences are derived from individuals' expectancies and evaluations concerning product beliefs (e.g. Lutz 1977). These beliefs are usually at the level of lower-level goals such as the product benefits and features desired by a consumer. The theory does not detail a process model for how and why the evaluative components of attitude structure can change. Further, in contrast to behavioral decision research, it does not account for consumer adaptation to proximal contextual factors such as the set of available alternatives. Instead, attitude theory considers contextual influence in the form of social norms and an individual's motivation to comply with those norms (Bagozzi and Warshaw 1990).

Summary

We summarize in Table 2.1 the theoretical issues that have been emphasized in each of the aforementioned approaches. Means-end research and social identity theory have focused on structural issues and linkages between goals at the level of being (or self) and lower-order goals such as preferred product features. These two paradigms have given relatively little attention to cognitive process issues. Behavioral decision theory and attitude theory have examined in some depth cognitive processes in goal determination, but have generally restricted themselves to lower-order consumer goals. Behavioral decision theory and social identity theory are inherently dynamic in their conceptualization (especially the former). In contrast, means-end models and attitude theory are relatively static in terms of their implications for consumer goals. The four approaches also vary in their emphasis on contextual factors. Behavioral decision theory heavily emphasizes the role of the immediate or proximal choice context, while social identity theory and attitude theory emphasize the social context of behavior. Means-end research is probably the most person-centered in terms of the locus of consumer behavior and, concomitantly, pays the least attention to contextual factors.

Table 2.1 Focus of prior research on consumer goals

	Goal determination process	*Dynamic aspects of goal determination*	*Role of higher-level goals and relationships between higher- and lower-level consumer goals*	*Impact of contextual factors on consumer goals*
Means-end chains	Low	Low	High	Low
Social identity theory	Moderate	Moderate	Moderate	Moderate
Behavioral decision theory	High	High	Low	High
Attitude theory	High	Low	Low	Moderate

Overview of the present framework

Our framework presented below adopts several key ideas from the different research paradigms discussed earlier, and it seeks to build on these ideas in order to present a more comprehensive and integrative view of consumer goal structures and goal-determination processes. As in means-end theory, social identity theory, and Carver and Scheier's action control theory (1996), we postulate a hierarchical goal structure (see also Bagozzi and Dholakia 1999). Discrete levels are integral to any hierarchical system, even though they must be viewed to some extent as simply a matter of epistemological convenience (Allen and Starr 1982). Therefore, our framework proposes six discrete levels of goals wherein higher-level (vs. lower-level) goals are more abstract, more inclusive, and less mutable. In descending order of abstraction, these goal levels are *life themes and values, life projects, current concerns, consumption intentions, benefits sought, and feature preferences* (see Figure 2.1). Later we define and discuss each level in detail with several examples and examine the interrelationships among goal levels.

We refer to the individual's conscious process of constructing and modifying goals as *goal determination*. In accordance with much recent research in social psychology (see, e.g., Cantor 1990; Carver and Scheier 1996; Gollwitzer 1996), we stress an intentional or purposive view of goal determination. We posit that the process of goal determination typically includes thinking about relations among goals (e.g. regarding their mutual consistency) and considering the implications of satisfying one goal for the achievement (or not) of other goals. Further, as implied by behavioral decision theory and social identity theory, we adopt a dynamic view of goal determination wherein consumer goals are formed and altered during decision-making in light of contextual information.

In our framework, there are two main psychological forces for goal determination, *goal alignment* and *goal adaptation* (see Figure 2.2). Alignment

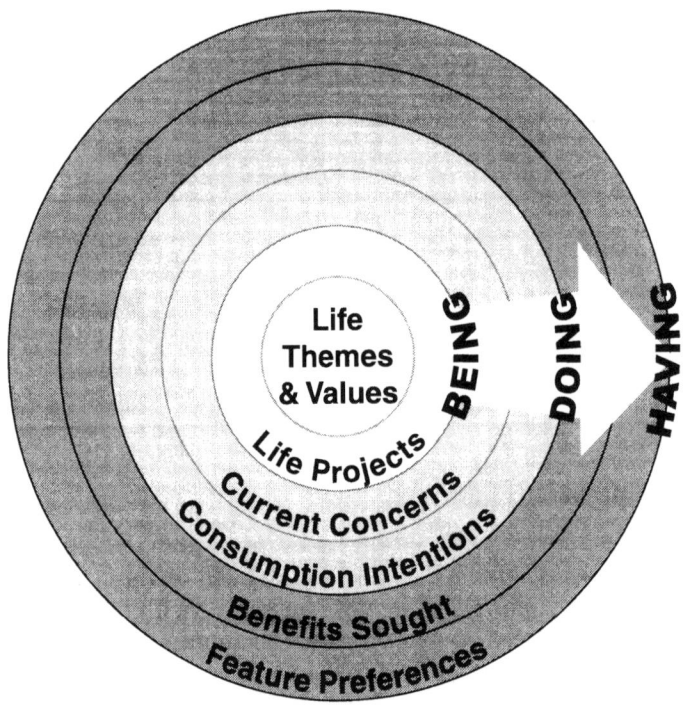

Figure 2.1 A hierarchical model of consumer goals.

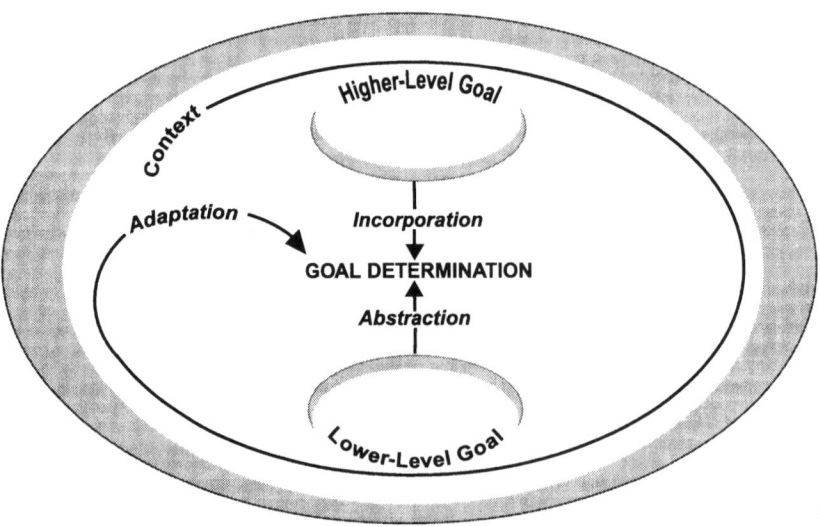

Figure 2.2 A model of goal-determination processes.

refers to processes by which goals at different levels in the hierarchy mutually influence each other such that the system as a whole tends towards consistency and congruence. The need for alignment is based on the concept that people find it functional to avoid inner conflict, and the stress and negative affect that ensue from such conflict, by maintaining harmony among various aspects of the self, including their goals (cf. Emmons 1986; Heider 1958).

Goal alignment is postulated to occur through both top-down and bottom-up processes. As is implicit in means-end theory and social identity theory, we propose that higher-level goals often shape and give meaning to goals at lower levels. This top-down goal alignment process is termed *incorporation* (see Figure 2.2). Although people would do well to regularly consider their higher-order goals in order to guide their day-to-day decisions, often the reverse is true. Considerable research in behavioral decision theory suggests that a decision situation can prompt an analysis of one's values (see, e.g., Keeney 1988). In such situations, lower-level goals such as revealed feature-preferences may shape and constrain higher-level goals. This type of bottom-up goal alignment process is termed goal *abstraction*.

The second main force for goal determination is adaptation, in which an individual's goals are shaped by contextual factors. In our framework, we provide for a wide range of macro and micro contextual influences on consumer goals; these include a person's general sociocultural environment, social and spatiotemporal aspects of product consumption situations, and the context of available choice alternatives.

A hierarchical model of consumer goal structure

We define and elaborate below each of the six goal levels in our structural model. We use the three consumer behavior vignettes in Table 2.2 to illustrate our key points. Our structural analysis of the goals of the consumers (Jack, Carol, and Marty) in these vignettes is summarized in Table 2.3.

Life themes and values

Life themes and values are defined as personal ideals of being, and they represent the highest goal level in our framework. According to Rokeach (1968), a terminal value is an enduring belief that an end-state of existence (e.g. freedom, wisdom, family unity) is preferable to other possible end-states (cf. Levy 1981). Life themes are related existential concerns that individuals address in daily life. Compared to sociocultural values, life themes are more distinctly rooted in personal history: individuals attempt to create a thematic coherence to their lives even as they undergo transformational experiences in childhood, family relations, schooling, and ongoing choices in adult life (Csikszentmihalyi and Beattie 1979).

Table 2.2 Three consumer behavior vignettes

Jack: Jack grew up on a farm in central Illinois, with three brothers and two sisters. Jack volunteered to serve in Vietnam in the late 1960s and then went to college on the G.I. Bill. He majored in agronomy and business. For the last 20 years Jack has been working as a sales representative in the Midwest for an agricultural machinery manufacturer. Jack's employer wants him to double the distribution of the line by entering new territories, so Jack has been considering the purchase of another automobile for making more frequent and longer trips to contact new potential distributors. Jack wants a car that is not likely to stand out or offend local sensibilities and will also be dependable and serviceable anywhere he goes. Jack visits the Ford, Chevrolet, Chrysler, Buick, Oldsmobile, and Pontiac dealerships in his area, but not Subaru, Honda, or Volkswagen. He also test drives ten different car models. After haggling over car prices with two dealerships and taking two models home for further test drives, Jack decides to buy a white Ford Taurus with grey cloth interior, automatic transmission, and cruise control.

Marty: Marty's mother is a painter and his father is an English professor. He himself excelled in art classes, developing a strong interest in art history and museum management. Marty has just arrived at State U. to study arts administration and has moved into a small three-bedroom apartment with two friends from high school. He has saved $200 for buying a new desk and a tall bookcase to accommodate his many books. Marty accompanies his roommates to a Wal-Mart store to shop for furniture. Both friends take a quick interest in some desks made from pressboard, priced at $89. While they decide to buy, Marty realizes he is not satisfied with them and chooses to wait and look further. Over the next week Marty visits six local antique shops, hoping to find a solid wood desk, one with craftsmanship quality and distinctiveness. However, Marty cannot seem to find anything he likes which he can afford. Then, one day he notices a full-page ad for the grand opening of a second-hand furniture shop. Grabbing his car keys, he heads out for the shop. Once there, Marty notices that the store has many desks. He finds several that are small and nondescript, while others are huge and bulky. Then, his eyes catch on to a medium-sized, wood desk of 1930s art deco design, with a matching two-shelf bookcase. The cost is $170. Next to it is a nice solid oak missionary style desk with a matching chair and a tall bookcase, for $300. Marty would rather have the tall bookcase in the second set for his many books, but he only has $200 to spend. He re-examines the art deco set and wonders how he can manage with only a two-shelf bookcase. Reasoning that he can probably leave most of his books at his parents' house, he purchases the art deco set.

Carol: Growing up the daughter of a veterinarian, Carol has always believed in being kind to all animals, and she became a vegetarian at an early age. Two months ago Carol and her husband, Steve, moved from Seattle to Pittsburgh. Carol has made some new friends, including a neighbor named Jane who casually mentioned one day that she was curious about vegetarianism. Carol has invited Jane over for lunch this coming Wednesday, along with another neighbor named Susan. She wants the two of them to experience a fresh and surprisingly tasty vegetarian lunch, and she believes she has a good idea. It is a meatless chili made from tofu, beans, tomatoes, onions, green pepper, and spices. Every time Carol makes this dish for unsuspecting guests, they never recognize the tofu and always like it. On Tuesday afternoon Carol drives to the grocery store to buy ingredients for cooking. However, the store is out of tofu. Carol feels frustrated and not certain what her next best option may be, especially since she doesn't have her recipe books with her. But a display of fresh herbs in the produce section catches her eye and jogs her memory. She recalls that she has occasionally fixed a spicy vegetable stew that has been very successful at past dinner parties and pot-lucks. Fortunately, the store has everything she needs to make the stew. She buys ingredients for the stew as well as for an appetizer, gets a light dessert from the bakery, and heads home.

Table 2.3 Examples of goal structures for three individuals

Goal level	Jack	Carol	Marty
Life themes and values	Be active; be patriotic	Be respectful and protective of all life	Be appreciative of art and style; be dedicated to learning
Life projects	Be a successful sales manager	Be a good neighbor	Be a successful college student; be an expert in arts administration
Current concerns	Distribute products in new territories in the Midwest	Host a lunch for my neighbor	Organize my apartment
Consumption intentions	Travel in my car for calling on new distributors	Serve and eat an entree at lunch	Study at a desk; store my books in a bookcase
Benefits sought	Comfortable, dependable, conservative, Midwest-acceptable	Moderately filling, tasty, novel	Distinctive looks, fit into limited space, fit my limited budget
Feature preferences	Made in USA, mid-priced, automatic transmission, cruise control, white exterior, grey cloth interior	Vegetarian, a tofu chili or a vegetable stew	A medium-sized desk; a tall bookcase; avoid mass-produced pressboard furniture; total price under $200

Life themes are fruitfully conceived in a dialectical fashion that reflects the existential tension experienced by individuals, e.g. being active versus being passive and being truthful versus being false (see Mick and Buhl 1992). For instance, Carol's childhood as the daughter of a veterinarian has fostered a life theme centered on being respectful versus disrespectful toward all living creatures. Similarly, Jack's maturation in a traditional farming family and later experiences as a soldier in Vietnam have engendered a strong work ethic and patriotic devotion, suggesting that one of his life themes concerns being faithful versus unfaithful to one's country.

Prior research suggests that both life themes and values are limited in number within the individual and are relatively invariant once developed (Csikszentmihalyi and Beattie 1979; Rokeach 1968). Together they represent core conceptions of self. Because they are so deeply embedded, interconnected, and central to maintaining the integrity of the self-system, they are likely to be relatively stable and accessible and thus easily activated across a variety of circumstances (Markus and Ruvolo 1989; Walker and Olson 1997). Moreover, once a value or life theme is internalized, it serves as a standard or yardstick to guide many lower-order goals and actions (Cantor *et al.* 1987; Markus and Ruvolo 1989; Rokeach 1968).

Life projects

Life projects are defined as the construction and maintenance of key life roles and identities (e.g. being a responsible mother, a loyal employee, a successful teacher). An individual may have several life projects at any given time (Kleine *et al.* 1993). Relative to life themes, life projects are somewhat in flux over the life span (though, relative to lower-level goals such as current concerns, life projects are still quite long-term). They are particularly likely to be modified when individuals go through life-stage transitions such as marriage, having a child, divorce, a new career, and retirement (Cantor *et al.* 1987). Carol's life projects include being a good neighbor and being a supportive wife, while Marty wants to be a successful college student.

Current concerns

Current concerns are defined as activities, tasks, or quests in which an individual wants to be engaged in the short term (cf. Klinger 1977). Compared to life projects, current concerns are briefer in duration and less inclusive in their scope. Such goals are typically cognized in an individual's consciousness as things that "need to be done" soon. Examples of current concerns include "find a job," "lose fifteen pounds," "go on a family vacation during the Christmas holidays," and "cheer myself up." As shown in Table 2.3, one of Jack's current concerns is to expand distribution for his company's products into new territories, while Carol's include hosting a lunch for a neighbor.

Our conceptualization of current concerns is based on the work of several social psychologists who have proposed a similar goal level. Cantor's "life tasks" (Cantor *et al.* 1987) are "problems that people are currently working on"; as such, they organize and give meaning to a person's everyday activities. Similarly, Little's "personal projects" are interrelated sequences of actions intended to achieve a personal goal (Little 1989). To assess current concerns, Cantor and her colleagues (Cantor *et al.* 1987; Zirkel and Cantor 1990) have successfully used interview probes such as "tell me about the things you are currently trying to do or accomplish."

In our framework, current concerns are things that are "on top of one's mind" in terms of activities and problems in which one chooses to be engaged, both mentally and physically. For example, Marty has a current concern of organizing his new apartment, while Carol is planning to host a lunch for a neighbor. Since satisfying current concerns requires the allocation of one's time for undertaking and completing specific activities or tasks, goals at this level play a critical role in guiding the consumption of discretionary time (see, e.g., Cotte and Ratneshwar, this volume).

Consumption intentions

Consumption intentions are defined as individuals' aims and desires to engage in particular product consumption and use behaviors (Belk 1975,

Belk *et al.*, this volume; Ratneshwar and Shocker 1991). For example, a consumption intention can refer to a person's aim to commute to work by using the subway or to invest retirement savings in a mutual fund; it can also refer to a person's desire to drink a glass of wine with dinner or to gamble at a casino.

Consumption intentions help break down or "unpack" a current concern into a set of specific action sub-goals; satisfying a current concern usually involves goals related to the purchase and consumption of multiple and complementary products and services. For example, Marty has a current concern of organizing his apartment. Given this current concern, he might aim to purchase and use a set of matching furniture for actions such as sitting, sleeping, studying, and storing. As another example, given her current concern of hosting a lunch for a neighbor, Carol might desire to make several complementary purchases such as an appetizer, the ingredients for an entree, dessert, beverages, and a decorative floral arrangement.

Benefits sought

Benefits sought are defined as the *consequences* that are desired from ownership, usage, and disposal of a product (Myers and Shocker 1981; Olson and Reynolds 1983; Young and Feigin 1975). For example, Marty seeks a desk and bookshelves that are attractive in appearance and therefore consistent with his aesthetic disposition; he also wants them to fit into a small space and a student's budget. Jack desires a car that is comfortable, dependable, and conservative.

Feature preferences

Feature preferences are defined as preferred product feature levels or values as stated in concrete physical or financial terms. In contrast to benefits sought, which are subjective and outcome-referent, feature preferences are relatively objective and product-referent (Myers and Shocker 1981; Ratneshwar *et al.* 1999; Zeithaml 1988). Feature preferences (e.g. the price of a car and whether it has anti-locking brakes) typically pertain to "search attributes," while benefits sought (e.g. a car's ride quality and safety) are more experiential (Nelson 1970).

Feature preferences often play an important role in consumer decision-making, largely on account of their concreteness and relative ease of cognitive processing. Obviously, feature preferences are likely to be highly influenced by pertinent benefits being sought by the consumer. Hence, Jack's feature preferences among cars, Carol's preferences among ingredients for her entree, and Marty's preferences regarding furniture features, are all shaped by the respective benefits these individuals are seeking.

Relationships among goal levels

A common view is that goals at lower levels are designed to achieve the realization of higher-level goals such as an ideal self (Markus and Ruvolo 1989), and a number of consumer researchers imply such relationships among goal levels when they link consumer purchases and preferences to higher-order goals (see, e.g., Bagozzi and Dholakia 1999; Belk 1988; Sirgy 1982; Walker and Olson 1997). The relationships among our goal levels are conceptualized in accordance with the work of Kleine *et al.* (1993) who state that, "Ontologically, the self reflects Sartre's (1943/1956) three states of existence (being, having, and doing) in the sense that one 'is' (has being) by virtue of what one does (which requires possessions, or 'having')" (p. 210). Therefore, in the simplest terms, the goal levels in our model are related by virtue of the fact that, over the long run, we *acquire* possessions to *perform* actions that move us closer to *realizing* our values and ideal selves (cf. Belk 1988).

In our framework, being goals are most closely associated with life themes and values (see Figure 2.1). This goal level refers to conceptions of cherished or desired self-states, that is, who a person is trying to be (see also Mick and Buhl 1992). Goals of doing signify purposeful activities and tasks in which people wish to be engaged; they often serve as behavioral means of achieving an ideal self. These goals are primarily represented in our framework by current concerns. In turn, goals of having are acquisitive means of facilitating or accomplishing a person's doing goals, often in a manner consistent with his/her being goals (see Belk 1988). Having goals in our framework are mainly at the levels of benefits sought and feature preferences.

We conceptualize life projects and consumption intentions as goals at the interfaces of being and doing, and doing and having, respectively. Hence, these two goal levels have a dual character to them. Life projects concern the roles and identities that are important in one's life; but in addition, since they are *projects*, they involve time- and effort-consuming actions. For example, Marty's life project of being a successful student not only relates to who Marty wants to *be* but also points to the kinds of things he needs to *do* (e.g. organize his life and study hard). Consumption intentions refer to doing goals (e.g. eating, writing, traveling, relaxing) that involve allocation and depletion of resources – primarily money, time, and energy – available to the consumer. Notwithstanding, performance of these actions also requires one to *have* the necessary products as "props": such things as food, a personal computer, a car, or a TV. Hence, Marty's consumption intention of studying at a desk denotes an intention to engage in a specific action as well as the type of product he needs to acquire for accomplishing that action.

Goal-determination processes

As stated earlier, goal determination refers to the cognitive processes involved in constructing and modifying goals. We assume that goals at the doing level (current concerns, consumption intentions) and having level (benefits sought, feature preferences) are the ones most proximal to purchase and consumption decisions. Further, we posit that consumer problem-solving typically begins with goal determination at the "things to do" level of current concerns and consumption intentions. Then, depending on various individual and situational factors such as perceived expertise and self-efficacy, involvement, accountability, desired decision confidence, and time pressure, the decision-maker may engage in varying degrees of goal determination involving additional goal levels (Alba and Hutchinson 1987; Celsi and Olson 1988; Tetlock and Boettger 1989). Consistent with Gollwitzer (1996), our model does *not* assume that each and every consumer behavior is preceded by conscious goal determination just before the behavior occurs. Many behaviors are initiated merely to resume a pattern or sequence of actions that was put in place some time earlier. The goals that drive the entire action pattern may have been determined well in the past. As a result, goal determination often can be temporally separated from specific consumer behaviors.

We note that in many everyday purchase situations, the decision facing the consumer may be a familiar problem that has been solved many times in the past (e.g. what snacks to serve friends who come over on a Saturday night). In these cases, goals may often be determined only at the consumption intention level, and such goals may directly activate goal-associated "solutions" (specific products and brands) in memory (Barsalou 1991; Park and Smith 1989; Warlop and Ratneshwar 1993). Consequently, consumer decisions in such situations often will be made simply on the basis of finding a match between such known solutions retrieved in memory and the alternatives actually available and perceived in the choice environment. This process essentially corresponds to what traditionally has been termed "routinized problem-solving" in the consumer behavior literature (Howard and Sheth 1969). Obviously, in such situations there is little need for extensive goal determination (e.g. at the level of benefits sought and feature preferences), as both the criteria for decision-making and acceptable solutions are already known.

Nonetheless, as exemplified by all three of our vignettes, there are numerous decision situations where the situation is new and non-routine, at least to some extent. Consumer decisions that fall in this category are conducive to more extensive goal determination. We posit that in the course of goal determination related to these decision situations, goals will be influenced in a dynamic manner by related goals at other levels (via incorporation and abstraction) as well as contextual information (via adaptation), processes we discuss in detail below.

Incorporation

Incorporation refers to the top-down process wherein higher-level goals shape goals at lower levels. Incorporation helps the consumer to achieve alignment (i.e. consistency and congruence) in the goal structure, and it enables the consumer to translate diffuse or ill-specified needs into relatively well-defined, actionable choice problems. Many life projects stem from and instantiate life themes. For example, Jack's patriotism and work ethic lead him into a challenging sales career for an American manufacturer of farm equipment. Current concerns, in turn, reflect incorporation from life projects. Hence, Carol's current concern of hosting lunch is considerably determined by her life project of being a good neighbor. Goals at lower levels such as benefits sought and feature preferences are subject to multiple incorporation influences from higher-level goals. For instance, consumption intentions often help determine which product benefits and features should be sought: Jack's intention of making long road trips in a car for calling on his new distributors influences desired benefits such as a comfortable, dependable, and conservative car. Life themes and values also aid in determining consumer preferences at the having level; Carol's life theme directly influences her choice of a vegetarian entree.

Incorporation involves several closely-related problem-solving processes. First, the individual may engage in means-end analysis, that is, he or she may assess the difference between a desired end-state (e.g. an important or salient higher-order goal) and the current state and devise means to reduce that difference (Carver and Scheier 1982; Miller *et al.* 1960). Cause-and-effect reasoning, scenario generation (simulation), and imagery are typical of the cognitive processes implicated in such means-end assessment (see Beach and Mitchell 1990; Markus and Ruvolo 1989; Sirsi *et al.* 1996; Walker and Olson 1997). For example, Jack may reason how owning and using a new car might facilitate his goal of expanding distribution; he might mentally simulate how his customers would react to a Cadillac versus a Ford Taurus; and he might draw conclusions about means-end fit by visualizing a BMW parked in his driveway and thinking "That's not me."

Constraint-setting is a related process of incorporation in which a high-level goal is broken down and refined into associated lower-level sub-goals, thereby facilitating problem solving (Barsalou 1991; Newell and Simon 1972). Barsalou (1991) theorizes that such constraints are often stored as a chain of associations among goals in connectionist networks in long-term memory. Incorporation occurs when activation of higher-order goals produces corresponding activation and retrieval into working memory of associated lower-order goals as well as related goal-derived category exemplars which are ideal for goal fulfillment (see also Ratneshwar *et al.* 1996).

An example of incorporation via constraint-setting and constraint chains could be Jack's search for an new car. His consumption intention of acquiring a car for long business trips is progressively refined and constrained in terms of more concrete goals at the benefits sought and feature preferences levels. Thus, he first decides on an American car, based on his life theme of patriotism. He further limits his search to conservative car models, thus incorporating his goal of not wanting to irritate his business customers by showing up in a flashy car. His feature preferences (e.g. cruise control, plain white exterior) are further constrained by consumption intention (a car for making long trips) and benefits sought (conservative appearance), respectively.

Abstraction

Abstraction refers to the bottom-up process wherein lower-level goals help determine what higher-level goals *must be*, if the lower-level goals are to hold and the lower and higher levels are to be consistent. Several models of the cognition–motivation interface in social psychology posit that in addition to the usual top-down processes (i.e. as in incorporation), goal influences may also flow upwards in a goal hierarchy (Carver and Scheier 1982; Emmons 1986; Vallacher and Wegner 1987).

Two general processes have been suggested in this regard. The first process holds when serendipitous discovery of a lower-level goal sensitizes a decision-maker to a related higher-level goal. Typically, this happens when a relatively concrete goal causes the recognition or activation of a pre-existing abstract goal that was previously not salient in consciousness (see Vallacher and Wegner 1987). For example, Marty's negative reactions to and rejection of the pressboard desks favored by his roommates may have prompted recognition or reinforcement of his higher-level goal of being appreciative of aesthetics.

The second mechanism for abstraction is the creation of new higher-level goals to provide a coherent organizational structure for lower-level goals (Carver and Scheier 1982; Emmons 1986). Carver and Scheier (1982), drawing upon Piaget, suggest that goal abstraction is often the result of an inherent tendency in human beings toward organization of one's cognitive structure in the service of self-assessment. For example, a consumer may reflect on her interest in high-risk leisure activities such as skydiving and use this behavior as a means of classifying herself at a life themes and values level (e.g. as thrill-seeking and adventurous; Celsi *et al.* 1993). A related notion is expressed in Anzai and Simon (1979), who demonstrate that inexperienced problem-solvers begin at a concrete level and over time organize their experiences into patterns of success and failure in order to derive more general and powerful problem-solving strategies. Both goal discovery and goal organization are likely to involve attribution processes, whereby an actor attempts to uncover higher-level, more abstract reasons for his/her lower-level goals (see Folkes 1984).

Adaptation

Adaptation refers to the goal determination process whereby goals are shaped by contextual factors. In our framework, these range from the macro cultural and social environment for higher levels of goals (i.e. life themes and values, life projects), to social, spatial, and temporal aspects of the consumer's environment for mid-level goals (i.e. current concerns, consumption intentions), to the context of available alternatives for lower-level goals (i.e. benefits sought, feature preferences). From a problem-solving perspective, adaptation denotes the adjustment of goals and problem representations to factors that are external to the individual.

We propose that contextual factors operate primarily in two ways. First, they may activate a subset of goals already established in one's memory. For example, prior research has demonstrated that different social contexts (e.g. work-place versus recreation with friends) activate different goal-related aspects of the self (e.g. competent versus fun-loving; see Cantor *et al.* 1987; Carver and Scheier 1982; Kleine *et al.* 1993). Similarly, Walker and Olson (1997) argue that aspects of the self should be related to consumer behavior only when the situation activates those aspects, and that the particular values that influence behavior may be situation-specific. At the middle level of doing goals, research on situational influences in consumer behavior has provided ample evidence that the social and spatiotemporal aspects of the context (usage situation) in which a product is consumed are likely to activate and determine goals at the consumption intention, benefits sought, and feature preferences levels (Barsalou 1991; Belk 1975; Levy 1981; Ratneshwar and Shocker 1991; Ratneshwar *et al.* 1996). For example, the need for a snack in mid-morning is likely to activate the benefits-sought goals of healthy and quick, whereas the need for a snack at midnight at a party with friends is likely to activate benefits such as filling and not messy to eat.

The strength with which specific goals are associated with particular contexts in long-term memory (e.g. the association of the work context with the goal of being competent) is likely to determine whether a certain goal is activated when the actor enters a given context. Associations between the context and particular goals may be learned in a variety of ways, including direct experience, word-of-mouth, and marketing communications. For example, one may learn from advertising that while any beer is okay to drink alone, drinking with friends requires a "special" beer. As argued persuasively by D'Andrade (1995), individuals tend to learn goals that are typical of a culture through vicarious observation of admired others and by experiencing a variety of gratifications for acting out culturally-sanctioned goals within particular contexts.

Second, the context may constrain a decision-maker's perception of *possible* goals. In the case of being-level goals, the sociocultural context constrains the set of available (or acceptable) values and life projects for an individual (see Csikszentmihalyi and Beattie 1979; McCracken 1986; Mick and Buhl 1992). Anthropological consumer research stresses that in most cases goals originate and are embedded within an indigenous cultural milieu that establishes the character, range, and practices of goals (see, e.g.,

Levy 1981; McCracken 1986). McCracken (1986), for example, has characterized life projects as each person's development of specific concepts (e.g.
manliness, professorhood) from a range of culturally-established alternatives; people create and modify roles in their social performances because
not all of the expectations and rules for enacting a role are prescribed.
Cantor and her colleagues (e.g. Zirkel and Cantor 1990) argue that the
cultural context, and the corresponding goals available for individuals, are
age-graded as well. That is, various stages of life are associated with
particular life projects and current concerns that are deemed appropriate
for adoption. Thus, students entering college are assumed to have goals of
establishing independence and a self-identity; graduating seniors are
assumed to have goals of establishing a successful career, etc. Similarly,
Levy's (1981) work illustrates how culture serves to establish goals related to
consumption actions (e.g. eating prime rib instead of hot dogs and
hamburgers) to which people adapt as the life span unfolds and different
roles or life projects are assumed.

The context of the choice alternatives available to the consumer can also
have a significant impact on the lower-level goals adopted (see, e.g.,
Simonson and Tversky 1992), particularly to the extent that the consumer
uses only the information that is explicitly displayed (see Slovic 1972). In
these cases, the consumer may adapt by fitting goals to what the alternatives offer. For example, when Marty realized that it was not possible to
satisfy both his goal for a large bookcase and his goal for a price under
$200, he adapted the goal that was more mutable, that of bookcase size. If
different alternatives were available, he might have adapted his goals in a
different manner. Similarly, because the grocery store did not have the
required ingredients for Carol's first choice for a lunch entree, she decided
to serve a vegetarian stew instead and adapted her purchases accordingly.

Relative likelihood of different goal-determination processes

Incorporation depends on the presence and salience of higher-level goals; it
is also fostered when lower-order goals are absent or weakly held. In
general, the salience or cognitive accessibility of higher-level goals will
depend on the frequency and recency with which they have been activated
in the past (Srull and Wyer 1986). Further, higher-level goals are also likely
to become salient as a person goes through transitions in life projects
(Cantor *et al.* 1987), thereby increasing the likelihood of incorporation. As
an example, a new life project such as motherhood could result in incorporation with respect to lower-level goals a woman holds with regard to the
purchase of a new car. The benefits sought might shift from sporty and fast
to safe and reliable, and her feature preference on the number of doors may
shift from two-door to four-door. Higher-level goals should also be more
salient and incorporation more likely when consumer involvement in a
purchase is relatively high (Celsi and Olson 1988; Walker and Olson 1997).

Correspondingly, abstraction is likely to play a substantial role in goal determination when problem-solving direction is not provided by salient higher-level goals (Park and Smith 1989). In addition, abstraction through discovery processes may be a strong possibility when concrete features of alternatives induce affective reactions in the decision-maker (Coombs, Dawes, and Tversky 1970; West 1996). Prior research suggests that three types of affective reactions enhance the chances that a consumer will abstract higher-level goals: (1) strong or extreme affect, (2) unexpected liking or disliking, and (3) negative affect in general. Research suggests that each of these outcomes is perceived as diagnostic and therefore may prompt an attribution analysis in order to identify likely causes; some of these causes may include higher-order goals (Folkes 1984; West 1996). Thus, Marty's affective response to the pressboard desk may have prompted abstraction to understand why he disliked those desks so much.

Johnson's (1984) findings regarding choice among "noncomparable" alternatives suggest still another factor that enhances the likelihood of abstraction. In his study, when subjects were given alternatives which were not easily comparable on concrete features, they tended to form more abstract representations of the features that were then more comparable across alternatives. Thus, the concrete features of a TV and a rowing machine might both be abstracted in a bottom-up fashion to a higher-level goal such as "entertainment" for making a decision. This relates to the organization process for abstraction that was discussed previously. Note, however, that consistent with our model's assumptions, Park and Smith (1989) and Ratneshwar *et al.* (1996) provide evidence that when consumers have salient, pre-existing goals at the consumption intention and benefits sought levels, abstraction of goals from concrete features is minimal.

As in the case of abstraction, adaptation may play a more significant role in goal determination when high-level goals are weak or insufficiently elaborated in terms of associations with low-level goals. This view is consistent with Bettman *et al.*'s (1998) view that constructive choice processes may be used more when the consumer has little experience with the decision task at hand. Also, in many situations, translating a higher-level goal into subordinate goals during problem-solving may be a difficult and cognitively challenging process (Carver and Scheier 1982). In contrast, since adaptation does not require extensive consideration of inter-goal relationships, it may be less effortful than incorporation or abstraction. Thus, adaptation may be more likely when decision-makers are satisficing rather than optimizing. Satisficing decision-makers are unlikely to adopt goals that they perceive as unattainable (Bandura 1989), so they may tend to rely on the context of available alternatives to "suggest" possible goals.

Consumers who are particularly knowledgeable about contextual information and for whom it is highly salient in a choice situation may rely heavily on such information in goal determination. For example, Jack appeared to be very cognizant of the Midwestern sociocultural context in which he operated as a sales manager, and he used his knowledge of his customers' sensitivities to help define his choice set of cars. Several individual and situational factors may enhance the salience of contextual information and, therefore, the role of adaptation in goal determination. First, prior research suggests that high self-monitors pay more attention to contextual information (see Snyder 1979); such individuals may be more likely to engage in adaptation than low self-monitors. Second, higher levels of accountability – the pressure to justify one's decisions to others – may motivate people to process contextual information more thoroughly, since such information may help defend or rationalize a particular choice (Simonson 1989; Tetlock and Boettger 1989). Hence, higher accountability may lead to adaptation being more likely in goal determination. Third, perceptible changes in the environment enhance the salience of contextual factors and, therefore, the likelihood of adaptation (see Carver and Scheier 1982; Zirkel and Cantor 1990).

Goal conflict and its resolution

Multiple goals across and within goal levels can be activated through the processes of incorporation, abstraction, and adaptation. These dynamics, and the inherent complexity of the goal system, often result in goal conflict or inconsistencies, as when, for example, pressures to adapt to situational factors clash with the mandates of higher-level goals such as an individual's values (Bell *et al.* 1988; Ratneshwar *et al.* 1996).

In cognitive terms, conflict may be avoided or approached during decision-making (Einhorn and Hogarth 1988; Luce *et al.*, this volume). Frequently, the consumer may not be sufficiently motivated to resolve goal conflict or may not consider himself or herself capable of such conflict resolution. Non-resolution of conflict in some cases can be "achieved" through ignoring the incoherence or living with it (Slovic *et al.* 1988); ignoring goal conflict often results in non-compensatory strategies for choice (Einhorn and Hogarth 1988). Similarly, Montgomery (1989) proposed that the choice process is essentially one of searching for, and creating where necessary, a dominance structure among the available alternatives whereby one option can be seen as clearly superior to the others. In goal conflict situations, dominance sometimes can be created by adjusting the relative importance of conflicting goals and thereby reducing cognitive dissonance or by adding new goals for cognitively bolstering a particular alternative (see Kunda 1990). Such conflict avoidance processes essentially bypass or avoid resolution of conflict among goals.

In contrast, conflict approach generally requires effortful consideration of the goals in question and how they are related to other goals the individual might have (Einhorn and Hogarth 1988; Keeney 1988). Scant research has been conducted on goal conflict resolution at higher goal levels, although researchers often mention the issue (e.g. Carver and Scheier 1982; Kleine *et al.* 1993). For example, social identity theory notes that people strive to attain consistency among their various identities (i.e. being-level goals) but does not specify how inconsistencies actually might be resolved (see Kleine *et al.* 1993). Carver and Scheier (1982) simply suggest that the goals associated with the more detailed plans for attainment, and/or the means associated with greater expectancies for goal attainment, are adopted over others (see also Bandura 1989). Conflict resolution has, however, been investigated at lower levels of goals in terms of how people make trade-offs among various product features (see, e.g., Bettman *et al.* 1998; Luce *et al.*, this volume).

In some cases, conflict might be approached by making the decision more concrete, with the general assumption that concrete trade-offs are easier to make than more abstract trade-offs. This may be particularly true when the higher-level goals involved are emotion-laden (see Luce *et al.*, this volume). For example, it may be easier to think about giving up a specific number of dollars for anti-lock brakes than it would be to think about trading off less wealth for more safety. Thus, an important avenue for future research is to determine how goals at various levels are traded off, and when and how goals at other levels in the goal structure are used to help resolve conflict. In addition, note that approaches other than simple approach/avoidance to goal conflict are also possible (Keeney 1988; Slovic *et al.* 1988). For example, the consumer may discover or synthesize new alternatives or approaches which allow conflicting goals to be satisfied. Consider Marty's behavior (Table 2.2) when he encountered goal conflict between his preferences regarding furniture appearance, size of bookcase, and price. He synthesized a new approach (leaving some books with his parents) which allowed him to reduce the importance of bookcase size while satisfying his other goals.

Summary

We discussed in detail the processes of incorporation, abstraction, and adaptation in goal determination. We suggested in each case underlying cognitive "building-block" processes and mechanisms; these include means-end analysis, constraint-setting, goal discovery, goal organization, and goal activation. Subsequently, we examined factors that moderate the likelihood of the three fundamental processes of goal determination. It is noteworthy that in our framework these processes are not mutually exclusive, thereby allowing for conflicting and/or inconsistent goals. We then briefly discussed the issue of goal conflict and its resolution within the rubric of goal-determination dynamics.

Discussion

We have proposed a framework for goal structure and goal-determination processes as it applies to the genre of consumer behavior referred to as problem-solving (cf. Alderson 1957; Howard and Sheth 1969). Our framework synthesizes and builds on recent ideas from several different areas of research, including social, cognitive, and humanistic psychology; behavioral decision theory; cultural anthropology; and prior consumer research. The result is a six-level hierarchical goal structure – spanning the being, doing, and having dimensions of life – which is fused by key goal-determination processes. These goal-determination processes encompass the interactions between goal levels, both top-down (incorporation) and bottom-up (abstraction), and the interaction of goals with numerous contextual factors (e.g. sociocultural environment, product usage situations, available alternatives) through adaptation. Overall, to our knowledge, it is the first broadly-applicable framework of consumer goals that explicitly melds goal structure and goal-determination processes in a parsimonious but principled manner. Inevitably, nonetheless, the framework harbors several limitations, some of which are discussed below.

Limitations

First, we note that each of the six goal levels in the framework was treated as a relatively unranked set of coterminous goals. In reality, within-level goals are likely to vary in their importance (e.g. a life project of being a loving father versus others such as being a helpful neighbor), and these variations deserve further consideration. For example, process explanations are needed for when and how one goal at a given level becomes more significant than another, and how conflicting goals at a given level (especially being- and doing-levels) are reconciled in relation to a given consumption event.

Second, we address here only consumer behavior that is goal driven in a relatively instrumental manner. Yet there is ample consumer behavior not explicitly guided by goals, notably autotelic activities, which can include attendance at sporting events (Holt 1995) or even substance abuse (Hirschman 1992). However, even activities that are highly experiential and seemingly for-their-own-sake can, in fact, be motivated by multiple goals, as Celsi *et al.* (1993) have astutely described with respect to sky diving. Indeed, several of their findings and interpretations readily conform to our structural model and goal-determination processes. For example, through the incorporation process, consumers with certain chronically-salient being goals (e.g. thrill-seeking, achievement) regularly engage in doing and having goals related to high-risk sport activities. Then, as their participation intensifies, they learn to associate other goals with the sub-cultural sport context and, through the adaptation process, they adopt other new goals accordingly (e.g. being-level goals of flow, communitas, and phatic communion with fellow enthusiasts; doing-level goals of riskier maneuvers; having-level goals of increasingly sophisticated sports gear).

Third, since our current framework takes a decidedly cognitive viewpoint on goals, there are many non-cognitive aspects of motivation that we have obviously not addressed (see Austin and Vancouver 1996). For example, at present the emotional processes and consequences associated with goal striving may be difficult to include in the model if parsimony remains an objective. However, based on the work of Bagozzi and his colleagues, it is possible that emotions and our framework could be potentially consolidated by extending the focus to include goal pursuit and "trying" (Bagozzi *et al.*, this volume; Bagozzi and Warshaw 1990). That research suggests that emotions elicited in anticipation of the consequences of achieving or not achieving a goal contribute to volitions; these volitions, in turn, guide the pursuit of the goal. Related to our framework, anticipatory emotions may serve key roles in goal determination, including whether incorporation, abstraction, or adaptation is the dominant process in goal determination. For example, Luce *et al.* (this volume) suggest that when consumers make trade-offs involving emotional attributes (e.g. family safety versus price), they tend to be conflict-avoiding rather than conflict-approaching. In terms of our framework, the implication might be that adaptation is more likely than incorporation or abstraction in such situations.

Finally, we emphasized the relatively cognizant activation of goals. An important future extension of the framework would be to consider sub-conscious goals in detail (e.g. as they relate to cultural myths or socially-sublimated desires). The determination, dynamics, and relationships of subconscious goals to conscious goals remain to be explored (see Coulter and Zaltman, this volume).

Looking ahead

It is our hope that our framework will serve as a theoretical foundation for empirical research in many different areas. For instance, our framework might be applied to goal-directed consumer behavior in domains as diverse as acculturation, gift-giving, household budget decisions, and time consumption. With this in mind, it seems appropriate to comment on some important methodological issues and challenges.

First, it is manifest that no single method such as participant observation, laddering interviews, scenarios, protocols, surveys, or experiments will be sufficient. Multiple methods are needed to fully appreciate goals that range from abstract life themes and values to concrete feature preferences, as well as processes that reflect adaptation to contextual aspects or goal alignment, up and down, across the various goal levels (see, e.g., Arnould and Price 1993; Sirsi *et al.* 1996). One could imagine, for instance, studies that include autobiographical interviews, surveys, laddering techniques, accompaniment by researchers on product searches and purchases, and experiments involving scenarios that consumers respond to on scales or through verbalized reactions (see also the chapters in this volume by Brownstein *et al.*; Coulter and Zaltman; Escalas and Bettman). There is little doubt that significant empirical efforts for advancing theory and substantive knowledge on consumer goals must involve multiple methods, threading qualitative and quantitative data into a fabric of understanding that justly reflects the variety and intricacy of consumer goals.

Second, our theorizing regarding goal-determination processes, and the vignettes we employed to bring the framework to life, indicate that most goals in real life are anything but fixed. If goals are inherently evolutionary, then investigating them empirically requires a commitment to longitudinal designs (see, e.g., Zirkel and Cantor 1990). An especially fruitful approach – but one with major operational challenges – would be to track consumers over time to examine how, when, and why their goal structures change. Fertile venues for studying these issues might include topics such as acculturation and household budget decisions. Future research endeavors on these lines may serve to validate the present theoretical framework. More importantly, such research may shed considerable light on how we can advance knowledge about consumer goals in a manner that is requisite with their complexity and dynamism.

Acknowledgments

We thank Richard Bagozzi, June Cotte, Jennifer Escalas, Wes Hutchinson, Mary Frances Luce, Brian Wansink, and Luk Warlop for their suggestions and constructive comments on earlier drafts of this chapter. We are also indebted to Luk for suggesting the term "incorporation" for a key construct. We are additionally grateful to participants in seminars at the University of Connecticut, University of Wisconsin, and K.U. (Leuven) for their helpful comments on this research.

References

Alba, J.W. and Hutchinson, J.W. (1987) "Dimensions of consumer expertise," *Journal of Consumer Research* 22 (August): 340–9.

Alderson, W. (1957) *Marketing Behavior and Executive Action*, Homewood, IL: Richard D. Irwin.

Allen, T.F.H. and Starr, T.B. (1982) *Hierarchy: Perspectives for Ecological Complexity*, Chicago, IL: University of Chicago Press.

Anzai, Y. and Simon, H.A. (1979) "The theory of learning by doing," *Psychological Review* 86 (March): 124–40.

Arnould, E.J. and Price, L.L. (1993) "River Magic: extraordinary experience and the extended service encounter," *Journal of Consumer Research* 20 (June): 24–45.

Austin, J.F. and Vancouver, J.B. (1996) "Goal constructs in psychology: structure, process, and content," *Psychological Bulletin* 120 (3): 338–75.

Bagozzi, R.P. and Warshaw, P.R. (1990) "Trying to consume," *Journal of Consumer Research* 17 (September): 127–40.

Bagozzi, R.P. and Dholakia, U. (1999) "Goal setting and goal striving in consumer behavior," *Journal of Marketing* 63 (special issue): 19–32.

Bandura, A. (1989) "Self-regulation of motivation and action through internal standards and goal systems," in L.A. Pervin (ed.) *Goal Concepts in Personality and Social Psychology*, Hillsdale, NJ: Lawrence Erlbaum Associates: 19–86.

Barsalou, Lawrence W. (1991) "Deriving categories to achieve goals," in G.H. Bower (ed.) *The Psychology of Learning and Motivation*, New York: Academic Press, vol. 27: 1–64.

Beach, L.R. and Mitchell, T.R. (1990) "Image theory: a behavioral theory of decisions in organizations," in B.M. Staw and L.L. Cummings (eds) *Research in Organizational Behavior*, Greenwich, CT: JAI Press, Vol. 12: 1–41.

Belk, R.W. (1988) "Possessions and the extended self," *Journal of Consumer Research* 15 (September): 139–68.

—— (1975) "Situational variables and consumer behavior," *Journal of Consumer Research* 2 (December): 157–64.

Bell, D.E., Raiffa, H., and Tversky, A. (1988) "Descriptive, normative, and prescriptive interactions in decision making," in D.E. Bell, H. Raiffa, and A. Tversky (eds) *Decision Making: Descriptive, Normative, and Prescriptive Interactions*, Cambridge: Cambridge University Press: 9–32.

Bettman, J.R. (1979) *An Information Processing Theory of Consumer Choice*, Reading, MA: Addison-Wesley.

Bettman, J.R., Luce, M.F., and Payne, J.W. (1998) "Constructive consumer choice processes," *Journal of Consumer Research* 25 (December): 187–217.

Cantor, N. (1990) "From thought to behavior: 'having' and 'doing' in the study of personality and cognition," *American Psychologist* 45: 735–50.

Cantor, N., Norem, J.K., Niedenthal, P.M., Langston, C., and Brower, A.M. (1987) "Life tasks, self-concept ideals, and cognitive strategies in a life transition," *Journal of Personality and Social Psychology* 53 (December): 1178–91.

Carver, C.S. and Scheier, M.F. (1982) "Control theory: a useful conceptual framework for personality – social, clinical, and health psychology," *Psychological Bulletin* 92 (1): 111–35.

—— (1996) *On the Self-Regulation of Behavior*, New York: Cambridge University Press.

Celsi, R.L. and Olson, J.C. (1988) "The role of involvement in attention and comprehension processes," *Journal of Consumer Research* 15 (September): 210–24.

Celsi, R.L., Rose, R.L. and Leigh, T.W. (1993) "An exploration of high-risk leisure consumption through skydiving," *Journal of Consumer Research* 20 (June): 1–23.

Coombs, C.H., Dawes, R.M., and Tversky, A. (1970) *Mathematical Psychology: An Elementary Introduction*, Englewood Cliffs, NJ: Prentice-Hall.

Csikszentmihalyi, M. and Beattie, O.V. (1979) "Life themes: a theoretical and empirical exploration of their origins and effects," *Journal of Humanistic Psychology* 19 (1): 45–63.

D'Andrade, R.G. (1995) "Cognitive processes and personality," in R.G. D'Andrade (ed.) *The Development of Cognitive Anthropology*, Cambridge: Cambridge University Press.

Einhorn, H.J. and Hogarth, R.M. (1988) "Behavioral decision theory: processes of judgment and choice," in D.E. Bell, H. Raiffa, and A. Tversky (eds) *Decision Making: Descriptive, Normative, and Prescriptive Interactions*, Cambridge: Cambridge University Press: 113–46.

Emmons, R.A. (1986) "Personal strivings: an approach to personality and subjective well-being," *Journal of Personality & Social Psychology* 51 (November): 1058–68.

Fishbein, M. and Ajzen, I. (1975) *Belief, Attitude, Intention and Behavior: An Introduction to Theory and Research*, Reading, MA: Addison-Wesley.

Folkes, V.S. (1984) "Consumer reactions to product failure: an attributional approach," *Journal of Consumer Research* 10 (March): 398–409.

Fournier, S. (1994) "A consumer-brand relationship framework for strategic brand management," PhD Dissertation, University of Florida.

Gollwitzer, P.M. (1996) "Planning and coordinating action," in P.M. Gollwitzer and J.A. Bargh (eds) *The Psychology of Action: Linking Cognition and Motivation to Behavior*, New York: Guilford Press: 283–312.

Gollwitzer, P.M. and Bargh, J.A. (eds) (1996) *The Psychology of Action: Linking Cognition and Motivation to Behavior*, New York: Guilford Press.

Heider, F. (1958) *The Psychology of Interpersonal Relations*, New York: Wiley.

Higgins, E.T. and Sorrentino, R.M. (eds) (1990) *Handbook of Motivation and Cognition: Foundations of Social Behavior*, vol. 2, New York: Guilford Press.

Hirschman, E.C. (1992) "The consciousness of addiction: toward a general theory of compulsive consumption," *Journal of Consumer Research* 19 (September): 155–79.

Holbrook, M.B. and Hirschman, E.C. (1982) "The experiential aspects of consumption: consumer fantasies, feelings, and fun," *Journal of Consumer Research* 9 (September): 32–140.

Holt, D.B. (1995) "How consumers consume: a typology of consumption practices," *Journal of Consumer Research* 22 (June): 1–16.

Howard, J.A. and Sheth, J.N. (1969) *The Theory of Buyer Behavior*, New York: Wiley.

Huffman, C. and Houston, M.J. (1993) "Goal-oriented experiences and the development of knowledge," *Journal of Consumer Research* 20 (September): 190–207.

Johnson, M.D. (1984) "Consumer choice strategies for comparing noncomparable alternatives," *Journal of Consumer Research* 11 (December): 741–53.

Kahle, L.R., Beatty, S.E. and Homer, P.M. (1986) "Alternative measurement approaches to consumer values: the list of values (LOV) and values and life style (VALS)," *Journal of Consumer Research* 13 (December): 405–9.

Kamakura, W. and Novak, T.P. (1992) "Value-system segmentation: exploring the meaning of LOV," *Journal of Consumer Research* 19 (June): 119–32.

Keeney, R.L. (1988) "Value-focused thinking and the study of values," in D.E. Bell, H. Raiffa, and A. Tversky (eds) *Decision Making: Descriptive, Normative, and Prescriptive Interactions*, Cambridge: Cambridge University Press: 465–96.

Kleine, III, R.E., Kleine, S.S. and Kernan. J.B. (1993) "Mundane consumption and the self: a social-identity perspective," *Journal of Consumer Psychology* 2 (3): 209–35.

Klinger, E. (1977) *Meaning and Void: Inner Experience and the Incentives in People's Lives*, Minneapolis: University of Minnesota Press.

Kunda, Z. (1990) "The case for motivated reasoning," *Psychological Bulletin* 108 (3): 480–98.

Levy, S.J. (1981) "Interpreting consumer mythology: a structural approach to consumer behavior, *Journal of Marketing* 45 (Summer): 49–61.

Little, B.R. (1989) "Personal projects analysis: trivial pursuits, magnificent obsessions, and the search for coherence," in D.M. Buss and N. Cantor (eds) *Personality Psychology: Recent Trends and Emerging Directions*, New York: Springer-Verlag.

Lutz, R.J. (1977) "An experimental investigation of causal relations among cognitions, affect, and behavioral intention," *Journal of Consumer Research* 3 (March): 197–208.

Markus, H. and Ruvolo, A. (1989) "Possible selves: personalized representations of goals," in L.A. Pervin (ed.) *Goal Concepts in Personality and Social Psychology*, Hillsdale, NJ: Lawrence Erlbaum Associates: 211–42.

McCracken, G. (1986) "Culture and consumption: a theoretical account of the structure and movement of the cultural meaning of consumer goods," *Journal of Consumer Research* 13 (June): 71–84.

Mick, D.G. and Buhl, C. (1992) "A meaning-based model of advertising experiences," *Journal of Consumer Research* 19 (December): 317–38.

Miller, G.A., Galanter, E., and Pribram, K.H. (1960) *Plans and the Structure of Behavior*, New York: Holt.

Montgomery, H. (1989) "From cognition to action: the search for dominance in decision making," in H. Montgomery and O. Svenson (eds) *Process and Structure in Decision Making*, New York: Wiley: 23–49.

Myers, J.H. and Shocker, A.D. (1981) "The nature of product-related attributes," in J.N. Sheth (ed.) *Research in Marketing*, Greenwich, CT: JAI Press, vol. 5: 211–36.

Nelson, P. (1970) "Information and consumer behavior," *Journal of Political Economy* 78 (March–April): 311–29.

Newell, A. and Simon, H.A. (1972) *Human Problem Solving*, Englewood Cliffs, NJ: Prentice-Hall.

Olson, J.C. and Reynolds, T.J. (1983) "Understanding consumers' cognitive structures: implications for advertising strategy," in L. Percy and A.G. Woodside (eds) *Advertising and Consumer Psychology*, Lexington, MA: Lexington Books.

Park, C.W. and Smith, D.C. (1989) "Product-level choice: a top-down or bottom-up process?" *Journal of Consumer Research* 16 (December): 289–99.

Pervin, L. A., (ed.) (1989) *Goal Concepts in Personality and Social Psychology*, Hillsdale, NJ: Lawrence Erlbaum Associates.

Pieters, R., Baumgartner, H., and Allen, D. (1995) "A means-end chain approach to consumer goal structures," *International Journal of Research in Marketing* 12 (October): 227–44.

Ratneshwar, S. and Shocker, A.D. (1991) "Substitution in use and the role of usage context in product category structures," *Journal of Marketing Research* 28 (August): 281–95.

Ratneshwar, S., Shocker, A.D., Cotte, J., and Srivastava, R.K. (1999) "Product, person, and purpose: putting the consumer back into theories of dynamic market behavior," *Journal of Strategic Marketing* 7 (3): 191–208.

Ratneshwar, S., Pechmann, C., and Shocker, A.D. (1996) "Goal-derived categories and the antecedents of across-category consideration," *Journal of Consumer Research* 23 (December): 240–50.

Reynolds, T.J. and Gutman, J. (1988) "Laddering theory, method, analysis, and interpretation, special issue: values," *Journal of Advertising Research* 28 (March): 11–31.

Richins, M.L. (1994) "Special possessions and the expression of material values," *Journal of Consumer Research* 21 (December): 522–33.

Rokeach, M. (1968) "A theory of organization and change within value-attitude systems," *Journal of Social Issues* 24: 13–33.

Rook, D.W. (1987) "The buying impulse," *Journal of Consumer Research* 14 (September): 189–99.

Sartre, J.P. (1956) *Being and Nothingness: A Phenomenological Essay on Ontology*, New York: Philosophical Library. (Original work published in 1943.)

Sherry, J.F. (1983) "Gift giving in anthropological perspective," *Journal of Consumer Research* 10 (September): 157–68.

Simonson, I. (1989) "Choice based on reasons: the case of attraction and compromise effects," *Journal of Consumer Research* 16 (September): 158–74.

Simonson, I. and Tversky, A. (1992) "Choice in context: tradeoff contrast and extremeness aversion," *Journal of Marketing Research* 29 (August): 281–95.

Sirgy, J.M. (1982) "Self-concept in consumer behavior: a critical review," *Journal of Consumer Behavior* 9 (December): 287–300.

Sirsi, A.K., Ward, J.C., and Reingen, P.H. (1996) "Microcultural analysis of variation in sharing of causal reasoning about behavior," *Journal of Consumer Research* 22 (March): 345–72.

Slovic, P. (1972) "From Shakespeare to Simon: speculations – and some evidence – about man's ability to process information," Oregon Research Institute Monograph 12 (April).

Slovic, P., Fischhoff, B., and Lichtenstein, S. (1988) "Contingent weighting in judgement and choices," *Psychological Review* 95 (July): 371–84.

Snyder, M. (1979) "Self-monitoring processes," *Advances in Experimental Social Psychology* 12: 85–128.

Sorrentino, R.M. and Higgins, E.T. (1986) "Motivation and cognition," in R.M. Sorrentino and E.T. Higgins (eds) *Handbook of Motivation and Cognition*, New York: Guilford Press: 3–19.

Srull, T.K. and Wyer, Jr., R.S. (1986) "The role of chronic and temporary goals in social information processing," in R.M. Sorrentino and E.T. Higgins (eds) *Motivation and Cognition: Foundations of Social Behavior*, New York: Guilford Press: 503–49.

Tetlock, P.E. and Boettger, R. (1989) "Accountability: a social magnifier of the dilution effect," *Journal of Personality and Social Psychology* 57 (3): 388–98.

Vallacher, R.R. and Wegner, D.M. (1987) "What do people think they're doing? action identification and human behavior," *Psychological Review* 94 (January): 3–15.

Walker, B.A. and Olson, J.C. (1997) "The activated self in consumer behavior: a cognitive structure perspective," in R.W. Belk (ed.) *Research in Consumer Behavior*, Greenwich, CT: JAI Press: 135–71.

Warlop, L. and Ratneshwar, S. (1993) "The role of usage context in consumer choice: a problem solving perspective," *Advances in Consumer Research* 20: 377–82.

West, P.M. (1996) "Predicting preferences: an examination of agent learning," *Journal of Consumer Research* 23 (June): 68–80.

Young, S. and Feigin, B. (1975) "Using the benefit chain for improved strategy formulation," *Journal of Marketing* 39 (July): 72–4.

Zeithaml, V.A. (1988) "Consumer perceptions of price, quality, and value: a means-end model and synthesis of evidence," *Journal of Marketing* 52 (July): 2–22.

Zirkel, S. and Cantor, N. (1990) "Personal construal of life tasks: those who struggle for independence," *Journal of Personality & Social Psychology* 58 (January): 172–85.

3 The role of emotions in goal-directed behavior

Richard P. Bagozzi, Hans Baumgartner,
Rik Pieters, and Marcel Zeelenberg

Introduction

Four components are frequently regarded as constitutive of an emotion: physiological changes, cognitive appraisals, subjective feelings, and behavioral reactions (Bagozzi, Gopinath, and Nyer 1999). In this chapter we will primarily be concerned with the behavioral effects of emotions. Emotional behavior consists of both unpremeditated, expressive behavior (including facial and vocal expressions) and emotionally motivated instrumental behavior (cf. Lazarus 1991; Mesquita and Frijda 1992). Our focus will be on the latter, and we will specifically emphasize the role of emotions in goal-directed behavior. Although Frijda (1993: 393) observed that "little systematic research exists on the actual relationships between emotions and corresponding changes in . . . goal-directed behaviors," we believe that such research offers many opportunities for enriching our understanding of human behavior in general and consumer behavior in particular.

We will not treat the large body of research about the relationship between attitudes and behavior (e.g. Fishbein and Ajzen 1975; Ajzen 1991; Fazio 1986) in any detail because affect (mood and emotions) and evaluation (attitude) are different constructs with independent effects on behavior (Cohen and Areni 1991). In support of this, studies have shown that affect (emotional responses and feelings engendered by an attitude object) and evaluation (thoughts, beliefs, and judgments about an attitude object) exhibit discriminant validity (Breckler and Wiggins 1989). In addition, affect can have direct effects on behavior that are not mediated by attitudes (Allen, Machleit, and Kleine 1992). Moreover, affect is often a better predictor of behavior than evaluation (Breckler and Wiggins 1989; Abelson *et al.* 1982). These and other findings justify independent and systematic research on the role of emotions in goal-directed behavior.

Emotional influences on goal-directed behavior

Our purpose in this section is to provide an overview of the psychological literature that is relevant to a consideration of the role of emotions in goal-directed behavior. We will focus on two functions of emotions. One is to provide feedback about the extent of goal attainment. This may be called the informational function of emotions in goal pursuit. The other is to direct and energize goal-directed behavior. This may be called the motivational function of emotions in goal pursuit. Some approaches focus more on the informational function, others on the motivational function, and still others on both. The theories covered in our review are quite varied, so it is necessary to impose some structure on the discussion. We will do this by classifying the frameworks along two dimensions. First, we will distinguish between approaches in which emotions are treated as broad underlying dimensions and approaches in which emotions are regarded as discrete categories. In the former approach, researchers have mostly studied the effects of positive versus negative emotions on behavior, although other dimensions such as degree of arousal have sometimes been discussed as well. In the latter approach, specific emotions such as happiness, sadness, anger, or fear are the focus of interest, and the idiosyncratic effects of these emotions on behavior are studied in greater detail. Second, we will differentiate between frameworks in which current (or past) emotional experiences have behavioral effects and frameworks in which the anticipation of future emotional experiences influences goal-directed behavior. In the former case, emotions are reactions to actual events that alert the organism to features of the environment that require attention. In the latter case, emotion-relevant events are imagined, but such mental simulations are assumed to have important effects on goal-directed behavior.

The two dimensions yield a 2 by 2 classification of theoretical frameworks dealing with the relationship between emotions and behavior. Table 3.1 lists representative approaches in each of the four cells. We will begin with a discussion of the various frameworks and indicate which function of emotions each approach emphasizes. We will then point out several important conceptual issues in research on the effects of emotions on goal-directed behavior and mention some requirements for a theory of goal-directed behavior in which emotions occupy a central place.

Behavioral effects of dimensions of currently experienced emotions

The control-process model of affect. In Carver and Scheier's (e.g. Carver and Scheier 1990; Carver, Lawrence, and Scheier 1996) model of affect, the informational value of emotions in goal-directed behavior is central. The model specifies that emotions arise as a by-product of people's movement toward goals, which is controlled by a negative feedback loop. In such a loop, the current state of the system is compared to a reference value and if a discrepancy is detected, adjustments are made in order to eliminate the discrepancy. Affect is hypothesized to be a function of the rate of reduction of the discrepancy and depends on a comparison of this rate with a desired

Table 3.1 A classification of frameworks dealing with the role of emotions in goal-directed behavior

	Emotions conceptualized in terms of underlying dimensions	*Emotions conceptualized as discrete categories*
Behavioral effects of currently experienced emotions	Control process model of affect (Carver and Scheier)	Psychoevolutionary theory of emotions (Plutchik)
	PAD model (Mehrabian and Russell)	Attribution theory (Weiner, Folkes)
	Mood effects on behavior (Gardner, Kahn and Isen)	Cognitive-motivational-relational theory of emotions (Lazarus)
		Communicative theory of emotions (Oatley and Johnson-Laird)
		Unfolding the emotion episode (Stein)
		Emotions and action readiness (Frijda)
		Regulatory focus (Higgins)
		Decision-making research (Zeelenberg, Pieters, etc.)
Behavioral effects of anticipated emotions	Positive and negative anticipatory affective reactions (Richard *et al.*, Parker *et al.*)	Decision-making research (Simonson, Zeelenberg, etc.)
		Prefactuals and behavior (Gleicher *et al.*)
	Goal-directed emotions (Bagozzi *et al.*)	
	Affective expectations and behavior (Wilson)	

rate of discrepancy reduction. If progress toward a goal is lower than the desired rate, negative affect is experienced; if it is higher, positive affect results. If no progress is being made, affect is also negative, and if progress equals the desired rate, no affect is experienced. Although the theory is mostly concerned with the informational value of affect, Carver, Lawrence, and Scheier (1996) offer some speculations about the influence of affect on behavior. For example, they argue that negative affect (if sufficiently strong) may lead to disengagement from the current goal and the reprioritization of a previously less important goal, or the adoption of an entirely new goal.

However, the behavioral implications of emotions have so far not been spelled out very clearly in the model and no empirical studies have addressed this aspect of the framework.

The PAD model. Mehrabian and Russell's (1974) environmental psychology model of approach-avoidance behavior emphasizes the directive function of emotions. Three emotional dimensions are distinguished in this framework: pleasure, arousal, and dominance (the so-called PAD dimensions). Pleasure refers to the valence of a feeling state (positive versus negative), arousal indicates the intensity of a feeling state (ranging from sleep to excitement), and dominance denotes a feeling state based on how much freedom to act a person has (dominance versus submissiveness). The term approach-avoidance behavior is used in a very broad sense and includes exploration, affiliation, performance, and preference. Emotional responses are assumed to arise from physical and social stimuli in the environment as well as characteristics of the person, and are specified to mediate their effects on approach-avoidance behavior. Specifically, Mehrabian and Russell (1974) suggest that pleasure (and possibly dominance) should lead to approach behavior and that arousal should have a curvilinear (inverted-U-shaped) relationship with approach-avoidance. In empirical studies, pleasure usually emerges as the most important determinant of approach-avoidance behavior, and it has displayed the most consistent results, although some evidence also supports the hypothesized curvilinear effect of arousal.

In marketing, the Mehrabian and Russell model has been used to investigate the effect of store atmosphere on approach-avoidance behaviors such as patronage and repurchase intentions, browsing, interactions with sales people, and amount of purchase. For example, Donovan and Rossiter (1982) showed that pleasure was the only significant predictor of an index of approach-avoidance intentions and unplanned spending, although there was also some evidence that arousal positively influenced approach in pleasant environments. In a follow-up study, Donovan, Rossiter, Marcoolyn, and Nesdale (1994) found that pleasure was a significant determinant of extra time spent in the store and unplanned spending, and that arousal was negatively related to unplanned spending in unpleasant environments.

Hui and Bateson (1991) used a variant of the Mehrabian and Russell model to study the role of perceived control and crowding in the service experience. They showed that perceived control (dominance) increased the pleasantness of the service experience, which in turn promoted approach behavior (desire to stay and desire to affiliate). In addition, perceptions of control lessened the negative effects of perceived crowding (submissiveness) on pleasure.

Olney, Holbrook, and Batra (1991) investigated the role of pleasure and arousal in consumer responses to advertising. They found that ad content influenced pleasure and arousal, which in turn affected the attitudinal components of hedonism, utilitarianism, and interestingness, and ultimately viewing time. In addition, arousal had a direct positive effect on viewing time. Several other studies have also shown that emotional reactions to ads are related to other dependent measures such as purchase likelihood (see Brown, Homer, and Inman 1998 for a review).

Mood effects on behavior. Although moods are different from emotions – moods are non-intentional and diffuse (cf. Frijda 1993) – the distinction becomes blurred when only dimensions of emotions (rather than discrete emotions) are considered and the source of the emotion is unrelated to the behavior in question (as in some studies discussed below). Gardner (1985) reviews research about the effects of moods states on behavior, and the general finding is that positive moods increase the likelihood of performance of certain behaviors (especially pro-social and helping behaviors). This effect may occur directly (e.g. moods may prime certain behaviors) or indirectly through the influence of moods on expectations, evaluations, and judgments (e.g. moods have been shown to bias judgments in a mood-congruent direction). Gardner (1985) specifically suggests that the effects of mood on behavior may be important in the service encounter, at the point of purchase, and in advertising communications contexts.

An interesting study by Kahn and Isen (1993) showed that positive mood may lead consumers to seek greater variety in their product choices (relative to a neutral-mood control condition). Variety seeking may be considered as a type of exploration in the Mehrabian and Russell model (see Steenkamp and Baumgartner 1992). However, the effect of positive mood on variety seeking was only obtained when the choice task did not make negative features of the choice options salient. The reason for this, presumably, is that subjects in a positive mood are more likely to recognize differences among brands and enjoy diversity in products as long as the experience is expected to be a pleasant one.

Behavioral effects of currently experienced discrete emotions

Plutchik's psychoevolutionary theory of emotions. Plutchik's (1980) psychoevolutionary theory of emotion proposes specific action tendencies in response to particular emotions. Drawing on Darwin, Plutchik (1989: 5) argues that the "fundamental function [of emotions] is to increase the chances of individual survival." He distinguishes eight basic emotions that can be arranged in a circle. Their subjective feeling states correspond to joy and sadness, anger and fear, acceptance and disgust, and surprise and anticipation. Associated with each primary emotion is a characteristic behavioral expression (cooperating, crying for help, attacking, escaping, affiliating, repulsing, stopping, and examining) that serves a particular adaptive function (reproduction, reintegration, destruction, protection, incorporation, rejection, orientation, exploration).

Holbrook (1986) provided illustrative examples of each of Plutchik's primary emotions in a consumption context (e.g. discovering that one has been misled by an auto salesman as an example of anger) and suggested that they should be related to marketing variables such as repeat purchase, audience share, and event attendance. He also presents empirical evidence that joy elicited by television commercials has a strong positive effect on purchase-likelihood intentions.

Attributional theories of emotion and action. In Weiner's (1985, 1986) attribution theory, situational appraisals and attributional thinking lead to the experience of different emotions, which in turn serve as motivators of behavior. Weiner assumes that the attainment or non-attainment of a valued goal evokes a general positive or negative reaction that is outcome-dependent but attribution-independent (e.g. happiness). However, a subsequent search for the cause of the outcome may result in more differentiated, attribution-dependent emotional experiences based on perceptions of locus (e.g. internal vs. external; buyer- vs. seller-related), controllability (e.g. personal vs. impersonal control), and stability (e.g. permanent or stable vs. temporary or unstable causes). For example, Weiner shows that pride and other feelings of self-worth are associated with internal attributions for success and that pity usually involves stable and uncontrollable causes, while anger tends to go with external and controllable causes. The various emotions then lead to characteristic actions. For example, perceived uncontrollability and pity promote helping-behavior, whereas controllability and anger imply a lack of help.

Folkes and her associates investigated some of these ideas in the context of product or service failure. For example, Folkes (1984) showed that locus and controllability influenced how much anger consumers experienced following product failure and how much they wanted to hurt the firm's business. Anger and desire for revenge were highest when the product failure was caused by the manufacturer or store and when it was controllable. In another study involving airline passengers whose flights were delayed, Folkes, Koletzky, and Graham (1987) found that both stability and control over product failure elicited anger at the firm, which in turn prompted a desire to complain about failure and lowered consumers' intention to repurchase the product. In addition, controllability had a direct effect on desire to complain, and stability influenced repeat purchase intentions. Folkes (1988) suggests that attribution theory might be applied to other emotions as well. For example, pride and embarrassment may be elicited depending on whether a certain purchase price is attributed to negotiating skill or negotiating ineptitude, and these emotions might lead to boasting about the purchase or reticence to talk about it.

The cognitive-motivational-relational theory of emotions. Lazarus (1991) explicitly set out to integrate the informational and directive roles of specific emotions in goal-directed behavior. He distinguishes between the goal-incongruent (negative) emotions of anger, fright-anxiety, guilt-shame, sadness, envy-jealousy, and disgust, and the goal-congruent (positive) emotions of happiness-joy, pride, love-affection, and relief. Each emotion is characterized by a core relational theme (i.e. the central harmful or beneficial relationship between the person and the environment underlying each emotion, such as making reasonable progress toward the realization of a goal in the case of happiness), an appraisal pattern (i.e. evaluations of the significance of events for one's well-being, in terms of such appraisal dimensions as goal relevance, goal congruence and ego-involvement), and an action tendency. The action tendencies that accompany specific emotions are as follows: attack (anger), escape (anxiety-fright), atonement (guilt), hiding (shame), withdrawal (sadness), possessing (envy), attack (jealousy), ejection (disgust), expansiveness (happiness-joy), expansiveness (pride), intimacy (love-affection), and relaxation (relief).

The communicative theory of emotions. In Oatley and Johnson-Laird's (1987: 35) influential theory, emotions occur "at a significant juncture of a plan; i.e. typically . . . when the evaluation (conscious or unconscious) of the likely success of a plan changes" (see also Johnson-Laird and Oatley 1992; Oatley and Johnson-Laird 1996). Emotions are seen as interrupt mechanisms that alert the cognitive system or others (in the case of mutual plans) to those parts of the goal structure that require attention. They prepare the organism for action appropriate to the juncture in the plan, eliminating the need for extensive, time-consuming deliberation and avoiding the inflexibility of reflex-like action patterns. In this view, the primary function of emotions is to assist organisms with limited resources in the management of multiple goals in an uncertain world.

In the original statement of the theory (Oatley and Johnson-Laird 1987), five basic emotions were distinguished: happiness, sadness, anxiety (or fear), anger, and disgust. Happiness arises when a subgoal is achieved, sadness when a major plan fails or an active goal is lost, anxiety when a self-preservation goal is threatened, anger when an active plan is frustrated, and disgust when a gustatory goal is violated. The theory treats the directive role of emotions as well. The behavioral consequences are: to continue with the plan for happiness; to do nothing or search for a plan for sadness; to stop, attend to the environment, or escape for anxiety; to try harder or aggress for anger; and to reject the substance or withdraw for disgust. Empirical research (summarized in Oatley and Johnson-Laird 1996) has supported the notions that different evaluations of goal-relevant events give rise to distinct emotions and that positive emotions lead to the continuation of a current plan and negative emotions to the formation of new plans. However, the theory required revisions in the specification of the basic emotions and now distinguishes four emotions that can be free-floating or non-intentional (happiness, sadness, anger, and fear) and five emotions that always have an object (attachment, parental love, sexual attraction, disgust, and personal rejection). The behavioral consequences of the intentional emotions are attraction and desire (for attachment, parental love, and sexual attraction) and rejection or withdrawal (disgust and personal rejection). In addition, the theory now allows for mixtures of basic emotions to occur in a given situation (e.g. the simultaneous experience of anger and sadness). This implies that conflicts might arise about which action to pursue at some juncture of a plan because of different evaluations of the goal-relevance of an event.

Stein's work on unfolding the emotion episode. Stein and her associates (e.g. Stein, Trabasso, and Liwag 1993; Stein, Liwag, and Wade 1996) have proposed a theory of goal-directed behavior in which the informational and directive role of (a small set of) specific emotions are integrated. Stein's theory makes the basic assumption that emotions are evoked by changes in the status of a valued goal and that they lead to attempts to attain or maintain pleasurable states and avoid or escape from aversive states. Stein considers four emotions (happiness, sadness, fear, and anger) and develops detailed process models of how each emotion episode unfolds. The process starts with a precipitating event that promises goal success or threatens goal failure. Depending on the type of appraisal and the perceived certainty of a change in the status of a valued goal, different emotions are experienced. For example, events that facilitate maintenance or attainment of goals and perceptions that goal success is certain lead to happiness. Certain goal failure, coupled with a wish to reinstate the goal and the belief that a course of action is available, evokes anger. Perceptions that goal failure is certain and that no plan is available to reinstate the goal result in sadness. Each emotional experience then leads to planning processes, the enactment of the plan, and the monitoring of results. Specifically, in the case of happiness, people will try to maintain the current state or attain new goals, in the case of anger they will attempt to reinstate the goal, and in the case of sadness they will abandon the goal, forfeit the goal, or substitute a new goal.

Frijda's work on emotional action readiness. Frijda's (1986) approach emphasizes the behavioral implications of specific emotions (see also Roseman, Wiest, and Swartz 1994). He argues and has found that a major component of the experience of an emotion is a felt state of action readiness. The modes of action readiness that he considers include approach, being with, protection, avoidance, attending, rejection, disinterest, antagonism, interruption, and inhibition. In two empirical studies, Frijda and his associates (Frijda 1987; Frijda, Kuipers, and ter Schure 1989) show that different emotions have different action readiness profiles and that emotions can therefore be predicted from action readiness cues. For example, fear is associated with not wanting something, protection, avoidance, and approach, while happiness involves approach, exuberance, and attending (cf. Frijda *et al.* 1989).

Higgins' work on regulatory focus. While much of life is devoted to the pursuit of pleasure and avoidance of pain, Higgins (1997) argues that *how* one regulates pleasure and pain determines emotional experience. Specifically, he proposes that, as a consequence of developmental experiences early in life, people exhibit one of two strategic orientations: a promotion focus or a prevention focus. Such individual differences in cognitive appraisal and action tendency moderate the effect of behavioral outcomes on emotional experience and subsequent behavior.

Under a promotion focus, a person is motivated to approach desired end-states (e.g. accomplishments, aspirations, hopes) by regulating behavior to achieve positive outcomes. Focus is upon ensuring the achievement of hopes or ideals and not missing opportunities in this regard. Under a prevention focus, in contrast, a person is also motivated to pursue desired end-states, but here end-states concern meeting one's responsibilities or guaranteeing safety. Focus is upon avoiding negative outcomes by not doing things forbidden or by doing things to meet expectations. Pleasure is experienced under a promotion focus by the presence of positive outcomes, pain by the absence of positive outcomes. Pleasure is experienced under a prevention focus by the absence of negative outcomes, pain by the presence of negative outcomes.

Higgins predicts different emotions result when discrepancies occur between current and desired end-states (Higgins 1987, 1996). When one falls short of aspirations, "dejection-related" emotions arise (e.g. disappointment, dissatisfaction, sadness). When one fails to live up to oughts or safety goals, "agitation-related" emotions emerge (e.g. afraid, anxious, worried).

Higgins' theory has not been applied in marketing, but a number of studies have been conducted in psychology. Consistent with the theory, Roney, Higgins, and Shah (1995) found that people with a promotion focus who succeeded on a task were happy, whereas those with a prevention focus were content. However, people with a promotion focus who failed to achieve a goal were dejected, whereas those with a prevention focus were agitated. Brendl, Higgins, and Lemm (1995) found similar results when gains and losses were monetary. Higgins, Shah, and Friedman (1997) showed that strength of regulatory focus moderates the relation between goal achievement and emotion. Specifically, the stronger the promotion focus, the happier people were when aspirations were achieved, and the more dejected people were when aspirations were not achieved; the stronger the prevention focus, the more content people were when oughts were fulfilled, and the more agitated people were when oughts were not fulfilled. Some research has examined the directive implications of the orientations. Crowe and Higgins (1997) demonstrated that a promotion versus prevention focus leads to greater vigilance and performance on difficult tasks, among other findings. It would be interesting to see how and to what extent a promotion focus and a prevention focus influence anticipated emotion and motivate instrumental behavior (see also Verbeke 1997).

Decision-making research on the behavioral effects of specific emotions. Recent research in behavioral decision-making and marketing has studied the behavioral effects of several specific discrete emotions in some detail. Most of this work has dealt with experienced regret (or its opposite, rejoicing), but disappointment (or its opposite, elation) has also been considered to some extent (see Zeelenberg, Inman, and Pieters 1999, and Zeelenberg, van Dijk, Manstead, and van der Pligt, forthcoming, for reviews). Regret and disappointment are closely related, negative emotions that occur when decisions take a bad turn. The difference between the two is that people tend to experience regret when a non-chosen alternative yields better outcomes than the chosen alternative, whereas they are likely to feel disappointment when the outcomes of a decision fall short of expectations. Research has shown that the regret following a bad decision influences subsequent decisions, and that experienced regret (rejoicing) is negatively (positively) correlated with satisfaction and repurchase intentions. Zeelenberg *et al.* (forthcoming) also argue that "whereas regret is likely to result in a focus on non-attained goals and promote goal persistence, disappointment may result in goal abandonment."

A study by Zeelenberg and Pieters (1999) is particularly relevant to the behavioral effects of regret and disappointment. Zeelenberg and Pieters suggest that regret and disappointment caused by a failed service encounter will result in dissatisfaction with the service encounter, but may also lead to particular behavioral responses. Specifically, they argue that consumers who experience regret are likely to switch service providers, whereas consumers who are disappointed will engage in negative word-of-mouth and complain. They used an experience sampling methodology to collect instances of failed service encounters by probing for either experiences where another service provider would have been a better choice or instances where the service was worse than expected. Their findings indicated that disappointment (but not regret) influenced dissatisfaction with the encounter, regret had a direct effect (not mediated by satisfaction) on switching, and disappointment had a direct effect (not mediated by satisfaction) on negative word-of-mouth. Neither of the two emotions had an effect on complaints.

Raghunatham and Pham (1999) recently contrasted the behavioral effects of anxiety and sadness. Based on appraisal theories of emotion (e.g. Lazarus 1991), they argued that sadness might prime reward acquisition goals because sadness is often associated with the loss or absence of a reward, whereas anxiety might prompt a goal of uncertainty reduction or risk avoidance because anxiety frequently involves uncertainty and lack of control. This suggests that in choice situations involving a trade-off between risks and rewards, sad individuals should prefer the high risk/high reward option and anxious individuals would prefer the low risk/low reward option. Raghunatham and Pham found support for these predictions in three experiments dealing with choices among gambles and jobs. It should be noted that in contrast to other studies about specific emotional effects on behavior, the research of Raghunatham and Pham dealt with affective states that were not relevant to the task at hand (sadness and anxiety were induced by asking subjects to project themselves into an emotional situation). Sadness and anxiety were thus more like moods than true emotions.

Behavioral effects of dimensions of anticipated emotions

Positive and negative anticipated affective reaction of behavior. Several recent studies have considered the effects of anticipated affective reactions on behavior within the context of Ajzen's (1991) theory of planned behavior. For example, Richard, van der Pligt, and de Vries (1995) investigated whether a summary measure of anticipated negative feelings of worry, regret, and tension following unprotected sex would influence behavioral expectations toward HIV preventive behaviors over and above attitudes, subjective norms, and perceived behavioral control. As hypothesized, anticipated affective reactions were a significant determinant of behavioral expectations for both refraining from sexual intercourse and condom use. In another study, Richard, van der Pligt, and de Vries (1996) showed that anticipated, post-behavioral affective reactions were distinct from general affective reactions toward a target behavior (even though they were both measured with the same scale of pleasant–unpleasant, nice–awful, and good–bad) and that anticipated feelings had a significant impact on behavioral expectations for three out of four target behaviors (eating junk food, using soft drugs, and drinking alcohol), even after the effects of attitudes, subjective norms, and perceived behavioral control were accounted for. A similar result was obtained by Parker, Manstead, and Stradling (1995), who found that anticipated negative affect had a significant impact on intentions to commit driving violations in addition to attitude, subjective norms, perceived behavioral control, and personal norms.

Perugini and Bagozzi (forthcoming) introduced a modification of the theory of planned behavior in which attitudes, subjective norms, and perceived behavioral control influence intentions indirectly through desires, and in which desires are additionally influenced by positive and negative anticipated emotions. In two empirical studies they showed that positive anticipated emotions influenced desires to exercise and diet, and negative anticipated emotions impacted desires to study.

A model of goal-directed emotions. Bagozzi, Baumgartner, and Pieters (1998) recently proposed a more integrated model of the behavioral effects of anticipated emotions. The model assumes that appraisals of a goal situation include an assessment of the prospects of goal success and goal failure and that this evaluation elicits anticipated emotions. Although, in principle, these appraisals could lead to the anticipation of specific discrete emotions (which would actually be most consistent with the appraisal theories from which the model is derived), as a first step only broad classes of positive and negative anticipated emotions were considered. Anticipated emotions that are sufficiently intense engender volitional processes concerned with the formation of behavioral intentions, decisions about how much effort to expend on goal pursuit, and planning and monitoring steps. Instrumental behaviors that are judged to have a high likelihood of goal attainment and are deemed both desirable and feasible are then implemented and will or will not lead to goal attainment. The process ends with an appraisal of the outcomes of goal pursuit and resulting goal-outcome emotions. The model was tested in a longitudinal study with 406 people who had either weight maintenance or weight loss goals, and the findings were largely consistent with the proposed model. In particular, positive and negative anticipatory emotions both influenced dieting and exercising volitions, which in turn led to dieting and exercising behaviors in an effort to lose weight or maintain one's weight.

Brown, Cron, and Slocum (1997) replicated and extended the study of Bagozzi *et al.* (1998) in a salesperson context. They explicitly considered what they termed "stakes" (interests in Frijda's theory) as an antecedent of positive and negative anticipatory emotions in their empirical work. Following Lazarus (1991), personal stakes are defined as "cognitive appraisals of the significance of the situation for a person's well-being" and are specified to serve as a "trigger initiating goal-directed emotions, intentions, and behavior" (Brown *et al.* 1997: 40). With the exception of the link between stakes and negative anticipatory emotions, Brown *et al.* (1997) supported the model proposed by Bagozzi *et al.* (1998), even though goal-directed behavior, goal attainment, and goal-outcome emotions were measured three months after the assessment of the wave-one constructs. Furthermore, in contrast to Bagozzi *et al.* (1998), who used a self-report measure of goal-attainment, Brown *et al.* (1997) assessed degree of goal attainment as the difference between a salesperson's stated goal and actual sales performance (number of units sold), which avoids the problem of self-report biases.

Affective expectations and behavior. Wilson and his associates (Wilson, Lisle, Kraft, and Wetzel 1989; Klaaren, Hodges, and Wilson 1994) have stressed the role that affective expectations play in affective experience and behavior. They argue that if an affective expectation is confirmed or if a discrepancy with an affective expectation is not noticed, judgments of one's affective experience can be made relatively quickly and will be consistent with one's expectations. They also suggest that when the discrepancy is noticed, judgments will be more effortful and one's affective experience might be contrasted away from affective expectations. They performed an experiment in which subjects who expected cartoons to be funny or not funny were exposed to objectively funny or non-funny cartoons. Ratings of the funniness of cartoons were generally consistent with expectations, even when subjects were thought to notice the discrepancy, and subjects' facial expressions of mirth mirrored their self-reports (Wilson *et al.* 1989). In another study (Klaaren *et al.* 1994), subjects who had either high or no expectations toward a movie watched the same movie under either pleasant or unpleasant viewing conditions. Compared to people with neutral expectations, those with positive expectations enjoyed the study more and indicated a greater willingness to participate in the study again when called three to four weeks later, while the objective pleasantness of the experience had no effect on subjects' willingness to repeat the activity. The authors argue that the result is due to selective reinterpretation, where people discount or reweigh memories of expectation-inconsistent events.

Behavioral effects of anticipated discrete emotions

Decision-making research on the behavioral effects of specific emotions. Recent studies have investigated the behavioral effects of anticipated regret (see Zeelenberg 1999 for a review). The idea is that people's decisions are not only influenced by the relative attractiveness of each choice alternative but also by the possibility of regretting the choice later on. So far, anticipated regret has been shown to impact people's decisions under two circumstances. The first is when post-decisional regret is made salient. For example, in an experiment by Simonson (1992), consumers who were reminded that they might later regret a bad decision were more likely to choose a higher-priced, brand-name products, presumably because they thought this would shield them from possible future regret. Indirect evidence comes from a field study on coupon use by Inman and McAlister (1994) in which they found that coupon redemption increased just prior to the expiration date. The second situation occurs when feedback on the foregone outcomes is made available. Since in choices between a sure thing and a gamble the sure thing is both the risk-averse and regret-averse option (because selection of the sure thing avoids feedback on the gamble and thus makes regret impossible), it was initially thought that the anticipation of regret promoted risk aversion. However, subsequent research by Zeelenberg (e.g. Zeelenberg and Beattie, 1997) showed that decisions can be framed in such a way that anticipated regret actually leads to risk-seeking. In his review, Zeelenberg (1999) proposes additional circumstances in which anticipated regret may be expected to influence decisions.

Zeelenberg *et al.* (forthcoming) also speculate about the behavioral effects of anticipated disappointment, although very little empirical work is available. They suggest that the desire to avoid disappointment may lead to risk aversion (when there is no uncertainty about an outcome, one cannot be disappointed), increased effort in goal pursuit or the lowering of expectations (to make it less likely that outcomes fall short of expectations), or the derogation of desired but uncertain outcomes. Future research will have to show under which conditions people engage in these disappointment-minimizing strategies.

Two field studies showing the effects of discrete emotion have been conducted in the salesforce context. In a study of mortgage salespeople, Verbeke and Bagozzi (2000a) showed that sales call anxiety (i.e. the fear of being negatively evaluated and rejected by customers) negatively affected the quality of sales interactions and the volume of sales. Sales call anxiety was found to consist of four factors: negative self-evaluations, negative evaluations perceived from customers, physiological symptoms, and felt urges to take protective actions. In a study of salespeople selling various financial services, Verbeke and Bagozzi (2000b) found that the tendency to experience embarrassment and shame leads to various coping responses (e.g. avoidance behaviors), and these in turn negatively impact sales performance.

Prefactuals and behavior. The research of Gleicher, Boninger, Strathman, and associates (summarized in Gleicher, Boninger, Strathman, Armor, and Ahn 1995) on prefactuals is also relevant to the discussion of anticipated emotions (especially regret). Prefactuals are like counterfactuals (i.e. imaginations of what might have been), except that the target event is imagined and has not happened (yet). Gleicher *et al.* (1995) argue that prefactuals can influence attitudes, intentions, and behavior in two different ways. First, imagining a counterfactual that reverses a negative outcome suggests an effective course of action for the future. Second, since a negative outcome is likely to lead to negative affect, the motivation to avoid this negative affect may influence future behavior. In a field study about prefactuals and condom use, Gleicher *et al.* showed that when subjects imagined engaging in unsafe sex and contracting HIV (including a consideration of the amount of regret for not having used a condom) they formed significantly more positive attitudes toward condoms, compared to a control condition in which subjects were only given information about the transmission of HIV. In another study, subjects given a pro-insurance prefactual (thinking about losing one's money because of not buying insurance) were more likely to buy insurance in an experimental game than subjects given an anti-insurance prefactual (thinking about buying insurance and not needing it).

Towards an integrated conceptualization of emotions in goal-directed behavior

So far, we have mainly tried to catalogue the progress that has been made in recent years in understanding the role of emotions in goal-directed behavior. In this last section of the chapter, we delineate four areas in which we believe additional research is particularly needed. Such research should promote a more refined and integrated conceptualization of the role of emotions in goal-directed behavior.

Emotions as dimensions or categories

Our review of the theoretical frameworks addressing the link between emotions and goal-directed behavior has shown that the different approaches can be readily classified as examples of the dimensional or categorical views of emotions. The question arises which one of the two views is more useful as a foundation for an integrated conceptualization of the role of emotions in goal-directed behavior.

Lazarus (1991: 59–68) has summarized the arguments in favor of each approach. The primary advantage of the dimensional view is that it is a more parsimonious account of emotional experience and that in many empirical studies a few dimensions (especially positive vs. negative valence) capture a large portion of the variation in more specific emotion ratings. In addition, it has been argued that feelings are frequently not experienced strongly enough to lead to full-fledged discrete emotions, that different positive or negative emotions tend to co-occur, and that people may only be able to discriminate emotions in terms of global dimensions such as valence or intensity. Proponents of the categorical view (including Lazarus) deny the plausibility of these arguments and contend that a focus on dimensions provides no unique insights into emotions because these dimensions are universal dimensions of meaning. Furthermore, only a categorical approach can yield rich insights into the eliciting conditions, subjective feelings, and behavioral consequences of different emotions.

An attempt at reconciling these positions was made by Frijda, and his views are particularly relevant to a consideration of the behavioral effects of emotions. Frijda (1986: 256) argues that the two views focus on two different levels of the emotion process. "Emotions are discrete states when considered at the level of actual response readiness – at the level of particular action tendencies. They are states varying along a set of continuous dimensions, however, when considered at the level of response to the event's valence and urgency." Future research will have to show under which conditions a dimensional (more abstract) or categorical (less abstract) view of emotions will be more useful in understanding the role of emotions in goal-directed behavior. One may speculate that in certain situations (e.g. atmospheric influences on purchase behavior) affective reactions are not differentiated enough to warrant a categorical perspective. Furthermore, if a situation evokes a mix of emotions (e.g. regret, disappointment, sadness, anger) or if the behavioral reactions tied to different emotions are similar (e.g. regret, disappointment, sadness, and anger in response to a bad experience with a service provider may all lead to avoidance of this service provider in the future), a dimensional approach might be sufficient. However, in general, there seems to be a lot of potential in exploring the behavioral effects of discrete emotions.

Anticipated versus experienced emotions

While research on the role of experienced emotions is relatively well established, systematic work on the role of anticipated emotions is in its infancy. Several issues provide opportunities for future research. First, empirical studies to date have only investigated the behavioral effects of anticipated positive and negative affect and regret. Little is known about other negative and especially positive anticipated emotions, even though it is likely that many consumer behaviors are the result of, say, the anticipation of future joy. The decisions to ride a rollercoaster or to go to a movie are obvious examples. Other behaviors, such as doing physical exercise, are also likely to be promoted by the anticipation of particular feelings afterwards.

Second, we do not know when people engage in the mental simulations of future emotional experiences. In previous studies subjects were prompted to anticipate their affective state following some behavior or outcome, and it remains to be seen to what extent people will naturally do these things. It would also be helpful to integrate research on anticipated emotions with research on mental simulation (e.g. Kahneman and Tversky 1982; Taylor and Schneider 1989; Taylor and Pham 1996). Taylor and her associates have discussed a variety of mechanisms by which simulations may bring about behavior, and more detailed discussions of the process of emotional simulation promise to enhance our understanding of the role of anticipated emotions in goal-directed behavior.

Third, affect in response to imagined future performance of a behavior (e.g. Parker *et al.* 1995; Richard *et al.* 1995, 1996; van der Pligt *et al.* 1998), goal-directed emotions (e.g. Bagozzi *et al.* 1998; Perugini and Bagozzi 1999), and prefactual judgments of regret (e.g. Gleicher *et al.* 1995) are all expected emotions that have been shown to affect decision-making. But exactly how do they do this? One possibility is that the emotions arise in response to a decision process wherein a person compares anticipated pleasant outcomes or expected goal achievement and anticipated unpleasant outcomes or expected goal failures with personal standards or reference values. Bagozzi (1992) termed these comparisons outcome-desire pursuits and outcome-desire avoidances, respectively, and, consistent with appraisal theories of emotions (e.g. Lazarus 1991), hypothesized that specific positive or negative emotions would arise and, in turn, stimulate corresponding coping responses, such as volition and action tendencies. Future research is needed to establish whether expected emotions function differently for discrepancy-reducing and discrepancy-enlarging goals (e.g. Carver *et al.* 1996) and for promotion and prevention regulatory focuses (e.g. Higgins 1997).

A fourth issue is whether expected emotions are experienced fully in terms of physiological and behavioral changes or only in terms of subjective feelings. That is, when imagining what one's positive and/or negative emotions would be toward goal attainment/failure, does the decision-maker experience these as "hot" (i.e. aroused) emotions or "cold" (i.e. cognitive) emotions? Do so-called hot or cold emotions influence volition and behavior to different degrees? In other words, do people "feel" at time 1 what they expect to "feel" at a later time 2, and how do such emotions affect decisions and enact behavior? A related question for future research is whether people compare at time 2, once they have achieved or failed to achieve a goal, their goal-outcome emotions to how they expected to feel when measured at time 1?

Directive influence of emotions on goal-directed behavior

Much progress has been made in understanding the antecedent conditions and cognitive appraisals that give rise to emotions. Much less is known about the directive effect of emotions on goal-directive behavior, particularly the process by which emotions influence behavior. For instance, structural approaches such as the Mehrabian and Russell model or the research that has attempted to incorporate affective influences into attitude-behavior models are silent about how emotions bring about behavior.

While several theories have proposed specific action tendencies in response to particular experienced or anticipated emotions, there has been no attempt to classify these action tendencies in an integrative way, and most action tendencies seem too abstract to be practically useful. With respect to the classification of action tendencies, for instance, several theories propose approach-avoidance tendencies (e.g. Mehrabian and Russell; Frijda, Higgins, and Oatley) or attack and affiliate tendencies (Plutchik; Lazarus). On the other hand, "hiding" appears to be specific to Lazarus, "crying for help" specific to Plutchik, and "reinstating the goal" specific to Stein. It seems fruitful to compare and contrast the emotion-specific action tendencies proposed by different authors and come up with an integrative framework. With regard to the level of abstractness of the action tendencies, few theories consider specific behaviors chosen from the behavioral repertoire that is actually available to the individual in a given situation. When the interest is in human behavior in general, it may be necessary to focus on fairly abstract action tendencies. However, in an applied discipline like consumer research, it is useful to know which avoidance behavior a consumer will select when experiencing a certain negative emotion in response to a service failure. Much can be learned from studying the specific behaviors associated with different discrete emotions evoked by different marketing situations. The studies of Folkes (1984; Folkes *et al.* 1987) and Zeelenberg and Pieters (1999) are good examples of the advantages of this approach.

Emotional influences in the action sequence

Most theories to date have examined the influence of emotions on behavior in general. A comprehensive model of the role of emotions in goal-directed behavior needs to distinguish different stages of the process of goal pursuit and investigate the influence of emotions on behavior at all stages of the process (see Huffman, Ratneshwar, and Mick, this volume). One useful distinction is between goal setting and goal striving (cf. Gollwitzer 1990; Bagozzi and Dholakia 1999). In the *goal-setting phase*, a person has to decide which goal(s) to pursue. This involves considerations of the desirability (i.e. goal attainment should lead to consequences that the person values) and feasibility (i.e. a person should have the ability to attain the goal and there should be environmental opportunities for reaching it) of different goals. Goal setting culminates in the formation of a goal intention, which expresses a commitment to achieve the chosen goal. In the *goal-striving phase*, a person considers how the desired goal can be attained, initiates actual goal-directed behaviors aimed at reaching the goal, deals with threats and opportunities that arise during goal pursuit, and eventually experiences goal attainment/failure. The reactions to goal attainment/failure and, more generally, the information gained during goal pursuit then serve as feedback in a new cycle of goal setting and goal striving.

Previous research investigating emotional influences on goal-directed behavior has mostly dealt with the goal-striving stage. However, emotions are also important at the goal-setting stage. First, an emotional experience may be the immediate goal object inspiring behavior, in the sense that the emotion expresses what the person is trying to achieve. For example, Emmons (undated) describes a category of personal strivings (i.e. goals that people typically try to accomplish) dealing with emotions and emotional well-being that includes such goals as "enjoy life and be happy," "avoid feeling dissatisfied with some aspects of life," and "not feel anxious about future career plans." In the consumer context, relevant emotional goals might be "enjoy my vacations" or "avoid stress while shopping." In addition, some purchase behaviors are strongly influenced by hedonic factors, as when people get the urge to buy something on impulse (e.g. Rook 1987) or go on a buying binge when they are depressed, upset, or angry (Faber and O'Guinn 1992; DeSarbo and Edwards 1996).

Second, emotional states may influence why the person decides to pursue a goal. In this case, the desirability of the goal is a function of the positive and negative emotional consequences of goal pursuit and goal achievement/failure. The work on anticipated affective reactions to outcomes of behavior, conducted within the context of the theory of reasoned action or theory of planned behavior, is relevant here (e.g. Richard *et al.* 1995). In addition, studies conducted from a means-end chain perspective often find that emotional states (e.g. feeling good about oneself, love, worrying less, etc.) are important motivators of product purchase because they provide the rationale for why consumers value certain product attributes (cf. Reynolds and Guttman 1988). Drawing on concepts from means-end chain theory, Pieters, Baumgartner, and Allen (1995) modeled consumers' goal structures for weight loss and found that happiness was an important superordinate goal motivating weight control behaviors (see also Bagozzi and Dholakia 1999).

In conclusion, there is solid evidence that emotions are an important component of people's pursuit of their goals. Many theoretical frameworks accord a central role to emotional influences on goal-directed behavior, but there has been little integration across the various streams of research. In this chapter we have reviewed the different frameworks using a simple 2 by 2 classification according to which experienced or anticipated emotions viewed as dimensions or categories affect people's pursuit of their goals. The next step will be to develop a comprehensive model of the influence of emotions on each stage of the goal-directed behavior process.

Acknowledgments

Thanks are due to Rajeev Batra, Steve Brown, and the editors for helpful comments on a previous version of this chapter

References

Abelson, R.P., Kinder, D.R., Peters, M.D., and Fiske, S.T. (1982) "Affective and semantic components in political person perception," *Journal of Personality and Social Psychology* 42: 619–30.

Ajzen, I. (1991) "The theory of planned behavior," *Organizational Behavior and Human Decision Processes* 50: 179–210.

Allen, C.T., Machleit, K.A., and Kleine, S.S. (1992) "A comparison of attitudes and emotions as predictors of behavior at diverse levels of behavioral experience," *Journal of Consumer Research* 18: 493–504.

Bagozzi, R.P. (1992) "The self-regulation of attitudes, intentions, and behavior," *Social Psychology Quarterly* 55: 178–204.

Bagozzi, R.P. and Dholakia, U. (1999) "Goal-setting and goal-striving in consumer behavior," *Journal of Marketing* 63 (special issue): 19–32.

Bagozzi, R.P., Baumgartner, H., and Pieters, R. (1998) "Goal-directed emotions," *Cognition and Emotion* 12: 1–26.

Bagozzi, R.P., Gopinath, M., and Nyer, P.U. (1999) "The role of emotions in marketing," *Journal of the Academy of Marketing Science* 27: 184–206.

Breckler, S.J. and Wiggins, E.C. (1989) "Affect versus evaluation in the structure of attitudes," *Journal of Experimental Social Psychology* 25: 253–71.

Brendl, C.M., Higgins, E.T., and Lemm, K.M. (1995) "Sensitivity to varying gains and losses: the role of self-discrepancies and event framing," *Journal of Personality and Social Psychology* 69: 1028–51.

Brown, S.P., Cron, W.L., and Slocum, J.W. Jr. (1997) "Effects of goal-directed emotions on salesperson volitions, behavior, and performance: a longitudinal study," *Journal of Marketing* 61: 39–50.

Brown, S.P., Homer, P.M., and Inman, J.J. (1998) "A meta-analysis of relationships between ad-evoked feelings and advertising responses," *Journal of Marketing Research* 35: 114–26.

Carver, C.S. and Scheier, M.F. (1990) "Origins and functions of positive and negative affect: a control-process view," *Psychology Review* 97: 19–35.

Carver, C.S., Lawrence, J.W., and Scheier, M.F. (1996) "A control-process perspective on the origins of affect," in L.L. Martin and A. Tesser (eds) *Striving and Feeling: Interactions among Goals, Affect, and Self-regulation*, Mahwah, NJ: Erlbaum.

Cohen, J.B. and Areni, C.S. (1991) "Affect and consumer behavior," in T.S. Robertson and H.H. Kassarjian (eds) *Handbook of Consumer Behavior*, Englewood Cliffs, NJ: Prentice-Hall.

Crowe, E. and Higgins, E.T. (1997) "Regulatory focus and strategic inclinations: promotion and prevention in decision-making," *Organizational Behavior and Human Decision Processes* 69: 117–32.

DeSarbo, W.S. and Edwards, E.A. (1996) "Typologies of compulsive buying behavior: a constrained clusterwise regression approach," *Journal of Consumer Psychology* 5: 231–62.

Donovan, R.J. and Rossiter, J.R. (1982) "Store atmosphere: an environmental psychology approach," *Journal of Retailing* 58: 34–57.

Donovan, R.J., Rossiter, J.R., Marcoolyn, G., and Nesdale, A. (1994) "Store atmosphere and purchasing behavior," *Journal of Retailing* 70: 283–94.

Emmons, R.A. (undated) "Personal striving coding manual," University of California at Davis.

Faber, R.J. and O'Guinn, T.C. (1992) "A clinical screener for compulsive buying," *Journal of Consumer Research* 19: 459–69.

Fazio, R.H. (1986) "How do attitudes guide behavior?" in R.M. Sorrentino and E.T. Higgins (eds) *Handbook of Motivation and Cognition: Foundations of Social Behavior*, New York: Guilford Press.

Fishbein, M. and Ajzen, I. (1975) *Belief, Attitude, Intention, and Behavior: An Introduction to Theory and Research*, Reading, MA: Addison-Wesley.

Folkes, V.S. (1984) "Consumer reactions to product failure: an attributional approach," *Journal of Consumer Research* 10: 398–409.

—— (1988) "Recent attribution research in consumer behavior: a review and new directions," *Journal of Consumer Research* 14: 548–65.

Folkes, V.S., Koletzky, S., and Graham, J.L. (1987) "A field study of causal inferences and consumer reaction: the view from the airport," *Journal of Consumer Research* 13: 534–39.

Frijda, N.H. (1986) *The Emotions*, Cambridge: Cambridge University Press.

—— (1987) "Emotion, cognitive structure, and action tendency," *Cognition and Emotion* 1: 115–43.

—— (1993) "Moods, emotion episodes, and emotions," in M. Lewis and J.M. Haviland (eds) *Handbook of Emotions*, New York: Guilford Press.

Frijda, N.H., Kuipers, P., and ter Schure, E. (1989) "Relations among emotion, appraisal, and emotional action readiness," *Journal of Personality and Social Psychology* 57: 212–28.

Gardner, M.P. (1985) "Mood states and consumer behavior: a critical review," *Journal of Consumer Research* 12: 281–300.

Gleicher, F., Boninger, D.S., Strathman, A., Armor, D., and Ahn, M. (1995) "With an eye toward the future: the impact of counterfactual thinking on affect, attitudes, and behavior," in N.J. Roese and J.M. Olson (eds) *What Might Have Been: The Social Psychology of Counterfactual Thinking*, Mahwah, NJ: Erlbaum.

Gollwitzer, P.M. (1990) "Action phases and mind sets," in E.T. Higgins and R.M. Sorrentino (eds) *Handbook of Motivation and Cognition*, vol. 2, New York: Guilford Press.

Higgins, E.T. (1987) "Self-discrepancy: a theory relating self and affect," *Psychological Bulletin* 94: 319–40.

—— (1996) "Emotional experiences: the pains and pleasures of distinct regulatory systems," in R.D. Kavanaugh, B. Zimmerberg, and S. Fein (eds) *Emotion: Interdisciplinary Perspectives*, Mahwah, NJ: Erlbaum.

—— (1997) "Beyond pleasure and pain," *American Psychologist* 52: 1280–300.

Higgins, E.T., Shah, J., and Friedman, R. (1997) "Emotional responses to goal attainment: strength of regulatory focus as moderator," *Journal of Personality and Social Psychology* 72: 515–25.

Holbrook, M.B. (1986) "Emotion in the consumption experience: toward a new model of the human consumer," in R.A. Peterson, W.D. Hoyer, and W.R. Wilson (eds) *The Role of Affect in Consumer Behavior: Emerging Theories and Applications*, Lexington, MA: Lexington Books.

Huffman, C., Ratneshwar, S., and Mick, D.G. (2000) "An integrative framework of consumer goal structure and goal determination processes," in S. Ratneshwar, D. Glen Mick, and C. Huffman (eds) *The Why of Consumption*, London: Routledge.

Hui, M.K. and Bateson, J.E.G. (1991) "Perceived control and the effects of crowding and consumer choice on the service experience," *Journal of Consumer Research* 18: 174–84.

Inman, J.J. and McAlister, L. (1994) "Do coupon expiration dates affect consumer behavior?" *Journal of Marketing Research* 31: 423–8.

Johnson-Laird, P.N. and Oatley, K. (1992) "Basic emotions, rationality, and folk theory," *Cognition and Emotion* 6: 201–23.

Kahn, B.E. and Isen, A.M. (1993) "The influence of positive affect on variety seeking among safe, enjoyable products," *Journal of Consumer Research* 20: 257–70.

Kahneman, D. and Tversky, A. (1982) "The simulation heuristic," in D. Kahneman, P. Slovic, and A. Tversky (eds) *Judgment Under Uncertainty: Heuristics and Biases*, New York: Cambridge University Press.

Klaaren, K.J., Hodges, S.D., and Wilson, T.D. (1994) "The role of affective expectations in subjective experience and decision-making," *Social Cognition* 12: 77–101.

Lazarus, R.S. (1991) *Emotion and Adaptation*, New York: Oxford University Press.

Mehrabian, A. and Russell, J.A. (1974) *An Approach to Environmental Psychology*, Cambridge, MA: MIT Press.

Mesquita, B. and Frijda, N.H. (1992) "Cultural variations in emotions: a review," *Psychological Bulletin* 112: 179–204.

Oatley, K. and Johnson-Laird, P.N. (1987) "Towards a cognitive theory of emotions," *Cognition and Emotion* 1: 29–50.

—— (1996) "The communicative theory of emotions: empirical tests, mental models, and implications for social interaction," in L.L. Martin and A. Tesser (eds) *Striving and Feeling: Interactions among Goals, Affect, and Self-Regulation*, Mahwah, NJ: Erlbaum.

Olney, T.J., Holbrook, M.B., and Batra, R. (1991) "Consumer responses to advertising: the effects of ad content, emotions, and attitude toward the ad on viewing time," *Journal of Consumer Research* 17: 440–53.

Parker, D., Manstead, A.S.R., and Stradling, S.G. (1995) "Extending the theory of planned behaviour: the role of personal norm," *British Journal of Social Psychology* 34: 127–37.

Perugini, M. and Bagozzi, R.P. (forthcoming) "The role of desires and anticipated emotions in goal-directed behaviours: broadening and deepening the theory of planned behaviour," *British Journal of Social Psychology*.

Pieters, R.G.M., Baumgartner, H., and Allen, D. (1995) "A means-end chain approach to consumer goal structures," *International Journal of Research in Marketing* 12: 227–44.

Plutchik, R. (1980) *Emotions: A Psychoevolutionary Synthesis*, New York: Harper & Row.

—— (1989) "Measuring emotions and their derivatives," in R. Plutchik and H. Kellerman (eds) *Emotion: Theory, Research, and Experience*, vol. 4, San Diego, CA: Academic Press.

Raghunathan, R. and Pham, M.T. (1999) "All negative moods are not equal: motivational influences of anxiety and sadness on decision making," *Organization Behavior and Human Decision Processes* 71 (July): 56–77.

Reynolds, T.J. and Gutman, J. (1988) "Laddering theory, method, analysis, and interpretation," *Journal of Advertising Research* 28: 11–31.

Richard, R., van der Pligt, J., and de Vries, N. (1995) "Anticipated affective reactions and prevention of AIDS," *British Journal of Social Psychology* 34: 9–21.

—— (1996) "Anticipated affect and behavioral choice," *Basic and Applied Social Psychology* 18: 111–29.

Roney, C.J.R., Higgins, E.T., and Shaw, J. (1995) "Goals and framing: how outcome focus influences motivation and emotion," *Personality and Social Psychology Bulletin* 21: 1151–60.

Rook, D.W. (1987) "The buying impulse," *Journal of Consumer Research* 14: 189–99.

Roseman, I.J., Wiest, C., and Swartz, T.S. (1994) "Phenomenology, behaviors, and goals differentiate discrete emotions," *Journal of Personality and Social Psychology* 67: 206–21.

Simonson, I. (1992) "The influence of anticipating regret and responsibility on purchase decisions," *Journal of Consumer Research* 19: 105–18.

Steenkamp, J.-B.E.M. and Baumgartner, H. (1992) "The role of optimum stimulation level in exploratory consumer behavior," *Journal of Consumer Research* 19: 434–48.

Stein, N.L., Liwag, M.D., and Wade, E. (1996) "A goal-based approach to memory for emotional events: implications for theories of understanding and socialization," in R.D. Kavanaugh, B. Zimmerberg, and S. Fein (eds) *Emotion: Interdisciplinary Perspectives*, Mahway, NJ: Erlbaum.

Stein, N.L., Trabasso, T., and Liwag, M. (1993) "The representation and organization of emotional experience: unfolding the emotion episode," in M. Lewis and J.M. Haviland (eds) *Handbook of Emotions*, New York: Guilford Press.

Taylor, S.E. and Pham, L.B. (1996) "Mental simulation, motivation, and action," in P.M. Gollwitzer and J.A. Bargh (eds) *The Psychology of Action: Linking Cognition and Motivation to Behavior*, New York: Guilford Press.

Taylor, S.E. and Schneider, S.K. (1989) "Coping and the simulation of events," *Social Cognition* 7: 174–94.

van der Pligt, J. Zeelenberg, M., van Dijk, W.W., de Vries, N.K., and Richard, R. (1998) "Affect, attitudes and decisions: let's be more specific," *European Review of Social Psychology* 8: 34–66.

Verbeke, W. (1997) "Individual differences in emotional contagion of salespersons: its effect on performance and burnout," *Psychology & Marketing* 14: 617–36.

Verbeke, W. and Bagozzi, R.P. (2000a) "Sales call anxiety: exploring what it means when fear rules a sales encounter," *Journal of Marketing* 64 (July): 88–101.

—— (2000b) "Self-conscious emotions in organizational boundary-spanning contexts: performance is a function of the ability to cope with shame and embarrassment," unpublished working paper, The University of Michigan Business School.

Weiner, B. (1985) "An attributional theory of achievement motivation and emotion," *Psychological Review* 92: 548–73.

—— (1986) "Attribution, emotion and action," in R.M. Sorrentino and E.T. Higgins (eds) *Handbook of Motivation and Cognition: Foundations of Social Behavior*, New York: Guilford Press.

Wilson, T.D., Lisle, D.J., Kraft, D., and Wetzel, C.G. (1989) "Preferences as expectation-driven inferences: effects of affective expectations on affective experience," *Journal of Personality and Social Psychology* 56: 519–30.

Zeelenberg, M. (1999) "Anticipated regret, expected feedback, and behavioral decision making," *Journal of Behavioral Decision Making* 12: 93–106.

Zeelenberg, M. and Beattie, J. (1997) "Consequences of regret aversion 2: additional evidence for effects of feedback on decision making," *Organization Behavior and Human Decision Processes* 72: 63–78.

Zeelenberg, M. and Pieters, R. (1999) "Comparing service delivery to what might have been: behavioral responses to regret and disappointment," *Journal of Service Research* 2: 86–97.

Zeelenberg, M., Inman, J.J., and Pieters, R.G.M. (1999) "What we do when decisions go awry: behavioral consequences of experienced regret," in J. Baron, G. Loomes, and E. Weber (eds) *Conflict and Tradeoffs in Decision Making: Essays in Honor of Jane Beattie*, Cambridge: Cambridge University Press.

Zeelenberg, M., van Dijk, W.W., Manstead, A.S.R., and van der Pligt, J. (2000) "On bad decisions and disconfirmed expectancies: the psychology of regret and disappointment," *Cognition and Emotion* 14: 521–41.

4 Minimizing negative emotion as a decision goal

Investigating emotional trade-off difficulty

Mary Frances Luce, James R. Bettman, and John W. Payne

Introduction

Imagine that you are purchasing a new car and have narrowed down your decision to two options. One of the cars is much safer, but costs more; the other is less safe but also less expensive. The car you select will depend on the trade-offs that you are willing to make between safety and cost. We are interested in how trade-offs such as this one generate different degrees of negative emotion and how decision makers cope with actual or potential choice-generated negative emotion. Trade-offs are a fundamental aspect of choice, as decision-making is essentially the process of accepting less of one choice attribute in order to get more of another (unless the choice is trivial, such as when a dominating alternative exists). Thus, much behavioral decision research (BDR) focuses on when and how people make trade-offs (see Bettman, Luce, and Payne 1998 for a recent review). This chapter outlines our research stream, specifically addressing the effects of *emotional* sources of trade-off difficulty on decision-processing patterns and choice outcomes.

Regarding emotional trade-off difficulty in choice, we propose that minimizing negative emotion is an important meta-goal in cognitive processing, shaping decision-processing behavior along with meta-goals involving effort minimization and accuracy maximization (Payne, Bettman, and Johnson 1993). Thus, the work we review in this chapter suggests an expansion of the effort-accuracy theoretical framework for understanding decision strategy selection (i.e. understanding how people decide how to decide; see Bettman, Luce, and Payne 1998 for further discussion of goals involving both minimizing negative emotion and maximizing ease of justification). Across a large number of studies conducted within the effort-accuracy paradigm, measurements of decision processing based on tracking of information acquisition indicate that decision strategy selection results from adaptive trade-offs of the accuracy provided by various possible decision strategies with the effort required by these strategies. For instance, when aspects of the environment increase the relative accuracy advantage of more normative decision strategies over more heuristic strategies, decision-makers tend to shift their processing behavior towards patterns that are more consistent with normative strategies. As a more specific example, when negative intercorrelation among attribute values increases the relative accuracy cost of heuristic (versus normative) decision processing, decision-makers adopt processing patterns that are more closely associated with normative processing (Bettman *et al.* 1993). Conversely, when environmental factors increase the relative effort cost of normative over heuristic strategies, decision-makers tend to shift towards more heuristic processing patterns; for instance, decisions involving more information both increase the relative degree to which normative strategies require more effort than heuristic strategies and are associated with more heuristic patterns of information processing (e.g. Payne 1976). Most of the research conducted within this framework utilizes decision contexts and manipulations that are likely to be associated with low levels of emotion, for instance choice among alternative gambles offering small, positive monetary payments. We believe that the effort-accuracy framework must be expanded in order to explain decision behavior in many consequential decision contexts (see Bettman, Luce, and Payne 1998). Specifically, we believe it necessary to add the meta-goal of coping with negative emotion to the framework in order to predict and explain decision strategy selection in potentially threatening decision environments. This represents an important extension of the effort-accuracy framework, as decisions that matter more (to both the decision-maker and to society) are almost by definition more threatening and therefore more likely to be influenced by coping goals. As we discuss next, the effort-accuracy framework, and our extension of this framework to emotion-laden choice, involves conceptualizing goals on at least two levels: meta-goals for decision processing shape decision strategy selection, while various detailed goals specifically describing choice outcomes determine whether these meta-goals are relevant to and/or satisfied by a decision.

Levels of goal conceptualization

Our extension of the effort-accuracy framework involves conceptualizing goals at two levels. First, as discussed above, we believe that emotion minimization (or equivalently the desire to engage in coping) is an important meta-goal guiding decision strategy selection. Thus, consistent with effort-accuracy BDR work, we conceptualize emotion minimization as a goal that helps shape decision-makers' reactions to task and context decision factors. As Huffman *et al.* (this volume) note, this theoretical framework pays limited attention to the nature of the more specific goals that are related to these meta-goals. For instance, the accuracy-maximization goal assumes that decision-makers have some underlying, directional preferences to be maximized (e.g. a preference for red over blue) such that decision outcomes more closely matching these underlying preferences (e.g. choice of a red car over an identical blue one) are more accurate. An implicit assumption made with respect to the proposition that a decision-maker is seeking to maximize decision accuracy is therefore that these directional preference(s) are implicated in the relevant choice. In much of the effort-accuracy work, researchers are able to successfully avoid *measuring* these underlying preferences by studying decisions among monetary gambles; in such decision situations it is straightforward to assume that all decision-makers have a simple underlying preference: to make more money (see Payne, Bettman, and Johnson 1993).

Just as some understanding of underlying preferences (e.g. purchase goals) is necessary in order to evaluate whether a decision-maker has maximized accuracy, an understanding of the decision-maker's individual goals (or values) is necessary to evaluate whether she has minimized negative emotion. In particular, some understanding of the decision-maker's specific goals and values is necessary in order to predict when emotion-minimization goals are likely to be relevant, as emotions are themselves typically defined as a function of goal states in that negative (positive) emotions result from threatened or actual non-attainment (attainment) of one's goals (e.g. Carver and Scheier 1990; Lazarus 1999). Thus, in order to study emotion minimization within a decision process, we must assume that important, higher-level goals (e.g. important values) are both relevant to and threatened by that decision process. Thus, by incorporating emotion minimization into our decision framework, we have brought our research interests more in line with the problem of consumer goal structures and determination. In our work, we have either used pretest measures or reasonable assumptions (e.g. safety would be related to an important goal of survival and therefore low levels of safety may generate negative emotion in an automobile purchase context) in order to manipulate negative emotion during decision processing and in order to predict the specific direction of emotion-minimization behavior. However, we believe that there is much more work to be done in order to integrate the idea of decision-makers' important goals and underlying values within our research framework, and we address some of the relevant research opportunities later in this chapter.

Chapter organization

In this chapter, we will discuss a series of experiments investigating the effects of emotional trade-off difficulty on decision behavior, specifically decision-processing patterns and decision outcomes. There are many different theoretical approaches to emotions; we use Lazarus' (1999) theory of emotion elicitation as a theoretical point of departure, and we briefly discuss that theory below. Then, we develop our theoretical framework regarding emotional trade-off difficulty and review some of the main empirical support for that framework. Finally, we outline what we believe are the major opportunities for future research that integrates the emotion-minimization metagoal with other decision goals or that investigates the links between underlying goals and emotion-generation in choice.

Theoretical background: Lazarus' theory of emotion elicitation

We use Lazarus' (1999) model of emotion elicitation as our theoretical background. This model argues that emotion results from two sets of cognitive appraisals. Primary appraisals assess the stakes one has in the outcome of an encounter by evaluating three components. *Goal relevance* assesses whether there is anything at stake in an encounter, i.e. whether the encounter has any potential relevance for valued goals and therefore any potential for emotion. *Goal congruence* assesses whether the encounter is expected to involve positive or negative outcomes and therefore determines whether the resultant emotions will be positive or negative; negative emotions can follow from actual non-attainment of goals (harms), but also, and more likely during decision-making, from potential non-attainment (threats). Finally, *goal content* assesses the particular goals that are at stake, influencing the exact form of emotional experience (e.g. whether guilt versus shame is felt).

Secondary appraisals assess options and prospects for coping. Specifically, secondary appraisals address whether the individual believes s/he can improve the relevant situation, whether future outcomes are expected to worsen, and whether blame or credit for oneself or another is warranted. The inclusion of secondary appraisal as a major proposed component of emotion elicitation reflects the view that emotion and coping enter into a dynamic process involving bi-directional causality.

Appraisals generating negative emotion also elicit coping behaviors that Lazarus classifies as either problem-focused or emotion-focused. Problem-focused coping involves attempts to solve the environmental problem leading to emotion, while emotion-focused coping involves attempts to directly alter experienced emotion without doing so. Emotion-focused coping is further classified into avoidance and changing the meaning of a situation. Both forms of coping are typically brought to bear on any individual stressful episode (e.g. Folkman and Lazarus 1988).

In summary, Lazarus defines primary appraisals of stakes and secondary appraisals of coping options as the major components of emotion elicitation. He further classifies coping behaviors into problem-focused and emotion-focused forms. In the following section, we outline several general propositions regarding emotional trade-off difficulty and decision behavior, and we provide an example of empirical support we have generated for each proposition. These propositions, and the related empirical work, are direct results of our adaptation of Lazarus' general emotion theory to the specific context of decision behavior.

Major propositions and findings regarding trade-off difficulty

Our theoretical framework for understanding the effects of emotional trade-off difficulty on decision behavior is associated with three main sets of propositions. First, decision characteristics (e.g. attribute identities and values) can generate decision-related emotions in general and emotional trade-off difficulty in particular. Second, emotional trade-off difficulty may influence patterns of information processing during choice deliberation. Third, emotional trade-off difficulty may influence choice outcomes. In this section, we briefly outline our rationale and support for each proposition. For simplicity, we focus on empirical results from four papers: (1) Luce, Bettman, and Payne (2000) report an exploratory study seeking to uncover attribute characteristics potentially eliciting trade-off difficulty; (2) Luce, Bettman, and Payne (1997) focus on decision-processing patterns and measures negative emotion as a manipulation check; (3) Luce (1998) focuses on choices such as status quo alternatives as coping strategies and measures how the availability of such coping options mitigates negative emotion; and (4) Luce, Payne, and Bettman (1999) focus on lexicographic choice as a coping strategy.

Antecedents of emotional trade-off difficulty

Along with others (e.g. Shepard 1964; Hogarth 1987), we believe that decision-makers may specifically respond to the emotional distress associated with choice trade-offs. Further, we believe that emotional sources of trade-off difficulty are an important and relatively overlooked source of influence on choice.

We define emotional trade-off difficulty as the level of *subjective threat* associated with an *explicit between-attribute trade-off* within the context of a particular choice. Following Lazarus, we believe that subjective threat is a function of the perceived likelihood of non-attainment of valued goals, and that this threat will be greater as relevant goals are either higher-level or more integrated with other goals. We believe that emotional trade-off difficulty is defined at the level of specific attribute pairs. For instance, trading off safety and purchase price in the context of an automobile purchase decision may be more threatening than trading off comfort and purchase price within the context of the same automobile purchase. Further, we believe that emotional trade-off difficulty is sensitive to the direction of contemplated trade-offs. For instance, completing a trade-off that sacrifices safety for money may be more threatening than completing a trade-off that sacrifices money for safety.

By defining emotional trade-off difficulty as the level of subjective threat, we distinguish this concept from the *emotion experienced* during a choice. We make this distinction because we believe that decision-makers often recognize the emotional potential of choice trade-offs and engage in coping strategies that forestall experienced emotion. For instance, a parent who anticipates that it will be very emotion-laden to trade off decreases in the quality of her child's health care with monetary savings can avoid the negative emotion inherent in that trade-off by taking actions that maximize her child's health, even if at great expense. In such a situation, the opportunity to engage in an effective coping strategy may result in decision behavior being influenced by emotion-relevant considerations, even though negative emotion resulting from decision tradeoffs is not actually experienced. Thus, we make propositions regarding both how the inherent properties of decision trade-offs will generate threat and how the availability of coping options will mitigate that threat.

Decision-threat proposition

We believe that attribute identities (i.e. the specific attributes along which alternatives are defined, such as safety or horsepower in a car purchase) and attribute values (i.e. the specific values each alternative possesses on each attribute, such as a value of 200 or 220 for horsepower) are two major factors influencing emotional trade-off difficulty by altering primary appraisals of decision tasks. Attribute identities should have a major impact on assessments of goal relevance and goal content during primary appraisal because attributes determine the goals that are implicated in a decision. For instance, the attribute automobile safety may implicate goals associated with personal survival while the attribute automobile styling may implicate goals associated with personal expression, and these differing goals may be associated with differing assessments of stakes by a particular decision-maker. To the degree that some goals are more important (e.g. survival is more important, or occupies a higher level in the typical goal hierarchy, than personal expression), the decision-maker should generate an appraisal of relatively higher stakes when these goals are threatened. We believe that these considerations regarding levels in one's goal hierarchy, and therefore regarding the emotionality of attributes, are separable from notions of attribute importance. For instance, some attributes (like price) may tend to be relatively important in purchase (e.g. perhaps due to budget constraints) while also being relatively distinct from high-level goals. Thus, attributes such as price may be important while not having much potential to elicit negative emotion, while other attributes (e.g. those associated with a rare but potentially catastrophic outcome such as safety features in a car) may be associated with moderate importance but high emotionality. In general, we believe that attribute identities will influence emotional trade-off difficulty.

Similarly, the relative or absolute values of choice alternatives on the relevant attribute(s) should influence primary appraisal by determining whether the goals implied by each attribute are appraised as likely to remain satisfied or unsatisfied. We believe that attribute values therefore have a major impact on assessments of goal congruence during primary appraisal. For example, choosing between a very safe car versus an extremely safe car is likely to involve a more positive primary appraisal than would choosing between a very unsafe versus an extremely unsafe car. We believe that both conflict among attribute values (the degree one attribute has to be sacrificed for another to be maximized) and the valence of attribute values (whether alternatives are seen as generally "good" or "bad") are likely to influence appraisals of goal content, potentially contributing to emotional trade-off difficulty. Similarly, the framing of attribute values (e.g. whether the decision-maker's reference point results in a particular set of attribute values being experienced as "gains" or "losses") should influence primary appraisal by altering the subjective valence of attribute values.

We believe that attribute identities and values will interact to determine emotional trade-off difficulty, as appraisals of both goal relevance and goal incongruence are necessary to generate negative emotion. Specifically, emotional trade-off difficulty is expected when attribute identities implicate valued goals and attribute values indicate that these goals may be blocked, as stated by our *Decision-threat proposition*:

> *Decision-threat proposition*: The potential for negative emotion will be associated with decision tasks involving low (or relatively low, e.g. loss) values on attributes with links to valued goals that conflict with one another.

The most straightforward evidence for our *Decision-threat proposition* is found in Experiment Two of Luce, Bettman, and Payne (1997). Using the decision context of choosing a job to take after graduation, we crossed manipulations regarding attribute identity (low- versus high-emotion) and attribute value (low- versus high-conflict). The within-subjects manipulation of attribute identity involved presenting each subject with two decisions comprised of five hypothetical jobs each defined across four attributes. The identity of two of the four attributes was manipulated on an individualized basis between the two decision tasks each subject completed. Specific attributes were chosen based on a preliminary, separate experimental session during which each subject responded to multiple measures of both importance and loss aversion for a set of fifteen potential attributes. Going from the low-emotion to the high-emotion attribute identity condition, we held attribute importance measures constant while replacing attributes relatively low in loss aversion with attributes relatively high in loss aversion. Consider an example subject who rated the attributes "yearly salary" and "job security" as equally important, but who also associated "job security" with greater levels of loss aversion. For that individual subject, the high-emotion decision task would involve alternative jobs defined in terms of differing levels of job security while the low-emotion task would involve alternatives defined in terms of yearly salary. A second attribute would be altered across high- versus low-emotion attribute identity conditions in the analogous manner, and finally each decision display would be filled out with two other attributes (held constant across attribute-identity conditions). The rationale behind using measures of loss aversion to operationalize our attribute identity manipulation was that trading off attributes involves accepting more of one for less of another, so that negative emotion generated by attribute trade-offs may be predicted by levels of loss aversion, especially when attribute importance is held constant. Thus, we used individualized pretests in order to assess the degree to which various decision attributes held the potential for negative emotion, presumably because these attributes were associated by the individual subject with important goals.

A second, between-subjects manipulation of conflict in attribute values altered the average correlation between values on different attributes within the decision matrix, therefore altering the degree to which one attribute had to be sacrificed in order for another to be maximized. Both high-conflict and high-emotion attribute identity, and particularly their combination, resulted in more self-reported negative emotion, as expected. That is, more loss-averse attributes were generally associated with more negative emotion, but this effect was stronger in the higher (versus the lower) conflict group, for whom losses on those attributes potentially had to be accepted.

Our success in manipulating emotional trade-off difficulty in part through attribute identities led us to consider the characteristics of attributes in a separate study. Specifically, in Luce, Bettman, and Payne (2000) we asked subjects to use 23 scales in order to rate a subset of 24 attributes associated with 3 decision domains (each subjects rated eight attributes related to health plans, to apartments, or to automobiles). Factor analysis of these ratings uncovered dimensions involving: (1) the overall importance or value of an attribute; (2) the emotional potential of an attribute; and (3) the cognitive ease with which an attribute can be considered. While this study was relatively exploratory, we find it interesting that subjects appear to view attributes in a multi-dimensional fashion, and we believe that more research investigating the links between various attribute characteristics and the elicitation of negative emotion during decision-making is warranted. For instance, while we were able to manipulate negative emotion based on measures of attribute-level loss aversion in Luce, Bettman, and Payne (1997), our more recent attribute characteristics work indicates that measures of attribute-level loss aversion actually correlate relatively highly with measures of attribute importance. The attribute characteristic work further indicates that more direct measures of the degree to which an attribute is associated with moral considerations or severe potential consequences define an emotionality dimension that is separable from attribute importance. Therefore, these latter measures may be more useful for determining which attributes will elicit trade-off difficulty, while holding constant more traditional considerations regarding attribute importance weights.

Coping-opportunity proposition

We predict that decisions characterized by potential losses on attributes with implications for important goals are high in emotional trade-off difficulty and will often generate negative emotion during decision processing. However, secondary appraisals identifying readily available coping options may mitigate primary appraisals associated with negative emotions (e.g. Lazarus 1999). Thus, we argue that avenues for coping (e.g. the ability to avoid a choice by delegating it to another) will mitigate the negative emotion associated with the threat of having to accept poor values on one or more attribute(s) with implications for important goals:

> *Coping-opportunity proposition*: An available option for coping will mitigate feelings of negative emotion associated with the potential necessity of accepting poor values on attributes with links to valued goals.

Within the context of emotionally difficult automobile purchase decisions, Luce (1998) investigated the effects of providing subjects with coping opportunities in the forms of 'avoidant options.' In that paper, two between-subjects manipulations addressed decision threat and the presence of avoidant options, respectively. First, similar to the method used in Luce, Bettman, and Payne (1997) and described above, attributes describing choice alternatives were manipulated, based on a pretest using a separate sample of subjects, such that decisions involved attributes associated with either higher or lower degrees of loss aversion, on average. Second, a manipulation of subjects' response options was crossed with the attribute identity manipulation. One group, denoted the control group below, simply indicated a choice among the available alternatives. A second group of subjects was given the opportunity to indicate they would maintain the status quo by choosing a 'previously' chosen alternative; that is, one alternative in the overall choice set was associated with a status quo label. Luce (1998) hypothesized that choosing the status quo was an avoidant option, satisfying emotion-focused coping goals, because it allowed the decision-maker to explain and justify her choice (to herself and others) in terms of the status quo label, which was independent of specific attribute importance weights or trade-offs. A second avoidant option was the option to report that one would prolong search instead of committing to one of the currently available choice options. Again, such a choice can be explained without the necessity of considering the relative merits of various alternatives, and therefore without a focus on specific attribute weights and trade-offs. A third avoidant option was the opportunity to choose an alternative that dominated a second alternative in the choice set. This alternative may satisfy emotion-focused coping goals in that the dominance relationship provides an objective justification for one's choice that does not rely on trade-offs (e.g. Simonson 1989).

In Experiment One of the Luce (1998) paper, negative emotion was assessed immediately after decision processing by asking subjects to report their expectations regarding the emotionality of the decision task if they were to repeat this same decision in the 'real world.' For this measure, the control group showed a significant increase in rated negative emotion with more loss averse attributes. However, emotion ratings in all three (non-control) avoidant option groups were insensitive to the attribute identity manipulation, supporting our *Coping-opportunity proposition*. Further mediation analyses indicated that subjects who actually chose an avoidant alternative were driving this lessened reactivity to attribute identity. That is, choice of an avoidant option (versus choice of another option) resulted in less assessed emotionality in the more threatening (more loss-averse-attribute) decision conditions. This finding is consistent with Lazarus' argument that primary appraisals of decision threat (which we propose are elicited by the manipulation of attribute identity) are moderated by secondary appraisals of anticipated coping opportunities (which we propose include the opportunity to choose an avoidant option).

Thus, our *Decision-threat proposition* and our *Coping-opportunity proposition* jointly specify how decision characteristics can affect negative emotion during choice. In the following section, we develop two propositions addressing how motivations to cope with these negative emotions can alter decision-processing patterns and decision outcomes.

Processing consequences of emotional trade-off difficulty

Processing-effort proposition

Once emotional trade-off difficulty is generated, we expect decision-makers to engage in both problem- and emotion-focused coping efforts. We believe that the major form of problem-focused coping relevant to choice behavior is the motivation to work harder, in order to do a "good job" solving the choice "problem" with which one is confronted. We expect decision-makers to generally associate more normative processing strategies with this motivation to do a good job, consistent with the finding that decision-makers use more normative processing strategies when explicitly instructed to maximize decision accuracy (e.g. Payne, Bettman, and Luce 1996). This more normative processing is both more extensive (effortful) and of a different form (i.e. involving explicit trade-offs) than is more heuristic processing. However, because effort feedback (rather than feedback regarding the normative accuracy of the form of one's particular decision strategy or outcome) is both available to the decision-maker and often relatively observable by others, we expect increased processing effort to be the major result of motivations to engage in problem-focused coping in decision situations.

> *Processing-effort proposition*: Problem-focused coping concerns will lead to increased effort in processing under increased emotional trade-off difficulty.

The *Processing-effort proposition* was supported in both Luce, Bettman, and Payne (1997) and in Luce (1998); in both papers, more emotion-laden decision environments were associated with greater processing effort in terms of decision response times. The former paper also found an effect on the total number of information acquisitions (using the Mouselab system to monitor information acquisition; see Payne, Bettman, and Johnson 1993 and our overview of Mouselab below). As noted above, our *Processing-effort proposition* above overlaps with an observed reaction to accuracy-maximization goals (e.g. Payne, Bettman, and Luce 1996), in that both an increased desire to maximize decision accuracy and an increased desire to cope with negative emotion are expected to cause increased decision effort. Thus, the above proposition does not by itself require a theoretical expansion of the effort-accuracy framework, as one could simply postulate that coping considerations cause an increased focus on accuracy goals. As is argued next, we believe that coping behavior may simultaneously involve problem-focused and emotion-focused efforts, and therefore increased effort in reaction to negative emotion will occur simultaneously with shifts in decision processing that are inconsistent with reactions to accuracy goals. The most novel aspect of our theoretical framework, as far as decision processing is concerned, is therefore that we expect this increased processing effort to co-occur with decision processing that is less normative in nature, contrary to typical findings where decision-makers who take longer to process also tend to process using more normative decision patterns.

Processing-pattern proposition

We believe that the major form of emotion-focused coping during decision-making involves attempts to avoid particularly distressing explicit trade-offs between attributes (e.g. Hogarth 1987; Shepard 1964). That is, if trade-off difficulty is elicited by the perception that valued goals must be given up, then the decision-maker should either avoid these sacrifices altogether or, at least, make them implicit (versus explicit). For example, an employee threatened by the possibility of giving up quality of medical care in choosing her benefits may shield herself from the problematic trade-off between medical care and money by considering only plans she can afford (screening on money) thus only considering quality of care for the "affordable" or "possible" plans. By considering attributes sequentially rather than simultaneously, this strategy makes the trade-off between medical care and money implicit in that the decision-maker never confronts the (perhaps higher) level of care she could have obtained by spending more money. Thus, we believe that decision-makers will adjust their patterns of decision processing to accommodate emotion-focused coping concerns.

> *Processing-pattern proposition:* Emotion-focused coping concerns will lead to decision processing patterns that avoid explicit, between-attribute trade-offs.

We test our *Processing-pattern proposition* by measuring decision-makers' information acquisition behaviors (i.e. which information is considered by a decision-maker and in what order). More generally, in order to measure the effects of trade-off difficulty on decision-processing patterns, it is necessary to have both a theoretical framework for understanding decision processing and a methodology for measuring it. We rely on Payne, Bettman, and Johnson's (1993) effort-accuracy framework for doing so, as this work provides a well-developed methodology for observing and describing individuals' decision-processing patterns with the Mouselab software system. This methodology provides choice information to subjects on a computer screen in matrix form, with the piece of information associated with each cell hidden behind an opaque box. For instance, research participants may be presented with a choice matrix for which decision attributes (e.g. safety, price, and styling within an automobile-choice context) define columns and decision alternatives (e.g. Car A, Car B, etc.) define rows. Subjects undertake decision processing by using a mouse-controlled cursor to open boxes one at a time, and the Mouselab software program records the order and timing of information acquisitions. Each cell of this matrix would be a covered box providing a specific piece of decision information when opened with the mouse-controlled pointer; for instance, the cell associated with the Price attribute for Car A may read "$16,000." Mouselab would record the time at which the subject opened and the time at which s/he closed this box. These information-acquisition data are used to construct dependent variables that characterize decision-processing patterns.

Within the Mouselab methodology, three main dependent measures capture much of the variance in decision processing. The first is simply how much information is processed, assessed using a count of total acquisitions (typically counting re-acquisitions) during choice and/or the overall response time of the choice. As discussed above, we used these measures in order to support our *Processing-effort proposition* in Luce, Bettman, and Payne (1997). The second is whether information is processed selectively across either attributes or alternatives (i.e. different amounts of information are processed for each attribute or alternative) or consistently (i.e. the same amount of information is processed for each attribute or alternative). The third is the pattern of decision processing. Processing may be organized more by alternative, where multiple attributes of a single alternative are considered before information about another alternative is processed. Processing may instead be organized more by attribute, in which the values of several alternatives on a single attribute are processed before information about another attribute is considered. Generally, compensatory decision rules, that is rules involving explicit trade-offs between decision attributes, are associated with less selective and more alternative-based decision processing (e.g. Payne 1976).

Extensive research has established theoretical links between these dependent variables and underlying decision strategies (Payne, Bettman, and Johnson 1993). For instance, the weighted adding strategy (i.e. expected-utility maximization) is typically taken as the normative standard for decision accuracy and is associated with alternative-based, extensive, and consistent decision processing. Similarly, Payne, Bettman, and Luce (1996) find that decision-makers given an explicit goal to maximize decision accuracy in the context of choices among simple monetary gambles display more extensive, less selective, and more alternative-based processing patterns than do subjects given an effort-minimization goal (see also Creyer, Bettman, and Payne 1990). These aspects of processing (i.e. extensive, consistent, and alternative-based processing) are also significantly correlated with the tendency to choose the expected-value-maximizing alternative, while the opposite processing patterns are correlated with choice of the lexicographic alternative (i.e. the alternative that is best on the most important attribute) (Payne, Bettman, and Luce 1996).

Recall that our above *Processing-pattern proposition* hypothesizes that decision-makers will use processing patterns that avoid explicit, between-attribute trade-offs in order to engage in emotion-focused coping during decision-making. Given our Mouselab methodology, we therefore expect that, under increasing emotional trade-off difficulty, decision-makers will engage in emotion-focused coping by considering different attributes sequentially rather than simultaneously, thereby keeping necessary trade-offs implicit rather than explicit. As expected, when we monitored subjects information acquisition patterns in Luce, Bettman, and Payne (1997), we found that more threatening decision environments were associated with more attribute-based patterns of processing. Thus, overall, decision behavior became *both* increasingly effortful and increasingly attribute-based as decision threat was increased through higher loss aversion in attribute identities and/or higher conflict in attribute values, supporting both our *Processing-effort proposition* and our *Processing-pattern proposition*. That is, in Luce, Bettman, and Payne (1997), we both hypothesize and find that problem-focused and emotion-focused coping motivations will influence the extent and the pattern of decision processing, respectively. We also conducted supplementary analyses of processing, for instance to rule out extensive use of the (attribute-based, but also trade-off-based) additive difference heuristic. Finally, a self-reported negative emotion measure partially mediated the above effects on processing effort and pattern, supporting our theoretical framework by indicating that the observed processing changes were motivated by desires to cope with decision-generated negative emotion.

In summary, consideration of emotion-focused coping behaviors, which leads to our *Processing-pattern proposition*, is one primary reason that we argue for an expansion of the effort-accuracy framework to incorporate emotion-minimization goals. That is, while problem-focused coping behaviors are likely to mirror accuracy-maximization behaviors, we expect emotion-focused coping to be undertaken simultaneously with problem-focused coping. These emotion-focused coping behaviors are similar to effort-minimization behaviors in that they are expected to involve avoidance of particularly emotion-laden or threatening processing operations. However, emotion-focused coping and effort-minimization are likely to diverge in that the specific processing operations that are most cognitively taxing (and are therefore avoided in the pursuit of effort minimization) will not necessarily be the operations that are most emotionally taxing (and are therefore avoided in pursuit of emotion minimization). Further, our joint prediction regarding decision-processing efforts and patterns in negatively emotion-laden environments runs counter to much work in less emotion-laden contexts, where environmental aspects that encourage more extensive processing typically also encourage more compensatory (alternative-based) processing (e.g. Payne, Bettman, and Johnson 1993). Of course, we also expect coping motivations to influence final choice outcomes, as discussed in the following section.

Outcome consequences of trade-off difficulty

Avoidant-choice proposition

We argue above that decision-makers will engage in emotion-focused coping through avoidance by altering the form of their decision processing. In addition, though, it may be possible to engage in avoidance by making particular choices in some situations. We call such directional choices "avoidant options," and specifically define an avoidant option as a choice recommended by some objective reason or label independent of value-based trade-offs; for instance, a status quo label is one such reason. Choice of these options may satisfy emotion-focused coping motivations to avoid distressing choice operations, as such choices can be made without engaging in difficult explicit trade-offs. Thus, we believe the choice share of these avoidant options will increase as trade-offs become more emotionally difficult.

Avoidant-choice proposition: Emotion-focused coping considerations will lead to increased choice of avoidant options under increased emotional trade-off difficulty.

As discussed above in terms of our *Coping-opportunity proposition*, Luce (1998) investigated avoidant choice by manipulating between-subjects whether decision-makers had a control (no avoidant-option) response option, or whether they had one of three avoidant options available to them. In the relevant experiment, choice shares of all three avoidant options increased (as compared to baseline, control-group choice shares where appropriate) when the decision task was defined in terms of more (versus less) loss averse attributes. These choice findings are consistent with our prediction that emotion-focused coping considerations would motivate increased choice of avoidant options.

Lexicographic-choice proposition

In some decision situations, the directional nature of emotional trade-off difficulty may also provide some opportunities to engage in emotion-focused coping through avoidance of distressing choice operations. For instance, an individual who is threatened by the potential of giving up medical care in order to save money (versus the prospect of giving up money in order to gain medical care) could engage in coping by choosing a health plan that maximizes perceived quality of care, despite the potential cost. Of course, the coping option of avoiding emotionally difficult trade-offs by making a lexicographic choice (i.e. a choice that maximizes one attribute) will only be attractive for decision situations involving one particularly emotionally difficult-to-trade attribute.

> *Lexicographic-choice proposition*: Emotion-focused coping considerations will lead to increased use of lexicographic choice based on an emotionally difficult-to-trade attribute.

We tested the above proposition in Luce, Payne, and Bettman (1999). In particular, we investigated the trade-off between higher quality and lower price in a highly simplified, two-attribute, two-alternative decision set. For example, a subject in this experiment may have been asked to choose between renting Apartment A characterized by $500 in monthly rent and a 25 percent yearly chance of being a crime victim and Apartment B characterized by $1000 rent but only an 11 percent chance of crime. We individually tailored choice stimuli to each subject based on his or her earlier response to a matching-task question, so that we could focus on difficult, value-revealing trade-offs. This matching question asked each subject to set a price for the high-quality alternative in the relevant stimulus pair (e.g. setting a rent for Apartment B in the example) such that he or she would be indifferent between that alternative and a lower-quality alternative (e.g. Apartment A). Either three or five individually tailored choice stimuli per alternative pair were then created for each subject such that the price of the high-quality alternative would be systematically arrayed around his or her earlier matching-task response.

In general, the Luce, Payne, and Bettman (1999) studies show that incorporating emotional trade-off difficulty into models predicting responses in difficult choice environments adds precision to these models. That is, across multiple experiments, we found that measures and manipulations related to increased trade-off difficulty predicted increased use of a lexicographic choice strategy. For instance, we found that providing subjects with a reference point framing quality attribute values as *losses* (versus gains) was associated with increased choice of the high-quality alternative, even in situations where such choice is inconsistent with earlier matching-task responses. Importantly, these findings did not generalize to losses involving attributes stated in generally less emotion-laden currency terms (i.e. purchase price for a car and commute time for an apartment). Thus, decision-makers appeared to cope with the emotional threat of quality-attribute losses by choosing the high-quality alternative, even at prices significantly higher than their stated matching price, but they did not show analogous behavior for price-attribute or time-attribute losses.

Summary of propositions

In summary, we have supported six basic propositions regarding emotional trade-off difficulty by adapting Lazarus' (1999) emotion framework to the particular situation of decision-making. We predict that choice situations will generate negative emotions when they require potential acceptance of low values on highly desired attributes (*Decision-threat proposition*). We further predict that this negative emotion will be mitigated by easily available coping options (*Coping-opportunity proposition*). We expect emotional trade-off difficulty to influence decision-processing patterns by motivating more extensive processing that avoids explicit between-attribute trade-offs (*Processing-effort* and *Processing-pattern propositions*). We further expect emotional trade-off difficulty to motivate increased choice of avoidant options where available (*Avoidant-choice proposition*) and to motivate lexicographic choices maximizing a particularly emotionally difficult to trade attribute where feasible (*Lexicographic-choice proposition*). In the following section, we discuss future research opportunities, with a particular focus on research opportunities related to better developing the implications of our work for understanding the impact of goals on consumer choice.

Future research directions

Our work to date provides evidence for the general notion that decision-makers consider emotion-minimization meta-goals during decision strategy selection. Although we have demonstrated that decision-makers avail themselves of opportunities for coping with negative emotion, we have not tended to put subjects in situations where they face obvious trade-offs between emotion minimization and other important meta-goals. Thus, to date, our emotional trade-off difficulty work has not produced as clear a link between concrete aspects of processing, underlying strategies, and emotion-minimizing meta-goals as in the effort-accuracy work. In addition, we have provided only minimal exploration of the links between underlying goals and values and the generation of emotional threat within a decision environment. These limitations of our work to date produce two major opportunities for future research: further understanding of emotion as a meta-goal, and understanding how the decision-maker's individual goals and values relate to decision threats and coping behavior. We discuss each below.

Further specification of the emotion-minimizing meta-goal

Our work on emotional trade-off difficulty has sought to expand the effort-accuracy framework by demonstrating the additional relevance of emotion-minimizing goals to decision strategy selection. Comparing our current work to the body of work comprising the effort-accuracy approach illustrates much opportunity for future work. In particular, we have only begun to explore whether and how decision-makers trade off between emotion, effort, and accuracy meta-goals. We speculate, however, that our initial results indicate decision-makers are less accurate as task-related emotion increases. For instance, the degree to which processing is extensive and the degree to which it attempts to accurately resolve tradeoffs between attributes are considered to be two important aspects of normatively accurate decision processing (e.g. Frisch and Clemen 1994). The finding that our subjects shifted to more attribute-based processing in more emotion-laden environments indicates that they may have been avoiding explicit trade-offs, and their performance could be expected to suffer as a result of such actions. An additional layer of complication involves the time course of trade-offs between meta-goals as the course of decision-making and coping unfolds. For example, emotion-focused coping strategies (e.g. putting off a decision) may engender long-term costs in terms of decision accuracy, while accuracy-maximization strategies (e.g. determining the probability of a dreaded outcome) might engender short-term costs in terms of emotion minimization. Thus, long- versus short-term considerations might often be at odds. Investigating these research questions would involve more specific calibration of some of the constructs in our emotional trade-off difficulty model. For instance, in order to determine whether decision-makers were constructing strategies that sacrificed long-run accuracy in the service of short-term emotion minimization, we would need to be able to specify the accuracy benefits and emotional costs of a range of possible decision strategies. While we have not made substantial progress on these calibration issues to date, we do believe that these are important theoretical issues. Once progress is made along these lines, we also believe that it would be useful to consider the relationship of the desire to construct an easily justifiable decision to the emotion, effort, and accuracy meta-goals.

Consideration of decision-makers' meta-goals is also complicated by presence of multiple definitions of utility. Kahneman and his colleagues (e.g. Kahneman, Wakker, and Sarin 1997) define four types of utility. Experienced utility is relevant to actual, post-choice consumption. Remembered utility is the recalled utility of that consumption experience. Predicted utility is the decision-maker's estimate of future experienced utility. Most choices must be based on predicted utility, as items are often not consumed until after choice, but this prediction is likely based at least in part on past, remembered utility. Decision utility is utility as inferred from decisions. Predicted utility is a primary determinant of decision utility, but other factors such as response mode are likely to be relevant as well. Finally, our work could be interpreted as indicating the relevance of a fifth type of utility, namely process utility, or the utility (or disutility) derived from the emotional aspects of implementing one's decision strategy. This idea regarding process utility is also consistent with Garbarino and Edell's (1997) finding that negative affect generated by (cognitively) difficult-to-evaluate alternatives influences choice outcomes. Thus, even a subject attempting to engage in 'accurate' utility maximization may show variance in behavior depending on his or her current notion of utility. Such issues will further complicate the measurement of accuracy and emotion levels associated with various decision strategies.

Understanding consumer goals and emotion-elicitation

Examining more specific emotions

Our work to date has taken a relatively undifferentiated view of negative emotion. Thus, opportunities exist for specifying how coping behavior is likely to differ depending on the presence of various types of negative emotion (and related constructs). For instance, it would be valuable to conduct decision-making research with a more direct tie to specific emotions. Anger involves a motivation to remove the relevant obstacle while fear involves a motivation to escape danger (Smith and Ellsworth 1985); these different motivations may tend to encourage more approach (anger) versus more avoidance (fear) in coping with trade-offs. Raghunathan (2000; Raghunathan and Pham 1999) has begun a promising program of research consistent with these notions. Raghunathan and Pham (1999) argue, for example, that anxiety and sadness prime different goals (uncertainty reduction and reward replacement respectively) and show that anxiety biases individuals toward low-risk/low-reward gambles whereas sadness biases people toward high-risk/high-reward gambles. Raghunathan (2000) investigates the effect of anger, sadness, and fear on consumer choice.

Lerner and Keltner (1999, 2000) have also examined the effects of specific emotions on choice. They show both that emotions with the same valence (anger and fear) can relate to risk perception and risk preferences in different ways and that emotions with different valence (anger and happiness) can relate to assessments of optimism about future life events in the same way. Although both these streams of research deal with mood effects rather than the sort of decision-task generated emotion that we consider, they are notable for their emphasis on the different goals associated with coping with differing negative emotions.

In addition to determining the differential aspects of negative emotion in choice, it would be interesting to address positive emotions as well. For instance, it would be interesting to determine whether potential opportunity or the likely upside represents an important dimension along which decision-makers respond to attributes. Decision-makers may even cope with positive emotions, for instance, by savoring the positive aspects of anticipation or by attempting to dampen the distraction associated with high-arousal positive emotions. In addition, it would be interesting to determine how decision-makers trade off between positive and negative aspects of a decision. For instance, Lopes (1987) argues that greed (focus on the upside) versus fear (focus on the downside) causes focus on different aspects of a decision.

Finally, future work should directly address subjects' lay theories of emotion, and should investigate the degree to which these theories are predictive of real-world decision behavior in emotion-laden settings. Future work should also address subjects' levels of insight into their own coping behaviors; for instance, it is unclear whether subjects in our studies consciously intended to minimize (hypothetical or real) negative emotion via their avoidant choices.

Individual differences

In addition to the great variance in types of emotion, there is also potentially great variance in the degree to which individuals experience and respond to negative emotion. Thus, there are opportunities for research involving individual differences and emotional decision difficulty. There are likely individual differences in the ease with which negative emotion is elicited; there are also likely individual differences in tendencies to engage in problem- and emotion-focused coping. For instance, individuals may vary in the degree to which they tend to delay, delegate, and so on. In particular, work on the tendency to use rational versus experiential decision styles (Pacini and Epstein 1999), the tendency to cope constructively (Epstein and Meier 1989), use of different methods for coping (Folkman *et al.* 1986), and the need and ability to achieve cognitive structuring (Bar-Tal, Raviv, and Spitzer 1999) seem potentially quite relevant.

Methodological issues

The topic of emotional trade-off difficulty, or of emotion-laden decisions in general, seems particularly appropriate to naturalistic research methods. For instance, in their book on decision conflict, Janis and Mann (1977) explicitly reject the notion that substantial decision conflict can be studied using laboratory methods and utilize a case study approach. We believe that we have been able to generate insight into our research questions by using laboratory settings allowing us to control for alternative hypotheses for observed behaviors. Given the real challenges associated with arousing emotion in the laboratory, however, our results may provide lower bounds on the magnitude of real emotional trade-off difficulty effects on choice.

More naturalistic methods may be necessary to explore the full impact of emotional trade-off difficulty on decision-makers. Interview or similar (e.g. diary, retrospective written reports) research techniques would be useful for uncovering the emotional appraisals and coping strategies used by individuals faced with extremely consequential real-world decisions. Analyses of these data are likely to be complicated by the fact that the exact nature of the threats involved is likely to vary, along with other factors, across decision domains. For instance, decisions about medical treatments for serious illnesses are likely to be associated with perceptions of extremely low attribute values. Conversely, decisions about how to invest one's retirement savings are likely to be associated with better perceived outcomes, yet very real threats.

It may also be possible to extend the range of the intensity of emotions under consideration by using quasi-experimental methods. For instance, it may be possible to manipulate the emotionality of hypothetical decisions by blocking on groups of subjects for whom the task is more or less emotional (e.g. children's health issues for parents and non-parents or decisions about hormone replacement therapy for women with varying anticipated time horizons before menopause). This would allow some experimental control of decision tasks, while still allowing for a relatively naturalistic manipulation of emotion.

Conclusions and implications

We believe that one of the driving forces behind decision behavior is the meta-goal of coping with or minimizing negative emotion inherent in choice. Thus, we have extended Payne, Bettman, and Johnson's (1993) effort-accuracy decision framework in order to incorporate emotion-minimization goals. It appears that the relevance of emotion-minimization considerations alters decision behavior and also complicates interpretation of existing relationships between processing characteristics and effort minimization or accuracy maximization. Of course, much remains to be learned regarding the causes and consequences of emotional trade-off difficulty in choice. Thus, we propose future research involving understanding how the meta-goal of emotion minimization is related to accuracy and effort goals in choice, and we also propose research further investigating the links between underlying decision goals and specific emotional reactions during decision-making.

References

Bar-Tal, Y., Amiram, R., and Spitzer, A. (1999) "The need and ability to achieve cognitive structuring: individual differences that moderate the effect of stress on information processing," *Journal of Personality and Social Psychology* 77 (July): 33–51.

Bettman, J.R., Luce, M.F., and Payne, J.W. (1998) "Consumer choice processes: an adaptive, constructive view," *Journal of Consumer Research* 25 (December).

Bettman, J.R., Johnson, E.J., Luce, M.F., and Payne, J.W. (1993) "Correlation, conflict, and choice," *Journal of Experimental Psychology: Learning, Memory and Cognition* (July): 931–51.

Carver, C.S. and Scheier, M.F. (1990) "Origins and functions of positive and negative affect: a control-process view," *Psychological Review* 97 (January): 19–35.

Creyer, E.H., Bettman, J.R., and Payne, J.W. (1990) "The impact of accuracy and effort feedback and goals on adaptive decision behavior," *Journal of Behavioral Decision Making* 3: 1–16.

Epstein, S. and Meier, P. (1989) "Constructive thinking: a broad coping variable with specific components," *Journal of Personality and Social Psychology* 57 (August): 332–50.

Folkman, S. and Lazarus, R.S. (1988) "Coping as a mediator of emotion," *Journal of Personality and Social Psychology* 54 (March): 466–75.

Folkman, S., Lazarus, R.S., Dunkel-Schetter, C., DeLongis, A., and Gruen, R.J. (1986) "Dynamics of a stressful encounter: cognitive appraisal, coping, and encounter outcomes," *Journal of Personality and Social Psychology* 50 (May): 992–1003.

Frisch, D. and Clemen, R.T. (1994) "Beyond expected utility: rethinking behavioral decision research," *Psychological Bulletin* 116 (July): 46–54.

Garbarino, E.C. and Edell, J.A. (1997) "Cognitive effort, affect, and choice," *Journal of Consumer Research* 24 (September): 147–58.

Hogarth, R.M. (1987) *Judgment and Choice*, 2nd edition, New York: Wiley.

Janis, I.L. and Mann, L. (1977) *Decision Making: A Psychological Analysis of Conflict, Choice, and Commitment*, New York: Free Press.

Kahneman, D., Wakker, P.P., and Sarin, R. (1997) "Back to Bentham? Explorations of experienced utility," *The Quarterly Journal of Economics* 112 (May): 375–405.

Lazarus, R.S. (1999) *Stress and Emotion: A New Synthesis*, New York: Springer.

Lerner, J.S. and Keltner, D. (1999) "Beyond valence: toward a model of emotion-specific influences on judgement and choice," *Cognition and Emotion* 13.

—— (2000) "How much risk can you handle? Testing the appraisal-tendency hypothesis with fearful, angry, and happy people," working paper, Department of Social and Decision Sciences, Carnegie-Mellon University, Pittsburgh, PA 15213.

Lopes, L.L. (1987) "Between hope and fear: the psychology of risk," in Leonard Berkowitz (ed.) *Advances in Experimental Social Psychology*, vol. 20, San Diego, CA: Academic Press: 255–95.

Luce, M.F. (1998) "Choosing to avoid: coping with negatively emotion-laden consumer decisions," *Journal of Consumer Research* 24 (March): 409–33.

Luce, M.F., Bettman, J.R., and Payne, J.W. (1997) "Choice processing in emotionally difficult decisions," *Journal of Experimental Psychology: Learning, Memory and Cognition* 23 (March): 384–405.

—— (2000) "Attribute identities matter: subjective perceptions of attribute characteristics," *Marketing Letters* 11 (2).

Luce, M.F., Payne, J.W., and Bettman, J.R. (1999) "Emotional trade-off difficulty and choice," *Journal of Marketing Research* 36 (May): 143–59.

Pacini, R. and Epstein, S. (1999) "The relation of rational and experiential processing styles to personality, basic beliefs, and the ratio-bias phenomenon," *Journal of Personality and Social Psychology* 76 (June): 972–87.

Payne, J.W. (1976) "Task complexity and contingent processing in decision making: an information search and protocol analysis," *Organizational Behavior and Human Performance* 16 (August): 366–87.

Payne, J.W., Bettman, J.R., and Johnson, E.J. (1993) *The Adaptive Decision Maker*, Cambridge: Cambridge University Press.

Payne, J.W., Bettman, J.R., and Luce, M.F. (1996) "When time is money: decision behavior under opportunity cost time pressure," *Organizational Behavior and Human Decision Processes* 66 (2) May: 131–52.

Raghunathan, R. (2000) "The motivational influence of negative affective states on consumption behaviors: the affective goal-priming hypothesis", unpublished doctoral dissertation, Stern School of Business, New York University.

Raghunathan, R. and Pham, M.T. (1999) "All negative moods are not equal: motivational influences of anxiety and sadness on decision making," *Organizational Behavior and Human Decision Processes* 79 (July): 56–77.

Shepard, R.N. (1964) "On subjectively optimum selection among multiattribute alternatives," in M.W. Shelley and G.L. Bryan (eds) *Human Judgments and Optimality*, New York: Wiley: 257–81.

Simonson, I. (1989) "Choice based on reasons: the case of attraction and compromise effects," *Journal of Consumer Research* 16 (September): 158–74.

Smith, C.A. and Ellsworth, P.C. (1985) "Patterns of cognitive appraisal in emotion," *Journal of Personality and Social Psychology* 48 (April): 813–38.

5 The role of approach/avoidance asymmetries in motivated belief formation and change

Frank R. Kardes and Maria L. Cronley

The interplay between motivation and cognition has occupied a central role in psychology for many decades. Questions such as "how do motives, goals, preferences, and desires influence beliefs" and "how do beliefs influence motives, goals, preferences, and desires" have fascinated psychologists since the turn of the century (e.g. McDougall 1908). More recently, consumer psychologists have attempted to develop a taxonomy of goals (Huffman 1996; Huffman and Houston 1993) and have attempted to illustrate how involvement, accountability, and other motivational variables influences each stage of information processing (Lee *et al.* forthcoming; Ratneshwar, Mick, and Reitinger 1990).

In this chapter, we adopt the perspective of "beliefs as possessions" (Abelson and Prentice 1989), because beliefs are functional and because people are often surprisingly reluctant to give them up. This reluctance is often apparent even when the evidence supporting beliefs is ambiguous or inconsistent (for a review, see Sanbonmatsu *et al.* 1998). Moreover, belief perseverance often occurs even when the original evidential basis for beliefs is discredited completely (Ross, Lepper, and Hubbard 1975). We suggest that people have many different motives or reasons for holding beliefs and that the strategy best suited for changing these beliefs depends on their functional bases (Katz 1960). More interestingly, we suggest that different types of beliefs imply different approach versus avoidance proclivities, and we suggest that asymmetries between these approach versus avoidance tendencies exist for each category of belief. This perspective offers many new insights because much prior theorizing and research has assumed that approach versus avoidance orientations are of equal importance.

We adopt Katz's (1960) belief taxonomy and expand it by linking it to theories of regulatory focus and by attempting to explain the reasons for approach/avoidance asymmetries for each type of belief. Katz (1960) suggests that there are four primary motives or reasons for holding beliefs and attitudes: knowledge, value expression, ego defense, and adjustment. Beliefs that serve the knowledge function give meaning and structure to the world and help the individual to understand their complex environments. Beliefs that serve the value-expressive function help the individual to interact more effectively with other people by communicating relevant values and goals to others and by increasing one's power and influence over other people having similar values and goals. Beliefs that serve the ego-defensive function help the individual to feel safe, secure, and protected from real or imagined threats. Finally, beliefs that serve the adjustment, utilitarian, or hedonic function help the individual to approach pleasure and to avoid pain.

Theories of regulatory focus suggest that people try to approach desired end-states and avoid undesired end-states (Carver and Sheier 1981; Higgins 1998; Miller, Galanter, and Pribram 1960). Self-regulation involves comparing current states to end-states. As Bagozzi, Baumgartner, Pieters, and Zeelenberg (this volume) point out, approach-avoidance behaviors can include a wide variety of actions including behaviors related to preference, affiliation, and performance. Approach involves attempting to decrease the discrepancy between current states and desired end-states, and avoidance involves attempting to increase the discrepancy between current states and undesired end-states. Cybernetic-control models (e.g. Carver and Sheier 1981), achievement motivation models (e.g. McClelland *et al.* 1953), implementational models (e.g. Gollwitzer and Moskowitz 1996), personality models (Higgins 1998), and even animal learning models (e.g. Hull 1952; Lang 1995) emphasize the importance of movement toward desired end-states (approach) and movement away from undesired end-states (avoidance).

An overview of our model is presented in Table 5.1. As Table 5.1 indicates, different belief functions imply different desired and undesired end-states, and different approach versus avoidance tendencies. Table 5.1 also highlights how recent research and theorizing fits into the classic Katz (1960) model. The implications of approach/avoidance asymmetries for persuasion are summarized in Table 5.2. As Table 5.2 indicates, a large set of persuasion strategies is available to those who wish to influence consumers.

Table 5.1 Belief functions, approach versus avoidance tendencies, and relevant theories

Function	Approach	Avoidance	Relevant theories
Knowledge	Certainty	Uncertainty	Theory of lay epistemology
Value expression	Indirect positive associations	Indirect negative associations	Impression management theory
Ego defense	Increase perceived likelihood of desired events	Decrease perceived likelihood of undesired events	Terror management theory
Adjustment	Pleasure	Pain	Promotion versus prevention focus

Table 5.2 Belief functions, approach versus avoidance tendencies, and persuasion

Function	Approach	Avoidance
Knowledge	Factual appeals Quality appeals Logical arguments	Hypothesis disconfirming ads Mystery ads Disrupt-then-reframe
Value expression	Image appeals Celebrity endorsers Attractive endorsers	Unattractive users of competing brands
Ego defense	Authority figures Expert endorsers	Fear appeals
Adjustment	Focus on the benefits of using the advertised brand (use comparative ads, classical and operant conditioning, and social modeling)	Focus on the costs of not using the advertised brand (use comparative ads, classical and operant conditioning, and social modeling)

Self-discrepancy theory

Although people are motivated to approach desired end-states and to avoid undesired end-states, recent research suggests that approach and avoidance motives are not always equally important (Higgins 1998). End-states are reference points, and people use different reference points in different situations. Whether people focus more heavily on desired or on undesired end-states depends on their regulatory focus. Focusing on desired end-states fosters a promotion focus and increases approach proclivities (e.g. pleasure-seeking). Focusing on undesired end-states encourages a prevention focus and enhances avoidance tendencies (e.g. avoiding pain).

Higgins' (1987) self-discrepancy theory suggests that there are two types of desired end-states that he refers to as self-guides. Ideal self-guides refer to an individual's representations of his or her ideal characteristics, hopes, wishes, aspirations, or maximal goals. Ought self-guides refer to an individual's representations of his or her duties, obligations, responsibilities, or minimal goals. The failure to achieve ideal end-states results in negative, dejection-related emotions, such as sadness, depression, or feelings of helplessness. The failure to achieve ought end-states results in negative, agitation-related emotions, such as anger, uneasiness, or tenseness. Chronically or situationally accessible ideal self-guides increase an individual's concern about approaching desired end-states, whereas chronically or situationally accessible ought self-guides increase an individual's concern about avoiding undesired end-states.

Chronic self-guide accessibility can be assessed by administering the Selves Questionnaire (Higgins *et al.* 1986), which asks respondents to list about ten attributes for their actual, ideal, and ought self-states, and rate the extent to which they actually possess, ideally want to possess, or ought to possess each category of attributes, respectively. Actual/ideal discrepancies are estimated by subtracting the number of matches from the number of mismatches between the actual and ideal attributes listed. Actual/ought discrepancies are estimated by subtracting the number of matches from the number of mismatches between the actual and ought attributes listed. When actual/ideal discrepancies are greater than actual/ought discrepancies, ideal self-guides are chronically accessible and individuals adopt a promotion focus that emphasizes advancement, growth, and accomplishment. When ought/ideal discrepancies are greater than actual/ideal discrepancies, ought self-guides are chronically accessible and individuals adopt a prevention focus that emphasizes protection, safety, and responsibility.

Situational accessibility of ideal versus ought self-guides can be manipulated by asking participants to indicate how their hopes and goals have changed over time or by asking participants to indicate how their sense of duty and obligation has changed over time. Situational accessibility can also be manipulated by priming ideal or ought attributes subjects listed earlier when completing the Selves Questionnaire. Chronically or situationally accessible ideal self-guides foster a promotion focus, an approach orientation, and an increased concern about errors of omission (inaction). Chronically or situationally accessible ought self-guides foster a prevention focus, an avoidance orientation, and an increased concern about errors of commission (action). Although Higgins (1998) applied his self-discrepancy theory primarily to the hedonic principle of approaching pleasure and avoiding pain, we suggest that his analysis can be extended from the adjustment/hedonic function to each of the four belief functions. Moreover, other factors in addition to ideal and ought self-guides can produce approach/avoidance asymmetries.

The knowledge function

Beliefs and attitudes that serve the knowledge function provide people with a stable, meaningful view of the world. Knowledge-based beliefs help people to organize and structure large amounts of information in order to understand and manage complex topics and issues. Knowledge-based beliefs are cognitively adaptive, helping people to make judgments and decisions more efficiently because they allow for the use of a person's established general beliefs and attitudes. For example, beliefs and attitudes related to brand loyalty often serve the knowledge function. Loyalty to a particular brand provides a simplified and quick purchase decision, reducing ambiguity and eliminating a need for an extensive search process for other alternatives.

Knowledge-based beliefs are more likely to be activated or retrieved from memory when ambiguous, complex, or confusing situations are encountered (Kardes 1999). The theory of lay epistemics, which examines how people acquire knowledge, suggests that individuals differ in their levels of motivation regarding information search and knowledge acquisition (Kruglanski 1980, 1989). This self-attributed motivational tendency to seek and acquire knowledge is referred to as the need for cognitive closure (Kruglanski 1989; Kruglanski and Webster 1996). More specifically, the need for (non-specific) cognitive closure is the desire for any definite answer or knowledge about a question or problem, as opposed to confusion and ambiguity (Kruglanski and Webster 1996). This individual difference variable has been shown to be both a stable, dispositional state and a situationally evocable motivational tendency. Individual differences in the need for cognitive closure are influenced by preferences for order, structure, and predictability, tolerance of ambiguity, decisiveness, and narrow or closed-mindedness. In addition, situations differ in the extent to which they elicit a high need for cognitive closure (Kruglanski and Webster 1996). Situational differences in the need for cognitive closure are influenced by time pressure, task aversiveness, fatigue, and accountability (i.e. the anticipation of explaining or justifying one's decision to others). Interestingly, all of these variables produce conceptually similar effects on judgment and decision-making (Kruglanski and Webster 1996). Specifically, when the need for cognitive closure is high (versus low), people consider fewer alternatives, consider smaller amounts of information about each alternative, draw snap conclusions that have immediate and obvious implications for action, are insensitive to information that is inconsistent with these conclusions, and exhibit overconfidence in the validity of these conclusions. Finally, need for cognitive closure has been shown to influence a variety of social psychological phenomena, including confidence in social information seeking (Kruglanski, Peri, and Zakai 1991); openness to persuasion given prior information (Kruglanski, Webster, and Klem 1993); confidence judgments (Mayseless and Kruglanski 1987); and over-attribution and correspondence biases (Webster 1993).

Knowledge-based beliefs help individuals attain closure and reduce uncertainty. Closure supplies an individual with order, stability, and predictability (Webster and Kruglanski 1994). When need for cognitive closure is high, individuals are motivated to come to a decision quickly, focusing on information that promotes closure, while neglecting or discounting information that may lead to confusion. This process is referred to as "seizing" and "freezing" by Kruglanski and Webster (1996; Kruglanksi 1989; Kruglanski, Webster, and Klem 1993; Webster 1993). When need for cognitive closure is high, a person "seizes" on readily available or prominent information to achieve closure and then "freezes" on that information to maintain it for as long as possible. When need for cognitive closure is low, a person may be more open to delaying judgment and examining more information.

The desire for closure creates an obvious potential trade-off between the speed of a decision and the accuracy of that decision. Closure promotes timely judgment. Under high need for closure conditions, because less information overall is considered, there is less uncertainty and ambiguity for the individual. Fewer hypotheses are generated and evaluated, and the decision or choice is made quickly. Unfortunately, this process of "seizing" and "freezing" on initial information under conditions of high need for closure may result in the individual's over-utilization of early cues, anchoring on initial information, and then failing to sufficiently adjust for subsequent judgment-relevant evidence (Kruglanski and Webster 1996). Thus, while the use of knowledge-based beliefs to attain closure provides less uncertainty and ambiguity for the decision-maker, it does not guarantee the quality of those judgments and decisions.

While a high need for cognitive closure may motivate people to draw upon knowledge-based beliefs in order to approach less ambiguous and more certain end-states, self-guides also play an important role. Chronically or situationally accessible ideal self-guides increase an individual's concern about achieving more desirable and certain end-states. When this is the case, factual and rational appeals are effective persuasive techniques because they can aid in the development of knowledge-based beliefs, especially when the need for cognitive closure is high. These types of appeals rely on factual details about the specific features and benefits of the product that are useful for generating an informed opinion. For example, an advertisement for a brand new category product, such as an in-home dry cleaning system, may contain a lot of technical information that is very important to consumers that have dry cleaning needs and are interested in using this new type of product.

Logical appeals are also likely to be very persuasive when ideal self-guides are chronically accessible and need for cognitive closure is high. In a study looking at how logical syllogistic argument structures influenced self-generated beliefs about products, Kardes *et al.* (in press), found that a persuasion-induced change in a single, specific belief about a product within a consumer's integrated belief system altered other related beliefs about the product, even when those other beliefs were not explicitly mentioned in the counter-persuasive argument. In addition, the logical structure or organization of a set of persuasive arguments also plays a role. For instance, persuasive arguments such as product claims that appear in an advertisement can be logically arranged in either a vertical or horizontal fashion. Logical arguments that are arranged vertically build upon one another in a dependent or chain-like fashion, where the conclusion of an argument acts as the premise for the next argument, culminating in a final conclusion. Logical arguments that are arranged horizontally have multiple sets of arguments arranged independently, with all of the arguments implying the same final conclusion. When persuasive arguments are arranged logically in a vertical fashion persuasion-induced changes in beliefs are much more likely than when persuasive arguments are arranged in a horizontal fashion. In other words, a belief about a product claim supported by a horizontal (vs. vertical) argument structure is more resistant to counter-persuasion. Therefore, logical persuasive arguments, such as horizontally organized product claims in an advertisement, that are independent and imply a singular conclusion, are resistant to counter-persuasion, allowing a consumer to gain cognitive closure and maintain a desired end-state.

When ought self-guides are chronically or situationally accessible, people are more concerned about avoiding undesired, uncertain end-states. In this situation, need for cognitive closure theory may actually work unilaterally, whereby, a person may actually respond to uncertainty. When this is the case, appeals that actually create a state of uncertainty or confusion, subsequently causing a state of heightened need for cognitive closure, can be very persuasive. This is due to the fact that a heightened need for cognitive closure may shorten external information-seeking and internal hypothesis generation and testing, which leads people to then rely more heavily on already formed beliefs and attitudes (Kruglanski and Webster 1996; Sanbonmatsu *et al.* 1998). This increases the use of knowledge-based beliefs to achieve closure and avoid uncertain and undesirable end-states. Hypothesis disconfirming advertising appeals, mystery ad appeals, and the disrupt-then-reframe approach can all be explained from this perspective.

Hypothesis disconfirming advertising appeals provide information that is inconsistent with a person's currently-held beliefs or hypotheses. A hypothesis refers broadly to one possible explanation, prediction, option, or solution to a question or problem. One way to facilitate judgment and belief formation is to create and test competing hypotheses. Because people often must deal with more information than they can efficiently process, a single hypothesis or belief is often used to guide information acquisition and interpretation. As a result, when need for cognitive closure is high, or when ought self-guides are chronically accessible, the tendency to confirm and then "freeze" on a hypothesis is high. Hypothesis disconfirming advertising appeals are interpreted as unexpected and potentially confusing information for the individual that threatens to "unfreeze" the belief or hypothesis. This unexpected information heightens the need for cognitive closure because once closure has been attained (i.e. "frozen") encountering new, disconfirming information might cause its disintegration. This possible disintegration represents an undesired and uncertain end-state. Subsequently, when need for cognitive closure is heightened, a person can become insensitive to the information that is inconsistent with the held belief or hypothesis and continue to maintain or reach the desired, certain end-state.

Mystery ad formats work in a similar manner as hypothesis disconfirming ads. Mystery ads are those in which the brand in question is not identified until the end of the advertisement (Fazio, Herr, and Powell 1992). Like hypothesis disconfirming appeals, mystery ads may heighten the need for cognitive closure, which subsequently leads to the consideration of fewer alternatives and to insensitivity to additional information. But, unlike hypothesis disconfirming ads, mystery ads may employ a combination of curiosity and disappointment to heighten the need for closure. In a study examining the use of mystery ad formats, Fazio, Herr, and Powell (1992) found that mystery ads were more effective than traditional ads (i.e. ads that identified the brand early on) in generating category and brand associations in memory. More interestingly, these results were moderated by brand familiarity. Mystery ads were more effective only for novel brands. The authors point out that curiosity, disappointment, and even feeling foolish may play a role in explaining these results. We contend that the lack of effect for familiar brands may be due to a lack of information processing due to a heightened state of need for cognitive closure. This heightened state of need for closure may result from the initial curiosity a person feels when encountering a mystery ad and then the subsequent disappointment that is felt when the brand turns out to be all too familiar. This upheaval of emotion during the mystery followed by the disappointment results in the person reverting back toward the original desired end-state.

The disrupt-then-reframe technique (DTR) is an influence tactic involving a disruption in a person's understanding of an event and a subsequent direct reframing of the event (Davis and Knowles 1999). For example, stating the price of a product in terms of time rather than money (disruption) and then saying the product is worth the time (reframe). In a series of experiments, Davis and Knowles (1999) successfully employed this technique to sell note cards door-to-door for a charity. The disruption was the price of the cards stated in pennies and the reframe stated that the price was a bargain. The authors identify action identification theory (Vallacher and Wegner 1985, 1987) and confusion techniques used in hypnosis (Erickson 1964) as potential contributors to the effectiveness of DTR. We offer an alternate interpretation based on the need for cognitive closure approach. We propose that, like mystery ads, a heightened need for cognitive closure may play a role. It is possible that in employing the DTR approach, disruption increases need for closure by presenting information in a disarming manner that temporarily "unfreezes" or disintegrates closure. This is an undesired and uncertain state. When the reframed argument is then presented, the individual, wanting to avoid this undesired state, readily "seizes" and then "re-freezes" on the reframed argument in the appeal. This allows the person to again approach the desired, more certain end-state.

The value-expressive function

Beliefs and attitudes that serve the value-expressive function help us to express our preferences, traits, and interests to others. Value-expressive beliefs help us to manage and control the impressions others form of us and help others to interact with us more effectively. Beliefs that allow us to demonstrate our standards and long-term orientations also serve the value-expressive function. For instance, a person's beliefs about a political party may reflect that person's long-term political affinity and a broad conservative or liberal orientation. Alternatively, products and services that are publicly used, conspicuous, or attention-drawing may also serve a value-expressive and self-presentation function. These products are considered image-oriented products. For example, the type of car a person drives, the clothes and accessories a person wears, or the type of store where a person shops, all may reflect beliefs that serve the value-expressive function.

People are generally very committed to their value-expressive based beliefs because there is a potential cost for holding those beliefs (Lydon and Zanna 1990). Impression management theory suggests that people are usually highly motivated to give the appearance that their beliefs and attitudes are consistent with their behaviors in order convey a favorable impression to others (Tedeschi, Schlenker, and Bonoma 1971). This motivation stems from the idea that inconsistency is a sign of inherent weakness. In other words, inconsistent people that say one thing but do another appear flaky and should not be taken seriously (Kardes 1999). Therefore, the use of value-expressive based beliefs to make a positive and consistent impression on others is very important to people. Further, the use of value-expressive based beliefs and impression management techniques may also influence self-perception (Greenwald and Breckler 1985). The self is an important recipient of beliefs that serve the value-expressive function. Value-expressive based beliefs that reflect a consistent and positive impression of oneself in order to maintain a positive sense of self and self-esteem may be as important, or more important, than impressing others.

One way to express value-expressive based beliefs is through indirect associations. An indirect association is a self-presentation technique that is aimed at influencing other's images of oneself indirectly. Image related information is not presented directly to others, but rather, is presented to others merely through one's association to an object or situation (Cialdini *et al.* 1976; Cialdini and Richardson 1980). Because of the desire to maintain a consistent image in the minds of others, individuals may attempt to be positively connected to positive stimuli and negatively connected to negative stimuli through indirect associations. Creating indirect positive associations to favorably evaluated stimuli (e.g. a brand, company, city, sports team, political party) allows a person to position themselves favorably in the eyes of others. In addition, indirect positive associations can increase perceived likability. Likability is related to the idea that a person can attain some degree of power over the people that like them. Cialdini *et al.* (1976) refer to these types of indirect positive associations as basking-in-reflected-glory. For instance, sports fans often wear clothing and apparel bearing their favorite team's colors and logos when the team is winning and having a successful season. The fans do not have any direct association with the team, but indirectly the team's success makes the individual appear successful.

While people may seek out desirable indirect associations, they may avoid undesirable indirect negative associations. This is the converse of Cialdini's basking-in-reflected-glory concept and is referred to as blasting. Blasting consists of creating a negative indirect association with an undesirable object or situation. When the favorite sports team begins to lose, fans suddenly become quite fickle and do not want to be associated with the team. Related to the idea of blasting is Snyder's concept of cutting-off-reflected-failure in order to lessen one's association with an unsuccessful person, object, or situation (Snyder, Lassegard, and Ford 1986). Snyder, Lassegard, and Ford (1986) found that when the group to which they belonged performed poorly, group members attempted to distance their self-assessed behaviors from the behaviors of the collective group. Interestingly, this cutting-off-reflected-failure was a stronger image maintenance tactic than the more positive associative process of basking-in-reflected-glory. These results suggest that the need to avoid indirect negative associations may be stronger than the need to create indirect positive associations.

While a desire for consistency and a positive impression of oneself may motivate people to draw upon value-expressive-based beliefs in making or avoiding indirect associations, self-guides provide similar results. Chronically or situationally accessible ideal self-guides increase an individual's concern about achieving consistent positive impression maintenance, whereas, chronically or situationally accessible ought self-guides increase an individual's concern about avoiding inconsistent impressions and negative associations. When this is the case, image-oriented appeals may be highly persuasive. Image-oriented appeals influence the beliefs and attitudes that serve the value-expressive function by activating salient cues associated with values (Kardes 1999). For example, seeing an attractive, healthy person drink an enriched sports drink may encourage some people to buy this type of product. Advertisements that use attractive spokespersons or celebrity endorsers are based on this idea. People that admire Tiger Woods or want to be like him buy products endorsed by him.

Image-oriented appeals often show a very attractive spokesperson or celebrity endorsing the brand. Likewise, highly unattractive or unpopular people are portrayed as using a competitor's brand. The success of these types of ads may be due, in part, to the inferences that people make about the endorser, which subsequently influence inferences and evaluations about the brand. Cronley *et al.* (1999) found this to be the case. In a study which examined correspondent inferences in celebrity endorsed print advertisements, the authors found that people exhibited correspondent inferences when evaluating celebrity endorsed ads, despite knowing the celebrity was paid a large endorsement fee. These inferences were subsequently related to brand evaluations. Other factors, such as physical attractiveness and credibility of the endorser, also influence the effectiveness of image-oriented, endorser appeals (e.g. Kamins 1990; Friedmen 1984). McCracken (1989) has also examined why particular endorsers are effective, proposing that it is the cultural meanings ascribed to endorsers which makes them effective. If there is a good "match" between the endorser and the product so that the transfer of cultural meaning is possible, then the endorser is effective.

The ego-defensive function

Beliefs that serve the ego-defensive function help the individual to feel safe, secure, and protected from real or imagined threats. Negative, stereotypic beliefs about members of various out-groups that are perceived to compete for desired resources (e.g. jobs, territories, status, influence) often serve this function. Beliefs about protective products and services (e.g. home and automobile security systems, law enforcement programs, insurance policies), religious beliefs that imply that believers are saved and non-believers are damned, and optimistic beliefs that good things will happen to us and bad things will not also serve the ego-defensive function.

Terror management theory (Pyszczynski, Greenberg, and Solomon 1997) suggests that the uniquely human cognizance of the inevitability of death creates the potential for paralyzing terror because it clashes with the powerful desire for continued existence. This terror is checked by an anxiety buffer provided by a cultural world-view that is benevolent to the ingroup, but not to outgroups. A cultural world-view is a schema or belief system that provides meaning and stability to an unpredictable world. It also provides a set of standards one needs to realize to achieve high self-esteem now or immortality later. Because one's cultural world-view is essential for managing terror, individuals are highly motivated to like people who believe in the same cultural world-view and to dislike those who do not. Differential perceptions of ingroup versus outgroup members are intensified when cues or symbols that remind people of their own mortality are salient.

Mortality salience results in more favorable responses to those who share one's beliefs and less favorable responses to those who do not. For example, mortality salience leads Christians to respond more favorably to other Christians and less favorably to Jews, and leads Americans to respond more favorably to foreigners who praise America and less favorably to foreigners who criticize America. Mortality salience also increases the magnitude of the false consensus effect, the dissonance effect, belief in a just world, and prejudice towards and intolerance of members of outgroups (Pyszczynski, Greenberg, and Solomon 1997). Mortality salience can be induced by exposing people to questions about death, or by incidental exposure to funeral homes, media reports on death (e.g. due to crime, disease, war), or death-related themes in movies, novels, or other entertainment media. Other types of anxiety (e.g. expecting to give a public speech, expecting to receive intense physical pain, expecting to fail an important exam) do not produce effects similar to those produced by death-specific anxiety.

People are generally motivated to believe that good things will happen to them and that bad things will not (optimistic bias or wishful thinking). Interestingly, mortality salience differentially influences people's concern about good events versus bad events. In general, the perceived likelihood of undesired events decreases as mortality salience increases. The effects of mortality salience on the perceived likelihood of desired events are more complex, however. In a provocative field experiment, German citizens were asked to indicate their opinions concerning a proposal to restrict the immigration of foreigners into Germany in a political opinion interview conducted on the street either directly in front of or 100 meters away from a funeral home (Pyszczynski *et al.* 1996). When the interview was conducted directly in front of the funeral home, citizens holding the minority view (against the proposal) overestimated the percentage of other Germans holding the same opinion. This false consensus effect was eliminated when the interview was conducted far away from the funeral home or when the participant believed in the majority opinion. In a follow-up study, US citizens were asked to express their opinions about the teaching of Christian values in public schools. When the interview was conducted in front of the funeral home, citizens holding the minority view (pro-Christian values in school) overestimated the percentage of other US citizens who would hold the same opinion. This false consensus effect was eliminated when the interview was conducted far away from the funeral home or when the citizen held the majority view. Those holding the minority view are more strongly motivated to believe that others believe as they do when mortality salience is high.

Mortality salience is not the only variable that motivates people to avoid thinking about unpleasant events. Chronically or situationally accessible ought self-guides also increase an individual's concern about avoiding undesired end-states. When people are highly motivated to avoid undesired end-states, fear appeals are likely to be particularly persuasive. Moreover, pairing fear appeals with specific suggestions for achieving effective self-protection also increases the effectiveness of fear appeals.

When mortality salience is low or when ideal self-guides are chronically accessible, people are more concerned about approaching desired end-states than about avoiding undesired end-states. Under these circumstances, experts and authority figures (e.g. religious, political, and opinion leaders) are likely to be very persuasive. Moreover, the message should focus on desired end-states (e.g. eternal bliss, national achievement, greater power and influence over others) rather than on undesired end-states.

The adjustment function

Higgins' (1998) theory of promotion versus prevention regulatory focus suggests that chronically or situationally accessible ideal self-guides foster a promotion focus, an approach orientation, and an increased concern about errors of omission (inaction). Chronically or situationally accessible ought self-guides foster a prevention focus, an avoidance orientation, and an increased concern about errors of commission (action). For example, in a study on differential sensitivity to gains versus losses in outcome framing, affective discrimination was reduced when there was a mismatch between chronic self-guides and regulatory focus (Higgins 1998). In one scenario, for example, participants were asked to imagine saving or losing $50 on the price of an airplane ticket for returning home after completing their final exams. In promotion conditions, the final exam schedule either permitted or did not permit them to take the less expensive flight. In prevention conditions, participants expected to have to take the more expensive flight, but later learned (after checking their schedule) that they would be able or unable to take the less expensive flight. Affective discrimination was lowest in ideal/prevention and in ought/promotion conditions, relative to the remaining conditions. Hence, sensitivity to framing manipulations depends critically on one's regulatory focus.

Recent research indicates that regulatory focus also influences performance on intellectual exercises, such as anagrams tasks (Higgins 1998). Participants were told to identify 90 percent of the words embedded in an anagrams puzzle, and they received $5 if they succeeded or $4 if they failed. In promotion frame conditions, participants were told that they would receive an extra dollar for success. In prevention frame conditions, participants were told that they could avoid losing a dollar they already possessed by not failing. The results revealed that performance on the anagrams task was better when chronically accessible self-guides matched (vs. mismatched) participants' regulatory focus.

Expectancy-value models of motivation assume that goal commitment increases as either expectancy or value increases. Moreover, these models assume that expectancy and value combine multiplicatively, so that the influence of one variable increases as the other increases. However, several studies in the expectancy-value model literature report a failure to find a positive expectancy X value interaction. Higgins (1998) hypothesized that people should be motivated to maximize the product of expectancy and value only in promotion focus conditions. A promotion focus should motivate people to approach matches to desired end-states and to pursue highly valued goals. By contrast, a prevention focus should motivate people to avoid mismatches to desired end-states and to avoid unnecessary risks. When a goal becomes a necessity, people must try to achieve it regardless of whether the likelihood of success is high or low. In several studies involving anagrams tasks or predictions about one's performance in a college course in one's major, Higgins (1998) found a positive expectancy X value interaction when participants were in a promotion focus, and found a negative expectancy X value interaction when participants were in a prevention focus.

In an unpublished study reported by Higgins (1998), Safer and Higgins investigated whether a promotion versus a prevention regulatory focus influenced the weighting of luxury versus safety attributes in apartments and cars. Participants were asked to give their impressions of and choose between two apartments or two cars. The luxury apartment was described as having grand, 12-foot-high ceilings and elegant, intricate wall moldings. The other safe apartment was described as having secure, solid-steel safety locks on the front door and reliable smoke detectors. Similarly, the luxury car was described as having plush, soft leather seats and a premium sound system, whereas the other car was described as having antilock brakes and a reliable battery backup for cold days. The results showed that the luxury products were more strongly preferred by participants with a promotion focus, whereas the safe/reliable products were more strongly preferred by participants with a prevention focus. Considered together, the studies reviewed by Higgins (1998) suggest that a promotion versus a prevention regulatory focus has an important influence on affective responses, performance, goal commitment, and decision-making.

We suggest that regulatory focus also has important implications for persuasion. When recipients are in a promotion focus, advertisements that emphasize the benefits of using the advertised brand are likely to be effective. Perhaps the advertised brand has deluxe, luxury features, or is attractively designed or easy to use. By contrast, when recipients are in a prevention focus, emphasizing the costs of not using the advertised brand is likely to be more effective. For example, in an ad that highlights the costs associated with not using a particular spray system for house painting, a neighbor uses old-fashioned buckets and brushes and gets paint everywhere, including in his hair, on the lawn, and so on. Similarly, ads for headache or stomachache pain relievers often depict foolish people using other brands that are almost completely ineffective.

Conclusion

This chapter examines the role of motivation in belief formation and change. As the model outlined in Tables 5.1 and 5.2 indicates, different belief functions imply different desired and undesired end-states, and different approach versus avoidance tendencies. The model has important implications for persuasion theory and practice, because beliefs that serve different functions require different strategies for belief change. Approaches that are effective for changing beliefs and attitudes that serve a particular function are likely to be remarkably ineffective for changing beliefs and attitudes that serve one of the other remaining functions.

Table 5.2 specifically outlines implications of approach/avoidance asymmetries for persuasion and shows that there is a large set of persuasion strategies available to those who wish to influence consumers. When consumers are motivated to approach certainty, impress others, feel safe, or enjoy the hedonic benefits of consumption, a number of approach-oriented persuasive appeals should be considered. When consumers are motivated to avoid uncertainty, not tarnish their image, avoid threatening events, or avoid the aversive hedonic consequences of consumption, several avoidance-oriented persuasive appeals should be considered. Selecting the most effective persuasion strategy requires a careful analysis of belief functions, approach versus avoidance tendencies, and reasons for approach/avoidance asymmetries.

Acknowledgments

The authors thank Cynthia Huffman and Sharon Shavitt for their helpful comments on an earlier draft of this chapter.

References

Abelson, R.P. and Prentice, D. (1989) "Beliefs as possessions: a functional perspective," in A.R. Pratkanis, S.J. Breckler, and A. G. Greenwald (eds) *Attitude Structure and Function,* Hillsdale, NJ: Erlbaum: 361–81.

Bagozzi, R.P., Baumgartner, H., Pieters, R., and Zeelenberg, M. (2000) "The role of emotions in goal-directed behavior," in S. Ratneshwar, D. Glen Mick, and C. Huffman (eds) *The Why of Consumption,* London: Routledge.

Carver, C.S. and Sheier, M.F. (1981) *Attention and Self-Regulation: A Control-Theory Approach to Human Behavior,* New York: Springer-Verlag.

Cialdini, R.B., Borden, R.J., Thorne, A., Walker, M.R., Freeman, S., and Sloan, L.R. (1976) "Basking in reflected glory: three (football) field studies," *Journal of Personality and Social Psychology* 34: 366–75.

Cialdini, R.B. and Richardson, K.D. (1980) "Two indirect tactics of image management: basking and blasting," *Journal of Personality and Social Psychology* 39 (3): 406–15.

Cronley, M.L., Houghton, D.M., Kardes, F.R., and Goddard, P. (forthcoming) "Endorsing products for the money: the role of the correspondence bias in celebrity advertising," *Advances in Consumer Research,* Montreal, Canada: Association for Consumer Research.

Davis, B.P. and Knowles, E.S. (1999) "A disrupt-then-reframe technique of social influence," *Journal of Personality and Social Psychology* 76 (2):192–9.

Erickson, M.H. (1964) "The confusion technique in hypnosis," *The American Journal of Clinical Hypnosis* 6: 183–207.

Fazio, R.H., Herr, P.M., and Powell, M.C. (1992) "On the development and strength of category-brand associations in memory: the case of mystery ads," *Journal of Consumer Psychology* 1 (1): 1–13.

Friedmen, J.B. (1984) "Advertising spokesperson effects: an examination of endorser type and gender on two audiences," *Journal of Advertising Research* 24 (5): 33–41.

Gollwitzer, P.M. and Moskowitz, G.B. (1996) "Goal effects on action and cognition," in E.T. Higgins and A.W. Kruglanski (eds) *Social Psychology: Handbook of Basic Principles,* New York: Guilford Press: 361–99.

Greenwald, A.G. and Breckler, S.J. (1985) "To whom is the self presented?," in B.R. Schlenker (ed.) *The Self and Social Life,* New York: McGraw Hill: 126–45.

Higgins, E.T. (1987) "Self-discrepancy: a theory relating self and affect," *Psychological Review* 94: 319–40.

—— (1998) "Promotion and prevention: regulatory focus as a motivational principle," in M.P. Zanna (ed.) *Advances in Experimental Social Psychology*, vol. 30, San Diego, CA: Academic Press: 1–46.

Higgins, E.T., Bond, R.N., Klein, Y.R., and Strauman, T. (1986) "Self-discrepancies and emotional vulnerability: how magnitude, accessibility, and type of discrepancy influence affect," *Journal of Personality and Social Psychology* 51: 5–15.

Huffman, C. (1996) "Goal change, information acquisition, and transfer," *Journal of Consumer Psychology* 5 (1): 1–26.

Huffman, C. and Houston, M.J. (1993) "Goal-oriented experiences and the development of knowledge," *Journal of Consumer Research* 20: 190–207.

Hull, C.L. (1952) *A Behavior System: An Introduction to Behavior Theory Concerning the Individual Organism*, New Haven: Yale University Press.

Kamins, M.A. (1990) "An investigation into the match-up hypothesis in celebrity advertising: when beauty may be only skin deep," *Journal of Advertising* 19 (1): 4–13.

Kardes, F.R. (1999) *Consumer Behavior and Managerial Decision Making*, Reading, MA: Addison Wesley.

Kardes, F.R., Cronley, M.L., Pontes, M.J., and Houghton, D.M. (in press) "Down the garden path: the role of conditional inference processes in self-persuasion," *Journal of Consumer Psychology*.

Katz, D. (1960) "The functional approach to the study of attitudes," *Public Opinion Quarterly* 24 (2): 163–204.

Kruglanski, A.W. (1980) "Lay epistemo-logic-process and contents: another look at attribution theory," *Psychological Review*, 87: 70–87.

—— (1989) *Lay Epistemics and Human Knowledge*, New York, NY: Plenum Press.

Kruglanski, A.W. and Webster, D.M. (1996) "Motivated closing of the mind: 'seizing' and 'freezing'," *Psychological Review* 103 (2): 263–83.

Kruglanski, A.W., Peri, N., and Zakai, D. (1991) "Interactive effects of need for closure and initial confidence on social information seeking," *Social Cognition* 9: 127–48.

Kruglanski, A.W., Webster, D.M., and Klem, A. (1993) "Motivated resistance and openness to persuasion in the presence or absence of prior information," *Journal of Personality and Social Psychology* 65 (November): 861–76.

Lang, P.J. (1995) "The emotion probe: studies of motivation and attention," *American Psychologist* 50 (3): 372–85.

Lee, H., Herr, P.M., Kardes, F.R., and Kim, C. (1999) "Motivated search: effects of choice accountability, issue involvement, and prior knowledge on information acquisition and use," *Journal of Business Research* 45 (May): 75–88.

Lydon, J.E. and Zanna, M.P. (1990) "Bolstering attitudes by autobiographical recall," *Personality and Social Psychology Bulletin* 14: 78–86.

McCracken, G. (1989) "Who is the celebrity endorser? Cultural foundations of the endorsement process," *Journal of Consumer Research* 16 (December): 310–21.

McClelland, D.C., Atkinson, J.W., Clark, R.A., and Lowell, E.L. (1953) *The Achievement Motive*, New York: Appleton-Century-Crofts.

McDougall, W. (1908) *Introduction to Social Psychology*, London: Methuen.

Mayseless, O. and Kruglanski, A.W. (1987) "What makes you so sure? Effects of epistemic motivations on judgmental confidence," *Organizational Behavior and Human Decision Processes* 39: 162–83.

Miller, G.A., Galanter, E., and Pribram, K.H. (1960) *Plans and the Structure of Behavior*, New York: Holt, Rinehart, and Winston.

Pyszczynski, T., Greenberg, J., and Solomon, S. (1997) "Why do we need what we need? A terror management perspective on the roots of human social motivation," *Psychological Inquiry* 8 (1): 1–20.

Pyszczynski, T., Wicklund, R.A., Floresku, S., Koch, H., Gauch, G., Sheldon, S., and Greenberg, J. (1996) "Whistling in the dark: exaggerated consensus estimates in response to incidental reminders of mortality," *Psychological Science* 7 (6): 332–6.

Ratneshwar, S., Mick, D.G., and Reitinger, G. (1990) "Selective attention in consumer information processing: the role of chronically accessible attitudes," in M.E. Goldberg, G. Gorn, and R.W. Pollay (eds) *Advances in Consumer Research*, vol. 17, Provo, UT: Association for Consumer Research: 547–53.

Ross, L., Lepper, M.R., and Hubbard, M. (1975) "Perseverance in self-perception and social perception: biased attributional processes in the debriefing paradigm," *Journal of Personality and Social Psychology* 32: 880–92.

Sanbonmatsu, D.M., Posavac, S.S., Kardes, F.R., and Mantel, S.P. (1998) "Selective hypothesis testing," *Psychonomic Bulletin and Review* 5 (2): 197–220.

Snyder, M. and DeBono, K.G. (1985) "Appeals to image and claim about quality: understanding the psychology of advertising," *Journal of Personality and Social Psychology* 49: 586–97.

Snyder, C.R., Lassegard, M., and Ford, C.E. (1986) "Distancing after group success and failure: basking in reflected glory and cutting off reflected failure," *Journal of Personality and Social Psychology* 51 (2): 382–8.

Tedeschi, J.T., Schlenker, B.R., and Bonoma, T.V. (1971) "Cognitive dissonance: private ratiocination or public spectacle?" *American Psychologist* 26: 685–95.

Vallacher, R.R. and Wegner, D.M. (1985) *A Theory of Action Identification*, Hillsdale, NJ: Erlbaum.

—— (1987) "What do people think they're doing? Action identification and human behavior," *Psychological Review* 94: 2–15.

Webster, D.M. (1993) "Motivated augmentation and reduction of the overattribution bias," *Journal of Personality and Social Psychology* 65: 261–71.

Webster, D.M. and Kruglanski, A.W. (1994) "Individual differences in need for cognitive closure," *Journal of Personality and Social Psychology* 67: 1049–62.

6 The missing streetcar named desire

Russell W. Belk, Güliz Ger, and Søren Askegaard

I don't want realism, I want magic.
(Blanch Dubois
in *A Streetcar Named Desire*)

Whatever lifts the body up–muscles,
sinews, joints; whatever wrestles against
gravity itself – the raised step, the lifted arm –
these form the body's hope. But also hunger,

selfishness, desire, all that leads us
to put one foot in front of the other,
these too form the body's hope, whatever
combats that urge to lie down – greed,

anger, lust – these feelings keep us going,
while the imagination sketches pictures
of the desired future, how we will look
in that new hat, how we will feel

with a belly full of cherries: anything
that shoves us from this moment to the next,
motivation like a flight of stairs, and hope
like a push at the top, not dissatisfaction

but eagerness to plunge into the next second
(Stephen Dobyns,
The Body's Hope, 1990)

Desire: introductory remarks

Desire has been a taboo word in consumer research. Two legacies of the economic and psychological parentage of the field of consumer research are its slowly disappearing cognitive information processing bias and its rationalization of consumer choice as a process of need fulfillment. The homeostatic tension-reducing model of consumer motivation that underlies this orientation has occasionally been challenged by pleas to consider hedonic pleasure seeking, variety seeking, or experiential consumption. But even in these cases it is more the object of needs rather than the nature of the motivational process itself that is questioned. In order to begin to envision an alternative to the needs paradigm, consider the descriptors used to characterize states of desire. We say in English that we burn and are aflame with desire; we are pierced by or riddled with desire; we are sick or ache with desire; we are tortured, tormented, and racked by desire; we are possessed, seized, ravished, and overcome by desire; we are mad, crazy, insane, giddy, blinded, or delirious with desire; we are enraptured, enchanted, suffused, and enveloped by desire; our desire is fierce, hot, intense, passionate, incandescent, and irresistible; and we pine, languish, waste away, or die of unfulfilled desire. Try substituting need or want in any of these metaphors and the distinction becomes immediately apparent. Needs are anticipated, controlled, denied, postponed, prioritized, planned for, addressed, satisfied, fulfilled, and gratified through logical instrumental processes. Desires, on the other hand, are overpowering; something we give in to; something that takes control of us and totally dominates our thoughts, feelings, and actions. Desire awakens, seizes, teases, titillates, and arouses. We battle, resist, and struggle with, or succumb, surrender, and indulge our desires. Passionate potential consumers are consumed by desire.

The difference between needs and desires is not simply their intensity or emotionality, but their basic perceived nature. Need is perceived to originate internally; desire externally. Needs push, desires pull. Needs offer a rational explanation of behavior (I bought it because I need it); desires do not. In a culture of abundance we often debate whether we *really* need something, but when we desire something we feel its unequivocal lure. While we might in retrospect question *how* we could have so strongly desired some, now inconsequential, object, we do not question *whether* we desired it. Desire is not an evolution of physical need as Elliott (1997) maintains, but is a categorically and qualitatively different phenomenon.

This is not at all to say that desires are not as compelling as needs; they are usually far more so. The lure of the desired object may cause us to suppress needs in order to pursue it, often rationalizing that we really need what we recognize as an irresistible desire. Desires are specific wishes inflamed by imagination, fantasy, and a longing for transcendent pleasure (Belk, Ger, and Askegaard 1996, 1997). Even though they are perceived to originate externally in the compelling object, the real locus of desire is the imagination of what it would be like if only we could have the desired object. Advertising, packaging, display, media representations, conversations, and the sight of certain others possessing an object help to fuel these fantasies, but desire exists only within the person or group who participates in creating, nurturing, and pursuing these illusions. No object

– whether a product, person, activity, or place – is inherently desirable. It may or may not be inherently pleasurable, but this does not make it an object of desire. We may even come to desire what is inherently painful as do sadists and masochists. More broadly we may act against our better judgment because of a strong contrary desire – what Aristotle termed Akrasia (Stocker 1986). Consider Klein's description of cigarette smoking:

> . . . cigarette smoking defies the economy of what Freud calls the pleasure principle. According to that principle, which interprets pleasure on the model of need, the satisfaction of a desire results in the elimination of the desire, the way an infant's demand for milk and desire for the breast are perfectly gratified by the mother's nursing. Cigarettes, however defy that economy of pleasure: they do not satisfy desire, they exasperate it. The more one yields to the excitation of smoking, the more deliciously, voluptuously, cruelly, and sweetly it awakens desire – it inflames what it presumes to extinguish . . . filling a lack hollows out an even greater lack that demands even more urgently to be filled
>
> (Klein 1993: 43, 45)

Even in these cases, however, we cling to the hope that the object will bring sublime transcendent pleasure. Desire is thus very much a social and personal construction. But just as much as we construct desire, desire constructs us. We are what we desire. Sartre (1956) observed that feeling an absence of being, we come to desire states of having and doing that we believe will construct and manifest our being.

Desire and consumption

The Latin *desiderium* meant the grief for the absence or loss of a person or thing. The verb form, *desiderare* is to desire, to long for. This sense of longing was associated with the stars: a yearning for the unreachable stars. *Sidus* means "star" and the verb *desidiris* refers to "expecting from the stars." The verb "consider" is closely allied to desire: con-siderare translates "to look closely at something, to contemplate," and originally it meant "to observe the stars."

> To enter the realm of desire cannot help but lead us into a relationship to what is all at once brilliant, attractive, and out of reach . . . Desire introduces us to an impossible situation – impossible of absolute fulfillment.
>
> (Jager 1989: 145–6)

With that distance of the stars, appetite (from *appetere* = to seek for, to strive after) or desire does not refer to physical fullness or emptiness and thus satisfaction is not the physical noticing of emptiness or fullness, not having our so-called "needs" filled. Simmel's views are consistent with Jager's. Simmel considers the distance between the subject and object to represent desire. He says, "we desire objects only if they are not immediately given to us for our use and enjoyment; that is to the extent that they resist our desire" (Simmel 1978 [1900]: 66).

Desire, in the ordinary and colloquial sense of the word, refers to a strong longing, to something that is strongly wanted or, as a verb, to the process of wanting something strongly. Its critical relevance to consumer behavior seems obvious. But in conceptualizations of consumer behavior similar phenomena are often presented as needs or "mere wants," and subsumed under psychological motivation models, such as the motivational hierarchy of Maslow (1954). Within this model various needs are like empty tanks to be filled sequentially; only when a more basic category of needs is fulfilled do we proceed the next higher-order need category. But such an approach tones down and hides the passion that we experience in connection with certain consumption activities. It also countenances the predominance of rational decision-making models within consumer research – only challenged within the last decade or so by alternative conceptualizations of the consumer's relationship with products and services, such as those of the extended self (Belk 1988), the sacred and profane (Belk, Wallendorf, and Sherry 1989), postmodernism (Firat and Venkatesh 1995), symbolic consumption (Hirschman and Holbrook 1981), hedonic consumption (Holbrook and Hirschman 1982), consumer mythology (Levy 1981), the cultural perspective (Sherry 1986), and existential phenomenology (Thompson, Locander, and Pollio 1989). By investigating consumer desires, consumer research may make yet another step in the direction of connecting feelings and personal experiences of the most passionate kind with the realm of consumption.

The saying that "everything good is either forbidden or fattening" bears witness to the fundamental link between desire, on the one hand, and sex(ual transgression) and eating, on the other. Metaphors from these fundamental domains of human existence point to the strong passions – "desires" – and represent an attempt to compare feelings of consumer desire to yearning for other delicious and arousing objects. Besides sex and eating, the other domains of passionate discourse commonly invoked by consumers in discussing their desires are addictive craving for drugs and transcendent religious passion (Belk, Ger, and Askegaard 1996). The use of such metaphors expresses the profound longing that characterizes desire by invoking a transfer of deep passions from the realms of our most intense emotions. Of these various metaphors we believe that sexual desire is most similar to consumer desire because the underlying state of arousal in both cases is positive rather than negative. As Scruton says of sexual desire:

> To see the orgasm as the aim of desire is as misguided as to see the exultation experienced by a player upon scoring a goal as the aim of football, rather than as a pleasurable offshoot of the aim fulfilled.
>
> (Scruton 1986: 91)

So it is with consumer desire in which purchase and use of the desired object is, at its best, only a pleasurable offshoot of the pursuit of desire. Consumer desire is also similar to sex in that it is more dependent on the mind and susceptible to fantasy than is the case with other metaphoric comparisons involving hunger and addiction. Furthermore, like sex at its best, consumer desire is not merely a person–thing relationship, but rather a person–person relationship. The material objects of consumer desires symbolically mediate or represent interpersonal relationships.

In addition to craving desire itself, we desire to be desired by certain others. This is Hegel's dialectics of desire:

> The end point of desire is not . . . the sensuous object – that is only a means – but the unity of the I with itself. Self-consciousness is desire, but what it desires . . . is itself: it desires its own desire. And that is why it will be able to attain itself only through finding another desire, another self-consciousness . . . Desire seeks itself in the other: man desires recognition from man.
>
> (Hyppolite 1996: 71)

Miller (1998) argues that normative sociability and relationships are objectified through consumption. Consumption is an expression of love and other relationships. It is a search for a relationship with the beloved, and entails devotion to the beloved. Conceptualizing shopping as a devotional rite, an act of sacrifice, he states that "What the shopper desires above all is for others to want and to appreciate what she brings" (Miller 1998: 149). Objects of desire come to matter as means for constituting people that matter. Consumption, like kinship, can objectify individualism and status competition as well as normative sociability, social relations, and commitment to family.

Desire and the psychoanalytic legacy

Desire has already for some time been a central focus in a number of fields without having had much impact on marketing and consumer research. Postmodernist, poststructuralist, feminist, and Marxist theorists across a wide array of social sciences and humanities have adopted an agenda in which deconstructing consumer desire plays a prominent role (see Hutcheon 1989 and Miller 1995). A brief review of some of these perspectives is a good starting point for envisioning a consumer behavior in which need fulfillment is supplanted by the pursuit of desires.

To the neo-Freudian psychoanalyst Jacques Lacan (1970), desire is a feeling of lacking something that is really a repressed and unconscious longing for the Other (our mothers with whom we once were/believed ourselves to be one) who is needed to take possession of the Self.

There is a need in the organism 'experienced' as an unpleasant tension, and this tension/need simply disappears when it is satisfied. . . . He hallucinates the satisfaction of his wish/desire. Desire . . . [is] the psychic impulse which is bound to a memory image of satisfaction and which thus orients the infant organism's quest to reestablish the situation of the original satisfaction.

(Ewens 1987: 305)

What Freud calls "wish," Lacan calls "desire" (Ewens 1987; Richardson 1987; Stewart 1986). In Freud's view, desire is an unconscious structure; for Lacan, the lost object is the mother as imaginary fullness (Richardson 1987). As Lacan explains:

Thus desire is neither the appetite for satisfaction [the infant's need for milk], nor the [underlying] demand for [mother's] love, but the difference that results from the subtraction of the first from the second.

(Lacan 1977: 287)

This lack or "want-to-be" is the nature of desire. The subject desires to restore the unity (Richardson 1987). The self that is lacking the object wants union with the object. But not knowing this, the self turns to imaginary fantasies as constructions of concealment. According to Lacan, when the infant begins to speak, a third dimension is introduced, the "symbolic order," and there is a rupture of the bipolar relationship with its imagined world (Richardson 1987). The symbolic realm of language transforms the fantasizing person into a person verbalizing his/her desires, thus constituting the subject.

Accordingly, Lacan insists that the "desire of man is desire of the Other," in a double sense: the subject desires to be the *desired* of the Other (at first mother), the object of the Other's desire; and the desire of the subject is to be the *desire* of the Other, insofar as the Other is the subject of the unconscious (Richardson 1987). In this sense, all consumer desire for things can be seen as a symbolic and ultimately ineffective attempt to complete the self by unconsciously signifying the Other (Leather 1983). To Lacan we are our desire: "desire is the metonymy of our being" (Lacan 1992: 321). But the self can only be known and completed through the Other. For Lacan, as for Freud, sexual desire is not simply a metaphor for other forms of desire, the libido, or the striving for *jouissance*, is the underlying source of all desire. Lacan sees Freud's pleasure principle as being allied with immediate and emotional primary process thinking while the reality principle instead involves more cognitive and constrained secondary process thinking (Lacan 1992). Freud's pleasure principle proves inadequate: "Desire does not subside with seeming satiation. Each orgasmic encounter merely whets the appetite in self-perpetuity. Memory as well as deliciousness of pleasure's ache gnaw at us, making it impossible to rest"

(Kakar and Ross 1987: 212). Although the *jouissance* sought is ultimately an Oedipal reunion with the mother, this unconscious motivation is repressed. We feel only an ill-defined lack resulting in displaced desires. What primary process thinking construes as a strongly felt, if vague, desire, secondary process thinking transforms into a rationalized need. Since it is impossible to obtain and maintain a state of *jouissance* in this way, all our striving to fill the empty feeling of lack is bound to fail. We pursue fantasies of fulfillment by sublimation and repetitive desire-pursuing rituals that cannot succeed. Thus, "we become affixed to repetitions rather than to satisfactions" (Ragland 1995: 152).

One attack on Lacan's extension of Freud's ideas is that it focuses on men as the subjects of desire and on women as the objects of desire (e.g. Doane 1987; Haskell 1999). Women's unspoken lack is the phallus (Silverman 1983). This does not mean that Lacan's conception leaves no room for female desire, but women are seen as desiring consumer goods in order to further turn themselves into objects of male desire. Men are seen to act and women to react in this view (Haskell 1999). Recent feminist criticism has, perhaps somewhat ironically, been directed at recasting women as agentic desiring subjects (e.g. Cixous and Clément 1986; Irigaray 1985; Kristeva 1984). The irony here is that women have long been castigated for being overly susceptible to consumer temptation and desire (e.g. Berry 1994).

Deleuze and Guattari (1972) attack Lacan's principle that desire is felt as a lack. They argue that desire is not a lack of something deep inside us, but a productive force. The underlying goal that our desire seeks to produce is the subject – the self of the person who experiences desire. By this it is not meant that what we desire defines who we are, but rather that the fact that we desire concrete things defines our being. The delusion is that when our desire focuses on a fantasy that we have been convinced we cannot do without, we are falsely made to fear a lack of something essential. The key metaphoric device that Deleuze and Guattari use to characterize desire as a productive process is that of the machine. We are desiring-machines they tell us. Just as "the breast is a machine that produces milk, and the mouth is a machine coupled to it" (1972: 7), the industry of capitalism is a machine that produces goods and the consumer is a machine that produces desire for these goods. As Bocock (1994) points out, however, the mechanistic reductionism of viewing consumers as desiring-machines is fundamentally problematic. Computers, robots, or other machines cannot discuss meanings, create religious rituals, yearn for love, or desire anything. They lack abilities to feel, to hope, and to pursue the transcendent. On the other hand, Deleuze and Guattari correctly discern that "desire does not lack anything; it does not lack its object. It is, rather, the *subject* that is missing in desire, or desire that lacks a fixed subject" (1972: 34). Coupled with the insight that desire keeps on producing itself, this means that desire keeps on attempting to produce the subject – our self. But since in order to do this there must be new things to desire, the consumer self that is produced is constantly changing as well as constantly eluding us.

Desire, need, and culture

Desires do not exist in a social vacuum however. We lack the self-knowledge and creativity to conjure our desires by ourselves alone. Nor will society condone or allow our pursuit of any peculiar desire. At the same time, we recognize that as consumers we are not mere pawns or machines that can be made to desire anything. Girard (1987) argues that desire is mimetic. We desire things because others desire them. Without other possibilities of knowing what we want, others become our models as we become their rivals. What is seen to be at stake in mimetic desire is prestige (Girard 1987). Mimetic desire is, then, a fundamental way of relating to the Other who becomes simultaneously a model and an obstacle.

The concept of desire, involving the passion with which we engage in many consumption activities, may be used to cast new light on the cultural embeddedness of our production and consumption system. Social philosophy, under the guidance of economics, has been concerned with freeing human societies from the constant fight to fulfill the needs of society. But the concept of need is not as illuminating as the concept of desire to explain the specific features of human society. According to Radkowski (1980), we can distinguish between desire, in the general sense, the human *ontological imagination,* and desires in their concrete expressions, *experienced desire.* The basis for the ontological imagination is the *power of otherness,* the fact that the human species can only perceive the reality of the world through the interpretation and *signification* attached to it – what Bouchet (1988) called "filling the void." This "power of Otherness" expresses the ability to see things not as they are ontologically (the extra-human world that Radkowski calls *the Same* because it only has one form of existence and cannot be otherwise), but rather as they can or could be: the ability and will to change natural objects into tools and other consumption objects, to form landscapes and habitat, to create a personal future by acting with a long-term perspective, to imagine life without illness and misery, to anticipate life after death, to communicate with the Gods, to form mythologies. Thus the power of otherness is also the power of *poesis,* of poetry, of human creation (Radkowski 1980).

The concept of need is hereby degraded to a secondary role in the explanation of cultures, in opposition to the axiom that all societies are (economically) organized in order to fulfill their needs. The necessary is always decided from above, on the basis of the surplus, never from below on the basis of survival (Baudrillard 1972). "Need," from one perspective, might be considered something that belongs to the realm of "the Same" (biophysical survival conditions) and as such would tell us very little about societies. When we import need in this sense to the social world we are mixing up logics and we imply "the Same" where, in fact, the power of Otherness rules. Alternatively "need" might be considered as a term that refers to domesticated desire, i.e. desires that have become socially instituted as necessities and placed in a social hierarchy. Need, in this sense, would refer to a set of norms attached to a system of social roles and not to a necessity that implies itself independently from culture. In contrast to such static needs, "desire always plays the mimetic game" (Radkowski 1989: 201). This mimesis helps to show how changes in society can create different desires. For example, in a Girardian triangulation of desire, the rarity of certain objects coupled with social stratification leads to competition, just as this competition in turn leads to the social construction and creation of rarity and scarcity.

As Girard (1987) specifies, the imagined pleasure of possessing an object depends upon the existence of others who desire it. It is this condition, "and not any intrinsic qualities of the object or even its context of origin, [that] determines its fetishistic value" (Stewart 1984: 163–4). The price of objects tells little about the objects and much about our collective appraisal of their worth as objects of desire. Colloquial terms evoke the existence of this domesticated desire in society. The terms *utilitarian, necessity* (obviously a pretended necessity since necessities strictly speaking are always biological, never cultural), *commodity* (indicating a so-called use and exchange value) or even *interesting, beautiful, good,* and *truthful* are all reflections of institutionalizations of desire. All are to a certain degree regarded as needs in our society, and suggest the basic cleavage between economic material philosophy and idealistic philosophy in our relative ranking of importance of these needs.

Desire, transgression, and control

There is another important sense in which desires are a social phenomenon rather than an individual phenomenon. Because desire is such a powerful emotional condition and in opposition to the socially desirable qualities of reason and rationality, it is also feared by many. Because the fervor of desire seems to be self-focused, and the longing most recognized is for things culturally defined as luxuries, desire is often regarded, especially in the West, as being a sinful transgression. While the transgression in desire is generally framed as sin and guilt – especially in Western cultures, it can also be framed as a matter of imbalance and loss of control – especially in Eastern cultures (Belk, Ger, and Askegaard 1997). Giving in to desire is seen as a loss of control – another socially valued quality. Attempts to control the exercise of desire take many forms at both an individual level (e.g. diets, exercise, savings) and societal levels (e.g. prohibition, drug laws, pornography laws). One argument against such controls, especially at the societal level, is that forbidden fruit seems much sweeter. That is, prohibiting something may make it all the more desirable. Bataille (1967 [1949]) is foremost among those who argue that transgression is a primary source of dangerous pleasure. The danger of desire emerges in battles between control and indulgence or rationality and animality. In Freudian terms, this is the battle between the id and the pleasure principle versus the ego and the reality principle. In terms of the sacred and profane, this tension is kratophany (Belk, Wallendorf, and Sherry 1989). Danger, whether felt in the form of guilt, sin, imbalance or loss of control, is thus a constitutive aspect of desire.

Desiring something unusual, extraordinary, beyond the normal, involves a desire to experience exciting differences and uncertainties. Pleasure comes from breaking taboos, engaging in the exotic, and satisfying the suppressed desire for disorder. The transgressive nature of desire is the desire to go beyond order – to break the prevailing boundaries (Bataille 1967 [1949]). The possibility of transgression is provided by the order, as in the object of temptation, the forbidden fruit, which is there to satisfy the order (Falk 1994). Thus, there is no lack in terms of needs, but a lack in terms of desire. The order or the boundary defines the object of desire. The forbidden element creates and articulates the lack. Hence, the pleasure is not only opposed by pain, but also by order, work, and duty (see also Mercer 1983). The political and cultural definition of desirability also involves what constitutes and is experienced as order and disorder.

Pursuing (apparently) "selfish" desires was also historically feared as opposing the social good. However, in the West, starting in the eighteenth century with Bernard Mandeville (1970 [1714]) and Adam Smith (1970 [1776]), selfishness in pursuit of desires began to be recast as potentially good. Not coincidentally, it was at about this time that Campbell detects a rise of contemporary imaginative hedonism which regards desire as "a state of enjoyable discomfort and . . . wanting rather than having is the main focus of pleasure-seeking" (1988: 86). Whether desire is more or less favorably evaluated at a specific time and place, it is accompanied by the concern that it is dangerous and must be controlled for the sake of the individual, social order, and the future of the planet. If danger and social order are so critical to the construction of desire, what is considered to be dangerous and disorderly in different cultures is key to the understanding of the social construction of desire.

Coping with desire in Western and Eastern moral philosophy

What is deemed desirable, what is pleasurable, is politically and historically defined. The appetite for consumer goods involves politics of the formation of pleasure (Jameson 1983), or definitions and judgments of desirability, with different implications for man and woman, for less versus more affluent societies and individuals, and for marketers and designers versus consumers. Desire, as well as the societal control or sanction of desire, differ over historic periods as well as cultures. Eastern and Western religious and philosophical histories shape the imagination about desires as well as objects of desire. All major world religions preach that desires should be controlled or given up. However, Eastern religions such as Hinduism and Islam, in spite of the fact that they exist in more ascetic versions as well, also demonstrate a certain acceptance of desires. This is in contrast to the condemning Christian approach to desire predominant in the West.

As hinted above, a key reason that desire has been overlooked is that it is too close to the "lower order" of the body and too distant from the "higher order" of the mind which has been deemed supreme, at least since the Enlightenment tore the two asunder. But the cause of the exclusion of desire goes farther back in Western history than the Enlightenment. Sahlins (1996) points to the Judeo-Christian concept of original sin and the Fall as being the reason we seem ashamed of our desires. The majority of the seven deadly sins of medieval Christianity have their basis in bodily desires. The program of Christianity can be seen as one of attempting to control and inhibit the presumably destructive effects of enacting these desires (Foucault 1985). This is accomplished both socially (via the external control of behavioral norms) and especially psychologically (via internalized self-control). While the Christian idea of asceticism has foundations in ancient Greek and Roman philosophies (Synott 1993), Christianity attached the notion of sinfulness to giving in to our bodily desires. Feelings of sin and guilt provide internal inhibitions and facilitate self-control of our inclinations to pursue what is pleasurable.

While he was primarily concerned with sexual desire, Foucault (1985) reveals the social processes of control whereby society inhibits the range and expression of our desires. This is done in such a way, however, that we become our own inhibitors. Desire and self-control are notions of Western culture, notions that produce us in their own image as desiring subjects (Alasuutari 1992). Self-control or restraint is made a virtue and we are made to feel noble and civilized by exercising it. Such control was especially evident in the Victorian era and later suppression of women's desires through the valorization of "purity" (Freedman 1987). What Foucault does with sexual desire, Berry (1994) does with more general desires for luxuries. Berry shows how societies at least from ancient Greek City States until the late eighteenth century constructed the quest for luxuries as decadent, feminine, and debilitating. Where we differ with Berry is in his stipulation that luxuries are not objects of fervent desire, but rather objects that, while they would be nice to have, we can do without. Berry nevertheless provides an insightful analysis of the social control of the exercise of desires, whether through sumptuary laws, luxury taxes, moral condemnation, or welfare restrictions of food stamp purchases to "necessities."

One societal basis for the condemnation of freely exercised desires is the charge that such indulgence is animalistic and gives in to lower-order feelings rather than higher-order thought (Berry 1994; Falk 1994).

However, Christian history left space for desire during carnivals, festivals, and holidays. Traditionally institutionalized rituals of inversion giving temporary free reign to normally taboo desires included medieval fairs, carnivals, and liminal holiday periods like contemporary Mardi Gras (Bahktin 1968). While hedonism was ostensibly against European morals, society also affirmed hedonism in other ways (Corbin 1995). Sensory hedonism became "civilized": placing more importance on sight and hearing (the "noble and social" senses) than the senses of proximity, of touch, taste and smell, which govern in depth the affective mechanisms. The discourse on the senses helped to establish and mark social order. Touch was a sign of the general populace's closeness to nature, to the animal, and taste and smell were the senses of survival; whereas among the bourgeoisie and the aristocracy, seduction required distance and the use of the senses (sight and hearing) required an assumed delicacy. Moreover, since the Enlightenment, the quest for satisfaction has become a more and more private quest, especially in the West. That is, Western consumers seek to define their desires without recourse to any collective cosmology or teleology. With the aid of psychoanalysis (also a very individualistic tool) they seek to find themselves "in the logic of childhood, dreams, and desires" (Soper 1990: 83).

Eastern religions that tell us we must overcome desire merely underline the seductive power of our desires and the still stronger power of our desire for desire. In various forms of both Hinduism and Islam, there is a simultaneity of the religious and the erotic or passionate, the body and the mind. In their more mystic forms, desire is seen to be an attachment that prevents freedom and joy if one remains attached to it and cannot move on. But desire, or pleasure, is not condemned as evil. There is also a situationalism in the Eastern sanction of desire: in some situations, for some men, some pleasures can be appropriate.

Hinduism accepts that all human beings have desires. It acknowledges four categories of essential aims that motivate individuals as they go through stages of life (Littleton 1996; Smith 1958): *dharma* (virtuous fulfillment of responsibilities, duty to community), *artha* (success, wealth), *kama* (pleasure), and *moksha* (spiritual fulfillment, liberation, "being" with awareness and bliss, achieved by release from attachment to worldly aims). The notion is that, although the highest ideal is *moksha*, repressing *artha* and *kama* will not work – if we think we want pleasure and success we should pursue them, with prudence and fair play. Rather than suppressed, desire should be fulfilled as richly and aesthetically as possible, and with good sense, before a person can advance to *moksha*. The Bhagavadgita expresses the paradox that things are created by desire and destroyed by desire. It also shows how to resolve paradoxes: act without acting for the sake of acting and don't be committed to action (Lipner 1997). If purified by *dharma*, the fruits of desire can be enjoyed. The lesson is to pursue the fruits of desiring, but to remain moral without greed, hypocrisy, cruelty, or arrogance, until one begins to seek eternal liberation, which is the ultimate fruit of desire. Thus, Indian cultural ethos swings from "bhogin" (the enjoyer or the sensualist) to "yogin" (the renouncer, the wise person) and the running theme is to be both at the same time (Venkatesh and Swamy 1994). In Indian thought, the body and the mind are not antagonistic to each other, the contemplation of the human form is as important as contemplating spiritual forms, and hence, there is room for joviality and desires as well as asceticism.

Islam also accepts that material things are important in life (e.g. Abdalati 1975; Smith 1958). If a person wants material things, he should work hard for such rewards, because unless he does, he cannot progress to more divine concerns. But acquisitiveness and competition must be balanced by fair play, compassion, generosity, and sharing wealth. Muslims must give *zekat* (poor due – a spiritual duty to society), by distributing 1/40 of the value of all possessions and property annually, to the have-nots. Thus, *zekat*, which purifies both the property of the owner and his/her heart from selfishness and greed, is a means of legitimation of desires for wealth and possessions. Moderation and balance are the guarantees of integrity and morality. Islam preaches unselfishness, moderation, and willpower (disciplining passion) in the pursuit of desires. Reason is seen to be supreme, but not to the exclusion of appetitive desire. As Kahlil Gibran suggests,

> Your reason and your passion are the rudder and the sails of your seafaring soul.
>
> If either your sails or your rudder be broken, you can but toss and drift, or else be held at a standstill in mid-seas.
>
> For reason, ruling alone, is a force confining; and passion, unattended, is a flame that burns to its own destruction.
>
> Therefore let your soul exalt your reason to the height of passion, that it may sing;
>
> And let it direct your passion with reason, that your passion may live through its own daily resurrection, and like the phoenix rise above its own ashes.
>
> (Gibran 1988: 50–1)

Hence, both Hindu and Muslim ethos seems to be one of realistic, honest, open, and ethical pursuit and enjoyment of desires, not a condemnation of desires. This is the Golden (or Harmonic) Mean once praised by Greek philosophers, but now largely lost in the West. The value of reconciliation and balancing of opposites based on the belief in the unity of the mind–body and acknowledgement of situationalism seem to underlie the Eastern acceptance of purified, moderate, and legitimate desires. Although desire is seen to be an attachment that prevents freedom and joy, it is to be experienced richly and aesthetically in order to be able to achieve detachment or self-control and move on along the path to the joyful bliss. Desires are to be pursued without becoming enslaved by passionate attachment and integrated with moral principles such as Hindu social responsibilities and caste duties or Muslim generosity and fairness. Such a pursuit is deemed to be moral and good, until one begins to seek eternal liberation.

In contrast to the more accepting and balanced beliefs about desire in Hinduism and Islam, Western Christianity can be seen as inhibiting and suppressing. It is also more individualistic. In the market economy of the Western societies where an individual is constructed to be individualistic, legitimization rests on transforming desire into an individualistic need or a "good" desire. Desires are naturalized into needs for essential decencies, as in the appetitive metaphors of eating, addiction, and lust, or rationalized to be the same as needs based on the notions of utility or benefit. Alternatively, desires are legitimized or purified by making a distinction between good (moral or aesthetic) and bad desires. However, in other societies where the individual is defined more by his or her public self, desires must be balanced according to interpersonal shame and honor, and purified and legitimized by fairness, generosity, preferring others' desires to one's own, moderation (e.g. in Islam) or by social responsibility, being virtuous and dutiful (e.g. in Hinduism). The point is not that one view of desire is more enlightened, effective, or correct. Rather, there are cultural differences in the experience, control, release, or cultivation of desire that need to be recognized in characterizing desire and analyzing its role in consumer behavior. These cultural contexts help to shape the nature of consumer desire and how this desire affects our behavior.

Objects of desire

Having looked at how the sacred realm of religion has tried to control desire in Eastern and Western societies, we now turn the problem around, and discuss how the desire for mass marketed consumer objects has taken on sacred dimensions in modern consumer society. Sacred and profane objects serve to link the community through its "collective reality." Radkowski (1980) refers to the distinction between the economy of everyday life and the economy of the feast, a dichotomy found in all societies. The first, he says, reflects the "masked desire" of profane consumption whereas sacred consumption is linked to the feast and is expressive of "unmasked desire."

The bane of abundance is the blurring of the sacred and profane, of masked and unmasked desire. What has been called "the waste of capitalism," the advertising junk pile, "superfluous" consumption and acquisitions, and accelerated obsolescence (Radkowski 1980) is, seen from the point of view of an economy of desires, both a cause and a logical consequence of this blurring. This process could be described as a crisis of legitimacy in the domestication of desires. If there is no longer any consensus as to which consumption goals are the most legitimate, and the society of abundance instead sets everyone free to pursue his or her own ends, this corresponds to the impetus for consumer research during the 1980s into what has been labeled "hedonic consumption" (cf. Holbrook and Hirschman 1982). On the surface, it looks like a shift in social focus from need to desire. But, seen from the perspective of the economy of desires, what is actually revealed is the initial primacy of desire, a primacy hidden by the technological and economical ideology under the more rational and reassuring concept of needs. Thus, the outburst of the interest in hedonic consumption reflects an epistemological breakthrough, hidden from its proselytes, that fundamentally challenges economic assumptions about human society. Our intent in this project has been to enlighten the key element for an alternative understanding of contemporary consumption: that of consumer desire.

Hedonism is not purely liberatory, though, as certain theorists highlighting the negative aspects of abundance have pointed out. In present consumer society, because we believe that we are what we desire (Fuery 1995) coupled with our social valorizing of self-actualization, we feel we *should* feel desire in order to be alive and like others. We attempt to fill our empty self (Cushman 1990) through mimetically aroused desire and through the auto-arousal of watching movies, reading catalogs, browsing the Internet, and window shopping. We do this because in a culture of abundance we have become alienated from our experienced desires (Alasuutari 1992) and feel only an objectless desire (Falk 1994). This endless desiring turns into a chronic deficiency (Falk 1994). The frustration of deficiency, having lost its enjoyable nature, becomes the permanent state. Falk argues that desire is constituted by the reciprocal effects of two movements of self-construction: pursuit of separateness and distinction, and pursuit of introjective self-fulfillment. The individual cannot achieve completeness, because she has to maintain her boundaries or separateness. This creates a state of lack that acts as an impetus for further pursuit of completion, identified by Wicklund and Gollwitzer (1982) as symbolic self-completion. Desire can thus be regarded as a quest for self-completion (Kakar and Ross 1987). The pursuit of completion is the core around which desire is constituted. "Self-building is simultaneously an act of separation or an articulation of self boundaries in relation to the outside, being thus both an 'addition' (complement) and a 'subtraction' with an effect of lack" (Falk 1994: 144). Just as Zeus split humans in half so that we must forever search for our other half, we seem doomed to wander in search of our lost desires.

While desire is experienced as an emotion focused on a certain object, it is also seen as a process during which emotions change, especially with the realization of desires. The process of desire tends to be seen as a cyclic process involving imagination, cultivation, and sacrifice. But when desire is realized, desire is quelled, if only until another focal object of longing is found. Often the joy of realizing a desire is short-lived and transforms itself into boredom or even negative feelings about the once beloved object. Disillusioned consumers seldom seem to learn however, and instead desire is commonly focused on some new desideratum. This is Campbell's (1987) "spirit of modern consumerism," that dooms us to a perpetual, but ultimately fruitless, quest for consumption euphoria.

But the reinitiation of desire focused on another object is not solely due to disappointment in the once longed for consumer good. It also appears to involve a more basic desire to desire. Thus the state of desire is simultaneously positive and negative for many consumers. While being out of control and feeling guilty about desires that seem compellingly self-indulgent is negative, desire is also a strongly positive feeling. This positive feeling seems to come from the excitement of desire and the anticipation of realizing a desire. Desire differs in this respect from idle wishful thinking for things we know cannot come true and planning for things that we can obtain without sacrifice and effort. The distance specified by Simmel cannot be too great. For the ultimate pleasure provided by the state of desire is hope. At the same time, actual realization of desires is sometimes anticlimactic or results in an elation that quickly fades. In either case, desire for desire is likely to lead to reinitiating the cycle of desire by focusing on a new object. Hope is reborn.

When this hope is linked not to beliefs in luck or magic, but rather is at least imperfectly linked to effort or beliefs that the desired object will be realized if we are just worthy enough to deserve it, the result is motivation. This process is seen to involve more than just hard work and planning; the sacrificial nature and feelings of worthiness or deservingness suggest elements of a religious pilgrimage or a chivalrous quest. Besides worthiness, accounts of deservingness also reveal that a sense of social justice may result in frustration when someone believes they deserve more than they have. In such cases the motivational consequences of desire may give way to questioning whether the world is a just place and to feelings of resignation and despondency.

More commonly. however, the frustration may be compensated by substituting a desire for something more likely to be achieved (even if it is unable to entirely ameliorate the underling feeling of frustrated desire). However, the notion of surrogate versus "true" objects of desire seems to us to involve a misreading of the nature of desire. When probed deeply enough, despite the intense focus on the desired object, what is really desired is some symbolic value that this object is thought to be able to represent or provide. The desire may be conceived and expressed in concrete terms, but it is essentially a longing for symbolic benefits that might be obtained in alternative ways or might not be obtained in any manner. The objects that we focus on are desired for what they represent –

their value inheres less in the object than in the culture, including such meaning-making cultural institutions as advertising.

Concluding remarks

Desire represents the reintroduction of the body in consumer research in two ways: by the reference to a human nature which is cultural and by the reference to bodily pleasures and sensations. Bodily sensations are, developmentally, the first building blocks of a symbolic order; in this sense, the most highly elaborated symbolic structures ultimately derive from bodily sensations (Brooks 1993). But we have already pointed out the linkage between the neglect of desire and the legacy of Enlightenment scientism and its primacy of (rational) mind over body, leading to an insensitivity to the intense feelings attached with desire. Consequently, whenever desire has been dealt with by Western scholars, they have given precedence to the imaginary theory or the idea (in the mind of the human being) of desire rather than the bodily rooted experience of it. Although symbolic and positional structural systems (class, status groups, ethnicity, gender) construct and limit desires (e.g. Bourdieu 1979), people neither are solely rationally utilitarian nor intellectually symbolizing creatures, they are also emotional and sensual creatures.

Consumers' somewhat misleading focus on the concrete rather than the symbolic as the object of their desires is likely one factor that leads to the cycle of desire and to our amazingly inexhaustible succession of intense desires. The other major factor seems to be our desire for desire, our hope for hope:

> Being happy is at the same time being able to desire, capable of feeling pleasure at the satisfaction of desire and well-being while satisfied, while waiting for desire to return to start over again. Nobody can be happy if they do not desire anything.
>
> (Laborit 1976: 96)

Here we have the most fundamental formulation of the role of desire in human well-being: to be happy is to be able to desire. Just as we are in love with love, we desire to desire.

A telling indication of what we experience as desire comes from our projective exercise asking people for desire antonyms (Belk, Ger, and Askegaard 1997). While one category of antonyms that emerged involved strong negatives (e.g. hate, loathing, disgust, fear), the dominant category was instead neutral (e.g. blandness, passivity, routine, boredom, dullness, nothingness, emptiness). Another antonym that emerged was that of death; to be without desire is to be dead to the world. All of these antonyms paint a portrait of bleakness, hopelessness, and joylessness. To desire is to live, to hope, to enjoy life and its promises. In short, to live a life beyond social orders and routines. But breaking the order is simultaneously to play with fire and to entertain the temptation to neglect the boundaries and duties of social life. Desire as a way of relating to the Other involves a dynamic interplay between the imaginary/symbolic and the deeply sensuous, between violent aggression and affectionate devotion, between activities which are at the same time dangerous and vitalizing or energizing. Hence, much in line with Kakar and Ross' (1987) notions of appetitive craving (sensory/destructive) and romantic affectionate longing (imaginary) as constitutive of desire, we can say that desire is embodied culture.

This approach to the human species' cultural and motivational capacities seems much closer to the empirical evidence found in ethnographic and anthropological research than *Homo oeconomicus.* Behind the reassuring name of *sapiens,* the true face of the human being appears, Morin (1973) writes. It is an animal of *hubris,* of strong and unstable feelings, an animal that invents demons and chimera, is ecstatic, violent, and loving, who knows death without being able to believe in it, an animal of pleasure and delirium, myth, magic and illusions. Consequently, Morin concludes, our more correct designation would be *Homo demens.*

Here, we may find the roots of the neglect of the concept of desire: it runs counter to the prevailing Western conceptualization of *Homo sapiens* during the total period of modern history since the Enlightenment. It threatens rationality as the basis of the social order. The reluctance to deal with desire is similar to the neglect of material culture within the social sciences (Miller 1995). Both have suffered from a general consensus that the topic is inherently morally "bad," whether this badness is labeled materialism, commodity fetishism, greed, or something else. Indeed, the word "desire" itself in its colloquial use evokes feelings of uncontrollable (and therefore potentially dangerous) acts and intentions. However, as we have seen, this can be regarded as denying culture: a symbolic system of socially instituted differences which individuals and groups use as a scheme for interpreting their life world, their possibilities of action, their past and future, and for establishing the relative importance of their needs. But all of these significations – life world, action, time, needs – are already manifestations of the ontological imagination, of the distance between human beings and their environment. Thus, according to Radkowski (1980), culture can be regarded as socially instituted desire, i.e. not individual images but imaginations pertaining to shared social reality.

Thus, on the theoretical level, we conclude that just as desire seems to be the embodiment of culture so can culture be seen as instituted desire. On the more phenomenological note of experienced desire, we find desire to be an overwhelmingly positive emotion, despite our occasional feelings of immorality and ambivalent feelings about our desires. It is an intense emotion that opposes what is ordinary and utilitarian. In order to provide us hope, desire focuses on something better; something that transcends the everyday; something magical. This is what Blanch means in saying "I don't want realism, I want magic." That these feelings depend upon the social imagination to construct objects that are sufficiently powerful symbols to become objects of obsessive desires, should neither be disillusioning nor a cause for rationalizing our existence. Perhaps the greatest miracle is that we collectively and individually find imaginative ways to re-enchant our world through desire.

Acknowledgments

The authors would like to thank A. Fuat Firat and Douglas Holt for their very helpful comments on an earlier draft of this chapter.

References

Abdalati, H. (1975) *Islam in Focus*, Indianapolis, IN: American Trust Publications.

Alasuutari, P. (1992) *Desire and Craving: A Cultural Theory of Alcoholism*, Buffalo, NY: State University of New York Press.

Bakhtin, M. (1968 [1965]) *Rabelais and His World*, Cambridge, MA: MIT Press.

Bataille, G. (1967 [1949]) *La part maudite*, Paris: Editions de Minuit.

Baudrillard, J. (1972) *Pour une critique de l'économie politique du signe*, Paris: Gallimard.

Belk, R. W, (1988) "Possessions and the extended self," *Journal of Consumer Research* 15 (September): 139–68.

Belk, R.W., Ger, G., and Askegaard, S. (1996) "Metaphors of consumer desire," in K. P. Corfman and J. G. Lynch, Jr. (eds) *Advances in Consumer Research*, vol. 23, Provo, UT: Association for Consumer Research: 368–73.

—— (1997) "Consumer desire in three cultures: results from projective research," in M. Brucks and D. MacInnis (eds) *Advances in Consumer Research*, vol. 24, Provo, UT: Association for Consumer Research: 24–8.

Belk, R.W., Wallendorf, M., and Sherry, J.F., Jr. (1989) "The sacred and the profane in consumer behavior: theodicy on the Odyssey," *Journal of Consumer Research* 15 (June): 1–38.

Berry, C.J. (1994) *The Idea of Luxury: A Conceptual and Historical Investigation*, Cambridge: Cambridge University Press.

Bocock, R. (1994) *Consumption*, London: Routledge.

Bouchet, D. (1988) "Skepsisen som højere bevidsthedstilstand," *Paradigma* 3 (1): 16–21.

Bourdieu, P. (1979) *La distinction. Critique sociale du jugement*, Paris: Editions de Minuit.

Brooks, P. (1993) *Body Work: Objects of Desire in Modern Narrative*, Cambridge, MA: Harvard University Press.

Campbell, C. (1987) *The Romantic Ethic and the Spirit of Modern Consumerism*, London: Blackwell.

Cixous, H. and Clément, C. (1986) *The Newly Born Woman*, trans. B. Wing, Minneapolis: University of Minnesota Press.

Corbin, A. (1995) *Time, Desire and Horror: Towards a History of the Senses*, trans. Jean Birrell, Cambridge: Polity Press.

Cushman, P. (1990) "Why the self is empty: towards a historically situated psychology," *American Psychologist* 45 (5): 599–611.

Deleuze, G. and Guattari, F. (1972) *L'Anti-Èdipe*, Paris: Editions de Minuit.

Doane, M.A. (1987) *The Desire to Desire: The Woman's Film of the 1940s*, Bloomington, IN: Indiana University Press.

Dobyns, S. (1990) "The body's hope," in *Body Traffic: Poems by Stephen Dobyns*, New York: Viking: 41–2.

Elliott, R. (1997) "Existential consumption and irrational desire," *European Journal of Marketing* 31 (3/4): 285–96.

Ewens, T. (1987) "Desire and the loss of object," *The American Journal of Psychoanalysis* 47 (4): 302–8.

Falk, P. (1994) *The Consuming Body*, London: Sage.

Firat, A.F. and Venkatesh, A. (1995) "Liberatory postmodernism and the reenchantment of consumption", *Journal of Consumer Research* 22 (December): 239–67.

Foucault, M. (1985) *The Use of Pleasure: The History of Sexuality*, vol. 2, trans. R. Hurley, New York: Random House (original, *L'Usage des plaisirs*, Paris: Editions Gallimard, 1984).

Freedman, E.B. (1987) "'Uncontrolled desires': the response to the sexual psychopath, 1920–1960," *Journal of American History* 74 (June): 83–106.

Fuery, P. (1995) *Theories of Desire*, Adelaide: Melbourne University Press.

Gibran, K. (1988) *The Prophet*, New York: Alfred A. Knopf.

Girard, R. (1977) *Violence and the Sacred*, trans. P. Gregory, Baltimore: Johns Hopkins University Press (original *La Violence et le sacré*, Paris: Editions Bernard Grasset, 1972).

—— (1987) *Things Hidden Since the Foundation of the World*, trans. S. Bann and M. Metteer, Stanford, CA: Stanford University Press (original *Des choses cachées depuis la fondation du monde*, Paris: Editions Grasset & Fasquelle, 1978).

Haskell, M. (1999) "Movies and the selling of desire," in Roger Rosenblatt (ed.) *Consuming Desires: Consumption, Culture, and the Pursuit of Happiness*, Washington, DC: Island Press: 125–35.

Hirschman, E.C. and Holbrook, M.B. (1981) "Hedonic consumption: emerging concepts, methods, and propositions," *Journal of Marketing* 46 (Summer): 92–101.

Holbrook, M.B. and Hirschman, E. (1982) "The experiential aspects of consumption: consumer fantasies, feelings, and fun," *Journal of Consumer Research* 9 (September): 132–40.

Hutcheon, L. (1989) *The Politics of Postmodernism*, London: Routledge.

Hyppolite, J. (1996) "Self-consciousness and life: the independence of self-consciousness," in John O'Neill (ed.) *Hegel's Dialectic of Desire and Recognition: Texts and Commentary*, Albany, NY: State University of New York Press: 67–86.

Irigaray, L. (1985) *The Sex Which Is Not One*, trans. C. Porter, Ithaca, NY: Cornell University Press.

Jager, B. (1989) "About desire and satisfaction," *Journal of Phenomenological Psychology* 20 (2): 145–50.

Jameson, F. (1983) "Pleasure: a political issue," in T. Bennett and J. Burin (eds) *Formations of Pleasure*, London: Routledge & Kegan Paul: 1–13.

Kakar, S. and Ross, J. Munder (1987) *Tales of Love, Sex, and Danger*, New York: Basil Blackwell.

Klein, R. (1993) *Cigarettes are Sublime*, Durham, NC: Duke University Press.

Kristeva, J. (1984) *Desire in Language: A Semiotic Approach to Literature and Art*, trans. T. Gora, A. Jardine, and L. Roudiez, Oxford: Basil Blackwell.

Laborit, H. (1976) *Eloge de la fuite*, Paris: Editions Robert Laffont.

Lacan, J. (1970) "Of structure as an inmixing of an otherness prerequisite to any subject whatever," in Richard Macksey and Eugenio Donato (eds) *The Languages of Criticism and the Sciences of Man*, Baltimore: Johns Hopkins University Press.

—— (1977) *Ecrits*, New York: Norton.

—— (1992) *The Seminar of Jacques Lacan, Book VII, The Ethics of Psychoanalysis, 1959–1960*, ed. J.-A. Miller, trans. D. Porter, New York: W. W. Norton (original, *Le Seminaire, Livre VII, L'ethique de la psychanalyse, 1959–1960*, Paris: Les Editions du Seuil, 1986).

Leather, P. (1983) "Desire: a structural model of motivation," *Human Relations* 36 (2): 109–22.

Levy, S. (1981) "Interpreting consumer mythology: a structural approach to consumer behavior", *Journal of Marketing* 45 (Summer): 49–61.

Lipner, J. (ed.) (1997) *The Fruits of Our Desiring: An Enquiry into the Ethics of the Bhagavadgita*, Calgary, Canada: Bayeux Arts.

Littleton, C.S. (ed.) (1996) *Eastern Wisdom: An Illustrated Guide to the Religions and Philosophies of the East*, New York: Henry Holt and Company.

Mandeville, B. (1970 [1714]) *The Fable of the Bees*, Harmondsworth: Penguin.

Maslow, A.H. (1954) *Motivation and Personality*, New York: Harper & Row.

Mercer, C. (1983) "A poverty of desire: pleasure and popular politics," in T. Bennett and J. Burin (eds) *Formations of Pleasure*, London: Routledge & Kegan Paul: 84–100.

Miller, D. (ed.) (1995) *Acknowledging Consumption: A Review of the New Studies*, London: Routledge.

Miller, D. (1998) *A Theory of Shopping*, Cambridge: Polity Press.

Morin, E. (1973) *Le paradigme perdu. La nature humaine*, Paris: Seuil.

Radkowski, G-H. de (1980) *Les jeux du désir*, Paris: Presses Universitaires de France.

Ragland, E. (1995) *Essays on the Pleasures of Death: From Freud to Lacan*, New York: Routledge.

Richardson, W. (1987) "Ethics and desire," *The American Journal of Psychoanalysis* 47 (4): 296–301.

Sahlins, M. (1996) "The sweetness of sadness: the native anthropology of Western cosmology", *Current Anthropology* 37 (June): 395–428.

Sartre, J.-P. (1956) "The meaning of 'to make' and 'to have': possession," in E.C. Moustakas and S.R. Jayaswal (eds) *The Self: Explorations in Personal Growth*, New York: Harper and Brothers: 140–6.

Scruton, R. (1986) *Sexual Desire: A Moral Philosophy of the Erotic*, New York: Free Press.

Sherry, J.F., Jr. (1986) "The cultural perspective in consumer research", in R.J. Lutz (ed.) *Advances in Consumer Research*, vol. 13, Provo, UT: Association for Consumer Research: 573–5.

Silverman, K. (1983) *The Subject of Semiotics*, New York: Oxford University Press.

Simmel, G. (1978 [1900]) *The Philosophy of Money*, trans. T. Bottomore and D. Frisby, London: Routledge & Kegan Paul.

Smith, A. (1970 [1776]) *The Wealth of Nations*, Harmondsworth: Penguin.

Smith, H. (1958) *The Religions of Man*, New York: Harper & Row.

Soper, K. (1990) *Troubled Pleasures: Writings on Politics, Gender and Hedonism*, London: Verso.

Stewart, D.W. (1986) "Lacan's linguistic unconscious and the language of desire," *Psychoanalytic Review* 73 (1) (Spring): 17–29.

Stewart, S. (1984) *On Longing: Narratives of the Miniature, the Gigantic, the Souvenir, the Collection*, Baltimore: Johns Hopkins University Press.

Stocker, M. (1986) "Akrasia and the object of desire," in J. Marks (ed.) *The Ways of Desire: New Essays in Philosophical Psychology on the Concept of Wanting*, Chicago: Precedent: 197–215.

Synott, A. (1993) *The Body Social: Symbolism, Self, and Society*, London: Routledge.

Thompson, C., Locander, W.B., and Pollio, H.R. (1989) "Putting consumer experience back into consumer research: the philosophy and method of existential-phenomenology," *Journal of Consumer Research* 16 (September): 133–46.

Venkatesh, A. and Swamy, S. (1994) "India as an emerging consumer society: a critical perspective," in C.J. Shultz, R.W. Belk, and G. Ge (eds) *Consumption in Marketizing Economies*, Greenwich, CT: JAI Press: 193–224.

Wicklund, R.A. and Gollwitzer, P.M. (1982) *Symbolic Self Completion*, Hillsdale, NJ: Lawrence Erlbaum Associates.

7 Postmodern consumer goals made easy!!!!

Craig J. Thompson

That was then and this is now

The last twenty-five years have witnessed a torrent of writings and theories on postmodernism and postmodernity. Architecture, the representational arts, and all branches of the humanities and the social science fields have been energized or travestied (depending on one's perspective) by the turn to things postmodern. Reciting the leading works across these multi-disciplinary considerations would easily fill the chapter. Suffice it to say that the writings of Baudrillard, deBord, Deleuze, Derrida, Jameson, Jencks, and Lyotard have set much of the intellectual tone and shaped the theoretical debates within this pluralistic pomo *oeuvre*.

Consumer research has also made a "postmodern turn." John Sherry's (1991) famed review chapter on the trembles beset by this tetonic postmodern movement is, in hindsight, a documentation of its nascency. The *fin-de-millennium* 1990s have witnessed a profligating, propagating, propagandizing, proliferation of pomo-ish research articles and conferences papers all aimed at displacing marketing's modernist 4Ps and its archaic models of the consumer. So, choose your favorite metaphor – a paradigm shift, an intellectual Zeitgeist, a sign of the apocalypse, a virus of the mind, an outbreak of millennial madness, heretical rantings from the lunatic fringe – postmodernism has claimed a prominent discursive space within consumer research. The *in-your-face* irreverence of Stephen Brown (1995, 1998, 1998a), the introspective, stereoscopic stylings of Morris Holbrook (1995, 1998, 1999) and the manifold expository replications of Firat and Venkatesh (1993, 1995, 1996) are without doubt the exemplary expressions of postmodernism in consumer research, though they differ so dramatically in rhetorical and intellectual tenor that only in the age of postmodernity could they all be classified as a common genre (but I'll get to that a bit later).

But wait, postmodernism is not just for interpretivists anymore. An academic cottage industry has emerged to explain the mysteries of postmodernism to marketing managers (see Cova 1996, 1997; Ogilvy 1990). This didactic enterprise has now attracted highly regarded marketing researchers whose names have not previously been invocative of the postmodern mood. To wit, Alice Tybout and Gregory Carpenter (1999: 104) propound "the postmodern buyer presents a serious challenge to classic and contemporary brands." Wait, there's more.

> Today's postmodern buyers see these [classic] brands as irrelevant. Indeed, many of today's buyers do not see consuming a brand for the sake of it as an objective, as previous generations might have done. Instead, postmodern buyers see brands as a means to an end.
>
> (p. 103)

Tybout and Carpenter (1999) bring clarity to this brave new postmodern world through this perspicacious insight: "Postmodern consumers seek to use brands to attain a remarkably broad array of goals – much broader than contemporary [modernist] goal sets" (p. 105). This unfathomable pomo consumer goal structure is

> a reflection of the larger number of roles postmodern buyers play. . . . A *striking* [emphasis added] characteristic of postmodern buyers is their willingness to turn to brands to satisfy many of these goals. . . . Aiming for a variety of goals simultaneously creates conflict and stress. . . . Brands have evolved from serving specific, functional goals to playing a central role in consumers' efforts at goal management.
>
> (p. 105)

Tybout and Carpenter further inform us that success in the postmodern marketplace now depends on brands helping consumers to reconcile conflicting goals and satisfy personal needs neglected due to "time famine." They praise "postmodern brands" like Harley-Davidson, Starbucks, Häagen-Daazs, and Watermen Pens that do heretofore unheard of things such as fulfilling the consumer goal of "self-indulgence" and enabling consumers to act out fantasy identities in their leisure time. Finally, they wisely caution all those impetuous marketing managers ready to leap blindly into the postmodern abyss: "When purchases are driven by abstract goals than by functional product properties, the nature of competition can be difficult to understand and it can shift – sometimes all too quickly" (p. 107). For the moment, I'll suspend the requisite pomo sarcasm (I'll get back to that a bit later).

Actually, I'm quite glad to see these two distinguished consumer researchers wanting to cross the postmodern divide. Scouts honor, I mean it. Alice and Greg welcome to Pomoville and here are a bunch of maps, books, articles, films, and music for you both right here in the welcome wagon. Gotta tell you though, the maps won't you help all that much. Here in Pomoville, the street names are constantly changing and all the buildings are mobile. Oh yeah, it can be kind of tough to get to know the Pomoville locals, such as they are, because their "goals" are a little schizoid. You know, Furs and Station Wagons by day, fetish wear and Harleys by night – that sort of thing. Neighborly pleasantries aside, one small question remains. Really, how is such an insipid conception of the postmodern consumer possible? How could anyone actually imply that until just a little while ago the competitive field was easy to understand and slow to change or that the "modern consumer" consumed brands as ends in themselves, bought products for functional properties alone, experienced almost no role conflict or time pressure, and pursued only a few, always compatible, always rational, always consonant goals.

What we have here is "Rip Van Winkle" theorization newly awakened from a long, deep econometric slumber. What we have here is "Nick at Nite" modernism where Father *Knows Best and Leave it To Beaver* provide the nostalgic *hyperreality* of how things used to be. What we have here is "old wine in a new decanter" postmodernism in which the staid, exhausted, and boringly familiar logic of means-end chain analysis is made new, exciting, radical, and flat out "PHAT" by *repackaging* it within trendy wrapping of "postmodernism." What we have here is a *pastiche* of trite cliches and marketing bromides simulating a profound understanding of cultural (and hence market) dynamism. What we have here is an audacious act of *self-referentiality* proclaiming that "postmodernism is whatever I say it is." What we have here is a shameless poaching of Dickens: "postmodernism – it is the best of times, the worst of times." Well, I'll be damned. Maybe they know their way around Pomoville better than I thought. Let me explain.

Been there, done that, bought the T-shirt or postmodernism redux

Many commentators on the "postmodern condition" in its many variegated forms espouse a "periodizing view," which portrays modernism and post-modernism as distinct historical/cultural/societal eras. Though some debate exists as to when this postmodern era dawned, a fairly common reference point is the 1960s. Why then? Let's take a quick stroll down memory lane. Andy Warhol canonized popular culture icons in a way that satirized modernist ideals of artistic authenticity, and thereby effaced the high art/popular culture boundary.[1] Genre blurring, self-consciously eclectic, post-industrial architecture came to prominence. The post-Fordist economy revolutionized the mode of production and fragmented the mode of consumption (see Harvey 1989). The cultural mood was colored by a widespread skepticism toward institutional authority and the modernist meta-narratives of technological progress and institutional societal progress. Large scale social challenges to modernist power structures (racism, sexism, imperialism, technocratic domination of nature) shook the cultural status quo. Youth movements brought individuals together in ways that seemingly transcended other social categories and boundaries. And every-day life was increasingly penetrated and transformed by mass media, marketing, and consumerism (see Jameson 1991). If the 1960s are the age of puerile postmodernism, the 1990s are the age of its millennial maturity. Here is how this epochal tale goes. Time-space compression is hyper-intensified by advances in information technologies and the digital revolu-tion. The accelerating currents of globalization are creating a diffusion of hybridized and creolized cultural forms (Hannerz 1996). The dissolution of modernist foundations/constraints (i.e. detraditionalization) is producing a radically new freedom of identity. We can now "virtually" be anywhere, and be virtually anyone, at "virtually" any time.

Hey, that's not all. The cultural scene is now one giant hyperreal amalgam which continually effaces modernist distinctions between fiction, fact, image, simulations, and the "real." You know those modernist ideals of continuity, depth, and originality? Forget about it! We have a new cultural (dis)order of fragmented, superficial signs and images whose only coherent linkage lies in their hyperstimulating, ephemerality. William James was almost 100 years ahead of his time when he coined the phrase "buzzing, blooming, confusion." Poor William, ever the modernist, he thought this to be a problem. Postmodernists celebrate and revel in the hedonic (no, make that heterodonic) pleasures of this endless, flittering, inchoate, imagistic pomo spectacle. Modernists called this debauchery; postmodermist call it *jouissance*. On MTV (the one-time epicenter of the pomo cultural universe), Michael Jackson's face morphs into twenty-five ethnicities and then into nostalgic irrelevance – displaced by "authentic gansta rappers" performing a bricolage identity, combining a calculated, urban street sensibility with elements drawn from Hollywood westerns and mob films – who then poly-morph into the dopest, white-boy simulations you ever saw (Beastie Boys to Eminem) – who then transmogrify into the precocious "grrrl power" of the Spice Girls – who then fragment to become Monica Lewinsky, Britney Spears, Ally McBeal, the Dixie Chicks, and the US Women's Soccer Team. And somehow it all makes us want to wear Nike. Some critical theory anachronists scandalize the postmodern condition as the ultimate form of capitalist exploitation; we now freely choose our forms of domination and joyously display our many overpriced signs of oppression. But wild-eyed pomo theorists celebrate this cultural implosion as one great carnival where everyone has the ultimate freedom to fashion (literally) themselves, un-impeded by modernist moralizations and societal constrictures. Anything goes; there is no fashion only fashions; viva la différence; doing the vida loca like it's 1999. Still others (and I ruefully confess to being one of these pomo party-pooping contrarians) say well, maybe these hyperbolic post-modernists are a tad giddy with Baudrillardian exuberance, are just a shade too devout in their Lyotardian disbelief, and a wee bit too enthralled by the abysmal expanse of endless simulacra. After all, when Sprite commercials lampoon the "image is everything" pomo mantra, you gotta wonder . . .

Same as it ever was?

It is with much trepidation that I suggest that these periodizing views of postmodernism make sense only within the encapsulated and provincially elitist social milieu of high culture and ivory tower academe. Characteristics supposedly definitive of the postmodern age have long been commonplace in the "debased" realm of popular culture (that is, until the postmodern turn gave it intellectual cachet). Popular fiction, comic books, vaudeville, radio and television shows, and, in fact, all forms of "mass" entertainment have mixed and matched stylistic genres, created hybrid cultural forms through acts of pastiche. Like, what else is rock 'n' roll? All these popular cultural forms made frequent use of simulation and parody, and elided cultural boundaries such as those between art and commerce (see Featherstone 1991).[2] Bakhtin's (1984) analyses of the medieval carnivals and folk spectacles suggest that many of these cultural characteristics may well predate modernism. Only in the "high culture" world of modernist art, design, and theory did we ever find the moralistic commitment to purity of form, the sanctification and mystification of authenticity, and the dream of a rationally ordered society free from irrational impulses and Dionysian excess (Bauman 1994).

Even here, the situation is a bit more complicated than evinced by that historical gloss. Theorists writing about the rise of the modern metropolis and the emerging modern marketplace (a period from, say, the mid-nineteenth century to the 1920s) articulated many of ideas that have now become *de rigeur* among postmodern theorists, though in their day these works were exiled to the margins of high intellectual culture. Baudelaire called attention to the fragmented, dehistoricized, aestheticized experiences of the nineteenth century urban flaneur and the visual spectacle of the city. Benjamin developed these Baudelairian themes in relation to his own notions of "aestheticized, consumer dream worlds" and he discussed the rupture between objects, meaning, and tradition created by mechanical reproduction (i.e. simulations) and capitalism's intertwining of aesthetics and the marketplace. Bataille offered urbane reflections on the paradox that capitalist production is based on an economy of waste. Simmel wrote brilliant essays on the pluralism and fragmentation of modern life, the multiplicity of modern identity, the hyperstimulating sensory complexity of the metropolitan milieu, and the creation of identity through the creative mixing of aesthetic styles[3]. Bahktin wrote extensively on the heteroglossia of popular culture and the spectacles of the marketplace. And last but not least, Nietzsche – the stark, raving avatar of postmodernism – rebuked the modernist faith in a rationally ordered universe, exalted the Dionysian impulse, proclaimed existence to be an endless simulacra of the "perpetual return" in which history repeats itself ad infinitum, and most scandalously of all, he deconstructed "truth" (i.e. the great modernist meta-narrative) showing it to be nothing but a will-to-power enforced by "a mobile army of metaphors."

"Postmodern theory" is a recognition of these formerly marginal, pre-postmodern intellectual currents and, more importantly, a calculated appropriation of the pop culture and countercultural diversity that have always thrived in modernity. These carnivalesque, debased, syncretic cultural forms had previously been ignored or disparaged because they did not the conform to the high ideals of modernist intellectuals. However, following trends set by the artistic community, high culture intellectuals began taking these popular elements seriously, as a topic of theory, as a source of theoretical tools and, here's the kicker, as a down payment on a premier plot of intellectual real estate located in that trendy neighborhood known as the cutting edge. Hence, Baudrillard transformed himself from a wannabe Marxian sociologist to the high priest of postmodernism by touring Las Vegas and writing like a fiend while suffering from an acute attack of intellectual vertigo precipitated by this massive consumer spectacle of endless neon lights, kitsch, pastiche, simulations, fragmentation, juxtapositions of opposites, and Elvis impersonators. "And the point is?" you ask. Well, I suggest that some highly regarded, well-established, well-tested, and theoretically elaborated models of the consumer and his/her goals also have been encapsulated in this elitist, rationalist, high modernist world-view, which has fallen hopelessly out of intellectual fashion. Mainstream consumer research remains a perennial late adopter, its sensibilities closer to *Ladies' Home Journal* than to *Vogue*. So, it is not so much that the consumer has suddenly and dramatically changed, as it is that the new intellectual *haute* fashion of postmodernism has finally trickled down to the J.C. Penney racks of consumer research. Lo and behold, consumer researchers are relegating their conventional models of consumer goals to the second-hand racks and have been working up the courage to try on something a tad more risque.

A matter of taste

In fairness to the postmodern periodizers, the contemporary mass-mediated, "wired" global village can quite justifiably described as a hypermodernism, marked by an accelerated pace of cultural change and heightened degree of social (and marketplace) fluidity and dynamism. And yes, Tybout and Carpenter (1999) were probably alluding to this very point in their rather pedestrian declarations about "new consumer goal structures." So no matter how you cut it, there's something about postmodernism. Let me explain. Let's call postmodernism a constellation of aesthetic and intellectual proclivities that celebrate rather than deride those once marginalized, irrational, unruly aspects of popular culture and the marketplace. A postmodernist no longer seeks unity and synthesis but instead revels in heterogeneity, polysemy, and difference. This aesthetic orientation demonstrates a cultivated self-awareness of the internal contradictions and caprice of contemporary life and uses them for purposes of play and parody (see that is what all this textual foreplay is about). A postmodern aesthetic is one that makes ironic comment on the ideals of high modernism rather than effecting a stern obedience to them or rejecting them as would anti-modernist luddites. A postmodern aesthetic takes pleasure in paradoxical inversions; the sacred is profaned, the profane is sacralized; the feminine is masculinized, the masculine is feminized; the staid and outdated becomes retro-fashionable. Most of all, a postmodern aesthetic defies all either/or classifications by, on occasion, being more modern than modernism and effecting a reflexively self-aware, ironically perfected simulation of modernist conventions, conceits, and confabulations. A shining popular culture example of this pomo aesthetic is offered by the cinematic auteur Gus Van Sant and his reproduction of Hitchcock's *Psycho*. Rather than aiming to rework this classic in his own authentic artistic vision, he aimed to create a perfect copy of this modernist masterpiece. An achievement that would have made a grand ironic comment on the artifice of artistic authenticity and, hence, attained the apogee of pomo mimeticism. Film critics in the pomo know, embraced the goal but resoundly panned the production for all the right reasons. Ann Heche was a poor facsimile of Janet Leigh's Marion Crane and Vince Vaughn was a flaccid imitation of Anthony Perkins' Norman Bates and the whole thing failed as a pomo simulation because it was far too literal and lacked ironic distance. Unquestionably, Mike Meyers created a far more successful simulacra with *Austin Powers: Man of Mystery* and *The Spy Who Shagged Me*; ironic parodies of British satires of James Bond films.[4]

Is it live or is it Memorex?

But what does this all have to do with consumer goals? More than you might suspect. My point is that you can't begin to understand the pomo consumer as long as you're tied to a modernist litany of characteristics that try to precisely define the enigma. No, you have to enter the realm of embodied knowledge. It is the difference between reading about how a musical instrument is played and actually learning to play it. And the better you get, the more you can improvise and adapt to say other musicians' riffs. Merleau Ponty (1962) – yes a modernist, but an especially brilliant one with lots of tacit pomo insights – talked about the "genius for ambiguity" that comes from learning how to understand the world in the manner of others; an intuitive, embodied, form of knowledge that does not put you "in the consumer's shoes" but better yet, allows you to understand how they feel, what they mean, the conditions of their desirableness, and why they will eventually be cast aside.

To cultivate this genius for ambiguity, a consumer researcher – yes, I am talking to you – must develop an intuitive "feel" for a postmodern aesthetic and the pleasures offered by seemingly contradictory, illogical, paradoxical turns and inversions. You have to understand that the ultimate goal of postmodern consumption is to avoid being typed, classified, predicted, and controlled. You have to understand that postmodern consumers do not strive to resolve or assuage goal conflict but instead use conflicting goals as vehicles of identity mobility; just when you think the pomo consumer is "there," safe and sound in the categorical box, he/she has gone underground and emerged in a very different place. You have to understand that postmodern consumers are not the kind who put down roots. No, the postmodern consumer is the nomad, the "tagger" on the subway, the thief in the night. You have to understand that postmodern consumers are self-conscious producers who use the marketplace for endless acts of self re-creation and who at times resist the ideology of consumerism by ironically playing at being "shopping mad consumers," and commodity fetishists. You have to understand that the postmodern consumer is motivated by a multiplicity of goals and desires, some of which are more modernist or hypermodernist (due to a reflexive self-awareness) than those taken for granted by traditional modern consumers. So, never putting down roots means sometimes you "play house" with the fervor of a paranoid recluse, lest you make the road your permanent residency. So, defying gender categories means that sometimes you adopt a macho pose or a Barbie Doll coquettishness, for those who only negate stereotypes become defined by their perpetual opposition. Finally, you have to understand that not everyone living in our fin-de-millennium is a postmodernist just as everyone is not a rap aficionado or a Trekkie.

Postmodernism is an aestheticized lifestyle that is only loosely and contingently related to cultural trends like "time famine." The paradoxical marketing challenge is that postmodern consumers are a market segment who only reveal themselves when it suits them, who are recognizable only by the signs they leave when moving on, whose travels are seldom arranged in advance or designed to follow a predictable path, whose predominant commonality is a self-conscious production of difference and change, and who resolutely resist being put into demographic "boxes" except when they want to play at being a type. The trendy nomenclature of "the postmodern consumer" is a convenient rhetorical fiction – as is any other abstract consumer classification – useful to describe a heteroglossic, polysemic ensemble of aesthetic tastes and potential identity positions. The always enticing project of defining the postmodern consumer as an "X, Y, Z" bundle of attributes is but a modernist exercise in futility and a source of amusement for the elusive, peripatetic pomo consumer. And so it is with great trepidation that I offer an ironic simulation of a modernist typology detailing the kind of consumption goals likely to be pursued by postmodern consumers. Think of these typological categories as distinct aesthetic preferences that pomo consumers can take up at different times, in different ways, and in different combinations. At the risk of unduly complicating my discussion (and by now you know I simply loathe any sort of postmodern perfidiousness or sesquipedalianism), I suggest that some of these pomo goals are *hypermodernist* in nature; that is, they are amplifications of modernist desires, fears, longings for something that seems to be missing in a fast-paced, hustle-bustle, depersonalized world. Other pomo consumer goals are *reflexive* in nature; that is, they manifest a playful, ironizing, self-aware stance toward the artifice of modernist socio-conventions and the many marketplace spectacles masquerading as "the real thing."

This typology, like all others, is an arbitrary and subjectively contingent, aggregation of things that could easily be constructed differently or discussed in relation to different organizing constructs. Rather than acknowledging this academic pretense, I could justify it with modernist panache by stating: "Postmodern consumers do not pull their aesthetic preferences out of thin air. Rather, they express discernible historical currents that have given rise to a reflexive and ironic stance toward modernist conventions. While postmodern consumers can enact these aesthetic preferences in a multitude of ways, their uniquely forged personal 'tastes' are situated within this cultural circuit. Their radical mobility derives not from an absence of cultural–historical structures but rather from a conscious effort to avoid becoming habituated in their consumer outlooks and consumption practices, with the one notable exception of habitually shifting among cultural positions and inhabiting these identity spaces in different ways." You know, that might have worked too.

The absolute, scientific truth about pomo consumer goals (yeah, baby!)

Hypermodernist goals

Re-enchantment

Jackson Lears (1994) persuasively argues that the dawn of modernism also ushered in a countervailing spirit of anti-modernism. Those who rejoiced in modernism's technological advances were opposed by those who lamented the demise of the artisan; those who celebrated the freedoms, conveniences, dynamism, and boundless opportunities of modern living were opposed by those who panegyrically pined for the timeless tradition-ality of continuity, communal ambiance, social stability and metaphysical security/certainty.[5] Anti-modernism lives in our pomo Zeitgeist as an insatiable hunger for something that seems to be lacking, something that we believe we once had but have lost, something we feel deeply nostalgic about and something that we hope to rediscover. A Lacanian lacunae made melodic by the soon-to-be-pomo Bono and the boys: "I still haven't found what I am looking for." You too? In our wired, high-tech, e-commerce pomo world, we long for the age of magic (Arnould, Price, and Otnes 1999). So it is that postmodernists often seek re-enchantment – that is, a simulation of the enchantment that we like to believe once animated everyday life – through consumption. In pursuit of this goal, pomo consumers often turn nostalgically toward a mythologized past (see Holbrook 1993; Holbrook and Schindler 1989; Stern 1992; Thompson *et al.* 1994).

They sit enthralled as *Riverdance* transports them to the Hibernian hinterlands of yore; they move into neo-traditional neighborhoods that simulate the *gemeinschaft* intimacy of small town life (see Cameron and Gatewood 1994); they seek out artisanship in expensive handcrafted trinkets; they tirelessly travel the globe in hopes of discovering little anachronistic pockets where the locals live as they always have lived (Thompson and Tambyah 1999); and they make pilgrimages to sacralized places seeking utopian fulfillment in the baroque splendor of nature or the "old-world" bazaar (and perhaps they even ignore the expertly sited McDonalds). In all these acts of re-enchantment, consumers take flight from entanglement in technological systems, capitalist commodification, McDisneyfication, and marketing artifice. They seek temporary respite in liminoid spaces offering magic, communion, spiritual enrichment, and the sublime aura of the authenticity (e.g. Arnould and Price 1993, 1999; Brown 1998a; Heilbrunn 1998; Holt 1995; MacClaran and Stevens 1998; Sherry 1998; Thompson and Tambyah 1999). And yes, all these paths of escape lead to the profane worlds of marketing, fashion, retailing, and the myriad forms of tourism. Pomo consumers desire to be seduced and captivated by the market for only then can they experience its magical reproductions of authentic traditions, as in the case of say "peasant chic" (see Brodman 1994; Craik 1994). By now, you realize that it can never be and never has been any other way. The marketplace is magical and it casts a hypermodern spell. Capitalism's holy trinity of advertising, marketing, and retailing enchant goods by shrouding them in symbolic meanings, ascribing them mystical, transformative powers, and invoking mythic ideals and images. Perhaps these hypermodern transubstantiations fulfill an even more primordial psychic need, as Twitchell (1999: 57) provocatively suggests: "In a most profound sense, advertising and religion are part of the same meaning-making process. They attempt to breach the gap between us and objects by providing a systematic order *and* a promise of salvation. They deliver the goods." Amen brother.

Communal consumption

Community is one of the great "feel good" words in the hypermodernist lexicon. Just as we turn apoplectic shades of red at the word "bureaucracy," we get all "doey-eyed" and "group-huggey" at the first mention of "community." Of course, this is not the "let-me-out-a-here" community of noisy, insufferable neighbors, mind-numbing conformity, byzantine codes of conduct, keeping up with Joneses automobile and lawn rivalries, or "Doom"-crazed, Marilyn Mansonite, machine-gun toting teenagers; nor is it the new "Fortress America" community of gated subdivisions, identification tags, laser activated alarm systems, private security guards, and border patrol checkpoints. No, this is the kinder, gentler, organic community from those halcyon days that your parents said their parents said their parents said their parents said their parents. . . . I mean, golly gee, someone must have lived in such an Edenic world waaaay back when. Oh yeah . . . Modernism has been haunted by the myth of the fall from its inception. We have bitten the apple of science and technology, and though this knowledge has provided unprecedented degrees of personal and social mobility, it must have come at a heavy price you know with original sin and all. Surely, we have lost that special, ineffable, inexplicable, wondrous feeling of "communitas" that permeated this imagined prelapsarian community, with its tightly knit, perfectly integrated, organically symbiotic way-of-life. So, Paradise has been Lost. Not to worry though, it can be simulated in ways that are maybe even better than the real thing (*gemeinschaft* with 500 digital channels and a cell phone!!!!). And so it is that pomo consumers go to great efforts to simulate this magical, mystical, communal solidarity. Of course, the virtual communities of pale-skinned, irradiated, internet junkies leap immediately to mind, but chalk that up to a synaptic misfire. No, virtual communities are too disembodied, too technologically mediated, too spatially and temporally segregated, and just too damn convenient. I mean, furiously typing on your computer at 3:00 A.M. in an insomniac trance isn't exactly Mayberry R.F.D. No, to attain this hypermodernist goal consumers must actually experience the kind of intimacy that only can come from face-to-face, "aren't you glad you use Dial" proximity and it requires individuals to cohere as a social collective, often in the face of challenge or hardship. Arnould and Price's (1993, 1999) "River Magic" questing, white water rafters are one prime example. Celsi *et al.* (1993) death-defying skydivers are another. Then, we have Schouten and McAlexander's (1995) famed Harley-Davidson subcultures of consumption in which consumers from all walks of life are brought together by their shared passion for the look, feel, and sound of these Hellacious machines.

But these canonical ethnographic studies have only broached the service of the hypermodern phenomenon of tribal consumption (see Cova 1996; Maffesoli 1996) such as "fan cultures" in all their many, many forms, from Trekkies, to the resurgent Star War communities, all stripes of soap opera followers, Barry Manilow devotees (O'Guinn 1991) and, God help us all, Ally McBeal-ites. Yes, fan cultures are linked together through the internet but also through conventions, parties, small group performances of fan literature/art (like the slash fiction which expounds on the homoerotic subtext of Spock and Kirk's "professional" relationships) and collective viewing/discussions of program episodes (see Jenkins 1992; Kozinets 1996). We also have youth cultures which are tied together by constellations of consumption interests in fashion, music, media, and leisure time activities; all-night dance "raves" bring it all together with just a touch of ecstasy. There are athletic communities – hardcore cyclists, extreme sports enthusiasts, runners, wind surfers – all of whom can feel intimately connected to each other in ways that can literally go without saying (Celsi *et al.* 1993) and that inspire feelings of spiritual epiphany (Arnould and Price 1993).

Spirituality and religion are now widely commodified. From the ethereally self-absorbed, glazed eye, new age disciples of Deepak Chopra to the "here, let me throw the first stone" fundamentalists, spiritual enlightenment is consumed though all forms of media, seminars, conventions, meetings and, all of which, creates a powerful sense of community. Finally, let us not forget that community requires the creation of symbolic boundaries that separate "us" from "them." The postmodern marketplace is remarkably proficient at separating us physically, socially, and culturally which means, of course, that only the marketplace can bring us together.

Reflexive consumption goals

Tactical flexibility (or not quite bricolage identity construction)

For many pomo theorists, constructing an identity through acts of bricolage (and the closely related pomo practice of poaching) are postmodernity's *raison d'être* (Bouchet 1995; Gergen 1991; Schouten and McAlexander 1993). These mix 'n' match acts of self-creation freely and compulsively borrow styles and preferences from all over the cultural map to produce personal identities that are idiosyncratic and constantly in flux. Plasticity triumphs over stability, consumption becomes identity production (Firat and Venkatesh 1995) and selfhood is decentralized in the grandest post-Fordist way. A liberating, exhilarating, and maybe even a little exhausting idea no doubt but one that those, pesky, persnickety, downright dour, pomo contrarians have called into question (see Brown and Rheid 1997; Holt 1997, 1998; Thompson and Hirschman 1995, 1999; Thompson 1998; Thompson and Tambyah 1999). Try as one might, histories of socialization, the materiality of embodiment (and its oh-so constraining habit of becoming habituated in what it does and likes), and the webs of interpersonal and social connections in which we live have an irritating tendency to anchor us to a limited number of identity positions. Sure, upper middle-class, paunchy (despite three times a week on the Stairmaster), Viagra popping, baby boomer executives can play Hell's Angels on the weekend with their other like-minded/bodied top-of-the-line-Harley riding cohorts, but if they venture too close to those who actually live in this marginalized socio-economic world, their daring act of bricolage may well earn them a comfy spot in triage.

Yet, don't think that I am dis(mis)sing bricolage as an important pomo idea. No, there is something about bricolage that makes it a captivating consumption goal, even if consumers never quite reach this nomadic apotheosis. Let me explain. Emily Martin (1994) argues that the dominant cultural ethos of postmodernity is flexibility. Similarly, Harvey (1989: 124) describes the post-Fordist economic order as a "regime of *flexible accumulation*" (1989: 124) that operates through "a direct confrontation with the rigidities of Fordism" and "rest on flexibility with respect to labour processes, labour markets, production, and consumption patterns." The ideal of flexibility has also transformed cultural conceptions of the morally ideal self. The personality type valorized by Riesman as the inner-directed individual because his/her preferences and beliefs are firmly carved in the bedrock of tradition, is now regarded as being pathetically inflexible, rigid, close-minded, insensitive to others, an inept self-monitor, insufferably parochial, pathologically phobic of difference, and flat-out xenophobic. In making sense of bricolage as a pomo identity practice, some insight can be gleaned from Claude Levi-Strauss who discussed how "non-moderns" (to eschew his modernist "pre" fixations) used bricolage to fashion new tools from available objects. Bricolage creations remained squarely within the boundaries of their conceptual and technological horizons. And so we have innovation within tradition, as creativity within conformity, and as novelty within the familiar. A perfect pomo paradox if there ever was one and it's the very one at work in bricolage identity construction. Consumers fashion new identities from the resources available to them and do so in ways that remain within the nexus of enduring predispositions, skills, knowledge, and social connections that have been forged through their personal histories. None-theless, bricolage – in this more constrained sense – enacts a mode of pomo flexibility whereby consumers can experiment with new looks and social practices and incorporate a broader range of experiences into their lives. Most of all, bricolage expresses that preeminent, predominant, damn near hegemonic, cultural metaphor of the *flexible system*. For postmodern con-sumers, proteanism, rather than promotheanism, is the identity mantra: "I am someone who can adapt to any cultural way-of-life, any fashion style, or any cultural good as I flexibly accumulate a broad range of diverse experiences."

To an outside observer, such acts may indeed look as if a whole new identity is being forged by an individual who is a schizoid composite of fragmented identities but, from the consumers' view, s/he is simply being what he/she always is: flexible and adaptable. Examples you want and examples you shall have. Holt's (1997) analysis of cosmopolitans – whom he describes as cultural omnivores – exemplifies this flexible ethos. Such consumers enjoy and appreciate a wide range of cultural styles in music, media, food, fashion, the fine arts, and architecture. You name it, they'll consume it, but always with a requisite degree of "high culture" sophistic-ation that focuses on the consumption objects' abstract intellectual qualities and its genealogical heritage ("you see, I appreciate WWF Wrestling for its Dadaist expressionism"). Thompson and Tambyah (1999) discuss the cosmopolitan sensibilities of entrepreneurial expatriates whose peripatetic lifestyles actually routinize the experience of adapting to new cultural contexts and, thereby, continually reaffirm their protean self-conceptions. Let's see, there was one other study, a clever one that everyone should cite profusely whether it is relevant or not. Oh what was it? Yes, that's it! Thompson and Haytko (1997) show that consumers often act as *fashion bricoleurs* who mix and match looks and brands to create relatively novel stylistic statements while also conforming to the aesthetic standards of their localized fashion norms. Only in this way, can they and their community of fashion peers adjudicate between an appealing sartorial innovation and a stylistic gaffe. Such acts of bricolage also afford consumers a feeling of autonomy over and against the machinations of the fashion industry. Rather than being dependent on pre-packaged looks or being a walking billboard for a specific fashion designer ("Look, there goes *Calvin*. Oh my Gawd, what a geek"), consumers create their own personalized styles and re-tailor brand images through a recondite, mix 'n' match logic guaranteed to baffle those on the micro-cultural outside: "Hey, you never mix Ralph Lauren with FUBU unless you're wearing Tommy Hilfiger socks or a neon pink discman spinning the latest Lauryn Hill CD. Where are you from anyway?"

And so there is a *tactical quality* (De Certeau 1984) to these acts of flexible consumption. That is, they are ways for consumers to evade the strategic operations of capitalist power or what is conventionally called a marketing strategy. By means of flexible consumption, pomo consumers become cultural chameleons who become very hard to find, identify, classify on appearances alone, such as the demographic characteristics and measures of consumption patterns, the *sturm and drang* of modern marketing strategists. Flexible pomo consumers appear to be ever changing because they don't always consume the same things or in the same way. If consumer researchers ever hope to comprehend a coherent pattern within this shifting consumptive repertoire, they must cultivate a highly localized, contextually nuanced, particularistic understanding of how consumers construct an identity. Holt's micro-detailed, hypercomplex, theoretically multi-textured interpretivist *tour de force* – demurely called a poststructuralist lifestyle analysis – offers the best conceptual prototype to date for making sense of the flexible consumer. Yes, such an analytic complexity may initially inspire right-thinking marketing managers to run screaming for the modernist hills. Once they get the feel for this postmodern aesthetic, they may sit redolent in amazement over how just how long they stayed happily cocooned in all those little VALS® boxes.

Ironic consumption

The old cliché about something "being so bad that it is good" has great resonance for postmodern consumers. Rather than reviling pop cultures' wealth of tackiness and triteness or denouncing its frontal assaults on good taste and aesthetic form, or proselytizing against the stupefying inauthenticity of its kitschy consumption worlds (I mean the kind of places that self-respecting tourists never admit going to because only "tourists go there"), or even furtively indulging these abominations as guilty pleasures, the postmodern consumer drops all supercilious pretense. Instead, s/he celebrates these cultural abominations as the absolute, epiphanic apogee of awfulness. They represent the points where Western civilization can descend no further; where consumption worlds are so absurdly self-parodying that simply experiencing them as they are meant to be consumed affords the ultimate irony. Think of watching Brady Bunch reruns, joining the Tony Danza fan club, collecting "Dukes of Hazard" action figures, listening to old Monkees records, planning your vacation around the most contrived, "tourist traps" you can find, wearing sky blue, double-knit polyester, eazy-fit slacks, eating dinner at Mr Steak's all-you-can-eat-salad bar (and gleefully complaining that the Miracle Whip dressing is not sickly sweet enough) and you will have the flavor of this highly refined appreciation for bad taste. Douglas Copland's (1991) *Generation X* tapped into this postmodern aesthetic with its notion of "recreational slumming." This orientation is also central to a much theorized orientation toward travel known as post-tourism (Feifer 1986) and shopping known as post-shopping (Sherry, McGrath, and Levy 1992). The post-tourist embodies the reflexive, ironizing, playful spirit of postmodernity: "the post-tourist knows that the apparently authentic local entertainment is as contrived as the ethnic bar and that the supposedly quaint and traditional fishing village could not survive without the income from tourism" (Urry 1990: 100). Post-tourists take ironic pleasure in playing tourists in all their stereotypical glory and in being immersed in McDisneyfied banalities (see Ritzer and Laska 1997; Urry 1990, 1995). As Belk discusses (1997), these same ironic propensities can also been seen in the phenomenon of post-shopping where consumers seek out the most tasteless, gawdiest, and splendidly tacky artifacts they can find; if you have ever scoured the second-hand clothing shops looking for an outrageously over-the-top 1970s outfit or hunted your favorite "junk shops" for the perfect, gag gift, you can appreciate this post-shopping ethos. (And if you haven't, well don't even try to make sense of postmodern consumers.) Both post-shopping and post-tourism effect the ultimate act of "if you can't beat 'em, appropriate 'em to your own ironic games." There is one other thing about these ironic acts of consumption: consumers almost never do them alone. No, ironic consumption is invariably far more enjoyable when it is a shared, social undertaking. Watching a laughably bad 1950s sci-fi B-film (think Roger Corman, think Ed Wood if you dare) is not much fun unless you are with others whom you know that they know that you know just what great ironic heights are being reached.

This is not a conclusion

There is so much more that could be written on consumer goals in the age of postmodernity. Suffice it to say for now that consumer researchers must embrace this ineffable postmodern aesthetic if they hope to understand the goals of pomo consumers. So, take pleasure in knowing that the joke is on us and that the sheer unpredictability of the postmodern consumer allows us to produce more discourse (which is of course what we do best) that is an ironic simulation of the modernist goal of pinning the consumer down. Realize that modernist metaphors of knowledge are all necrophilic. All turn on ideas of capturing, dissecting, and fetishizing the inert, unchanging, immobilized (and to reveal the dark secret of modernist consumer research), decaying consumer. Postmodernist consumer researchers, who self-consciously know what they will never know, are at least enamored with a live, mobile and exciting, dare I say decadent, body of consumers. Sure we're closer to the paparazzi, voyeurs, peeping Toms, and obsessive fans but, in the end, we simply want be at the right place and the right time to record what happens when our beloved pomo consumers arrive for a brief visit at their autotelic destinations.

Finally, my fellow community of consumer researchers, don't despair over the unpredictability of the pomo consumer or his/ her refusal to make a permanent home in our easily explained, easily applied, analytic categories for this is the very thing that makes us valuable. The only thing that builds demand for our new models of the consumer is the inevitably dismal failures of our old ones (see Nietzsche's ideas on the perpetual turn). If consumers were actually predictable and controllable, no one would need consumer researchers to create theories and models for predicting and controlling them, not that we are always "hitting 'em where they ain't." The wondrous abundance of our theoretical models and tests assures that consumers often happen to be at the very place that we predict, though it may be right before their departure to new identity locales. Those felicitous coincidences afford a compelling illusion of precision and progressive knowledge accumulation. But these admittedly more than by-chance correspondences inevitably break down creating dire needs for new models, theories and paradigms and fueling the whole "crisis" industry of marketing consulting (see Brown 1998). Proto-postmodernist Georges Bataille (1985) famously proclaimed that the capitalist market depends on a cultural logic of waste. To this insight I add that the market for consumer research depends on a logic of immanent failure. If consumer research ever coalesced as a bona fide predictive model, we could all bask in the glories of having reached "the truth" while helping Alice and Greg serve up lattes and chai to our fully understood customers at that pomo haven Starbucks. Fortunately, in postmodernity, getting it right means getting it wrong time and time again. "Falsification" is our Keynesian multiplier. So rather than having to find personal fulfillment as baristas, we always have something more to do as consumer researchers. Now, don't you love Pomoville?

Acknowledgments

I wish to thank Eric Arnould, Beth Hirschman, and Barbara Stern for their very helpful comments on an earlier version of this chapter.

Notes

1 Warhol also ironically (and profitably) subverted the romantic image of the unrecognized, suffering artist/genius/martyr by being blatantly self-promotional, banausic, and above all else an avid collector and shopper.
2 As just one little example, in a recording of a 1951 radio performance by country-and-western legend Hank Williams, he pitches his book *How to Write Folk and Country Music to Sell* (The Complete Hank Williams Box Set: Disc 8).
3 Arch modernist Emile Durkheim commenting on Simmel's *Philosophy of Money*: "Imagination, personal feelings are thus given free reign here and rigorous demonstrations have no relevance. For my own part, I confess to not attaching a very high value to this kind of *hybrid*, illegitimate speculation where reality is expressed in subjective terms, as in art, but also abstractly as in science" (quoted in Weinstein and Weinstein 1993: 9).
4 Yes, exactly! If Van Sant were to direct a parody of his simulation of Hitchcock's *Psycho*, then he would be well on the way to invoking the imbricated waves self-referentiality (a copy of a copy of a copy of a . . .) that is the *sin qua non* of pomo artistry.
5 Famed *fin de siècle* social scientists Max Weber and Thorstein Veblen gave these anti-modernist sentiments enduring theoretical credibility through their writings on the iron cage of rationality, disenchantment, and the spiritual vacuousness of conspicuous consumption.

References

Arnould, E.J. and Price, L.L. (1993) "'River Magic': extraordinary experience and the service encounter," *Journal of Consumer Research* 20 (June): 24–46.

Arnould, E.J., Price, L.L., and Otnes, C. (1999) "Making consumption magic: a study of river rafting, " *Journal of Contemporary Ethnography* 28 (1): 33–68.

Bakhtin, M. (1984) *Rabelais and His World*, Bloomington, IN: Indiana University Press.

Bataille, G. (1985) *Visions of Excess: Selected Writings 1927–1939*, ed. A. Stoekl, Minneapolis, MN: University of Minnesota Press.

Bauman, Z. (1994) "Is there a postmodern sociology?" in S. Siedman (ed.) *The Postmodern Turn*, New York: Cambridge University Press: 184–207.

Belk, R.W. (1997) "Been there, done that, bought the souvenirs: of journeys and boundary crossing," in S. Brown and D. Turley (eds) *Consumer Research: Postcards from The Edge*, New York: Routledge.

Bouchet, D. (1995) "Marketing and the redefinition of ethnicity," in J.A. Costa and G.J. Bamossy (eds) *Marketing in a Multicultural World*, Thousand Oaks, CA: Sage: 68–104.

Brodman, B. (1994) "Paris or perish: the plight of the Latin American Indian in a Westernized world," in S. Benstock and S. Ferris (eds) *On Fashion*, New Brunswick, NJ: Rutgers University Press: 267–83.

Brown, S. (1995) *Postmodern Marketing*, London: Routledge.

—— (1998) *Postmodern Marketing 2: Telling Tales*, London: ITB Press.

—— (1998a) "What's love got to do with it: sex, shopping, and personal introspection," in S. Brown, A.M. Doherty, and B. Clarke (eds) *Romancing the Market*, London: Routledge: 137–71.

—— (1998b) "Feats don't fail me now: a Bakhtinian interpretation of *Riverdance*," in *Postmodern Marketing 2: Telling Tales*, London: ITB Press: 156–67.

Brown, S. and Rhona Reid (1997) "Shoppers on the verge of a nervous breakdown: chronicle, composition and confabulation in consumer research," in S. Brown and D. Turley (eds) *Consumer Research: Postcards from the Edge*, London: Routledge: 79–149.

Cameron, C.M and Gatewood, J.B. (1994) "The authentic interior: questing gemeinschaft in post-industrial society," *Human Organization* 53 (1): 21–32.

Celsi, R. L., Rose, R., and Leigh, T. (1993) "An exploration of high-risk leisure consumption through skydiving," *Journal of Consumer Research* 20 (June): 1–21.

Copland, D. (1991) *Generation X*, New York: St. Martin's Press.

Cova, B. (1996) "What postmodernism means to marketing managers," *European Management Journal* 14 (5): 494–9.

—— (1997) "The postmodern explained to managers: implications for marketing," *Business Horizons* 31 (3/4): 297–316.

Craik, J. (1994) *The Face of Fashion*, New York: Routledge.

De Certeau, M. (1984) *The Practice of Everyday Life*, Berkeley, CA: University of California Press.

Featherstone, M. (1991) *Consumer Culture & Postmodernism*, London: Sage.

Feifer, M. (1986) *Tourism in History: From Imperial Rome to the Present Day*, New York: Stein and Day.

Firat, A.F. and Venkatesh, A. (1993) "Postmodernity: the age of marketing," *International Journal of Research in Marketing* 10 (3): 227–49.

—— (1995) "Liberatory postmodernism and the reenchantment of consumption," *Journal of Consumer Research* 22 (December): 239–67.

—— (1996) "Postmodern perspectives on consumption," in R. W. Belk, N. Dholakia, and A. Venkatesh (eds) *Consumption and Marketing: Macro Dimensions*, Cincinnati, OH: South-Western: 234–65.

Gergen, K.J. (1991) *The Saturated Self*, New York: Basic Books.

Hannerz, U. (1996) *Transnational Connections*, London: Routledge.

Harvey, D. (1989) *The Condition of Postmodernity*, Cambridge, MA: Blackwell.

Heilbrunn, B. (1998) "In search of the lost aura: the object in the age of marketing romanticism," in S. Brown, A. M. Doherty, and B. Clarke (eds) *Romancing the Market*, London: Routledge: 187–201.

Holbrook, M.B. (1993) "Nostalgia and consumption preferences: some emerging patterns of consumer tastes, "*Journal of Consumer Research* 20 (June): 245–56.

—— (1995) *Consumer Research: Introspective Essays on the Study of Consumption*, Thousand Oaks, CA: Sage.

—— (1997) "Walking on the edge: a stereographic essay on the verge of consumer research," in S. Brown and D. Turley (eds) *Consumer Research: Postcards from the Edge*, London: Routledge: 46–78.

—— (1998) "Illuminations, impressions, and ruminations on romanticism: some magical moments concepts and mystical comments from Morris the Catoptric on the superiority of stereoscopy in visual representations of marketing and consumer research," in S. Brown, A.M. Doherty, and B. Clarke (eds) *Romancing the Market*, London: Routledge: 86–125.

Holbrook, M.B. and Schindler, R.M. (1989) "Some exploratory findings on the development of musical tastes," *Journal of Consumer Research* 16 (June): 119–24.

Holt, D. (1995) "How consumers consume: a typology of consumption practices," *Journal of Consumer Research* 22 (June): 1–16.

—— (1997) "Poststructuralist lifestyle analysis: conceptualizing the social patterning of consumption," *Journal of Consumer Research* 23 (March): 326–50.

—— (1998) "Does cultural capital structure American consumption?" *Journal of Consumer Research* 25 (June): 1–26.

Jameson, F. (1991) *Postmodernism or the Cultural Logic of Late Capitalism*, Durham, NC: Duke University Press.

Jenkins, H. (1992) *Textual Poachers: Television Fans and Participatory Culture*, New York: Routledge.

Kozinets, R.V. (1996) "I want to believe: a netography of X-philes subculture of consumption," presentation given at the Association for Consumer Research Conference, Tucson, AZ.

Lears, T.J.J. (1994) *No Place of Grace*, 2nd edition, Chicago: University of Chicago Press.

MacLaran, P. and Stevens, L. (1998) "Romancing the utopian marketplace: dallying with Bakhtin in the Powerscourt Townhouse Center," in S. Brown, A.M. Doherty, and B. Clarke (eds) *Romancing the Market*, New York: Routledge: 172–86.

Maffesoli, M. (1996) *The Time of Tribes: The Decline of Individualism in Mass Society*, London: Sage.

Martin, E. (1994) *Flexible Bodies*, Boston, MA: Beacon Press.

Merleau-Ponty, M. (1962) *The Phenomenology of Perception*, London: Routledge & Kegan Paul.

Ogilvy, J. (1990) "This postmodern business," *Marketing and Research Today* 8 (1): 4–21.

O'Guinn, T.C. (1991) "Touching greatness: the Central Midwest Barry Manilow fan club," in R.W. Belk (ed.) *Highways and Buyways: Naturalistic Research From the Consumer Behavior Odyssey*, Provo, UT: Association for Consumer Research: 102–11.

Ritzer, G. and Liska, A. (1997) "McDisneyization and Post-Tourism," in C. Rojek and J. Urry (eds) *Touring Cultures: Transformation of Travel and History*, New York: Routledge: 96–109.

Schouten, J. and McAlexander, J. (1995) "Subcultures of consumption: an ethnography of new bikers," *Journal of Consumer Research* 22 (June): 43–61.

Sherry, J.F. (1998) "The soul of the company store: Nike Town Chicago and the emplaced brandscape," in J.F. Sherry (ed.) *Servicescapes: The Concept of Place in Contemporary Markets*, Lincolnwood, IL: NTC Business Books: 109–46.

—— (1991) "Postmodern alternatives: the interpretive turn in consumer research," in T.S. Robertson and H.K. Kassarjian (eds) *Handbook of Consumer Research*, Englewood Cliffs, NJ: Prentice-Hall: 548–91.

Sherry, J.F., McGrath, M.A., and Levy, S. (1992) "The disposition of the gift and many unhappy returns," *Journal of Retailing* 68 (Spring): 40–65.

Stern, B. (1992) "Historical and personal nostalgia in advertising text: the fin de siècle effect," *Journal of Advertising* 21 (4): 11–22.

Thompson, C.J. (1998) "Living the texts of everyday life: a hermeneutic perspective on the relationships between narrative and life-world structures," in B. Stern (ed.) *Representing Consumers: Voices, Views, and Visions*, New York: Routledge: 127–55.

Thompson, C.J., Pollio, H.R., and Locander, W.B. (1994) "The spoken and the unspoken: a hermeneutic approach to understanding the cultural viewpoints that underlie expressed consumer meanings," *Journal of Consumer Research* 21 (December): 432–52.

Thompson, C.J. and Hirschman, E.C (1995) "Understanding the socialized body: a poststructuralist analysis of consumers' self-conceptions, body images, and self-care practices," *Journal of Consumer Research* 22 (September): 139–53.

—— (1999) "An existential analysis of the body as a consumption project," *Consumption, Markets, & Culture* 2 (4): 401–48.

Thompson, C.J. and Haytko, D. (1997) "Speaking of fashion: consumers use of fashion discourse and the appropriation of countervailing cultural meanings," *Journal of Consumer Research* 24 (June): 15–42.

Thompson, C.J. and Tambyah, S.K. (1999) "Trying to be cosmopolitan," *Journal of Consumer Research* 26 (December): 214–41.

Twitchell, J.B. (1999) *Lead Us Into Temptation,* New York: Columbia University Press.

Tybout, A.M. and Carpenter, G.S. (1999) "Meeting the challenge of the postmodern consumer," in T. Dickson and N. Hawcock (eds) *Mastering Marketing: The Complete MBA Companion in Marketing,* London: Financial Times: 103–7.

Urry, J. (1990) *The Tourist Gaze: Leisure and Travel in Contemporary Societies,* London: Sage.

—— (1995) *Consuming Places,* London: Sage.

Weinstein, D. and Weinstein, M.A. (1993) *Postmodern(ized) Simmel,* New York: Routledge.

8 Authenticating acts and authoritative performances

Questing for self and community

Eric J. Arnould and Linda L. Price

> The challenge in this era of globalization – for countries and individuals – is to find a healthy balance between preserving a sense of identity, home and community and doing what it takes to survive within the globalization system.
>
> (Friedman 1999: 35)

This chapter examines the role of consumption in people's quest for self-authentication and community in contemporary Western culture. Specifically, we posit that authenticating acts and authoritative performances represent two primary drivers of consumer behavior. Authenticating acts are self-referential behaviors actors feel reveal or produce the "true" self. Authoritative performances are collective displays aimed at inventing or refashioning cultural traditions. Consumers use narratives or "stories of the self" (Gergen and Gergen 1985: 17) to give these acts a sense of cohesion and integration (see Escalas and Bettman this volume). Personal narratives simultaneously enable people to accommodate multiple selves and mitigate or render comprehensible events and performances that deviate from presupposed collective norms.

Many authors argue the current historical period – postmodernity involves a number of processes that create new problems for selfhood and collective identity (Baumeister 1987; Gergen 1991; Giddens 1991; Grodin and Lindlof 1996). The term postmodernity refers to the post-industrial, information age, to an economy dominated by marketing, and to fundamental shifts in the values idealized in the arts and in popular culture (Firat and Venkatesh 1995; see Thompson this volume). However, postmodernity is a "portmanteau" term, encompassing too much too loosely. We deal here only with some of the effects of this historical period on the self and community (Cushman 1990; De Certeau 1984; Ewen and Ewen 1992; Firat 1991).

Commentators across the political spectrum agree personal meaninglessness has become a fundamental psychic problem in postmodernity (Cushman 1990; Ewen and Ewen 1992; Giddens 1991; Lasch 1985).

Despite considerable theorizing about the consequences of postmodernity for self and relationship between self and community, the techniques that individuals use to cope with contemporary Western society and attain self-fulfillment "are relatively unstudied" (Baumeister 1987: 174). We demonstrate empirically that many consumers embrace authenticating acts and authoritative performances to restore a sense of community, tradition, and self. In contrast to the dark view of consumers offered by some (Baudrillard 1983; Ferrara 1993; Firat 1991), we harbor a more optimistic view of people who actively and creatively carve out their identities in the midst of the challenges posed by postmodernity.

In eras past, identity and relations to the community were fixed institutionally according to family, lineage or rank. Postmodernity induces more awareness regarding self and identity formation, more experimentation and risk (Grodin and Lindlof 1996: 7; Kellner 1992). Individuals, freed of archaic or modern social links, are reflexively recomposing their social universe (Cova 1997: 300; Maffesoli 1996). Some argue that mass consumption frustrates identity creation (Baudrillard 1983; Ewen and Ewen 1992). But consumption can be "a mean's of *producing* one's self and self-image" (Firat 1991: 72).

The chapter is divided into three parts. First, we briefly overview select characteristics of postmodernity that affect self and community. Second, we draw on a broad range of empirical research to posit authenticating acts and authoritative performances as prevalent consumer mechanisms for constructing the narrative of self-identity and relation to community. We conclude by identifying circumstances that frustrate the objectives of authenticating acts and authoritative performances.

Self and community in postmodernity

> Under modernism, the individual seemed an isolated, machinelike entity
> – reliable, predictable, and authentic, propelled by a core mechanism
> embedded not too deeply within the interior. But today's increasing
> cacophony of competing voices creates a pervasive challenge to the
> assumption of "things (including people) in themselves." . . . There is no
> voice now trusted to rescue the "real person" from the sea of portrayals.
>
> (Gergen 1991: 140)

The self-concept is always situated in a social space (Turner 1976: 990). The integration of an individual into solidary groups is the ultimate source of a sense of reality concerning experience; "human life is, in important respects, life in community" (Swanson 1985: 332; Turner 1976: 1001). Self and society arise to facilitate human adaptation and both are continuously modified in the course of adaptation (Swanson 1985). We believe three conditions of postmodernity have had particularly severe implications for the construction of the self in relationship to a social space: globalization, deterritorialization, and hyperreality. Here we briefly describe how they have influenced construction of the self.

Globalization

> If globalization were a sport, it would be the 100-meter dash, over and over and over
>
> (Friedman 1999: 10)

Globalization is an unprecedented feature of contemporary society that influences construction of the self. All cultures, before the modern epoch, were particular, time bound and expressive, and their holism operated within strict cultural constraints (i.e. ethnocentrism) that gave form to self and community (Smith 1990: 178). Globalization detaches labor, capital, technology, ideology and other shared elements of culture from particular times and places. Globalization also increases the volume and speed of their movement through global systems (Waters 1995). In the singular, highly mobile, highly segmented society that results from globalization, disjunctures between culture, community, and selfhood become pervasive (Appadurai 1990; Gergen 1992; Lash and Urry 1987; Turner 1976: 1002). Boundaries between key reference points for identity like community, nation and people become fluid and contentious. As a consequence, global culture is often said to be "contextless" (Smith 1990: 177).

New globalizing technologies have a remarkable decontextualizing potential. "The ability to populate ourselves with a multitude of identities, all constructed in the ever expanding relational possibilities we engage, changes our traditional notion of identity" (McNamee 1996: 41). Cyberspace may produce an unbounded range of social relational possibilities. For example, the Internet is a very effective medium for accomplishing time-space compression. It integrates even tiny communities into global info- and technoscapes, as in the case of schooling illustrated by the following excerpt from a depth interview-based study of Greenlandic immigrants to mainland Denmark:

> Now, with the introduction of the Internet – there are schools in the little villages that receive teaching through the net. Places with maybe 8 pupils, and they don't have a teacher for a certain course, then they get it through the net. You almost can't believe it, but that is reality today.
>
> (Female, age 60; Askegaard and Arnould 1999)

The world is much more singular than it was even recently and it is difficult for individuals to understand the global system and their place in it. We lack organizing metaphors and shared global memories to do so (Smith 1990). Unstable, anonymous economic and technological forces create a sense that identities, families, jobs and communities could be changed at any moment (Friedman 1999: 11).

Deterritorialization

Deterritorialization represents a process of spatial and temporal dislocation Deterritorialization melds together objects, people, rituals and cultures as people cross borders that formerly divided civilizations and separated traditions. Further, popular culture emphasizes "spectacles and visualizations" that alienate individuals from participation in community, and produce "non-linear contours in time and space" experience (Venkatesh, Sherry, and Firat 1993: 217). Frameworks for action and interpretation become relativized and contested.

Destabilization of traditional "master narratives" may shake individuals' foundation of identity. For example, informants in the study of Greenlandic immigrants found that the question of "what makes one Greenlandic?" has become uncertain. The following excerpt indicates that ethnicity becomes more complex than taken for granted emic models:

> I felt a little strange in relation to my own culture, when I started working in the Greenlandic Community House in Odense; I felt I had acquired some prejudice about Greenlandic people. Suddenly some Danes came and were entitled to receive scholarships from the Greenlandic Home Rule, and I was astonished. And one of them spoke Greenlandic! Good grief, what's going on, I thought to myself, is this Greenland. And of course it is Greenland. It is Greenland today. In the beginning I had difficulties finding whether some of these things are possible, but of course it is possible . . .
>
> (Female, age 37; Askegaard and Arnould 1999)

The world is increasingly a shifting landscape of tourists, migrants, refugees, business travelers and ethnic diaspora. Everywhere the fabric of community is strained by persons whose experiences, and expectations contest, and are contested by, those of the communities through which they move. Reinforced by media technology that erodes linkages between place and cultural identities, today's cultures are becoming territory-less. We are moving toward a global society in which the adoption of consumer lifestyles that are/ were fixed to specific groups has been surpassed (Featherstone 1991: 83).

For the individual, the continuity of tradition and sureties of habit that previously anchored identity are replaced by pervasive uncertainty and a dreadful multiplicity of existential choices (Gergen 1991). Thus, a middle-aged American laments what she perceives as a loss of tradition in holiday feast preparation:

> I don't think there are very many families that probably do all the Swedish foods from scratch any more. Um, I think a lot of times you're, you're not around grandparents, ah. And I think grandparents and parents are the ones that instill these traditions, and you're just not

around them enough to learn all the skills and I think with women working they don't have time to do both, to passing on this because they're so busy. And I think the kids are really, really busy.

(Female, age 51; Price and Arnould 2000)

Hyperreality

Commercial media confront people with dream images catering to every desire simultaneously and pushing people toward a global order that effaces the distinction between reality and image and the stylization of everyday life. Time is fragmented into a series of parallel present moments of equal value. Fashion, architecture, and music draw on a repertoire of themes from anyplace and anytime. These trends create a simulation world or hyperreality (Firat and Venkatesh 1995). Hyperreality is a product of the dense barrage of images that continuously (re)creates ostensibly "fresh images and meanings based on the same signifiers" (Firat 1991: 73). The continuous flow of diverse, specialized images makes it difficult for individuals to chain them together into a meaningful message. The saturation of images defies systematization and the traditional logic of narrative (Featherstone 1991: 65). One effect of hyperreality is that a kind of unintentional parody and uncertainty hovers over social life.

Faced with a loss of their moorings, people proliferate ways of creating anchors, e.g. myths of origin, signs of reality, and second-hand truths (Baudrillard 1983: 12–13). Attempts to overcome the sense of loss and parody fuel the appetite for authentic images anchored outside of the self (e.g. in nativism, nationalism, and fundamentalism). Examples can be found in the depth interview study of Greenlandic immigrants to Denmark who purposefully adopt "native" costume, carry a *tupilaak* (fetish figure), or consume "native" food:

> Informant: I use my national costume at festive occasions, and formerly – I hadn't used it for several years, nor while I've been down here, but now I simply have to call my mom and ask whether she has all the parts, right? So that I am sure they'll be ready, if ever I need them. I also use it a lot more now, I'm more into traditions, I think. Now, I go to church for Christmas and I have to wear it. I wasn't so much into these things before.

> Interviewer: "Does that mean that through the years you attach more importance to Greenlandic culture?

> Informant: Yes, I would say so. I definitely am very conscious about preserving it.

(Female, age 25; Askegaard and Arnould 1999)

In an expatriate context, hyperreal consumption of "native" culture aims to produce a sense of authentic identity (Firat and Venkatesh 1995).

Responses to postmodernity: authenticating acts and authoritative performances

Some social scientists point to the fluidity, deterritorialization, and lack of authority of contemporary institutions to explain alienation and to infer self-estrangement. However, evidence of alienation and anomia tell us only where the self is not. We ask whether the self is lodged somewhere other than where investigators have looked (Turner 1976: 997). In the midst of multiple identities, and in the absence of the authority and continuity formerly provided by tradition, consumers actively foster a sense of continuity and integration. In postmodernity, creative consumption can provide the foundation for individuals' authentic selves and a connection to community.

Individuals labor to construct autobiographical or emergent self-narratives that organize their life experiences to produce integrated (but not unitary) selves. In this vein, Giddens writes:

> A person's identity is not to be found in behavior, nor – important though this is – in the reactions of others, but in the capacity *to keep a particular narrative going*.
>
> (1991: 54)

A self-narrative refers to an individual's account of the relationship among self-relevant events over time. Weaving together past, present, and future conceptions of self and relations with others, the narrative promotes integration while allowing for different selves and multiple discourses (Hermans 1996). Narratives provide a means for expressing and understanding the self, its change over time and across contexts. By providing a flexible configuration to which an individual attaches his or her evolving life experiences, narrative provides a cartography society no longer supplies (see Escalas and Bettman this volume).

Individual self-narratives are created and sustained through what we call authenticating acts and authoritative performances (Abrahams 1986). In different ways, each contributes to a sense of narrative identity. Neither the distinction between authenticating acts and authoritative performances, nor the links between them as a source for self-narratives have been discussed previously. Figure 8.1 outlines orientations and outcomes of effective authenticating acts and authoritative performances.

Authenticating acts

Authenticating acts concern the expression of the "true self, our individual existence, not as we might present it to others, but as it 'really is,' apart from any roles we play" (Handler 1986: 2). Thus, authenticating acts require transcendence of roles and may be emptied of meaning if the role becomes visible. Authenticating acts affirm uniqueness, and hold power because they

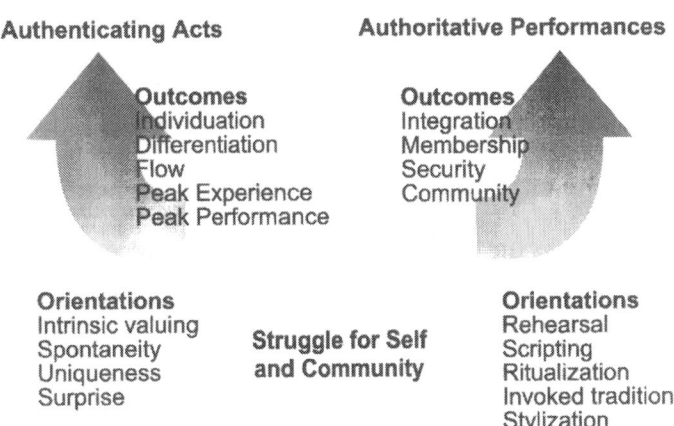

Figure 8.1 Authenticating acts and authoritative performances.

echo a Romantic Western conception of personhood (Geertz 1976: 225). They emerge from the integration of life experiences within a narrative of self-development: the creation of a personal belief system through which the individual acknowledges that "his[/her] first loyalty is to [her/]himself."

Activities that induce flow (the unity between thought and action), peak experience (intense joy), or peak performance (superior functioning) may be experienced as authenticating (Arnould and Price 1993; Celsi, Rose, and Leigh 1993; Csikszentmihalyi 1990). With each event, individuals experience integration of personal identity. Present in all is an awareness of power and a clarity that comes from the structure of the activity. Enabling orientations productive of authenticating outcomes include intrinsic valuing of action, openness to spontaneity and feelings of uniqueness and surprise.

The key reference points are set "from the inside," in terms of how individuals construct/ reconstruct their life history. The issue is not whether the individual "really" has an authentic experience, but rather whether the individual endows the experience with authenticity (Cohen 1988: 378). As Geertz (1976: 225) argues, we view individuals' experiences "within the framework of their own idea of what selfhood is." In other words, "authenticity is life as a readable first-person narrative, individuated in its authorship, integrated through its employment and creative by dint of its ongoing invention" (Handler and Saxton 1988: 250). Thus, the authentic postmodern self is constructed.

Authoritative performances

Authoritative performances are cultural displays like festivals and rituals that make explicit what the membership of the community of participants regard as significant life moments and that invite adherence to the values portrayed (Abrahams 1986: 50). To be authoritative, "experience-in-common" is privileged. Authoritative performances represent a "primitive" quest for unity between self and society (Cohen 1988: 373–4). To understand them requires attention to purposively devised social units rather than institutional practices (Abrahams 1986; Maffesoli 1996).

Effective authoritative performances offer integration among participants, a collective sense of identity, and the security and feelings of community that flow from this integration (Turner 1987). The units of activity – lifestyle or affinity group, club, family, household, community, ethnic group – are valued because they are agreed on through participation; performances can be "learned, rehearsed and practiced together" (Abrahams 1986: 60). Enabling orientations also include receptivity to scripting and stylized behavior, and invocations of imagined traditions (Arnould, Price, and Tierney 1998).

Successful authoritative performances are redressive activities that recognize and repair breaches in social order. Breaches may be cyclical; aging evokes a concern for family legacy in the flat temporal space of postmodernity:

> We are reaching a point that we don't need all this that we have. We need to get rid of it. And we are. Slowly – You know, when you get to a certain stage in life, you're trying, you don't want to – But see, as you get older, we have all this stuff that we don't really use. And we would like to, not all of a sudden –. Tell you what, I go to estate sales all the time. And when I go, every time I go, I realize that I have to do something. I must get rid of what I have. It is so *sad* [stresses the word sad] and there are these beautiful items that are being sold – And I think of these people, and of how they must have felt. They had all of this, and it meant so much to them. So, every time I go, I think that's not going to happen to me . . .
>
> (Female, married, age 78; Price, Arnould, and Curasi 1999)

Breaches may be episodic; doubts about group ties, values, and symbols engendered by hyperreal representations prompt organization of a festival to reassert them. The Florida Classic football bowl game serves a redressive goal for the African-American community fractured by class differences and negative media stereotypes:

> I mean, you're there; you're *rejuvenated*. You're seeing all these people doing well. I mean, if you just listen to the news two days out of the year, you think that black people did everything wrong with America, but if you go to this one game, you're *rejuvenated*, you know there are people doing positive things. You've been in this huge group of people, you know, 40,000–45,000–50,000 people and nothing went wrong, *everything was perfect*
>
> (Focus group informant, black, 20s; Stamps and Arnould 1998;
> emphasis added)

Authoritative performances involve scripting, stylization, rehearsal, and the invocation of tradition, and then enactments that involve "deep play": dramatic ritualization of symbols and values (as also in sports; Ségalen 1998). They deploy verbal and behavioral rhetoric to assert power in uncertain systems of meaning and representation (Abrahams 1986; Cheal 1989). Authoritative performance provides meaning by redefining boundaries so that chaotic cultural difference lies, if contingently, outside the imagined community of participants (Maffesoli 1996):

> . . . you've got all the majority of the black members of the Florida Legislature – they come back for the game – and they're very visible walking around. You've got people who are in corporate America where they're walking around having fun. You've got people from all walks of life and everyone is right there. No one feels that they're better than anyone else.
>
> (Focus group informant, black, 20s;
> Stamps and Arnould 1998: 581)

The distinction in postmodernity is individuals and organizations craft traditions, customs and rituals and agree to participate in potentially recurring group activities (Ségalen 1998). In this way, authoritative performances invoke the "absolute discrepancy" between that which takes place in ritual and in everyday life (Smith 1978: 109–10). This new rituality expresses the creativity of postmodern society and its numerous tribes (Cova 1997). We read authoritative performances as communal resistance to globalization, deterritorialization and hyperreality.

Consumption in authenticating acts and authoritative performances

In this section we argue consumption objects and experiences may assume a positive role in the adaptive and iterative processes of construction of self and community, and we specify conditions that facilitate authentication. We organize our discussion to clarify the distinctive and non-interchangeable roles of authenticating acts and authoritative performances. For authenticating acts we illustrate specific ways in which consumers effectively appropriate individual meanings (e.g. create agency) from products and services. For authoritative performances, we depict how individuals invent collective consumption traditions that stabilize a sense of time and space through idealization and participation.

Authenticating acts

Two types of authenticating acts illustrate (but do not exhaust) the use of consumption to create personal agency. In one type, the consumer works creatively with products or consumption experiences to obtain self-authentication; purchase and consumption is transformed into production. In the other type, a consumption object or experience is transformed into an individuated possession or experience by linking it to self-narrative.

Use of products in self-authentication

An example of the first type of experience recounts completion of a consumption set that yields a totalizing, and highly personal self-conception (Price and Walker 1991):

> In a remote corner of the store, on a low shelf, I found my dream shoes. They are not 9 West, but Italian, with a 1¾" heel, and are multi-colored patchwork leather in gray, black, cranberry and navy blue, and when I put them next to the jacket they looked perfect. They even had a great size selection. I told the sales person that I was so excited because I had been looking for shoes to go with the suit for 2 years. She looked at me like I was out of my mind. . . . I will feel very well put together when I wear the shoes and they are also comfortable. If I get the job, they will be my favorite business shoes. . . . Because of the job interview and because they are unique and they are part of a total look which has been tough to achieve . . .

Here there is a focus on a "tough" extended creative effort, that contributes to feelings of unique and "put together" individual qualities. Even though both suit and shoes were mass-produced, through work they embody individuation and self-identity (Giddens 1991: 200).

Production and giving to others are at play in the authenticating act of making horseradish. Our informant describes at length his ritual production of horseradish from garden to jar. He answers the question of what make this food special saying:

> I've done it myself! You know, I think that's much better! Whether it's any better than what you can buy is questionable, but the fact that I've done it myself and put my own work and labor and talents into making it, to me it makes it more enjoyable. And I enjoy giving that to family members. And I think they like it better. Whether it's actually any better, that's questionable. Some might say it is and some might say it isn't.
>
> (Male, married, age 58; Price and Arnould 2000)

Many stories that emphasize the role of productive consumption in creating narratives of the self are told by customers of commercial river rafting trips. For example,

> [You] develop a personal enrichment especially if you encounter a situation in which you become frightened and overcome the obstacle of the situation. And finally, long after its done, even years later, you'll find your mind escaping, returning back to the journey and reliving the thrill and when you encounter a situation in life where you're afraid or unsure the river experience often enables you to overcome it because you are inevitably more self-assured
>
> (Arnould and Price 1993)

Across these examples individuals attain a sense of authenticity from active, individuated productive consumption. Our data abound with examples of consumers making something their own by repainting, reconstructing, and reusing commodities in novel ways. The unique and natural quality of consumers' creations contributes to their individuation. Also evident is the weaving of production and consumption together into life stories.

Appropriation of authenticating meanings

In a second type of authenticating act, consumers appropriate authenticating meanings by transforming commodities or experiences into highly *individuated* icons of personal meaning. One example is a story about a pair of cowboy boots. The episode represents a reaction to deterritorialization and suggests how multiple selves are woven into a coherent, meaningful story (Price and Walker 1991):

> I lived in Texas most of my life. My mother's family grew up on a farm. As a child I used to love to go to the ranch and enjoy the country. . . . I stayed in Texas for college, but I went to a Republican, yuppie university that didn't value the simpler life. Since I graduated 3 years ago, I've lived in Boston, Sacramento and now in Denver. While being away from home, I've begun to long for things which remind me of simpler things not careers. . . . *On my* visit home to Texas around Christmas time I went into a country western store. I saw these blue-gray Justin Roper boots. Immediately got this feeling that I should buy them. . . . During my visit, we had a large family get together – It was there that I saw most of my cousins who are about the same age wearing Justin Ropers. I knew then that I would go back to the store and buy those blue Ropers regardless of the cost. . . . I like to think those boots show my down-home nature. I sometimes feel that I get too caught up in becoming this ambitious professional. . . . I love knowing that they are in my closet. . . . The boots reinforce my idea that I'm a true Texan at heart and that no matter what I do or become, I will always love the country and the good down home life.

The story of the mass-produced boots not only illustrates how meanings are appropriate from commodities but also shows how they become repositories of personal meanings. The consumer seems to look ahead to times when the boots will reinforce and remind him of his personal sense of identity.

In other cases, possessions may be purchased without special meanings, but through manipulation or product nurturing acquire a history that is intertwined with the self-narrative of their owners. Our example shows how an elderly respondent transforms an object into an heirloom totem of personal history:

> Ok . . . See this picture on the wall? That's me when I was about 4 and your father when he was about 5. Then my picture has a spoon under it and your dad's has a fork. You can hardly see the writing any more cause they have tarnished, but they have our names on it. This is a keepsake I made up from the pictures and spoon and fork that both parents gave me. Did I create a heirloom? I think it looks nice
>
> (Female, married, age 50)

These examples from large data sets illustrate how over time people imbue commodities with personalized meanings linked to life narratives (Price, Arnould, and Curasi 1990). The use of personal photographs in the case of the spoons facilitates this transformation. What begin as mass-produced commodities become intertwined with individuals' life histories. In the examples, linkage of self and a group is frequently evoked, but in a highly individuated form; meanings are personal, even private, unrehearsed, fitting our conception of authenticating acts. We now turn to consumption activities that involve experiences in common, e.g. authoritative performances, and their linkage to self-narrative.

Authoritative performances

Like authenticating acts, people engage in and derive meanings from authoritative performances. Authoritative performances focus on creating and sustaining shared traditions and connections between individual and community. In authoritative performances, identity emerges from community. To the extent that these contemporary authoritative performances sustain elements of extrinsic traditionality, they hold out the promise of community revival, and recentering of meaning and self-identity.

Against deterritorialization

Deterritorialization is a profound process of spatial and temporal dislocation, the proliferation of "premature endings and the dislocation of endings and beginnings" in Cheal's (1989: 284) phrasing. Authoritative performances combat deterritorialization by reorienting the temporal perspective of participants towards the future (Cheal 1989). Illustrative examples of relocating an authoritative emotional community in the future can be found in the ritualization process through which inheritance creates descent groups (Arnould, Price, and Curasi 1999). The following excerpt is typical of our heirloom data. The young informant imagines a tradition by projecting a behavior into the future:

> R: Okay, one heirloom I inherited from my grandmother, is a ring. A heart shaped ring has rubies and diamonds in it. Another heirloom I got, was from my mother that was a ring I got for my sixteenth birthday. That contains diamonds and sapphires, Actually both of the rings I got for my sixteenth birthday.
>
> I: Okay, so the one that was from your grandmother she gave it to you on your sixteenth birthday?
>
> R: Well no, my grandmother had bought this ring when she was living. And she always said that when I turned sixteen she was gonna give it to me. Okay my grandmother passed away therefore, my mother kept the rings for me. And as my grandmother wished she gave it to me on my sixteenth birthday. . . . The ring that my mother gave me, was one that she purchased for me for my sweet sixteen, well when I turned sixteen. And the reason why she I guess gave one, gave a ring to me is because I am her only daughter and I am the youngest child. The story goes the same for my grandmother, I am her only granddaughter and I am her youngest grandchild. So I think that's why I was passed along. And like the other people in my family are males, they wouldn't wear women's rings.
>
> And later . . .
>
> I plan on passing them on a, I'm gonna pass on the ring my grandmother gave me to my grandchild. The ring my mother gave me to my daughter, my child. I am gonna try to keep that traditional. You know, granddaughter from grandmother, I mean daughter from mother.
>
> (Female, single, age 20)

Alternatively, the success of authoritative performances in combating the effects of deterritorialization may be predicated on successfully inserting a band of stability into the present by re-inventing tradition. Examples of this are found in a variety of community performances. For example,

> What is particularly striking about the expressive events in Bethlehem [PA] is that people, both locals and visitors, seem to care little about whether they [the events] really are old. There seems to be a willing suspension of disbelief, a collective amnesia about authenticity. This response is related to what Cohen (1988: 379) describes as "emergent authenticity," that is a negotiated agreement about what is perceived as genuine.
>
> (Cameron and Gatewood 1994: 23)

Similarly in Japan, the process of *furusato-zukuri* (old village making) involves a similar suspension of disbelief and redefinition of the past in the interest of creating a shared present:

> Visually, *furusato*, is depicted as a rural landscape consisting of a forested mountain range enclosing fields dotted with thatch-roof farmhouses and cut by a meandering river. The term, *furusato*, however, is not confined to such landscapes, but is used to signify a variety of places, real or imagined, where individuals or groups have experienced – or feel they can experience – some order of belongingness or insideness. The evocation of *furasato* in conjunction with the staging of citizen's festivals is an increasingly cogent means of fostering we-feelings among a citizenry . . . *Furasato-zukuri* aims to achieve what Frederic Jameson . . . terms a "cultural dominant," or a "new systemic cultural norm and its reproduction" – "new" in the sense of a resurrected and "improved" connotation of pastness and historicity.
>
> (Robertson 1987: 126)

This suspension of time and belief, of participants remaking the past to suit the needs of the present, is observed elsewhere, in a study of Quebecois folklore celebrations for example (Handler and Linnekin 1984).

Against hyperreality

Hyperreality involves a flattening of images that are fragmented in space, and juxtaposed in parallel temporal moments, with a resultant draining of emotional value and discursive meaning. The Rock Creek, Montana Home of Champions Rodeo derives emotional power and symbolic significance by evoking the liminality common to effective rituals, thus combating hyper-reality:

> The experience of liminality, of being outside normal society, could have a special, indeed *augmented*, significance for those Americans who are likely to regard community with ambivalence, believing that it requires at least the partial loss of that individuality which is a major source of self worth. I suggest, therefore, that the oscillations in performances (and other rituals) between the normal and liminal may well have *by virtue of their structure*, their movement *in and out of society*, a particular salience in this American context; they lend themselves to being experienced in terms of what are regarded as the linked processes of individual and social ontology – those focusing on the negotiation (however tacit) of the social compact.
>
> (Errington 1990: 640)

Research on Bethlehem, Pennsylvania's Christmas pageant, also provides evidence of this liminal condition participants experience: "The print coverage provide additional evidence that visitors believe that they have slipped into a *gemeinschaft time warp* . . . Nostalgia and longing are transparent in the prose . . ." (Cameron and Gatewood 1994: 25; emphasis added).

Liminality inserts a separate space of attachment between participants and prescribes a temporal sequence of events with a beginning, middle and end that suspends the hyperreality and detachment experienced in everyday life. Authoritative performances also depend for their success on emergent idealization and participation as we discuss below.

Idealization

Idealization refers to a process of selection from diverse sources and reification of desirable values. Like other contemporary authoritative performances, the vitality and ability to provide meaningful linkages between self and community of the Christmas program in Bethlehem, Pennsylvania, depends on idealization couched within, and evolving from a temporal sequencing or narrative:

> Ethnicity, history, and music are the three most important themes of the tourism program, and all of them are closely linked to the Moravians. . . . It is apparent that the Moravians symbolically "own" Christmas. . . . Moravian values are praised . . . historical antipathy to racism . . . lauded for their emphasis on equality and human dignity . . . hospitality and generosity . . . the spiritual emphasis that Moravians give to Christmas . . . the continuity of custom and tradition among Moravians . . . community integration and spirit is given much emphasis. . . . The effect of this text . . . is to communicate a vivid and integrated image of Bethlehem. . . . Another is that the traditions are timeless and that the past pervades the present.
>
> (Cameron and Gatewood 1994: 24–5)

Without this emergent idealization the program would be nothing more than a sham spectacle perpetuated on visitors. Emergent idealization is also evident in river rafting trips where guides create a sense of tradition, acting as purveyors of "ancient" myths and initiators of rituals for willing participants (Arnould, Price, and Tierney 1998).

Just because authoritative performances partake of disparate commodities and traditions, people do not find themselves lost in a world with no meaning. Borrowing of traditions from separate chronotopes does not necessarily result in hyperreality, but instead these borrowings may be nested into a cohesive, idealized, and shared narrative space. Apparent contradictions are unified through the "difference" the performance itself creates.

Domestic group rituals illustrate emergent idealization that anchors individuals within a "little community." Field notes recorded at Thanksgiving feasts illustrate the way particular commodities become traditions, constitutive of authoritative performance. An example of transforming commodities into blended domestic tradition is provided in the following excerpt from Thanksgiving field notes (Wallendorf and Arnould 1991):

> Violet had prepared the cabbage. She told of how it is a traditional Yugoslavian dish. My mom brought the shortbread and the carrot cake because they are two of her specialties and they were easy to bring on our trip over. Shortbread is traditional of the British Isles and both my dad and my Uncle grew up with it. Turkey and stuffing were unanimously the most traditional dishes served. The stuffing was an old family recipe of Ruth's [NB: Ruth is a new family member and also the host, is allowed to stuff the bird].

Rather than descending into kitsch or a clash of traditions, this international bricolage of invoked tradition is idealized. The blend becomes a sign of membership and community. The following interview excerpt suggests another example of how a commodity may become a repository for emergent idealization in a little community. The narrative genre is a common one in this data, a story of hard times overcome. It illustrates how narrative is temporally layered onto a single object over the generations:

> I: How about the one-hundred-two-year-old gold watch which to my amazement still runs, perfectly to the second?
>
> R: Yeah. (laughs). That was really a masterpiece kind of thing. And I know when I see my mother wear it that she's *connecting herself* to her own family. She was not real close to her own mother and these were kind of women who helped raise her and so I think it was not just a family heirloom as much, it was a symbol of the kind of people they were. They were precise. They were, they valued things; they hung onto things and *after going through the Depression*, they placed a lot of value on something like a fine watch. It probably was one of the few symbols of any kind of maybe, wealth that they might have had.
>
> (Female, married, age 46)

Common to the above examples is the evocation of archetypes or idealization to imbue rehearsed, shared events with cultural meaning. Also common, is the narrative and emergent quality of idealization, relying on the active engagement of participants and audience for meaning. The emergent idealization relies on a sensitivity of the focal performances to salient cultural and historical roots of participants and on the present terrain and future hopes shared by those participants.

Participation

Across many cases, it becomes clear that temporal sequencing and idealization weave together with participation to produce successful authoritative performances. The sense that the performance is not merely acting or a commercial show, but rather a shared living re-presentation, is central to the performance's success. The more widespread the participation, the more likely the success. The Rock Creek Rodeo and its Festival of Nations involve a majority of community members; men's roles are highlighted in the former, and women's in the latter (Errington 1990: 1987). Cameron (1987) notes there is a very high rate of volunteerism for Bethlehem's Musikfest and that volunteers come from all ranks in the community. She argues "The festival appears stable because many people are committed to making it endure" (Cameron 1987: 170). Finally, the Florida Classic football bowl pageant provides ample opportunities for many people to participate and spectate by turns (Stamps and Arnould 1998). High levels of volunteerism communicates to participants that events are real and not merely play-acting for commercial ends.

In a study of a Japanese commuter village's *furusato-zukuri* movement-inspired spectacle, Ari-Ben emphasizes the importance of participation directly. Unlike living history spectacles, the participants are not perceived to be actors. But participants play a dual role:

> Just as the coaches and initiates are representatives of pre-Meiji samurai traditions, so too the villagers, with their comments and jokes are purportedly examples of the way locals historically took part in the cooperative staging of communal rites. Along these lines, the villagers carry out a dual role: as participative audience to the youths, and as actors to an external audience.
>
> (Ari-Ben 1991: 143)

The villagers as performers for an outside audience also become exemplars or idealizations of the traditional *(denototeki)* which in postmodern Japan imbues them with cultural authenticity regardless of the actual history or vintage of the performance (Robertson 1987: 124).

Similarly, in Bethlehem's Christmas pageant and the Florida Classic, participants perceive themselves to be engaged in a real, living tradition. The fact that each is slightly different each year is evidence of the "living faith" of the "Moravians," or the evolution of the African-American "community," respectively (Cameron and Gatewood 1994: 25; Stamps and Arnould 1998). In each case, events produce a remarkably homogenous response among visitors from dramatically different social environments:

> Tourists consume this image [continuity in belief and customs over time]; their experience appears to be spiritual, rich, and meaningful. Bethlehem at Christmas seems to connect people . . . to their ideas of what a community should be.
>
> (Cameron and Gatewood 1994: 28)

Participation in shared rituals also transpires within "little communities." The first example portrays a family ritual characteristic of our data about homemade food:

> R: For Christmas especially cookies. We have a special um, ah, sugar cookie that ah, which has *been in the family for, for many years* and ah, we always make that ah, sugar cookie.
>
> I: What makes it so special?
>
> R: Well, because um, my mother made it and ah, ah, her, her mother made it and ah, ah, so I *just naturally* ah, make it myself and, and made it with my girls when, when they were little as, as my mother made it with me when, when I was little. So that's I guess what makes it special.
> (Female, married, age 53; emphasis added)

Like the community celebrations discussed above, this little tradition appears stable because of the enacted commitment. By invoking tradition, and through scripted participation, actors preserve values that they believe. These performances are at contrast with contemporary pressures that estrange these small communities, as illustrated in another informant's comment about ritualized food preparation at Christmas-time.

> I, I think it, because it makes me think of my childhood and um, how I'd always help my mom cook and how everybody in the family was involved with that and now the boys help me cook and like Laurie helps me cook when she's home. So it's the kind of thing that everybody does together as a family. We usually don't have time to do that any other time of year because everybody's going every which way
> (Female, married, age 51)

Many excellent examples of idealized participation occur in Thanksgiving data, as in the following exchange:

> We *always* had Thanksgiving at our house. *All* the kids would come and bring their husbands and children. Sometimes we would have up to 24 people over for dinner. The kids would *usually* sit in the foyer for dinner because the floor was marble and they could spill and nobody would care. You could mop the floor with a special chemical that they recommended. The parents would sometimes sit on the stairs that overlooked the foyer and watch their children eat. My husband was *always* the initiator in family gatherings. They called him "leader" he *always* made sure *everyone* came home for Thanksgiving. It was a lot of work; sometimes it took over two days to do the preparations for the dinner. My daughters would bring salads *usually*. I *always* cooked the turkey. The turkey was the center of attention. *Always* the main focus of the meal [emphasis added].

The description takes the form of a conventionalized narrative. The declarative tone and the words "always," "usually," "all," "everyone," are cues that the informant is describing idealized goals. It is unlikely that her statements are categorically true. Instead, her statements use over-generalization, signs, and iconic relationships to redefine the variety of the past into meaningful authoritative experience (Arnould 1998).

Each of the above examples captures a "living" presentation of a shared, rehearsed and idealized tradition. Participation breathes life into these performances by connecting past, present and future through evoked archetypes, associations and recollections. Participation (as contrasted with acting) gives the performance an authoritative voice and links those so engaged to community and tradition. Without participation, these performances may be entertaining, but not authoritative – filled with actors and separated from their temporal sequencing they lapse into kitsch or empty nostalgia. It is to the potential for failure of authenticating acts and authoritative performances that we now turn our attention.

Failure of authenticating acts and authoritative performances

We identify three obstacles to authentication through authenticating acts and authoritative performances. The first is the ongoing *commodification* of productive consumption. Authenticating acts from grass-roots innovation in costume, recreations, or lifestyles are constantly coopted by marketers and repackaged as mass-produced commodities. The commodification of experience leads to *passivity* rather than participation. For example, at living history spectacles and ethnic cultural centers, active engagement is frustrated by the repetition of displays, and the constraints on interactions with mere performers, not real historical figures or native craftsfolk, (Handler and Saxton 1988: 252). Absent community participation, commodification, leads to the *decontextualization* of objects and behavior. With decontextualization, consumption dissolves into pastiche as in nostalgic consumption, and promotes the second obstacle to authentication, reflexivity.

Reflexivity refers to the self-consciousness that breaks down the unity of thought and action in authenticating acts or the suspension of disbelief in authoritative performances. Reflexivity leads to studied protocol or to role enactment rather than participation. One factor that leads to reflexivity is *typicality*, or the possibility of multiple instantiations of a role that preclude authorship. Another factor that leads to reflexivity is *routinization*, the possibility of mere re-enactment without authorship. Routinization undermines the sense that authenticating acts or authoritative performances are produced by the interaction of convergent tendencies, are creative moments of life-in-process (Handler and Saxton 1988: 253–7). Finally, episodicity leads to reflexivity. *Episodicity* is the bracketing of the facticity of authenticating acts or authoritative performances by the disempowerment and fragmentation of ordinary experience. Bracketing separates the act or performance from the broader life narrative and drains it of meaning.

A final obstacle is confusion of the orientations of authentication through authenticating acts with authoritative performances and vice versa (see Figure 8.1). If individuals seek a sense of real self through authoritative acts, they forego the possibility for individuated authorship, differentiated experience, and flow that characterize authenticating acts. This happens to participants in living history programs, where the typicality, episodicity, and routinization of re-enactment defeat the phenomenological emplotment to which they aspire (Handler and Saxton 1988: 251, 254). If individuals seek community through authenticating acts, they forfeit the integration, membership, and security that is manifest only through shared authorship, evoked archetypes, and communitas proffered by authoritative performances. This is a dilemma experienced by participants in extreme sports. Initially, shared knowledge of the flow experience creates a bond between participants in extreme sports that constitutes a sense of belonging and a sharing of transcendent information (Celsi *et al.* 1993: 12; Turner 1987). However, as an individual pursues more individuating peak experiences, the "shared flow" community becomes smaller until the individual, again, stands alone.

Conclusion

> The modernist world view urges us to tell a unified story of who we are . . . . Alternatively, a more constitutive, contingent, provisional view of communication would lead us to identify not with our present story but with the storyteller; not with one's current identity but with the generative process of sense making from which numerous possible life stories might arise.
>
> (Eisenberg 1998: 99)

Globalization, deterritorialization, and hyperreality are postmodern conditions that consumers face. Interpretations of their effects on the self and motivation emphasize the negative. Some authors believe people abandon the search for self; others posit an empty postmodern self. Still others argue fragmented selves produce an absence of meaning and purpose. Thoroughgoing commodification and the radical globalization of identity markers at once make possible and desirable consumer behaviors that swing between two motivational poles. Consumers are motivated to mark differences between self and others, to engage in authenticating acts redolent of personal style. Consumers are also motivated to express their shared participation in temporary emotional communities through authoritative ritualized performances. Together, these practices describe the motivational contours of behaviors that consumers employ to create a narrative sense of self. Commodification, reflexivity, and the confusion of one for the other may frustrate the objectives of both practices. Active narrative construction of self and community creates the sense of sequence, order, and individuated meanings postmodern society no longer supplies.

Authenticating acts and authoritative performances are not interchangeable. Authenticating acts emphasize self-referential behaviors, uniqueness and individuality. Although they may be fleeting moments in a life story, they can provide powerful contingent confirmation of a true self. Two types of authenticating acts illustrate the use of consumption to create agency in personal life: purchases and commodities are transformed into production, and commodities and commodified experiences are individuated through links to self-narrative.

Authoritative performances focus on creating and sustaining shared traditions and the connection between individual and community. Authoritative performances reorient the temporal perspective of participants toward the future, re-invent the past or redefine it in the interests of a shared present. Authoritative performances depend for their success on emergent idealization and active participation. Emergent idealization creates narrative order through evoked archetypes, associations and glorified recollections. Participation gives performances their authoritative voice and achieves community for those engaged.

Acknowledgments

We would like to thank Professor Beth Walker, Arizona State University, for her contributions to an ancient version of this article and to some of the original research that inspired it. Craig Thompson and Søren Askegaard both waded through a disgracefully long and untidy version of the current paper and helped us sculpt it into a more reasonable size and shape. None of these colleagues should be held responsible for the inevitable shortcomings in the final product. Eric would like to thank Linda for getting him involved in this project. Linda would like to thank Eric for insisting we bring it to closure.

References

Abrahams, R.D. (1986) "Ordinary and extraordinary experience," in V.W. Turner and E.M. Bruner (eds) *The Anthropology of Experience*, Urbana: University of Illinois Press: 45–73.

Appadurai, A. (1990) "Disjuncture and difference in the global cultural economy," in M. Featherstone (ed.) *Global Culture*, London: Sage Publications: 295–310.

Ari-Ben, E. (1991) "Transformation in ritual, transformation of ritual: audiences and rites in a Japanese commuter village," *Ethnology* (April): 135–47.

Arnould, E.J. (1998) "Daring consumer ethnography," in B.B. Stern (ed.) *Representing Consumers*, London and New York: Routledge.

Arnould, E.J. and Price, L.L. (1993) "River Magic: hedonic consumption and the extended service encounter," *Journal of Consumer Research* 20 (June): 24–45.

Arnould, E.J., Price, L.L., and Curasi, C. (1999) "Ritual longing, ritual latitude: shaping household descent," paper presented at the Conference "Consumption and Ritual," 18–21 August, Bilkent University, Ankara, Turkey.

Arnould, E.J., Price, L.L., and Tierney, P. (1998) "Communicative staging of the wilderness servicescape," *Service Industries Journal* 18 (3): 90–115.

Askegaard S. and Arnould, E.J. (1999) "Consumer acculturation of Greenlandic people in Denmark," paper presented at the 1999 European ACR Conference, 23–26 April, HEC, Jouy-es-Josas, France.

Baudrillard, J. (1983) *Simulations*, New York: Semiotext(e).

Baumeister, R.F. (1987) "How the self became a problem: a psychological review of historical research," *Journal of Personality and Social Psychology* 52 (January): 163–76.

Cameron, C.M. (1987) "The marketing of tradition: the value of culture in American life," *City and Society* 1 (December): 162–74.

Cameron, C.M. and Gatewood, J.B. (1994) "The authentic interior: questing for *gemeinschaft* in post-industrial society," *Human Organization* 53 (spring): 21–32.

Celsi, R.L., Rose, R.L., and Leigh, T. (1993) "An exploration of high risk leisure consumption through skydiving," *Journal of Consumer Research* 20 (June): 1–23.

Cheal, D. (1989) "The postmodern origin of ritual," *Journal for the Theory of Social Behavior* 18 (3): 269–90.

Cohen, E. (1988) "Authenticity and commoditization in tourism," *Annals of Tourism Research* 15: 371–86.

Cova, B. (1997) "Community and consumption: towards a definition of the 'linking value' of product or services," *European Journal of marketing* 31 (3/4): 297–316.

Csikszentmihalyi, M. (1990) *Flow: The Psychology of Optimal Experience*, New York: Harper & Row.

Cushman, P. (1990) "Why the self is empty: towards a historically situated psychology," *American Psychologist* 45 (May): 599–611.

De Certeau, M. (1984) *The Practice of Everyday Life*, trans. S. Randall, Berkeley: University of California Press.

Eisenberg, E.M. (1998) "Flirting with meaning," *Journal of Language and Social Psychology* 17 (March): 97–108

Errington, F. (1987) "Reflexivity deflected: the festival of nations as an American cultural performance," *American Ethnologist* 14 (November): 654–67.

—— (1990) "The Rock Creek Rodeo: excess and constraint in men's lives," *American Ethnologist* 17 (November): 628–45.

Ewen S. and E. Ewen (1992) *Channels of Desire: Mass Images and the Shaping of American Consciousness*, Minneapolis: University of Minnesota.

Featherstone, M. (1991) *Consumer Culture & Postmodernism*, Newbury Park, CA: Sage Publications.

Ferrara, A. (1993) *Modernity and Authenticity*, Albany, NY: State University of New York.

Firat, A.F. (1991) "The consumer in postmodernity," in R.H. Holman and M.R. Solomon (eds) *Advances in Consumer Research*, Provo, UT: Association for Consumer Research: 70–6.

Firat, A.F. and Venkatesh, A. (1995) "Liberatory postmodernism and the re-enchantment of consumption," *Journal of Consumer Research* 22 (December): 239–67.

Friedman, T.L. (1999) *The Lexus and The Olive Tree: Understanding Globalization*, New York: Farrar, Straus and Giroux.

Geertz, C. (1976) "From the natives' point of view: on the nature of anthropological understanding," in K. Basso and H. Selby (eds) *Meaning in Anthropology*, Albuquerque: University of New Mexico Press: 221–38.

Gergen, K. (1991) *The Saturated Self: Dilemmas of Identity in Contemporary Life*, New York: Basic Books.

—— (1996) "Technology and the self: from the essential to the sublime," in D. Grodin and T.R. Lindlof (eds) *Constructing the Self in a Mediated World*, Thousand Oaks, CA: Sage Publications: 127–40.

Gergen, K. and Gergen, M.K. (1988) "Narrative and the self and relationship," in L. Berkowitz (ed.) *Advances in Experimental Social Psychology*, vol. 21, San Diego: Academic Press: 17–56.

Giddens, A. (1991) *Modernity and Self-identity: Self and Society in the Late Modern Age*, Stanford, CA: Stanford University Press.

Grodin, D. and Lindlof, T.R. (eds) (1996) *Constructing the Self in a Mediated World*, Thousand Oaks: Sage Publications.

Handler, R. and Linnekin, J. (1984) "Tradition, genuine or spurious," *Journal of American Folklore* 97 (385): 273–90.

Handler, R. and Saxton, W. (1988) "Dyssimulation: reflexivity, narrative, and the quest for authenticity in 'living history,'" *Cultural Anthropology* 3 (August): 242–60.

Hermans, H. (1996) "Voicing the self: from information processing to dialogical interchange," *Psychological Bulletin* 119 (January): 31–50.

Kellner, D. (1992) "Popular culture and the construction of postmodern identities" in S. Lash and J. Friedman (eds) *Modernity and Identity*, Oxford: Basil Blackwell: 141–77.

Lasch, C. (1985) *The Minimal Self: Psychic Survival in Troubled Times*, New York: W.W. Norton & Co.

Lash, S. and Urry, J. (1987) *The End of Organized Capitalism*, Oxford: Polity Press.

Maffesoli, M. (1996) *The Time of the Tribes: The Decline of Individualism in Mass Society*, trans. D. Smith, Cambridge: Cambridge University Press.

McNamee, S. (1996) "Therapy and identity construction in a postmodern world," in D. Grodin and T.R. Lindlof (eds) *Constructing the Self in a Mediated World*, Thousand Oaks, CA: Sage Publications: 141–55.

Price, L.L. and Walker, B. (1991) " 'This is really me!' The consumer's search for the authentic self," paper presented at the Annual Meeting of Association for Consumer Research, October, Chicago: 11.

Price, L.L. and Arnould, E.J. (2000) "The meaning and production of 'homemade,'" paper presented at the AMA Winter Educator's Meetings, San Antonio, TX.

Price, L.L., Arnould, E.J., and Curasi, C. (1999) "Older consumers' disposition of valued possessions," working paper, Lincoln: University of Nebraska.

Robertson, J. (1987) "A dialectic of native and newcomer," *Anthropology Quarterly* 60 (July): 124–36.

Ségalen, M. (1998) *Rites and Rituels Contemporains*, Paris: Editions Nathans.

Smith, A.D. (1990) "Toward a global culture?" in M. Featherstone (ed.) *Global Culture*, Newbury Park, CA: Sage Publications: 171–92.

Smith, B.M. (1978) "Perspectives on selfhood," *American Psychologist* (December): 1053–63.

Stamps, M.B. and Arnould, E.J. (1998) "The Florida classic: performing African American community," in J.W. Alba and W. Hutchinson (eds) *Advances in Consumer Research*, vol. 25, Provo, UT: Association for Consumer Research: 578–84.

Swanson, G. (1985) "The powers and capabilities of selves: social and collective approaches," *Journal for the Theory of Social Behavior* 15 (October): 331–54.

Turner, R.H. (1976) "The real self: from institution to impulse," *American Journal of Sociology* 81 (March): 989–1016.

Turner, V.W. (1987) "Dewey, dilthey, and drama: an essay in the anthropology of experience," in V.W. Turner and E.M. Bruner (eds) *The Anthropology of Experience*, Urbana, IL: University of Illinois Press: 33–44.

Venkatesh, A., Sherry, J.F. Jr., and Firat, A.F. (1993) "Postmodernism and the marketing imaginary," *International Journal of Research in Marketing* 10 (August): 215–24.

Wallendorf, M. and Arnould, E.J. (1991) "'We gather together': the consumption rituals of Thanksgiving Day," *Journal of Consumer Research* 18 (June): 13–31.

Waters, M. (1995) *Globalization*, London: Routledge.

9 Representations of women's identities and goals

The past fifty years in film and television

Elizabeth C. Hirschman and Barbara B. Stern

Introduction

> Analyses have suggested that in a postmodern image culture, the images, scenes, stories, cultural texts of so-called popular culture offer a wealth of subject positions which in turn help structure individual identity. The images project role and gender models, appropriate and inappropriate forms of behavior, style, and fashion, and subtle enticements to emulate and identify with certain subject positions while avoiding others.
>
> (Kellner 1991: 177)

One of the primary projects of feminism, from the 1950s onward, has been to make women aware of how cultural representations influence gender identities. Writers from Freidan (1963) and Greer (1971) to Wolf (1991) and Faludi (1991) have argued that how women are depicted in mass-media vehicles such as motion pictures, television shows, newspaper accounts and advertisements can affect the goals women set for themselves in terms of relationships, careers and appearance.

Reader response (Fetterley 1978) and postmodern theorists (Culler 1982; Derrida 1974 [1986]) propose that women are free to pick and choose among the pantheon of female images available, constructing a bricolage identity that combines desired attributes from a cross-section of representations (see Hirschman and Thompson 1997 and Thompson and Tambyeh 2000 for reviews of this position). While this position is supported by empirical evidence (see, e.g., Hirschman and Thompson 1997), it is important not to lose sight of the fact that women must pick and choose from the bounded collection of those images that are culturally available at a given point in time. Thus, women's identities, and hence their goals, desires and motives, are determined by the representations accessible during particular historic periods. Yet few studies have examined the stock-of-images at hand during different epochs. After first reviewing ancient images of women, we shall show how these have been carried forward in mass-media portrayals during the past sixty years.

People have constructed representations of women since prehistoric times (Campbell 1970a, 1970b, 1973; Leeming 1990), and archaeologists believe that female figures were the first embodiments of divine power (Campbell 1973; Leeming 1990). In Gimbutas' *The Language of the Goddess* (1989) a survey of Neolithic female representations includes images of women as Nurturant Goddesses who promote life and health, provide material goods, protect human life and the home, and serve as wise guides and seers. Coexisting with these images are those of women as Destructive Goddesses who wield death and destruction, using violence or natural disasters (storms, fire, earthquakes) to destroy life and property.

The later cultures of Sumer and Akkad (2500 BC) divided generic goddess attributes into birth givers versus life destroyers, among whom were maidens/virgins, seductresses/whores, fairy godmothers, and hags/crones/ witches. As noted above, we will show that this pantheon of female representations continues to inform current images of women, which play two vital roles in contemporary culture. First, these images contribute to the ideological content of mass produced and mass consumed media products such as television shows, motion pictures, novels, plays, and advertisements (Schroeder and Borgerson 1998). Second, these same images serve as the ideological backdrop against which individual lives are played out. As women, we are embedded within a larger cultural template that shapes our expectations about who women are and what women do. That is, women's sense of their goals, desires, and motives as humans – and as consumers – are influenced by contemporary redactions of ancient female imagery.

Our purpose is to examine these images in selected popular movies and television shows of the past sixty years and to discuss how they may have helped mold women's goals and identities during a given time period. This chapter uses a subset of data gathered for a larger study (Hirschman 2000) previously used in a gender-based sub-study focused on images of men (Hirschman 1999). The full data set consists of the top fifty motion pictures (measured by box office receipts) and the top thirty-five television shows (measured by Nielsen statistics) in the United States since 1939. The analytical method is structural-syntactical analysis (see Hirschman 1988), with special emphasis on bi-polar oppositional patterns and Jungian archetypes (Campbell 1970a; Jung 1958, 1959, 1967, 1968). Our analysis traces the availability of various women's representations decade by decade.

The 1930s and 1940s

Three films from the 1930s were among the century's most popular and present a cross-section of the images available during that time period: *Snow White and the Seven Dwarfs* (1937), a Disney studios animated feature; *Fantasia* (1939), a second Disney animated film; and *Gone With the Wind* (1939). *Snow White* portrays two female characters in opposition to one another: the first, Snow White, represents the Nurturant Goddess and virginity. She embodies romantic and courtly images from the Middle Ages, in which a passive princess is endowed with beauty, gentleness, and kindness and is given a life-sustaining mission (Campbell 1970b). Snow White also serves as catalyst for civilization among the seven male dwarfs who adopt her in the forest. Her opposite is the evil, vain, and powerful Queen/Stepmother, who transforms herself into a hag/witch and uses black magic to concoct a sleeping potion (symbolizing Death) for Snow White. In the Disney version, the hag is destroyed by nature (a violent thunderstorm), and Snow White is restored to life by the prince's kiss.

These oppositional roles vivify the ideology of female fertility, for Snow White is a young woman in training for the Nurturant Goddess roles of wife and mother. In contrast, the Queen is a dessicated old woman, mateless, and bent on destroying her potential successor. Her ability to transform herself into a hag/witch and concoct poisons signifies her role as Destructive Goddess. Nonetheless, the story teaches us that nature, the all-powerful female deity, champions life over death, for the Destructive Goddess is herself destroyed, allowing the young woman to marry, mate, and procreate. This story clearly plays to women's traditional roles as mothers and caretakers.

Even though *Fantasia* (1940) has no overarching plot – it is a series of vignettes – it features several significant female images. In one sequence, the feminine aspect of nature is represented by diaphanous goldfish with large dark eyes and petite red mouths and sprightly fairies with lithe nude bodies and gossamer wings. Here Nature is equated with Mother Earth, the fertile womb from which all life springs (Gimbutas 1989), while womanhood is presented as delicate and diminutive, reminiscent of medieval womanhood in the courtly love literature (Campbell 1970a).

However, 1939 also witnessed a profoundly different media role model, one who foretells the androgynous woman of a generation later (albeit in a decidely negative form) – Scarlett O'Hara in *Gone With the Wind*. Set in the Civil War, a time of cataclysmic social change, *Gone With the Wind* presents the demise of the courtly love ideals of masculinity and femininity. The chivalric man, Ashley Wilkes, and his passive princess mate, Melanie Hamilton, give way as icons to two Modern/Industrial Age characters – Scarlett O'Hara and Rhett Butler. Scarlett merges the Nurturant Goddess and Destructive Goddess into a single all-powerful female deity who can create and destroy life, both helping and harming humanity. In this sense, she is a reincarnation of the Mesolithic Great Goddess (Gimbutas 1989) and a forerunner of the androgynous women of the 1980s and 1990s. Unfortunately, although Scarlett is portrayed as powerful and successful, she is crippled as a desirable role model by her barrenness and vanity. Women of this period were warned by her example that if they ventured too far from the passive princess identity, they risked losing home and family.

The 1950s

The disempowerment of women was aided and abetted by most media images from the 1950s and 1960s. We consider two iconic characters –

Sleeping Beauty and Lucy in *I Love Lucy*. The Disney animated film *Sleeping Beauty* (1959) appeared twenty years after *Snow White*, but is essentially a reprise of the medieval Nurturant Goddess who is beautiful, kind, and passive. The story, drawn from the Grimm's compilation of Germanic folk tales, begins when Aurora, a royal princess, is betrothed at birth to Phillip, the infant son of a neighboring king. Three good fairies – Flora, Fauna and Merriweather – represent the female attributes of beauty and song, with which they endow Aurora. They are prevented from adding a third gift by Maleficent, the evil female fairy who represents the Destructive Goddess analogous to the evil Queen/ Stepmother in *Snow White*. She places a curse on Aurora, declaring that at age 16 (the cusp of womanhood) she will prick her finger on a spinning wheel spindle and die. The remaining good fairy has the power to adjust the curse from death to sleep, with the caveat that Aurora can only be awakened by her true love's kiss.

Aurora closely resembles Snow White, for both are young girls cast as beautiful but passive pawns caught in a power struggle between the positive and negative aspects of female power – nurturance versus destructiveness. Aurora is saved by the heroism of Prince Phillip, who challenges Maleficent to battle, during which Maleficent transforms herself into a fire-breathing dragon. Phillip – armed with the shield of justice and the sword of virtue – is able to defeat her. The movie displays beauty, nurturance, and passivity as desirable womanly goals and encourages protection by a brave and chivalrous male suitor, a formula constructed during the Middle Ages and still applicable.

The Passive Princess of the 1950s was joined by another popular female figure who debuted in a 1952 television series, *I Love Lucy*. However, Lucy fit none of the traditional female representations for she was neither Nurturant nor Destructive; Lucy was not vain and materialistic like Scarlett O'Hara, nor passive and virginal like Snow White and Sleeping Beauty. Further, her habitual costume – she often wore slacks rather than dresses – indicated that she was rather asexual. It is this asexuality that sustains her status as the first female exemplar of a comedic archetype more often associated with males (Jerry Lewis, Jim Carrey) – the enfant terrible or misbehaving child.

In one of the show's most memorable episodes, Lucy and Ethel begin work at a candy factory – and end by stuffing their clothes and mouths with chocolate, just like children in a sweet shop. Lucy's comedic persona fit into the 1950s chauvinistic mindset that relegated women to childish roles as silly creatures in need of constant supervision, unable to manage money or to understand life in the real world, irrational and subject to emotional whims and excesses.

The 1960s

The 1960s featured two popular television shows which continued the Nurturant Goddess image – *The Dick Van Dyke Show* and *Bewitched*. Both shows depicted the white, suburban, middle-class lifestyle, with attractive, stay-at-home suburban wives as the aspirational goal for American women. In the *Dick Van Dyke Show*, Laura Petrie (Mary Tyler Moore) often used her intuition to foresee problems or predict events, thus revitalizing women's ancient representations as seers and prophetesses. However, the pagan belief in women's magical powers had long since been coopted by Catholic and Puritan theology, which transformed the concept of women magicians into that of women witches. Witches were considered consorts of the Devil, and their magical powers viewed as evil. By the 1960s, the witch image had been recategorized as less malign, enabling Samantha, the heroine of *Bewitched*, to be portrayed as a "good" witch.

Like the Nurturant Goddess, she was not only beautiful, kind, and caring, but also a woman with supernatural abilities in regard to natural phenomena. Samantha was immortal, able to fly and move objects, create wind, fire, rain, and thunder, and transform humans into animals and vice versa.

The image of a powerful Destructive Goddess reappeared in Disney's *101 Dalmatians*, where Cruella DeVille's self-centered vanity, violence, and power were analogous to *Sleeping Beauty's* Maleficent and *Snow White's* Queen/Stepmother. This time, instead of magical power, the modernized version wields great wealth to wreak havoc. But like her predecessors, she is cruel to the young – in this case the Dalmatian puppies whose skin she intends to use for a fur coat. Once again, women are instructed that if they seek material wealth and power, they risk losing their suitability as wives and mothers and becoming transformed into ugly witches.

The pendulum swung between Nurturant and Destructive Goddesses throughout the 1960s, a time when American culture veered between oppositional role models for women. Julie Andrews portrayed two memorable Nurturant Goddesses in *Mary Poppins* and *The Sound of Music*, in which she was a Heaven-sent female figure who transformed dysfunctional families into harmonious ones. In, *Mary Poppins*, she teaches the father and mother to pay less attention to work and politics and more to their children and each other. In *The Sound of Music*, Maria, a former nun, becomes a mother-figure who transforms the household from one ruled by paternal military discipline into one softened by kindness and caring. Once again, desirable women's goals are depicted as revolving around the maternal and caregiver roles.

The end of the 1960s was defined by Mrs Robinson (*The Graduate*), another Destructive Goddess who provides us with a searing image of what an aging, alcoholic Scarlet O'Hara might look like. In 1967, when *The Graduate* was released, Mrs Robinson (Ann Bancroft) symbolized female sexual sophistication – a 40-ish woman with streaked blonde hair, glamorous clothes, and an ever-present cigarette. She is the first modern Destructive Goddess who openly expresses sexual wilfullness, perhaps as a result of the emerging Feminist movement's challenge to the Passive Princess stereotype and demand for sexual liberation (Schroeder and Borgerson 1998).

Although feminist ideas hardly penetrate the movie, there is some modification of the core male and female representations. The princess remains a passive virgin willing to let her parents and boyfriend determine the outcome of her life, but, the prince is a minority male (Jewish), and able to be corrupted by Mrs R's offers of sex, alcohol, and cigarettes.

However, the major modification is the character of Mrs Robinson. When the film first appeared, audiences found her a frightening figure of what a woman should *not* become – a country club version of the fairy tale witch, oozing predatory sexuality, drinking alcohol and smoking cigarettes. However, we (the authors) now view Mrs Robinson as a misogynistic cultural stereotype. Even though she is said to be an alcoholic, we do not see her behaving like one – she is never drunk or out-of-control. Rather, she is presented as a powerful sexual predator who happens to drink and smoke. The moviemakers constructed a sexualized witch out of American fears of powerful women – the cigarette smoke is Mrs Robinson's witch's fire, the liquor her magic potion, and the expensive lingerie and erotic body the source of her power to corrupt men.

But recall that it is the prince who calls Mrs. Robinson to arrange their first date; who regularly has sex with her; and who dumps her immediately after an innocent date with her beautiful daughter. Whereas 1960s audiences despised and feared Mrs Robinson, we see her as a repository of failed dreams, a prisoner of a patriarchal system that defined women in terms of 'marrying well' and staying married, and a sex-starved wife whose husband's lack of interest forces her to turn to liquor, cigarettes, and the pursuit of young men. In many ways, we now see Mrs Robinson as more the victim, than the villain. She represents the 'unhappily-ever-after' version of the discarded passive princess.

The 1970s

The 1970s were a watershed decade when women's long submerged goals of sexual liberation and careers beyond marriage "came out of the closet" and were openly displayed. One of the decade's most popular films, *The Exorcist* (1973), merged sexual liberation with mythological motifs of Good and Evil. Here, a working mother takes her virginal twelve-year-old daughter on a business trip, where a demonic spirit transforms the girl from a budding Nurturant Goddess to a violent, profane, sexually aggressive Destructive one. Although the demon is eventually exorcised, the priests who perform the rites die. On a metaphoric level, the transformed girl represented our society's deepest fears about the potential of women's sexuality to transform innocent girls into man-devouring monsters.

By the second half of the 1970s, more positive portrayals of the liberated woman emerged. Even though *Star Wars* (1977) featured three men as main characters – Luke Skywalker, Han Solo, and Darth Vader – it also presented a competent, intelligent, courageous (and beautiful) female character –

Princess Leia. Of the four, Leia is the most consistently reasonable and professional: she organizes troops, oversees a government, formulates strategy, and deploys resources. In short, she is an excellent *manager*, a goal that only a decade before was depicted as inappropriate for women.

Nonetheless, Leia was asexual, and it was not until 1978 that the film *Grease* showed the transformation of a Passive Princess into a sexually liberated spirit of the 1970s. *Grease* breaks with the longstanding iconic tradition of Active Prince/Passive Princess by depicting the heroine not only as a classic nurturant goddess – beautiful, demure, well-bred, and shy – but also as sexually uninhibited. Unlike previous princesses guarding their virginity until a proposal of marriage, Sandy parades her sexuality in public. The abandonment of passive virginity as the appropriate goal for women represents a major shift in the popular culture of the 1970s after which women were never the same – at least on film and television.

Two television shows exemplified the change – *Laverne and Shirley* and *Three's Company*. The first was set in the 1950s and 1960s and featured two working-class single women who shared a basement apartment and worked at a brewery. The show located 1970s issues of women's economic freedom and sexuality in a "bygone" era, which defused contemporary anxieties and enabled an exploration of the feminist issues of job success and dating. Rather than emphasizing women's destructive competition for men and money, the show focused on women's cooperativeness and mutual support.

The 1970s ended with a sexual "bang," not a whimper, in the "swinging seventies" production of *Three's Company*. The show featured over-the-top characterizations of two young women and a young man rooming together in a Los Angeles condominium. Even though its ostensible aim was the exploration of changing male–female relations, most of the episodes featured one-night stands, breast-and-pickle humor, disco dancing, and the typical 1970s stud in gold neck chains, open-necked shirts, and flared polyester pants.

Still, despite its shallowness and gross humor, the show did expose cultural uneasiness about gender and sexuality. Women's goals were changing, for now women as well as men worked at jobs that paid enough to permit partying on weekends. Economic independence was necessary, though not sufficient, for women to be freed from the conservatism of earlier generations. A paycheck plus more accessible birth control methods contributed to providing women with personal goals and identities that were historically novel.

The 1980s

By the end of the 1970s, political and social unrest had calmed: the Vietnam War was over; the leaders of the radical left and Black Power movements were dead, retired, or imprisoned; and student rebels, both male and female, were married and working. However, social uneasiness about changing gender goals grew in proportion to the increasing numbers of women entering the workforce, which raised the possibility of female masculinization and corresponding male feminization.

Ironically, Dustin Hoffman, the actor portraying the prince in the *The Graduate*, was again the symbol of contemporary manhood, this time in *Tootsie* (1982), where he played a character in search of sexual identity. His quest is played out in terms of the Jungian archetypes of femininity (anima) and masculinity (animus), posited to exist in every human regardless of biological sex. Jung argued that the goal of human completeness required integration of the anima and animus, a process that could be achieved in one of two ways. The first is the traditional Passive Princess and Heroic Prince model, in which the woman's anima and man's animus were united when they formed a couple. The alternative way is the modern androgynous model in which each man and woman develops both his/her anima and animus and then mates (unites) with a similarly developed member of the opposite sex.

Dustin Hoffman's character, Michael Dorsey, represents the 1980s version of androgyny. He is an unemployed actor (a profession that itself requires frequent role-shifting) whose lack of success is due to his rebellion against conventional stereotypes. He is an animus-driven social misfit searching for the right goal in life and work. In a rebellious effort to prove his acting talent, Michael tries out for the role of a woman in a television soap opera. He adopts the apparel, hairstyle, and voice inflection of a woman and changes his name to Dorothy Michaels.

When Michael takes on the woman's role, his long-dormant anima begins to develop and he starts viewing the world as a woman would. As Dorothy, Michael falls in love with Julie (Jessica Lange), who is in many ways an inversion of the traditional passive princess: she is self-supporting, financially well off, and a single mother, all of which suggest she has a developing animus. However, her animus is still embryonic, for she is sexually involved with the show's producer, a domineering, abusive man. Thus, the movie presents a man with a developing anima and a woman with developing animus who are emotionally drawn to each other.

Tootsie then takes the examination of personal goals to a subtler level. Julie's anima is attracted to Dorothy's animus, for she trusts "Dorothy" precisely because she believes him to be a self-reliant woman. She wants a friendly relationship with a strong woman so that she can continue to develop her own animus and free herself from dependence on masculine men. In this, she is the mirror image of Dorothy's newly developed anima which is attracted to Julie's animus. Michael as a woman is able to feel feminine attachment and romantic love and to admire Julie's independence. Drawing strength from Dorothy/Michael's animus, Julie breaks up with the abusive producer and becomes independent enough to complete her own animus.

Tootsie reveals new aspects of the 1980s reconstruction of masculine/feminine identities and goals. To begin, the film suggests that people who seek to complete themselves by developing only their traditional gender-consistent identities and then finding a complementary opposite-sex partner are likely to be unsuccessful. The reason is that the sea-change in sex roles made it now culturally inappropriate to be an all-animus man or all-anima woman. The correlative is that those who first complete themselves by developing both their anima and animus, regardless of gender, are more likely to succeed in developing a relationship with a similar fully-developed person. By the 1980s, mainstream cultural representations suggested that two half-people cannot form a successful couple – only two whole people can. Androgyny became the preferred goal for both men and women.

Consistent with *Tootsie*, television representations of women were generally androgynous during the 1980s. Women held a variety of blue collar and professional jobs; some were wives and mothers; all displayed varying degrees of androgyny. In *Dynasty*, the most fearsome female figure is Alexis Colby Carrington, a fertile (four children) reincarnation of Scarlett O'Hara. She is beautiful, competitive, intelligent, materialistic, and utterly ruthless in achieving her goals as a woman and a business mogul. Like her vain predecessor, Alexis is always fashionably dressed; however, unlike Scarlett, Alexis is shown to be capable of successful mothering, often advancing her children's careers in her corporate enterprises. Even though her portrayal suggests that powerful – even unscrupulous – female executives can still be effective parents, her multiple divorces suggest that she is unable to form a lasting relationship with a man. Perhaps from a radical feminist perspective Alexis did not really need a man because she was fully self-sufficient and when she wanted sex, she found desirable men readily available.

Later in the 1980s, two television programs echoed the domestic settings of situation comedies decades earlier: *The Cosby Show* and *Roseanne*. Like *I Love Lucy* and *The Dick Van Dyke Show*, these programs illustrated life in the American family, albeit remarkably different ones. *The Cosby Show* is the more traditional, but it reflects cultural changes in identitites and goals since the 1960s *Dick Van Dyke Show*. First, Mom and Dad are different: Mom works as a lawyer, and even though Dad also works, he is directly involved in parenting. Second, Mom and Dad are African-Americans, not WASPs – evidence of the 1970s turn toward multiculturalism.

However, some things remain the same: each episode presents a family problem such as dating, grades, or money, that must be resolved. Now that mother, father and children tackle problems on an equitable basis, parental responsibility and family decision-making are shared rather than paternally controlled. *The Cosby Show* presents models of healthy child–parent and husband–wife relationships that exemplify respected values in our culture. Cliff and Claire Huxtable serve as a visible set of icons for a newly enlarged cultural constituency; they demonstrate that African-Americans can have creative and demanding careers, be loving parents, and enable their children to become productive, happy individuals.

Like the Huxtables, the Connors in *Roseanne* must cope with issues of child rearing and family cohesion, but unlike them, must do so with less money and more frustration. The Connor household typifies present-day blue collar life in a small town. Dan Connor (John Goodman) is a skilled worker who has lost his job running a bicycle shop. To support the family, his wife, Roseanne (Roseanne Barr), has opened a restaurant with the help of her mother and unmarried sister. The Connors have two children: Darlene, a brilliant, depressive 16-year-old with liberal ideals and literary talent and D.J., a lovable 12-year-old whose doltishness resembles his father's.

The Connors and the Huxtables represent different visions of the American family. The Huxtables embody the American Dream – the belief that if one works hard, acts honestly and perseveres, one can achieve any goal. The Connors embody the dark side of the dream – not everyone is able to grab the golden ring.

The 1990s

By the 1990s, women motivated by androgynous goals were commonplace in television and motion pictures. Popular shows such as *E.R.*, *Seinfeld*, and *Friends* featured women in a variety of professional and domestic roles. Women were portrayed as equal partners in relationships at work and home, where they were decision-makers in matters critical (how to save an accident victim's life) and trivial (how to bake a lasagna).

One measure of women's liberation from traditional social constraints was the increasing representation of heroines who were no longer "merely" young princesses. When former Vice-President Dan Quayle criticized Murphy Brown's out-of-wedlock birth, the rejoinder – that Murphy was not a 'real' woman, but a fictional character – was less relevant than the fact that she was a fully functional adult. Murphy Brown was a significant departure from the traditional female image, and her actions, however fictive, did count. The public discussion of *Murphy Brown* demonstrated unequivocally that popular television shows and movies are powerful forms of representation able to influence social mores and personal goals.

At the end of the 1991 season, Murphy is pregnant but unmarried, and faced with the decision either to get an abortion or have the baby out of wedlock. She chooses the latter, and the opening 1992 episode begins with Murphy's interviews of nannies to care for her new-born son, so that she can resume her career as a television investigative reporter. A nice competent nanny is scared off by Murphy's paranoid questions and her lament about having to leave her infant with a stranger. When Murphy returns to work, she is disheveled and dressed in pajamas; her explanation is that she feels overwhelmed and incompetent at motherhood. Her friend Jim tells her that she is lucky that times have changed for the better – at least she wasn't stoned for having an illegitimate child! When her friend Frank comes to visit, he has to teach her how to hold and rock the baby, and she takes notes on his lesson. The note-taking illustrates her masculine side, as well as the feelings of incompetence common to all new mothers.

Later in the episode, Murphy's news station features a clip of Dan Quayle stating that she "glamorizes single motherhood," followed by clips of the real-world media debate generated by Quayle's comments. In response, Murphy invites several non-traditional families, including ones with single parents, to appear on her program; she tells the audience: "Families come in all shapes and sizes; they are based on commitment and love." Murphy's behavior illustrates well the evolution of women's images and identities across 40 years of television from ditsy housewives (*I Love Lucy*) to competent, self-sufficient media professionals (*Murphy Brown*).

The most remarkable program in this respect is *Murder, She Wrote*, starring Angela Lansbury, which was one of the top ten television series from 1984 until 1995. What is especially striking is that its heroine, Jessica Fletcher, is a middle-aged mystery writer who has neither husband nor family, does not work in an office or live an apartment building filled with interesting people, and behaves neither like a warrior-goddess nor a superwoman. Instead, she roves from crime scene to crime scene using her intelligence to identify criminals. Jessica is the female version of the 'wise old man/ guide/seer' archetype. Rather than enforcing law and order as a warrior would, she advises and counsels law enforcement officials, who are invariably fixated on the wrong culprit. The series is innovative not only in terms of feminizing the wise guide, but also in featuring women criminals. It displays both constructive and destructive women, often older, and even features one episode in which the youngest male and female characters are in their fifties. Unlike earlier series, this one does not "disappear" people over fifty.

A cinematic representation that exemplifies the 1990s version of androgyny is Sarah Connor in *Terminator II* (1990). At the outset, Sarah is locked in a high security psychiatric facility because she believes that machines/computers are destined to take over the world and destroy human life. Her belief is well-founded, because in an earlier film, the original *Terminator* (1983), she was visited by a handsome young warrior from the future who impregnated her with a son, John, now 13 years old. At that time, her lover and several others were killed by an android-machine – the Terminator – who had also come from the future.

In the sequel, Sarah is intent on saving the world – and her son – by preventing technological Armageddon. She frees herself from the psychiatric institution and enlists the aid of her son and a helpful Terminator to do battle with an apparently indestructible molten-metal machine capable of assuming human form. Sarah displays courage, compassion, physical strength, ingenuity, competence at weaponry, and commitment to her goal – in short, she embodies the Great Goddess figure described by Gimbutas (1989).

Note that the modifiers "Destructive" or "Nurturant" are unneeded, for Sarah is both. She represents "the mythological One Great Goddess who is all-powerful – she controls life, regeneration, renewal, and death" (Gimbutas 1989: 318). The character of Sarah Connor is all of these; she embodies both the Good Mother who protects and nurtures her child and puts his needs above her own survival, as well as being a courageous warrior, an Amazon who competently employs the destructive technology which is usually the province of men – guns, bombs, fists, cars, trucks, and grenades – to advance her humanitarian agenda. In her most essential form, Sarah is nature personified: the life-giving and life-destroying figure who sustains life itself. A millenial figure, Sarah represents the return to humanity's mythological roots – the archetypal female who combines the diverse aspects of femininity and masculinity into a single figure.

Another memorable 1990s heroine also encapsulates the goals, desires, and motives of women over the past sixty years: Rose in *Titanic*. When the movie begins, Rose seems to be a classic passive princess: beautiful, well-bred, virginal, and betrothed to a wealthy, handsome prince. Yet unlike Snow White or Sleeping Beauty, she is despondent, unwilling merely to marry well and live happily ever after in a Victorian castle. Rose is willful, intelligent, and passionate, intent on following her emotional and sexual desires by choosing her own lover, a penniless commoner. She wants to see the world and live freely, abandoning the passive princess identity, and jumping ship (literally) so that she can recreate herself.

Rose's movement toward her goal evokes the evolution of women's representations over the twentieth century. In early films such as *Snow White* and *Sleeping Beauty*, women were shown to be normatively confined to the domestic sphere. When a prince risked his life to rescue a princess, she was saved only for a life as his wife. During the lengthy "happily ever after" period, the princess-cum-wife was expected to sacrifice her goals and aspirations by assuming a subservient role as caretaker for the prince's career. *Titanic* turned this traditional fairy tale upside down by showing the princess's lover, Jack, sacrificing *his* life for *her* career. This film is the first one in which the princess's goals are given preference, perhaps an explanation for its popularity among young women, the majority of repeat-viewers.

We have come a tremendous distance in the representation of women's goals and identities. From 1939 to 1999 we have witnessed the joining of formerly-masculine with formerly-feminine properties to create a powerful and positive image of womanhood. Yet remarkably, we have journeyed back in time, as well. Back to the ancient origins of female representation which incorporated life-giving, life-destroying elements into one all-powerful figure: the Great Goddess. Our hope is that from here forward women's goals will be directed toward achieving this identity for themselves – an identity of fullness, completion and integration.

References

Campbell, J. (1970a) "Mythological themes in creative literature and art," in Joseph Campbell (ed.) *Myths, Dreams, and Religion* New York: E.P. Dutton.

_____ (1970b) *Myths, Dreams, and Religion*, New York: E.P. Dutton.

_____ (1973) *Creative Mythology: The Masks of God*, New York: Penguin Books.

Culler, J. (1982) *Theory and Criticism after Structuralism*, Ithaca, NY: Cornell University Press.

Derrida, J. (1974 [1986]) *Glas*, trans. J.P. Leavey, Jr. and R. Rand, Lincoln: University of Nebraska Press.

Faludi, S. (1991) *Backlash: The Undeclared War Against American Women*, New York: Crown.

Fetterley, J. (1978) *The Resisting Reader: A Feminist Approach to American Fiction*, Bloomington: Indiana University Press.

Friedan, B. (1963) *The Feminine Mystique*, New York: Bantam Books.

Gimbutas, M. (1989) *The Language of the Goddess*, San Francisco: Harper and Row.

Greer, G. (1971) *The Female Eunuch*, New York: McGraw-Hill.

Hirschman, E.C. (1988) "The ideology of consumption: a structural-syntactical analysis of 'Dallas' and 'Dynasty'," *Journal of Consumer Research* 15 (December): 344–59.

—— (1999) "The meanings of men," *Semiotica* 37 (spring): 161–82.

—— (2000) *Heroes, Monsters and Messiahs: The Mythology of Highly Successful Motion Pictures and Television Shows*, Kansas City, MO: Andrews-McMeel.

Jung, C.G. (1958) *Psychology and Religion*, New York and London: Hogarth.

—— (1959) *The Archetypes and the Collective Unconscious*, trans. by R.F.C. Hull, Princeton, NJ: Princeton University Press.

—— (1967) *Symbols of Transformation*, trans. by R.F.C. Hull, Princeton, NJ: Princeton University Press.

—— (1968) *Man and His Symbols*, New York: Dell Books.

Kellner, D. (1991) "Popular culture and the construction of postmodern identities," in S. Lash and J. Friedman (eds) *Modernity & Identity*, London: Blackwell: 141–77.

Leeming, D.A. (1990) *The World of Myth*, New York: Oxford University Press.

Schroeder, J.E. and Borgerson, J.L. (1998) "Marketing images of gender: a visual analysis," *Consumption, Markets and Culture* 2 (2): 161–201.

Wolf, N. (1991) *The Beauty Myth: How Images of Beauty are Used Against Women*, New York: W. Morrow.

10 The urge to buy

A uses and gratifications perspective on compulsive buying

Ronald J. Faber

Although compulsive buying was first reported in the psychiatric literature in the early part of the twentieth century (Kraepelin 1915; Bleuler 1924), the vast majority of our knowledge regarding this problem has emerged in the past decade. During this time, compulsive buying has been studied by researchers from a range of disciplines, and through a number of different research techniques. What has emerged is a realization that this problem can stem from a variety of causes and may take on several different forms. This is consistent with research across a number of various addictive or excessive behaviors that suggest that each disorder can serve many different functions for different individuals or even for a single person (Orford 1985).

This chapter will attempt to examine the different motivations that may lead someone to become a compulsive buyer and the various gratifications that the behavior can serve. In doing so, a uses and gratifications framework borrowed from research in mass communications will be employed. This model is concerned with the reasons why people engage in a behavior as well as their antecedents and consequences. Consistent with the framework of this book, it is suggested here that compulsive buying may occur as a result of different motivations and that these differing motivations may be related to different underlying causes and result in differential behavior patterns.

Compulsive buying

Compulsive buying has commonly been characterized as involving an irresistible urge to buy or shop which leads to spending far more time than intended and/or purchasing more than can be afforded or needed (Goldsmith and McElroy, in press; McElroy *et al.* 1994). This behavior leads to a temporary reduction in tension for compulsive buyers, but ultimately results in social and/or financial problems (Christenson *et al.* 1994; McElroy *et al.* 1994; Valence *et al.* 1988).

Compulsive buying has been variously viewed as an addiction, an obsessive-compulsive disorder, an impulse control disorder, an affective-spectrum disorder, or an extreme form of normal buying. Indeed, debate has raged in the compulsive buying literature regarding the most appropriate way to categorize this phenomenon (Nataraajan and Goff 1991). Some researchers view compulsive buying as representing one side of a normal continuum of buying behavior (d'Astous 1990; Dittmar, in press; Nataraajan and Goff 1991). For example, Nataraajan and Goff (1991) suggested that all buyer behaviors can be categorized in a four-fold table with control and motive as the two dimensions. People in the low control, high motive cell are labeled as compulsive buyers.

Other researchers view compulsive buying as a qualitatively different phenomenon from normal buying (O'Guinn and Faber 1989; McElroy *et al.* 1994). This approach is taken by most of the researchers viewing compulsive buying from a medical perspective. The disorder is seen as related to a broader spectrum of psychiatric disorders each having many characteristics in common. Those who support the notion that compulsive buying is qualitatively different from normal buying see the motivations behind this behavior as stemming from these common psychiatric characteristics and unrelated to a functional desire for the item purchased. To support this belief, several researchers have pointed out the comorbidity, or co-occurrence, of several different disorders in the same individual or in the same biological family. For example, compulsive buying is significantly more common among women suffering from binge eating disorder than for a similar weight non-bingeing group. Additionally, binge eating is more common among compulsive buyers than in a matched control group (Christenson *et al.* 1994; Faber *et al.* 1995; McElroy *et al.* 1994). Compulsive buyers have also been reported to have higher than average levels of alcoholism, drug addiction, pathological gambling, and kleptomania (Christenson *et al.* 1994; McElroy *et al.* 1994; Schlosser *et al.* 1994).

The belief that there is a difference between people who are at the high-end of normal consumption and those who might be termed "true compulsive buyers" is also consistent with results from efforts to identify different clusters of compulsive buyers (DeSarbo and Edwards 1996). This study found a 2-cluster solution was optimal. Cluster 1 seems most characteristic of compulsive buyers and people with other addictions or impulse control disorders. They tended to have low self-esteem, and greater dependence and anxiety. The second cluster seemed more motivated by impulsiveness and materialism. These people resemble people who are more likely to be at the high-end of normal consumption rather than driven to buy because of deeper needs.

The viewpoint adopted in this chapter is most consistent with a psychiatric perspective of compulsive buying. However, it will also attempt to explain the motivations behind people who engage in excessive buying because they are at the high-end of a normal buying continuum. In some cases, these high-end normal buyers may share common attributes and motivations with people who are true compulsive buyers. In other cases, however, the buying motivations of high-end normal consumers and those with a compulsive buying disorder will differ.

Characteristics of compulsive buyers

Consistent with research in other areas of addiction and excessive behavior, compulsive buying has been viewed as emerging from a biopsychosocial model (Faber 1992). This model assumes that these excessive behaviors stem from multiple factors rather than from one common cause. Some compulsive buyers may, therefore, share some traits in common, while others have different traits. The factors thought to influence compulsive buying include biological conditions, psychological characteristics, and sociological circumstances. Prior work has suggested that elements of each may be related to compulsive buying (Elliot 1994; Faber 1992; McElroy *et al.* 1991; Scherhorn, Reisch, and Raab 1990).

A number of commonalties have emerged across different studies of compulsive buyers. For example, several studies have found that compulsive buyers have low levels of self-esteem (Elliott 1994; O'Guinn and Faber 1989; Scherhorn *et al.* 1990). Compulsive buyers have also been found to have higher than average levels of depression (Christenson *et al.* 1994; Schlosser *et al.* 1994) and anxiety (Christenson *et al.* 1994; Scherhorn *et al.* 1990). Similar findings have emerged from studies of people with other forms of addictions or impulse control disorders (Marlatt *et al.* 1988; Mitchell 1990). However, it is unclear whether these factors are potential causes of compulsive buying or are consequences of this problem.

While commonalties appear to exist in compulsive buyers, there also appears to be differences in the way the behavior is manifested. Some compulsive buyers have a need to go shopping and/or buy something everyday. They feel tense and anxious on days they don't go shopping (O'Guinn and Faber 1989). Others engage in episodic compulsive buying, ranging from several times a week to only a few times each year (Christenson *et al.* 1994; Schlosser *et al.* 1994). Although most compulsive buyers state that they experience an uncontrollable urge to purchase something, some experience an urge to shop, but do not feel compelled to buy. The majority of compulsive buyers report these urges are undesirable and intrusive and lead to a mounting tension that can only be relieved by shopping or making a purchase (Christenson *et al.* 1994; McElroy *et al.* 1994). However, others do not experience it in this way. Some, but certainly not all, compulsive buyers report making multiple purchases of specific items, such as eight tee-shirts or three raincoats at one time (Christenson *et al.* 1994; O'Guinn and Faber 1989). Most compulsive buyers primarily buy just for themselves, but a small subgroup buys almost exclusively for other people (Faber, O'Guinn, and Krych 1987). The fact that the behavior appears in different forms suggests the possibility that there may be different motivations creating different types of compulsive buying behaviors.

Uses and gratifications

The uses and gratifications model has been successfully employed to study the motivations behind people's choices in media use and the success of these choices in meeting underlying needs. More specifically, the uses and gratifications model has been said to be concerned with: "(1) the social and psychological origins of (2) needs, which generate (3) expectations of (4) the mass-media or other sources, which lead to (5) differential patterns of media exposure (or engagement in other activities), resulting in (6) need gratifications and (7) other consequences, perhaps mostly unintended ones" (Katz, Blumler, and Gurevitch 1974: 20). This model assumes that media use (and other activities) plays a functional role for people. They engage in activities in order to try to achieve desired goals.

Although developed to explain mass media consumption, the model suggests that it can be used to analyze other activities or behaviors (including compulsive buying). Using this perspective, compulsive buying may be viewed as serving a functional need for individuals. This problematic behavior therefore stems from the expectations compulsive buyers develop regarding shopping's ability to meet needs that have their origin in the social and psychological background of the individual. Seen in this light, compulsive buying which is frequently perceived by the public as a "dumb" or "foolish" behavior that an individual should be able to control, may, instead, be seen as motivated by the functional needs it meets even though it ultimately leads to "unintended" negative effects. Uses and gratifications research has gone through several stages in its development. In its earliest stage, it was primarily concerned with determining why people used different media or different types of media content. For example, Herzog (1941) found that regular listeners to radio soap operas did not all do so for the same reason. She found that some listened in order to experience emotional release ("for a good cry"). Others reported listening for escape ("to avoid drudgery" or "for excitement") or to gain advice for their own lives.

During its second stage, researchers began to try to create categories, or typologies, to represent the various reasons people had for their media use. Studies found numerous clusters of motivations for television use. These included: to pass time/habit; for companionship; for arousal or excitement; for specific content; for relaxation; for information/learning; to escape; for entertainment/enjoyment and for social interaction (Rubin 1981). McQuail, Blumler, and Brown (1972) proposed that motivations could be further reduced down to four basic categories. They labeled these categories: diversion, personal relationships, personal identity and surveillance.

Diversion refers to motivations that involve escapism or enjoyment. Included here are escaping from personal problems or daily routines, and attempting to relax, fill time, or overcome boredom. Diversion can also refer to the desire to experience an emotional release.

Personal relationships involve both fostering actual interpersonal relationships and substituting for these interactions. Thus, media use may be motivated by a desire to share an activity with other people or to provide something to talk about with others at a later time. These motivations would promote actual ties and meaningful human interactions. Alternatively, one may be motivated to use the media to replace other people by serving as a companion, or by providing a sense of belonging or community.

The third category of motivations is for personal identity. These motivations refer to gaining self-awareness and reinforcing personal values. Here, one engages in media use (or some other activity) in order to foster or express a sense of self.

Finally, surveillance motives involve a desire to be aware of what is new and what is happening. The person engages in a behavior in order to be informed and to be engaged with the world. This motivation may arise out of curiosity, interest, need, or for some other reason.

In its most recent stage, uses and gratifications research has attempted to relate motives with other parts of the model (Rubin 1994). For example, some researchers have attempted to link specific motives for media use with particular needs and the underlying origin of these needs. Others have tried to compare the goals sought with the benefits actually obtained from media use. Finally, some have sought to examine the relationship between motives for media use and the consequences of these activities. The remainder of this chapter will first attempt to identify the motives for compulsive buying. Then it will try to link these motivations with prior needs and the origins of those needs. Finally, it will briefly relate motives to both the intended and unintended consequences of compulsive buying.

Applying uses and gratifications motivations to compulsive buying

Researchers examining compulsive buying have suggested many different motivations for this problem. Therefore, an important first step here is to identify and classify these motivations. The primary motivations for both compulsive buying and more typical shopping can be fit into the same four categories of media use motivations developed by McQuail *et al.* (1972).

Surveillance

On the face of it, one of the most likely motivations for compulsive buying might be surveillance. This is particularly true for those compulsive buyers that are driven to engage in compulsive shopping. Some may find pleasure in being aware of all that is available (Campbell, in press). Others may engage in compulsive shopping as a way of finding out about new products, staying aware of the latest fashions or trends, or finding the best possible bargain. Either perceiving one's self, or being seen by others as being a trendsetter or bargain hunter may be an important source of gratification. Indeed, each of these motivations can be found in depth interviews with compulsive buyers. However, for some, surveillance may actually be an indicator of other underlying motivations, rather than the primary reason for compulsive buying.

Surveillance motivations may also be particularly germane to people who are on the high-end of a normal buying continuum. They may be motivated by a desire to know about, and perhaps own, the latest fads. These people may enjoy shopping and gain pleasure from it. Alternatively, they may be frequent shoppers who are particularly susceptible to impulse purchasing. Impulse buying has been defined as occurring when desire for something outweighs one's level of willpower (Hoch and Lowenstein 1991). Most conceptions of impulse buying stress that it is reactive, triggered at least partially, if not fully, from the item purchased. For some excessive buyers, owning specific items may be the underlying motivation for the behavior. However, compulsive buyers indicate that they often purchase items and then never use them (Faber, O'Guinn and Krych 1987; McElroy *et al.* 1991; O'Guinn and Faber 1989; Scherhorn *et al.* 1990). This suggests that the desire to own specific items may not be the prime motivation for many compulsive buyers. A more direct examination of the desire for objects as a motive for compulsive buying can be found from the studies looking at the relationship between materialism and compulsive buying.

O'Guinn and Faber (1989) used Belk's 24-item materialism scale to examine differences between compulsive buyers and more general consumers. They found that compulsive buyers score higher on this dimension than did the general consumers. However, the Belk scale is designed to assess three different dimensions of materialism – possessiveness, envy and non-generosity. If a desire to own goods is the primary motivation for compulsive buying, then these groups should demonstrate a significant difference on the possessiveness scale. Results, however, indicated that compulsive buyers were no different from other consumers in regard to possessiveness. Instead, the overall difference in materialism was due to differences on the other two dimensions. Later in their study, these authors also examined scores on a scale that assessed a person's desire for an object as the reason for buying. Interestingly, general consumers actually scored significantly higher on this measure than did the compulsive buying sample. Similar findings by other authors further supports the belief that a desire to own things is not a key motivation in compulsive buying (Edwards 1992; Scherhorn *et al.* 1990). On the other hand, materialism and possessiveness are found to be related to excessive (the high-end of normal consumption) and impulsive buying (Dittmar, in press).

While it appears most compulsive buyers do not buy purely for the desire to have specific items, it is also true that most do not buy things indiscriminately. Instead, they tend to buy specific types of items or from specific types of outlets. For example, female compulsive buyers have been found to frequently buy clothing, shoes, jewelry, and cosmetics, while males report frequently purchasing clothing, electronics, and auto related products (Christenson *et al.* 1994; Faber *et al.* 1987; O'Guinn and Faber 1989; Schlosser *et al.* 1994). Similarly, some people engage in problematic buying in malls or department stores, while others report that for them compulsive purchases occur almost exclusively in other locations such as specialty shops; second-hand stores; through catalogues; via shop-at-home TV programs; on the internet or from garage sales (Benson, in press; Faber *et al.* 1987). The choice of specific items or shopping environments may best be explained by looking at the other categories of motivations.

Personal identity

One motivational category that might account for the specific items that people purchase is personal identity. Specific items may be purchased in order to enhance one's self-perception. For example, items such as clothes, jewelry, or cosmetics are closely linked with appearance and self-image (Dittmar, in press). Those who compulsively buy such items may do so because a large part of their identity is wrapped up in their looks or their sense of fashion. Others may spend exclusively on items like auto parts or electronic goods in order to support their feelings of competence or expertise in these areas. Thus, for some compulsive buyers, purchasing specific types of goods may represent a way of "buying an identity" (Shields 1992).

Where one shops can also be related to a sense of identity. Some compulsive buyers shop only in exclusive stores in order to reinforce their feelings of importance. Others define their identity in the opposite way by shopping garage sales and discount stores in order to demonstrate their ability to find bargains and thereby strengthen their image of being intelligent or thrifty consumers. Finally, for some people, the act of shopping or buying, rather than the item or location, may be a key element of their identity. Just as playing music, collecting stamps, coins, or other items, rooting for a sports team or any of a number of other activities can become a key component of one's identity, so too can buying or shopping.

Personal relationships

While some compulsive buyers may buy specific goods in order to help define their own identity, others may do so in order to enhance inter-personal relationships. People who shop sales may anticipate gaining praise and respect from others who admire their ability to find good deals. The specific items purchased may also represent a way of getting attention from others. Purchasing clothes, jewelry, and cosmetics enhance one's looks and this, in turn, may attract other people or earn compliments from others. Alternatively, the items purchased may help the person to gain inter-personal contacts:

> One compulsive buyer we interviewed bought predominantly expensive stereo and television equipment but demonstrated little affect when discussing the types of music or programs he liked. Eventually, it came out that his motivation for buying came mainly from the fact that

> neighbors recognized him as an expert in electronic equipment and came to him for advice when making their purchases.
>
> (Faber 1992: 815)

Another way compulsive buying can serve to meet personal relationship needs is by substituting for ties with friends and family. This may occur by perceiving one's self as having a temporarily satisfying relationship with sale personnel or others in the shopping environment. Interviews with compulsive buyers have indicated that several get pleasure from the attention they receive from sales people (O'Guinn and Faber 1989; Krueger, in press; McElroy *et al.* 1991).

The interaction with others in the shopping or buying situation may be even more remote. This may be particularly true for people who watch shop-at-home TV shows or shop by phone. Operators are often taught to talk to the shopper as they would with a friend and to reference previous purchases when they look up the caller on their computer. This forms a sense of intimacy without an actual relationship. It is similar to a notion in the uses and gratifications literature known as parasocial interaction. Parasocial interaction refers to the bond TV viewers can form with a person repeatedly see on TV such as David Letterman or Tom Brokaw. These personalities come into our homes daily and almost seem like friends. For viewers who are lonely or isolated, television provides this parasocial interaction. For compulsive buyers, the same may be true of people in the retail environment. The most obvious example of this is shop-at-home programs where hosts not only become familiar faces, but take it a step further by mentioning shoppers on the air and even talking to some of them during the program. Thus, it seems like viewers are interacting with the people on the show. Compulsive buyers can also develop parasocial interactions with other retail personnel such as store clerks, advertising spokespersons and delivery people. One woman reported:

> I know the UPS drivers in my neighborhood real well. They all wave and say hello by first name.
>
> (O'Guinn and Faber 1989: 154)

Although we generally think in terms of desiring positive interpersonal relations with others, negative attention may also serve to motivate compulsive buying. Calls from creditors and the strife caused for parents and spouses over mounting bills can produce this negative attention (Faber 1992; Goldman, in press). Some compulsive buyers may find receiving any type of attention better than getting no attention at all. Additionally, engaging in negative interactions can be used as a way of communicating anger or displeasure. Other compulsive buyers may use the problems they encounter from buying as a way of maintaining a bond with others (Krueger, in press). This is similar to the co-dependency alcoholics often form with others in their life.

Given the motivation for interpersonal interaction, it is interesting that most compulsive buyers prefer to shop alone (Elliott 1994; O'Guinn and Faber 1989). This may be because compulsive buyers are embarrassed by their behavior and don't want others to know, or because they find that others interfere with the particular gratifications they are receiving from this behavior. As one compulsive buyer stated:

> I deliberately cancel shopping trips with friends if I know I want a serious shop and don't want any outsiders' interference and comments.
>
> (Elliott 1994: 171)

Shopping with others can be unpleasant when their shopping styles differ. In interviews with general consumers, Prus (1993) found that one of the most common complaints about shopping with others was that there was a difference among the companions in level of intensity, speed, or stamina in shopping. Given the level of intensity and arousal expressed by compulsive buyers, it is unlikely many others would be able to match them.

Diversion

Diversion is a frequent excuse for going shopping. It is seen as relaxing, something to do when bored, or as a way to temporarily escape from one's problems. These motivations are common among many normal buyers. Shopping to combat boredom has also been found among compulsive buyers (Faber, in press; Faber and Christenson 1996). However, what may distinguish compulsive buyers from other shoppers is the degree to which the behavior is motivated by a desire to alleviate negative affective feelings (Krueger, in press; Scherhorn *et al.* 1990).

Compulsive buying seems to serve as a way of improving negative mood states. One study asked compulsive buyers to complete the following sentence fragment, "When I don't feel good about myself, I am likely to . . ." (Faber *et al.* 1987). "Spend money/shop" was tied with "sleep/withdraw" as the most common response to this question. Using the same sentence fragment with a non-compulsive buying sample, Belk (1985) reports the most common responses to be "act depressed," "try to feel better," and "withdraw from others." He doesn't mention any responses related to buying or shopping. An even stronger indication of the degree to which buying may represent a way of improving negative feelings comes from a response to another sentence fragment, "I am most likely to buy myself something when . . .". Almost three-quarters of all of the compulsive buyers examined finished the sentence with a negative emotions such as "I'm depressed," or "I feel bad about myself." Belk reported that only 20 percent of his respondents mentioned any type of emotion (either negative or positive). Other researchers have also examined the degree to which compulsive buying may be related to negative mood states. Elliott (1994) developed a mood repair scale to determine the degree to which shopping served to alleviate depressive mood states. He found that this measure was highly correlated with compulsive buying. Emotional mood states have also been reported to increase compulsive buyers' desire to buy (Christenson *et al.* 1994).

While negative mood states often precede buying for compulsive buyers, the actual act of buying is frequently described in extreme positive terms. Compulsive buyers use terms like "high," "intoxicated," "elated," and "powerful" to describe their buying experience (Elliott 1994; Faber *et al.* 1987; McElroy *et al.* 1991). Some of these informants have stated that the only time they escape from negative feelings is when they are shopping (Elliott 1994; Friese and Koenig 1993). For them, buying serves as a way of altering their mood state.

Comparisons of compulsive buyers with a matched control sample found that the compulsive buyers indicated they experienced most mood states more often than the comparison group both prior to and during shopping (Faber and Christenson 1996). However, closer examination found that the biggest differences were that compulsive buyers feel negative mood states more often prior to shopping and positive mood states more while shopping than did the control group. Additionally, respondents were directly asked if buying changed their mood. Only about one-fourth of the comparison sample stated that purchasing changed their mood. However, almost all of the compulsive buyers (95.8 percent) indicated buying did change their mood. Furthermore, among those who indicated their mood state did change as a result of buying, compulsive buyers were more likely than the comparison sample to say that this change was in a positive direction.

Closely tied to the notion that compulsive buyers use buying to improve or repair their mood state, is the idea that this behavior serves to change arousal levels. Arousal is generally viewed as one component of emotion or mood. It has been proposed that a need or desire to change arousal level is a key component in some forms of addiction (Jacobs 1989). Some activities like gambling or buying may increase arousal level, while others such as television watching may decrease arousal. The adjectives used by compulsive buyers to describe their experiences while buying are clearly reflective of a high arousal level (Faber and Christenson 1996; Faber *et al.* 1987; Scherhorn *et al.* 1990). These include terms such as "feeling high," "getting a rush," "being alive," "elated," and "out of control." Others describe physiological changes when buying that included increased pulse rate, faster breathing, and heightened awareness. An informant describing a specific buying trip perhaps best captured these feelings:

> It was almost like my heart was palpitating, I couldn't wait to get in to see what was there. It was such a sensation. In the store, the lights, the people; they were playing Christmas music. I was hyperventilating and my hands were starting to sweat, and all of the sudden I was touching sweaters and the whole of it was just beckoning to me.
>
> (O'Guinn and Faber 1989: 154)

A more complete uses and gratifications model

Uses and gratifications theory states that the motivations for a behavior come from the desire to fill specific needs, and that these needs stem from social and psychological factors (Katz *et al.* 1974). Thus, looking at the needs compulsive buyers have and where they stem from, may give us a better understanding of the motivations for this behavior. The full model also suggests that motivations will lead to both intended and unintended consequences. This may help us to better recognize how buying becomes a repetitive activity for compulsive buyers even though it ultimately leads to undesirable consequences.

Needs and their antecedents

One of the most frequently reported findings regarding compulsive buyers is that they have low self-esteem compared to other consumers (Elliott 1994; O'Guinn and Faber 1989; Scherhorn *et al.* 1990). As with other psychological variables, it is difficult to determine if this is a cause or an effect of compulsive buying. However, Christenson *et al.* (1994) report that the mean estimate of the age of onset of compulsive buying is 17.5 years of age. Compulsive buyers often state that their buying problems first started when they began to live on their own or started earning their own money. These interviews, however, suggest that the development of low self-esteem may be traced to childhood and early family experiences (Elliott 1994; Faber 1992; Friese and Koenig 1993). Informants indicated that that they couldn't please their parents; that siblings are perceived as being better or more favored than they are; or that their parents didn't provide them with much praise or feelings of love (Edwards 1992; Faber and O'Guinn 1988). As one respondent told interviewers: "And then there is [informant's name] and my mother did all of my schoolwork, even my college papers. It's not much to be proud of" (O'Guinn and Faber 1989: 153). Quotes from two other informants also illustrate the life-long feelings of low self-esteem:

> I always refer to myself as being very shallow and superficial. I don't feel there's much more behind me than what you see.

> So I never really knew who I was or how people really liked me because I was never – I've never been fully represented.

> (Faber, in press)

It therefore seems plausible that for many compulsive buyers, childhood and family experiences were the origin of their low self-esteem. Another characteristic associated with compulsive buyers is perfectionism (O'Guinn and Faber 1989). Holding themselves to an impossibly high standard may contribute to experiencing low levels of self-esteem. This is perceived as a painful state and creates a need or desire to overcome the feeling. Through trial and error and/or via socialization, some compulsive buyers discover that buying is a way to temporarily overcome their feelings of low self-esteem (Elliott 1994; Faber 1992). This can occur in several different ways. For some it is the ability to use a charge card that makes them feel good about themselves. In the words of one compulsive buyer:

> I got this great high. It was like you couldn't have given me more of a rush just for the power of having that card.
>
> (Faber, in press)

In this case, the need to overcome feelings of low self-esteem may lead to buying since it serves as a diversion, allowing a temporary respite from poor self-feelings. For others, self-esteem may be enhanced by temporarily being able to imagine themselves differently. It is interesting to note that several researchers have reported that compulsive buyers have a particularly high propensity to fantasize (Edwards 1992; O'Guinn and Faber 1989; Goldman, in press). This may allow people to both imagine themselves as able to afford the purchase, as well as to imagine that the purchase will make them better or perceived differently by others (Goldman, in press). For these individuals, personal identity is the motivation for engaging in compulsive buying. When buying, they can temporarily imagine themselves as being different than how they generally view themselves. Low self-esteem can also be countered by positive responses from others. For some people, when they feel down, a reminder that they look attractive or that they are desirable, can be obtained from an attentive sales person. Others may go to people they know with the trophies of bargains they have found in order to receive praise and admiration. Differences in the specific motivation people seek may depend on their childhood socialization, their interpersonal network, and trial and error experiences.

Postmodernists suggest that the break-up of the family structure and the loss of a sense of community in modern life have seriously affected our ability to establish a clear identity (Langman 1992). Consumption and commodification become our expression of identity directed toward a generalized "other" in a new form of parasocial interaction. Thus, the changing social structure creates personal identity and personal relationship needs which motivates some people to engage in compulsive buying behaviors to try to fulfill these needs.

Another commonality among compulsive buyers is that they experience high levels of anxiety and stress (Christenson *et al.* 1994; Edwards 1992; Valence *et al.* 1988). DeSarbo and Edwards (1996) suggest that compulsive buyers may be particularly likely to respond to stress with greater feelings of anxiety. While there are a number of ways to cope with feelings of stress and anxiety, compulsive buyers utilize escape as a coping mechanism more frequently than other methods (Edwards 1992). This would lead them to seek out diversion. Thus, for compulsive buyers who are particularly prone to stress and anxiety, diversionary motives may be the most important factor underlying their buying behavior. Compulsive buyers have been asked to indicate what cues trigger an episode of compulsive buying (Faber *et al.* 1996). Over 400 objects, activities, feeling states, locations and circumstances were examined. Items that were found to trigger episodes of compulsive buying for at least one-third of the sample were then factor analyzed, resulting in a two-factor solution. One factor contained objects and places associated with buying like money, shopping malls, wanting something, and credit cards. The other factor represented negative emotional states and events such as feeling stressed, feeling angry, weighing one's self, and feeling overweight. These negative feelings thus serve as immediate cues that trigger buying behaviors that can temporarily divert these moods.

Poor interpersonal relationships are common among many compulsive buyers. This is seen both in family relationships and romantic relationships. Compulsive buyers are more likely to come from families with greater discord and are more likely than other consumers to feel neglected by their parents (Friese and Koenig 1993). Low self-esteem in compulsive buyers is readily apparent in discussions of their family relationships, and for many it seems that this is where their poor self-concept emanated.

> I had acne, braces and glasses and she [sister] was gorgeous.
> (Faber and O'Guinn 1988: 9)

> She [youngest sister] was running wild. She did whatever she wanted . . . Things that I wasn't allowed to do she was doing all the time. And this would generally be great with them [parents].
> (Faber and O'Guinn 1988: 9)

> All those years that I tried and tried and tried to have a relationship with him [Dad], he was too busy to be bothered.
> (Friese and Koenig 1993: 28)

> My other sister has never grown up. She's 36 years old and my father is still supporting her. They live very close by. They baby-sit her children all the time. They never did that for me. They give her things. They never did that for me. So my sister was given everything. Both of them [sisters] were given help and my brother too. And I was given nothing.
> (Faber and O'Guinn 1988: 9)

In some cases material goods were used to replace this lack of attention. The use of gifts or money to reward behavior during their childhood was found to be more common among compulsive buyers than for other consumers (Faber and O'Guinn 1988). In other cases, the feelings of being included and loved may be tied to purchasing situations. For example, one informant reported:

> My grandmother was just like me, exactly. When I was a kid and she'd
> get her check, we'd go downtown and spend all day. And I absolutely
> loved it. It was so much fun.
>
> (Friese and Koenig 1993: 28)

These childhood experiences can further increase the likelihood that
people will try to use purchasing as a means of coping with negative
feelings in later life. A number of compulsive buyers have remarked that
their first response to a negative interpersonal encounter is to go buy
something. In this way, compulsive buyers may be motivated to buy in
order to replace negative interpersonal relationships with more positive
ones. If your family, boyfriend, or spouse makes you feel bad or unloved, a
salesperson may make you feel more wanted and desirable. This is likely to
lead people who are motivated by a desire to cope with negative feelings to
become episodic buyers who only buy compulsively in response to a
negative event. Other compulsive buyers may be more socially isolated or
chronically depressed. These people may utilize buying as a way to have
social or parasocial contact with others. People who are particularly lonely
may watch home shopping programs on television to feel more connected
to others. Their purchasing may be a way of gaining attention or having
contact to other people. One recently interviewed compulsive buyer told of
buying predominantly from home shopping programs. She was divorced
and had custody of her daughter. She reported that she most frequently
watched and bought when her daughter was staying with her ex-husband.
The absence of her daughter from home made her feel lonely and this was
filled by seeing familiar people on TV and by purchasing.

Although the initial conception of the origin of needs in the uses and
gratifications model referred just to psychological and social origins,
Rosengren (1974) suggested adding biological origins and the structure of
society as well. Both of these have also been hypothesized to play a role in
understanding motives for compulsive buying as well (Elliott 1994; Faber
1992; Goldsmith and McElroy, in press; Scherhorn 1990). One proposed
theory suggests that a key factor that makes people susceptible to a range
of addictive behaviors is an undesirable level of arousal (Jacobs 1989).
Jacobs believes that people at risk for developing addictions have a
physiological resting state that they experience as aversive. In an effort to
achieve a more pleasant state, people engage in activities or use substances
to alter their arousal level. Several studies have suggested that compulsive
buyers experience heightened arousal during shopping as well as when
confronted with negative consequences of this behavior (Faber 1992; Faber
et al. 1987; McElroy *et al.* 1994). Thus, biological factors may account for a
chronically hypotensive or hyertensive arousal level which creates a need
for change to a more optimal level. This need leads to a diversion
motivation for compulsive buying since it is capable of temporarily
changing the level of arousal one feels.

Jacobs' model states that addictions can occur when problems with arousal level are combined with feelings of inadequacy or low self-esteem. The fact that compulsive buying can alter both of these situations further increases the likelihood the behavior will become problematic. Social system and cultural characteristics are another source of antecedents of needs that can ultimately be link to compulsive buying. Compulsive buying has been readily found to exist in numerous Western developed nations, such as Canada (d'Astous 1990; Valence *et al.* 1988); England (Elliott 1994); Germany (Scherhorn *et al.* 1990); France (Lejoyeux *et al.* 1996); and the United States (Edwards 1992; O'Guinn and Faber 1989; Schlosser *et al.* 1994). This has lead some authors to suggest that it might be an outcome of the alienation and lack of community that is common in the modern urban existence in developed nations (Cushman 1990; Elliott 1994; Shields 1992). Others have suggested it is caused by the disintegrating social order in postmodern society which is replaced by the consumption not just of products but of symbolic meanings (Elliott 1994; Baudrillard 1981; Langman 1992; Scherhorn 1990).

Changes in modern society have also created changing family environments that may create needs ultimately filled through compulsive buying (Langman 1992; Scherhorn 1990). Modern society has removed children from many of the close adult relationships that existed in earlier times. Extended families no longer live together and children are taught at an early age to distrust unknown adults. Divorce and families with two working parents further remove children from adult comfort and support. This can serve to increase children's feelings of depression, low self-esteem, and the development of poor coping skills.

Gender differences

Studies have consistently reported that far more women experience compulsive buying problems than men (Black 1996; O'Guinn and Faber 1989; Scherhorn *et al.* 1990). One explanation for this gender difference is that in most Western nations shopping is defined as a woman's role. Additionally, women are socialized to enjoy shopping. They are more likely to receive praise and recognition for being good shoppers than men.

Campbell (in press) has suggested that men approach shopping with a "work frame" using a problem-solution framework that involves as little cost and time as possible. Women, however, view shopping through a "leisure frame" in which this activity is seen as recreation – something to be enjoyed, savored, and prolonged. They are taught that shopping is "good therapy" and something to do when feeling bored or depressed. As a result, women are more likely to engage in buying when in mood states that might make them vulnerable to the short-term benefits that compulsive buying can provide. Additionally, they shop more frequently, allowing for repeated reinforcement of this behavior. For people who are susceptible to developing an addiction, opportunity and reinforcement may help to indicate what activity will become problematic. Most addictions and problematic behaviors are not equally divided among the genders. Men traditionally have been more likely to develop alcoholism and drug addiction, gambling problems, and sexual addictions. Women are reported to more frequently develop eating disorders and kleptomania. Recently, however, the proportions are beginning to change. More women report gambling and alcohol problems and more men are beginning to show signs of eating disorders. The same may well hold for compulsive buying.

Consequences of compulsive buying

The uses and gratifications model suggests that actions will lead to intended and unintended consequences (McQuail *et al.* 1972). Intended consequences occur by achieving the needs that motivated the behavior. For example, people who engage in compulsive buying to achieve personal identity are able to view themselves differently while buying than they normally do. Similarly, compulsive buyers who seek interpersonal relations are able to overcome loneliness or gain praise from others for their shopping. Those who seek diversion can temporarily overcome boredom, change their mood state or their arousal level, or escape from their problems. Thus, compulsive buying serves a functional purpose by achieving the goal that motivated the behavior. It is the success of meeting these needs that makes the behavior repetitive and problematic. Intended consequences are generally short-term outcomes of problem buying. Compulsive buyers experience these benefits, but they are often quickly replaced with feelings of remorse, guilt and fear (Faber and Christenson 1996; Scherhorn *et al.* 1990). Unintended consequences, on the other hand, are generally long-term outcomes of repeatedly engaging in compulsive buying. These include mounting debt and financial problems, bankruptcy, interpersonal conflicts with family members, divorce, passing on this behavioral problem to children, as well as other legal, emotional, and even physical problems (Christenson *et al.* 1994; Faber, in press; McElroy *et al.* 1994). This pattern of having a short-term positive effect, followed by an ultimately dysfunctional outcome, is characteristic of addictions in general (Elliott 1994; Marlatt *et al.* 1988). The specific behavior becomes repetitive and problematic because immediate outcomes play a disproportionally large role in learning compared to more long-term effects (Elliott 1994). With compulsive buying, the short-term, intended consequences are sufficiently able to satisfy the motivations thereby acting to reinforce and extend the behavior even in the face of severe unintended negative consequences.

Conclusion

This chapter has attempted to utilize the uses and gratifications model to explain compulsive buying behavior. This model allows us to examine specific motivations that underlie compulsive buying and how these different motivations can produce the different types of compulsive buying patterns reported in prior studies. For example, some people buy almost exclusively for others. These individuals are most likely motivated by a desire to maintain interpersonal relationships. Buying provides a way of maintaining another person's attention and serves as a form of "buying love." This need for interpersonal attention and the fear that one cannot receive it without buying things for others is likely to have come from childhood experiences and low self-esteem. There may be several different ways in which early family experiences contribute to this. For example, the individual may have had parents who gave gifts rather than their time or affection. Alternatively, they may have only gotten attention from their parents if they "gave" something such as work around the home, good grades, appropriate behavior, etc. Thus, they learned that love and attention only come as the result of giving. Buying things for others may initially serve to maintain a relationship, but has the unintended consequence of further lowering self-esteem and probably undermining the relationship.

Some compulsive buyers have reported the need to buy something everyday, while others indicate their behavior is more episodic. These alternative patterns may be the result of two different sets of underlying motivations or needs. Those compulsive buyers who buy every day may be more driven by physiological needs. They may be the people who experience an undesirable baseline level of arousal. As a result, they are motivated to seek experiences to alter their arousal level in order to reach a more optimal point. They engage in compulsive buying because it creates a "high" or "rush," that provides short-term relief from their undesirably low arousal state. Days when altered arousal is not achieved may be experienced as the feeling of "mounting tension" reported by some compulsive buyers (Christenson *et al*. 1994). However, compulsive buying is only a short-term solution to a chronic problem and will therefore require frequent repetition. Habituation to higher levels of arousal may also occur leading to a need for greater excitement through more expensive or more numerous purchases. Ultimately, this will result in unintended financial problems. Episodic buying behavior may be motivated more from a need for occasional mood repair. When things are going well, these compulsive buyers are able to resist buying impulses. However, when negative events occur, they feel greater than normal levels of stress, anxiety, and depression. To cope with this anxiety or depression they seek diversion or try to alter their self-image. These motives lead to buying either as a way of feeling differently about one's self, or as a way to forget problems. In the short-term this may have the intended result, leading to an increased probability that buying will again occur the next time these negative feelings emerge. Ultimately, however, buying becomes the primary response to anxiety and depression.

The hypothetical examples above may help to better understand the phenomenon of compulsive buying and the different ways it can manifest itself. Prior research has shown that the various motivations discussed here are common among compulsive buyers. This research has also found that compulsive buying is displayed in different ways. Future research needs to try to validate the linkages proposed here to determine if different needs do lead to differing motivations and buying patterns and if these motivations can be related to particular biological, sociological, and psychological origins. In keeping with the central theme of this book, the uses and gratifications model helps to tie motivations to their consequences as well as to show how they relate to specific antecedents. Better understanding of the various motivations for compulsive buying and their linkage with different antecedents, behavior patterns, and consequences can help in building a broader and more complete theory of compulsive consumption. It is also important in explaining comorbidity among compulsive buyers and people with other disorders. This will be critical in developing effective treatment programs. It is time for research in compulsive buying to move toward understanding how varying motivations lead to specific problem behaviors and to determine where these motivations stem from.

Acknowledgments

I would like to thank April Benson and Tom O'Guinn for their helpful comments, insights, and suggestions on an earlier draft of this manuscript. I would also like to thank Tom O'Guinn, Jim Mitchell, and Gary Christenson for their collaboration on much of the work I've done on compulsive buying.

References

Baudrillard, J. (1981) *For a Critique of the Political Economy of the Sign*, St Louis, MO: Telos Press.

Belk, R.W. (1985) "Materialism: trait aspects of living in the material world," *Journal of Consumer Research* 12: 265–80.

Benson, A.L. (in press) "Introduction," in A.L. Benson (ed.) *I Shop, Therefore I Am: Compulsive Buying and the Search for Self*, Northvale, NJ: Aronson Press.

Black, D.W. (1996) "Compulsive buying: a review," *Journal of Clinical Psychiatry* 57 (suppl 8): 50–4.

Bleuler, E. (1924) *Textbook of Psychiatry*, New York: Macmillan.

Campbell, C. (in press) "Shopaholics, spendaholics, and the question of gender," in A.L. Benson (ed.) *I Shop, Therefore I Am: Compulsive Buying and the Search for Self*, Northvale, NJ: Aronson Press.

Christenson, G.A., Faber, R.J., de Zwaan, M., Raymond, N., Specker, S.,Eckert, M.D., Mackenzie, T.B., Crosby, R.D., Crow, S.J., Eckert, E.D., Mussell, M.P. and Mitchell, J. (1994) "Compulsive buying: descriptive characteristics and psychiatric comorbidity," *Journal of Clinical Psychiatry* 55: 5–11.

Cushman, P. (1990) "Why the self is empty," *American Psychologist* 45: 599–611.

d'Astous, A. (1990) "An inquiry into the compulsive side of 'normal' consumers," *Journal of Consumer Policy* 13: 15–31.

DeSarbo, W.S. and Edwards, E.A. (1996) "Typologies of compulsive buying behavior: a constrained clusterwise regression approach," *Journal of Consumer Psychology* 5 (3): 231–62.

Dittmar, H. (in press) "The role of self-image in excessive buying: a social psychological model," in A.L. Benson (ed.) *I Shop, Therefore I Am: Compulsive Buying and the Search for Self*, Northvale, NJ: Aronson Press.

Edwards, E.A. (1992) "The measurement and modeling of compulsive buying behavior," *Dissertation Abstracts International* 53 (11–A).

Elliott, R. (1994) "Addictive consumption: function and fragmentation in post-modernity," *Journal of Consumer Policy* 17: 159–79.

Faber, R.J. (1992) "Money changes everything: compulsive buying from a biopsy-chosocial perspective," *American Behavioral Scientist* 35: 809–19.

—— (in press) "A systematic investigation into compulsive buying," in A.L. Benson (ed.) *I Shop, Therefore I Am: Compulsive Buying and the Search for Self*, Northvale, NJ: Aronson Press.

Faber, R.J. and Christenson, G.A. (1996) "In the mood to buy: differences in the mood states experienced by compulsive buyers and other consumers," *Psychology and Marketing* 13: 803–20.

Faber, R.J. and O'Guinn, T.C. (1988) "Dysfunctional consumer socialization: a search for the roots of compulsive buying," in P. Vanden Abeele (ed.) *Psychology in Micro and Macro Economics*, vol. 1, Leuven, Belgium: International Association for Research in Economic Psychology.

Faber, R.J., O'Guinn, T.C., and Krych, R. (1987) "Compulsive consumption," in M. Wallendorf and P. Anderson (eds) *Advances in Consumer Research*, Provo, UT: Association for Consumer Research: 132–5.

Faber, R.J., Christenson, G.A., de Zwaan, M., and Mitchell, J.E. (1995) "Two forms of compulsive consumption: comorbidity of compulsive buying and binge eating," *Journal of Consumer Research* 22: 296–304.

Faber, R.J., Ristvedt, S.L., Mackenzie, T.B., and Christenson, G.A. (1996) "Cues that trigger compulsive buying," paper presented at the Association for Consumer Research Conference, Tucson, AZ, Oct.

Friese, S. and Koenig, H. (1993) "Shopping for trouble," *Advancing the Consumer Interest* 5 (1): 24–9.

Goldman, R. (in press) "Compulsive buying as an addiction," in A.L. Benson (ed.) *I Shop, Therefore I Am: Compulsive Buying and the Search for Self*, Northvale, NJ: Aronson Press.

Goldsmith, T. and McElroy, S. (in press) "Compulsive buying: associated disorders and drug treatment," in A.L. Benson (ed.) *I Shop, Therefore I Am: Compulsive Buying and the Search for Self*, Northvale, NJ: Aronson Press.

Hoch, S.J. and Loewenstein, G.F. (1991) "Time inconsistent preferences and consumer self-control," *Journal of Consumer Research* 18: 492–507.

Herzog, H. (1941) "On borrowed experience: an analysis of listening to daytime sketches," *Studies in Philosophy and Social Science* 9: 65–96.

Jacobs, D.F. (1989) "A general theory of addictions: rationale for and evidence supporting a new approach for understanding and treating addictive behaviors," in H.J. Shaffer, S.A. Stein, B. Gambino, and T.N. Cummings (eds) *Compulsive Gambling: Theory, Research and Practice*, Lexington, MA: D.C. Heath.

Katz, E., Blumler, J.G., and Gurevitch, M. (1974) "Utilization of mass communication by the individual," in J.G. Blumler and E. Katz (eds) *The Uses of Mass Communication: Current Perspective on Gratifications Research*, Beverly Hills, CA: Sage, 19–32.

Kraeplin, E. (1915) *Psychiatrie*, 8th edition, Leipzig: Verlag Von Johann Ambrosius Barth.

Krueger, D. (in press) "The use of money as an action symptom," in A.L. Benson (ed.) *I Shop, Therefore I Am: Compulsive Buying and the Search for Self*, Northvale, NJ: Aronson Press.

Langman, L. (1992) "Neon cages: shopping for subjectivity," in R. Shields (ed.) *Lifestyle Shopping: The Subject of Consumption*, London: Routledge: 40–82.

Lejoyeux, M., Ades, J., Tassain, V., and Solomon, J. (1996) "Phenomenology and psychopathology of uncontrolled buying," *American Journal of Psychiatry* 153: 1524–9.

McElroy, S.L., Keck Jr., P.E., Pope Jr., H.J., Smith, J.M., and Strakowski, S.M. (1994) "Compulsive buying: a report of 20 cases," *Journal of Clinical Psychiatry* 55 (June): 242–8.

McElroy, S.L., Satlin, A., Pope, H.G., Keck, P.E., and Hudson, J.I. (1991) "Treatment of compulsive shopping with antidepressants: a report of three cases," *Annals of Clinical Psychiatry* 3: 199–204.

McQuail, D., Blumler, J.G., and Brown, J.R. (1972) "The television audience: a revised perspective," in D. McQuail (ed.) *Sociology of Mass Communications*, Harmondsworth: Penguin: 135–65.

Marlatt, G.A., Baer, J.S., Donovan, D.M., and Kivlahan, D.R. (1988) "Addictive behaviors: etiology and treatment," *Annual Review of Psychology* 39: 223–52.

Mitchell, J.E. (1990) *Bulimia Nervosa*, Minneapolis: University of Minnesota Press.

Nataraajan, R. and Goff, B.G. (1991) "Compulsive buying: toward a reconceptualization," *Journal of Social Behavior and Personality* 6 (6): 307–28.

O'Guinn, T.C. and Faber, R.J. (1989) "Compulsive buying: a phenomenological exploration," *Journal of Consumer Research* 16: 147–57.

Orford, J. (1985) *Excessive Appetites: A Psychological View of Addictions*, Chichester: Wiley.

Prus, R. (1993) "Shopping with companions: images, influences and interpersonal dilemmas," *Qualitative Sociology* 16 (2): 87–110.

Rosengren, K.E. (1974) "Uses and gratifications: a paradigm outline," in J.G. Blumler and E. Katz (eds) *The Uses of Mass Communication: Current Perspective on Gratifications Research*, Beverly Hills, CA: Sage: 269–86.

Rubin, A.M. (1994) "Uses, gratifications and media effects research," in J. Bryant and D. Zillmann (eds) *Media Effects: Advances in Theory and Research*, Hillsdale, NJ: Lawrence Erlbaum Associates: 281–301.

Rubin, A.M. (1981) "An examination of television viewing motives," *Communication Research* 8: 141–65.

Scherhorn, G. (1990) "The addictive trait in buying behavior," *Journal of Consumer Policy* 13: 33–51.

Scherhorn, G., Reisch, L.A., and Raab, G. (1990) "Addictive buying in West Germany: an empirical study," *Journal of Consumer Policy* 13: 355–87.

Schlosser, S., Black, D.W., Repertinger, S., and Freet, D. (1994) "Compulsive buying: demography, phenomenology, and comorbidity in 46 subjects," *General Hospital Psychiatry* 16: 205–12.

Shields, R. (1992) "The individual consumption cultures and the fate of community," in R. Shields (ed.) *Lifestyle Shopping: The Subject of Consumption*, London: Routledge: 99–113.

Valence, G., d'Astous, A., and Fortier, L. (1988) "Compulsive buying: concept and measurement," *Journal of Consumer Policy* 11: 419–33.

11 On selling brotherhood like soap

Influencing everyday disposal decisions

Luk Warlop, Dirk Smeesters, and Piet Vanden Abeele

In most societies, citizens are expected to protect and respect the well-being of their fellow citizens. But they often fail to do so, despite the high value societies attach to their members acting as their "brother's keeper." Not surprisingly, Rothschild (1979) has labeled "selling brotherhood" as one of the most important, yet one of the most difficult tasks for the social marketer.

One threat to the common good of current and future generations is the household production of waste. In industrialized nations, the annual per capita production of household garbage ranges between approximately 400 kilograms in Europe (Bogaert and Van Ootegem 1997), and 800 kilograms in the US (Pelton *et al.* 1993). Incineration and landfill capacity is severely limited and under increased public scrutiny. The corresponding social marketing task is to reduce the societal problem of processing and storing the waste. Recycling reduces the strain on processing resources, but requires separation of garbage fractions at the source. Social marketers need to convince consumers to do the sorting themselves. Using paid labor would currently render recycling economically unfeasible.

Rothschild (1979) argued that it is "hard to sell brotherhood like soap." He observed that behavior in many social dilemma situations is relatively thoughtless, while the dominant response tendency is to maximize one's own gains. In order to produce prosocial behavior the social marketer should try to make the consumer reconsider the social implications of his behavior, and convince him of the attractiveness of the prosocial option. This view permeates the literature on social marketing. For example, Andreasen (1995) wrote that social marketers are in the business of trying to influence high involvement consumer decisions. Prosocial behavior, in his view, requires "active contemplation," which is hard to produce when consumers are not spontaneously inclined to do so.

We want to offer an alternative point of view, and will use our findings on household recycling in Belgium as a source of inspiration. The alternative is based on the observation that for individual consumers recycling can be characterized as routine behavior. Recycling decisions occur several times each day, when a consumer throws something in the trash. These molecular choices are not necessarily driven by explicit consideration of goals or values of any kind. But when a consumer wants to reflect about justifications for his decision, several (and possibly conflicting) values and goals are available for justification. Making people think about their choices, like social marketers propose, is likely to activate several of these value considerations and awaken a decisional conflict that may not be spontaneously experienced. Sometimes, therefore, social marketers may be better off not promoting elaborative thought. We will examine the implications of this alternative perspective, and discuss the research questions it raises. Our recommendations and research propositions are rooted in theories regarding the nature of low-involvement decision-making and judgment (Alba, Hutchinson, and Lynch 1991; Clore 1992).

Characteristics of Belgian recycling behavior

Belgium installed mandatory recycling of major waste fractions in the early 1990s. Local governments mandate the use of different waste bags or bins for glass, paper, plastics, metal, and organic waste. Separated fraction should be "pure" to be used for recycling. Below a certain purity threshold, it would cost too much to recycle the contents of a waste bag. Control, however, is imperfect and not all garbage is sorted well. A recent field study in Flanders (Bogaert and van Ootegem 1997) found that on average only 62 percent of recyclable waste is appropriately sorted.

This finding contrasts with our own observations of household recycling behavior in the Flemish part of Belgium (Smeesters *et al.* 1999). The data are based on focus groups and individual depth interviews, and relatively "raw." Our respondents report on a highly routinized behavior, in which conflict is rarely experienced.

Recycling is procedurally simple. People are asked to sort recyclable waste in three or four categories; one additional category is for non-recyclables, which we term "rest waste." Though a number of garbage items constitute problems for some (e.g. not all plastic materials belong to the "plastic" category; some belong to the rest waste category), overall it is fairly obvious what goes where.

Recycling is rarely a major consideration in one's life. Recycling has a cost, in terms of space and money, but very few respondents experienced these costs as serious. Recipients for each waste fraction are made available by the local government at a price covering the waste processing cost of its contents. For example, plastic bags for rest waste typically cost about 1.50 Euro for a 60-liter bag, while 100-liter containers for organic waste can be rented for an annual 35 Euro. Sorting different waste categories also implies that people have to store a number of collection bins or bags in their house. Many people have a garden or garage where they would store garbage until it was collected anyway. Even people living in smaller dwellings reported handling the recycling guidelines pretty well.

The recycling dilemma is not commonly experienced as a personal conflict. Most of our informants reported on a good organization for storing waste bags and sorting the waste fractions. They remembered problems when the mandatory programs had just been introduced, but reported that they had been able to develop routines that minimized the strain on the household fairly rapidly.

Reflection easily produces justifications for non-compliance. Spontaneous narratives about household garbage handling activities revealed surprisingly little reference to values or purposes. Respondents concentrated on how rather than why they recycle. When asked to reflect about reasons, however, justifications were easily produced for both compliance and non-compliance with the recycling guidelines, and related to basic values or motivations. Most informants reported a high degree of compliance, but no one had any difficulties to retrieve episodes of defection, which were justified by referring to situational constraints on the appropriate behavior or to witnessing successful defection by others.

A range of intrinsic motivations. The installation of a mandatory program did not seem to produce "burn-out" as described by economists and psychologists when extrinsic motivation replaces intrinsic motivation (Frey 1993). In fact, our observations indicated that the installation of the mandatory program broadens the set of intrinsic values that seem applicable to the behavior. While most of the literature on values and recycling (e.g. Bagozzi and Dabholkar 1994; McCarty and Shrum 1994) emphasizes environmental values, we found that our informants referred to morality, fairness, and social duty as more important drivers.

There is an obvious contradiction between the ease and routinization of the reported recycling behavior of our informants and the aggregate observation that so much of the garbage is inappropriately sorted. Government studies of recycling (e.g. Bogaert and van Ootegem 1997) suggest that the problem is not associated with specific groups of individuals. While there are individual differences, inappropriate sorting occurs in virtually every household. Can existing consumer theories provide an explanation for this phenomenon?

Recycling as intentional and volitional behavior

The dominant theoretical framework in the research on recycling behavior have been Fishbein and Ajzen's (1975) Theory of Reasoned Action (TRA) and its successors. These theories model the cognitive structure of beliefs about behavioral consequences and their importance weights, which jointly determine the attitude towards a particular behavior. Consequences are incorporated at the level of abstraction most salient to the individual. Typically, they are conceptualized as fairly proximal to the behavior. The intention to perform this behavior is a function of the attitude and the social norms surrounding the behavior. The values underlying the behavior are incorporated as determinants of importance weights. A behavioral consequence that appeals to a higher value in one's life will receive a higher weight and have more impact on the attitude towards the act. The potential conflict between goals is left out of the discussion.

Counter to what many recycling researchers have assumed (e.g. Bagozzi and Dabholkar 1994), the theory of reasoned action does not assume that every single decision is necessarily based on thoughtful consideration of the consequences of the behavioral alternatives. Actual behavior may be based on retrieved attitudes that are stored in memory. It does assume, however, that the attitude has formed through thoughtful reasoning at some point prior to the act. Choices are made by comparing retrieved attitudes about the competing alternatives (see Eagly and Chaiken 1993 for an extensive discussion). These theories adhere to what Wilson, Lisle, and Kraft (1990) have called the "file drawer analogy" of behavior. Like in a file drawer, a person's values, attitudes, beliefs, and relevant knowledge about a target object or act are stored in a systematic fashion. The "file" with all these potential decision inputs is opened when it is called for by a pending decision involving the target object or behavior. Its entire content is then available for use in the decision, and will be used in the decision. The contents of the file drawer may change over time, through learning and experience, but this learning process is slow and gradual. Stored beliefs, attitudes, and values are accessed and combined on the basis of some implicit calculation on their weighted relevance to the target object or behavior; this calculation rule itself is assumed to be stable. Therefore, in the short term the consumer's recycling behavior is highly predictable from the contents of his "file" only.

The only source of variability in behavior, according to these models, is when a consumer changes intentions: a non-recycler decides to become a recycler, or vice versa. Intentions can only change if the consumers' beliefs are changed. These beliefs can be about the costs and benefits of behavior, about the norms of the social environments, or about one's own ability to perform the behavior. The model assumes that changing these beliefs is an all-or-nothing process. It is a volitional and voluntary act on the part of the consumer, who has to be convinced that his previous conviction was wrong. Once a consumer has adapted a belief, the changed belief will always be active and influence each subsequent recycling act, unless it is changed again by a new, successful, marketing effort.

Recycling research (see Pieters 1989; Hornik *et al.* 1995, for reviews) has adapted to the constraints imposed by this model. All hitherto published studies have investigated recycling at a fairly high level of abstraction. Criterion variables in most of the studies have been measures of intention, or self-reports of past behavior. Self-reported recycling behavior is a summary measure of a series of consecutive discarding decisions over a specified or unspecified stretch of time. Even the few studies that used observational measures (e.g. Pieters' (1989) household-level garbology studies) could only observe the aggregate result of consumers' recycling decisions over the previous week or weeks, as reflected in the contents of garbage containers they put out for curbside collection.

Not surprisingly, the bulk of recycling research studies individual differences in motivation and knowledge, or situational factors that can be assumed constant over the period implied by the level of aggregation of the dependent measures. Pieters (1989), Thøgersen (1994), and Hornik *et al.* (1995) have called attention to the role of ability-related and opportunity-related determinants of recycling behavior. Intentions to recycle may or may not translate into behavior, depending on the consumer's recycling knowledge and stable constraints imposed by the environment. TRA-based models have been fairly successful in predicting whether an individual, based on his beliefs, will report to be a recycler or not (e.g. Allen, Davis, and Soskin 1993; Goldenhar and O'Connell 1992–3; Grunert 1996). The theory cannot account well for intra-individual variation in behavior. Recyclers are assumed to be always recyclers; non-recyclers never have a reason to recycle. The application of the theory of reasoned action to the recycling problem illustrates how difficult the social marketing task can be. One is asking the social marketer to make "recyclers" out of "non-recyclers," or to convert "sinners" to "the good faith." This difficulty has inspired the statement that "brotherhood can not be sold like soap" (Rothschild 1979).

Recycling as a social dilemma

Most prosocial behaviors, including recycling, are not all-or-nothing phenomena. The prosocial option competes at all times with other concerns, or may not even be salient in the mind of the consumer. From this perspective, the social marketing goal would be to minimize the number of selfish choices, while realizing that most individuals will defect some of the time. The decisional conflict can also be characterized as a social dilemma or commons dilemma, because the needs and desires of the individual (self-interest) conflict with the needs and desires of human beings in general (collective interest). It is, however, an intra-personal conflict to the extent that both types of interests are simultaneously salient within one individual.

Social dilemma research studies molecular choices, which only after accumulation may result in negative consequences for the group. The approach allows for situational determinants of these molecular decisions, which can vary within individuals over time. Most social dilemma research uses experimental games, such as the Prisoners Dilemma game or one of several resource dilemma games, in which subjects take resources from a common pool and try to maintain it over a series of trials. Each player's task is to use the pool efficiently while trying to do well individually. In experimental games, the pay-off matrix of alternative courses of action is usually very salient. Participants are uncertain about the outcome, but they know all possible consequences of their cooperative and non-cooperative choices. The major situational influences on behavior are due to the interdependent relationship of each participant with the other players in the game. Behavior in such games has been shown to depend on the anticipation and perception of the strategies of other players (see Komorita and Parks 1994 for an extensive review of this literature).

These findings are easily applicable to behavior in small-group dilemmas (e.g. negotiation behavior). Only a few studies (e.g. Cialdini, Kallgren, and Reno 1990; Van Vugt, Meertens, and Van Lange 1995) have looked at societal social dilemmas. These are more problematic because they imply a large number of social actors, and a much longer time perspective, obscuring the social consequences of one's personal decisions. For example, in a metropolitan area several millions of actors make daily discarding decisions, affecting the lives of many more millions belonging to current and future generations. Each individual decision has a minimal impact on the collective outcome. Individual consumers cannot know whether sufficient others would be willing to participate, and they are uncertain about whether the collective outcome will ever materialize (Wiener and Doesher 1994). As a result, they feel less personally responsible. They easily attribute the responsibility for a clean environment to other "players" like "industry" or the government (Pieters *et al.* 1998), or assume that future generations will develop the technology for solving the problems created by their current behavior (Stern 1992).

Wiener and Doescher (1991) proposed several social marketing strategies to overcome these barriers. Social marketers should convince consumers that the collective goal is worth pursuing, and will be achieved with high probability. They should also try to enhance individual consumers' identification with the collective and emphasize the importance of the individual's contribution. These are all changes in beliefs or cognitive structure, which are hard to obtain.

It should therefore not be surprising that, just like in TRA-based recycling research, research efforts have concentrated on individual differences that help to explain differences in cooperation. While the social marketing research is looking to identify segments which will respond positively to social marketing action, the emphasis in social dilemma research was initially more theoretical. Messick and McClintock (1968) identified cooperation, individualism, and competition as three social value orientations (SVO). Cooperators prefer to maximize own and others' outcomes, individualists tend to maximize own outcomes without reference to other's gain, and competitors prefer to maximize the relative advantage of self over others. Cooperators are typically the largest group, and the two others are often collapsed in one, contrasting, "pro-self" group. Social value orientation is a measurable and stable individual difference variable, rooted in socialization processes starting in early childhood (Van Lange *et al.*

1997). Previous research has shown that people with cooperative SVO (pro-socials) cooperate more frequently in experimental games than individuals with individualistic or competitive SVO (pro-selves) (e.g. Allison and Messick 1990). More applied research has shown, for example, that they would also prefer to commute by public transportation if other commuters do the same, while proselves prefer public transport only if other people travel by car (Van Vugt *et al.* 1995). Another important observation in these studies is that prosocials are very sensitive to the perceived behavior of others. Prosocials are willing to cooperate only when the other players also cooperate. Otherwise, even prosocials might turn to a more defective kind of behavior or tit-for-tat strategies (McClintock and Liebrand 1988).

Summary of current approaches

We have identified two psychological accounts for recycling (and other prosocial) behavior. The theory of reasoned action and (large-scale) social dilemma theory can both be used as a basis for designing social marketing interventions. In both cases the proposed interventions need thoughtful consideration and changes in beliefs or attitudes. Because these are so difficult to achieve, researchers working in these paradigms look primarily for individual-difference variables as explanations for behavior. This 'all-or-nothing' position is hard to square with the low intra-personal consistency observed in garbology studies (Bogaert and Van Ootegem 1997).

Just like many other prosocial behaviors, recycling consists of a series of molecular recycling acts, embedded in an ongoing stream of household behaviors. Our own observations suggest that the molecular acts are rarely very thoughtful. They are the result of a very simple decision by an individual at a particular time to throw the empty bottle or the read newspaper in the appropriate recyclable waste bin or not. On the other hand, prosocial behavior, such as recycling, assumes and requires that the consumer perceives the behavior (decision situation) as consistent with prosocial goals. How then can these simple and non-involving behaviors be linked with the "appropriate" social goals?

Linking means and ends

It is generally accepted that consumer behavior is goal-directed, and that goals at different levels of abstraction are hierarchically related. In consumer research, means-end chain models have proposed a structural link between values and higher-order goals, immediate concerns, and actual behaviors or preferences (Gutman 1982; Huffman, Ratneshwar, and Mick, this volume). Means-end chains can be considered schemas or knowledge structures that may or may not be used to interpret a current situation (Walker and Olson 1991). Throwing the empty bottle in the glass recyclables bin may be construed as socially responsible or environmentally friendly, through the perceived social consequences of choosing for recycling or non-recycling. The alternative, throwing the bottle with the non-recyclable waste, may be construed as smart and time-efficient, because "nobody would find out anyway, and it saves me a trip to the neighborhood glass collector." When both types of values are active, the decision-maker experiences the social dilemma as a personal conflict. This does not have to happen. In some cases, only one value or corresponding means-end chain might be salient to the decision-maker, or none at all. In those cases, there is no conflict, but there may also be no prosocial action.

Huffman *et al.* (this volume) have proposed two different, but not necessarily mutually exclusive processes by which molecular behaviors are linked with higher-order values. One process, they have labeled "goal alignment." Here it is assumed that consumers are motivated to achieve consistency among the different goal concepts they carry at different levels, and their actual behaviors. Goal alignment is achieved by extensive problem-solving based on top-down processes (finding behavioral options consistent with one's goals) and bottom-up processes (finding goal constructs that are consistent with behavioral alternatives that one is considering). The other process is one of adaptation. The consumer constructs a motivation or purpose for his behavior by considering the constraints imposed by the environment. Goal alignment is a thoughtful and resource-consuming process. For some brotherly behaviors a lot of thought may be necessary, such as when a potential choice for prosocial behavior carries a lot of personal risk. Huffman *et al.* (this volume) suggest that goal-alignment processes will occur for high involvement decisions, such as when a consumer believes he will be held accountable for his choices. In other circumstances, goals are constructed by adaptation to the environment (Bettman, Luce, and Payne 1998; Huffman *et al.* this volume). The optimal course of action and its justification are jointly constructed on the basis of the choice set, or salient constraints (e.g. time pressure) on the decision. The proposed constructive heuristics are still resource-consuming and require considerable issue relevant thought.

The drawbacks of issue-relevant thought

For the recycling activities considered here, social marketers will not gain much by facilitating the problem-solving processes that are assumed in the goal-determination framework. Recycling is one activity in a continuous stream of household tasks, many of which require considerable planning, problem solving and social interaction. The individual mental capacity for such mental control tasks is limited. For example, Baumeister *et al.* (1998) recently demonstrated that performance in mental control tasks seriously deteriorates when the mental load imposed by a preceding self-control task (e.g. not eating from a plate of cookies) is high. In other words, consumers may have limited mental capacity for virtue.

We argue that promoting consideration of prosocial values may even be counterproductive. Making consumers think about why they should recycle, will also make more salient why they should not. When consumers think about courses of action in a commons dilemma, private costs of the prosocial option and private benefits of the more selfish alternative are more a priori salient than the public costs and benefits of each behavior. Concrete public benefits of recycling or the public costs of not recycling are fairly abstract, and further removed from one's daily considerations. In a heuristic decision process, based on the available problem representation, they may not even come to mind at all, or will be out-weighted by more proximal and salient personal consequences.

If social marketers would succeed in starting a more involving goal-determination process, one should take into account that there is no reason why constructive thought should be selective. An individual, who is trying to construct or retrieve reasons to recycle or act brotherly, will also retrieve or be able to construct reasons why he should not. Consideration may make the prosocial consequences of one option more salient, but it will also make the costs of the prosocial behavior for the self more salient. Similarly, it will make more salient that one's own contribution to the public good is extremely limited, and would not make much of a difference. Consideration may also promote speculation about what others will do or should do (Pieters *et al.* 1998), or render observed defective behaviors of others more salient (Smeesters *et al.* 1999).

Some writers have suggested an additional way in which purposive consumer behavior may be influenced, especially when the behavior is relatively thoughtless, as in the case we are examining. Huffman *et al.* (this volume; see also Walker and Olson 1991) have suggested that one may influence behavior by merely making relevant goals more accessible in the mind of the decision-maker. This idea, although not elaborated in detail by these authors, is consistent with a body of research in social cognition and low-involvement consumer decision-making. We will examine the implications of this possibility in the remainder of this paper.

Extremely simple prosocial decisions

Alba, Hutchinson, and Lynch (1991) characterized many consumer choices as extremely simple, incorporating only minimal informational inputs, and only those that tend to be salient and are perceived to be relevant at the time of the decision. Their "accessibility–diagnosticity" framework suggests that consumer choices are often based on minimal inputs as long as these inputs are more accessible and more diagnostic than their alternatives (Alba *et al.* 1991). We argue that social dilemmas of the less involving kind are similar. The decision to throw an item of garbage in the "prosocial garbage bin" or in the "selfish garbage bin" may be based on the first discriminating thought that comes to mind. While higher order values usually do not enable to discriminate among brands of consumer products, they do discriminate among the behavioral alternatives in a garbage disposal decision. Therefore, the best option for social marketers may be to make prosocial values accessible in the mind of the consumer at the moment of discarding, while avoiding further thought and consideration (which would make alternative and more selfish considerations more salient).

Some writers in social cognition go one step further, by suggesting that mere accessibility of decisional inputs may be interpreted as relevance. In the field of organizational theory, Cohen, March, and Olson (1972) have proposed a "garbage can model" of decision-making (pun not intended). They argued that in organizations momentarily available information will be considered important and will drive decisions, resulting in a marked lack of consistency over time. Clore (1992) claims that it applies equally well to individual decision-making. The model assumes that decision-making is like the "art of found objects" (Clore 1992): the decision-maker makes the best possible use of whatever is at the top of one's mind. People want their judgments and choices to be justifiable, but the acceptable justifications may be heavily dependent on what is cognitively salient at any particular time (Sedikides and Skowronski 1991).

Recycling values, beliefs, attitudes, and intentions to recycle not only have to be traded off against competing concerns in housekeeping tasks; they may not even come to mind at all. Whether or not they are used in any discarding/recycling decision will depend to a large extent on whether they are accessible for the behavior at the time of the decision. Communication policies to facilitate recycling behavior should be evaluated on the basis of their ability to bring relevant thought to the consumer's mind, while s/he is engaging in the specific household tasks that involve the discarding of garbage. Unfortunately, no empirical research to date has investigated these issues.

Increasing the activation level of prosocial values for recycling decisions

Social psychologists (e.g. Langer, Blank, and Chanowitz 1978) have long demonstrated that behavior in complex social situations may be mindless and under the control of environmental cues. The mechanism by which the environment may control decisions and behavior is the formation of direct mental links between representations of motives and values in memory and the behaviors associated with them. The motive-goal-plan structure becomes activated whenever the relevant triggering situational features are present in the environment (Barsalou 1991). Similarly, consumer researchers have argued that in familiar decision contexts, the activation of a goal or value may make the products or behaviors directly accessible as solutions to the problem (Warlop and Ratneshwar 1993). This formulation assumes that goals and intents are represented in the mind in the same fashion as social constructs, stereotypes, and schemas. Higgins (1997) referred to mental representations of goal values as "guides," and to mental representations of the behaviors to reach those goals as "procedures." For both types of representations, the probability of activation is a joint function of their applicability to the situation and their accessibility in memory (Higgins 1997).

The choice between actual prosocial and selfish behaviors is ambiguous. Both choice options have costs and benefits, positive and negative aspects. Behavior may be strongly dependent on how the choice options are interpreted. Several authors have suggested that these interpretations may be "primed" by the environment (Cialdini *et al.* 1990; Herr 1986; Hertel and Fiedler 1998; Sattler and Kerr 1991). Priming refers to the incidental activation of knowledge structures, by the current situational context. Many studies have shown that the recent use of a trait construct, a social stereotype, or an action schema, even in an earlier unrelated situation, carries over to exert an unintended passive influence on the interpretation of a social situation (see, e.g., Higgins 1997 for a recent review). In ambiguous situations, a priori open to multiple interpretations, Higgins (1997) has suggested that primes serve as disambiguators. Priming will influence which of two applicable alternative knowledge structures will be used to interpret the decision situation, resulting in prime consistent behavior. Bargh (1990) has argued that a motive or goal consistently activated in a general type of situation may become activated by the general features of that situation. "Habitual" recyclers' motives may therefore be triggered each time they are confronted with the situational features of a typical discarding decision. They may cease to experience discarding as a decision, because the alternative courses of action would never come to mind. In Bargh's (1990) words, motives start to function as "auto-motives," guiding behavior without requiring intervening conscious deliberation.

When the "choice nature" of a behavioral choice is not salient, several authors have shown that action schemas can be directly activated by contextual "primes." Bargh, Chen, and Burrows (1996) primed participants in a study with either an elderly or a youthful stereotype, and observed marked differences in the speed with which the participants crossed a hallway after leaving the experimenter room. "Primable" action schemata can consist of relatively complex procedural knowledge. Dijksterhuis and Van Knippenberg (1998) found that priming subjects with a "professor" stereotype increased performance in a Trivial Pursuit game, while priming with a "supermodel" stereotype reduced performance.

More common should be the case in which the consumer still faces a decision each time he has to discard an item. By definition, "decisions" require deliberation, although the process might be extremely simple. The decision task is ambiguous in the sense that multiple values or "guides" can be applied in its interpretation. The "prosocial" option, in fact, has many different possible labels. It can be identified as the environmental choice, the morally just choice, the socially responsible choice, the civic choice, and so on. But it can also be labeled negatively, as the "dumb choice," if somebody uses more individualistic, cost minimizing, motivations as a frame of reference. The environment may exert a considerable influence on the interpretation of the decision task, which in turn will make some behavioral decisions more likely than others.

Herr (1986) found that altering the accessibility of "hostile" categories influenced people's competitiveness in a Prisoner's Dilemma game. He argued that influencing the relative accessibility of one's cognitive categories can alter the interpretation of other players' behavior and, consequently, influence one's own behavior. Sattler and Kerr (1991) have conceptualized social motives (e.g. a cooperative social motive, an individualistic social motive, etc.) as a structured set of cognitions (i.e. a schema). They primed social motive schemas by presenting prescriptive messages (messages with either a "moral" theme or with a "power" theme) in a context unrelated to the choice task. They found that a moral message activated the prosocial social motive schema and resulted in more prosocial behavior, but only under some circumstances (see below). Similarly, Cialdini *et al.* (1990) primed exiting library visitors by handing them a leaflet that featured a pro-environmental of unrelated message, and found that receivers of environmental messages were much less likely to toss it on the floor of the parking garage.

In social dilemmas, not only the semantic (cooperative vs. individualistic) meaning of a prime is important, but also its valence. Both cooperative and individualistic behavior can be framed positively or negatively. Hertel and Fiedler (1998) suggested that semantic priming activates the representation of a specific type of behavior, whereas affective priming activates an orientation to approach or to avoid that type of behavior. They found, for example, that prosocial behavior in a dilemma game was not only influenced by primes suggesting positive connotations of cooperation but also by primes suggesting negative connotations of competition.

Boundary conditions for the priming effect

Priming effects can be due to simple situational cues that could be put in place by social marketers. In the Cialdini *et al.* (1990) study, the prime was a message on a leaflet, which was at the same time the to-be-discarded item. Other priming studies have used involuntary overheard conversations by confederates or "radio messages" as priming stimuli. Laboratory manipulations often use less mundane tasks, but they always are designed to present the priming message in a way that makes the content active without suggesting that its meaning is related to the central task.

A lot of research needs to be done before a theory can be developed of "low involvement" behavior and social marketing intervention in social dilemmas, which can complement the well-established work on high involvement prosocial behavior. We suggest that laboratory consumer research using priming paradigms can be used to develop such theory. Initially, researchers should concentrate on documenting the effectiveness of priming, and its sensitivity to a number of boundary conditions. In the priming literature, boundary conditions are derived from the finding that priming only works when the to-be-primed mental structures are (1) available to the individual, (2) accessible for use, and (3) perceived as applicable to the behavioral context. Below, we discuss a number of such limiting findings as a start for further inquiry.

Availability

Providing subtle cues in the environment cannot create motivations that the person does not at all have. An important boundary condition to the priming effects is that the mental structure or script linking the behavior to the value is present in the person. Bargh, Chen, and Burrows (1996) suggested that behavior can only be under control of the situation (prime) if the behavioral representation is already associated with the situation by the individual. In their experiments all the primed behaviors were likely part of the behavioral repertoire of the participants.

One crucial element of the theory we are looking for should be the required level of specificity of the relationship between value and behavior. Social dilemma research suggests the use of very general social value orientations (Hertel and Fiedler 1998; Sattler and Kerr 1991). Van Lange *et al.* (1997) found that prosocial value orientations dominate for the largest group of individuals, and that they are an important aspect of socialization starting in early childhood. However, the more general and abstract the primed values, the more extensive the chain of associations that needs to be activated in order to affect behavior. It is also possible, but has never been empirically examined, that effective prime stimuli activate more task- and person-specific social values. Our own qualitative research (Smeesters, *et al.* 1999) suggests that qualitatively different value orientations dominate reflections about the "why of recycling" for different individuals. If primes were only effective if the primed values are task specific, segmented approaches would be called for, which makes the life of the social marketer much more difficult.

Base-line accessibility of primed constructs

Arguably, the most speculative part of our conceptualization is the assumed schematic link between values and value-consistent behaviors. Moreover, these associations should be strong enough activate situation specific action plans, upon mere triggering by value consistent cues in the environment.

The availability of these strong scripts is easily assumed in current work on social cognition and in much current means-end chain work in marketing (Grunert and Grunert 1995). Cohen and Warlop (in press) have lamented the absence of good evidence and theory on precisely this aspect of means-end chain conceptualizations of human motivation. Good evidence exists for the effect of prosocial value primes in abstract resource or prisoners dilemma games (Herr 1986; Hertel and Fiedler 1998; Sattler and Kerr 1991). Whether the same results would be obtained in more specific pro-social contexts remains to be demonstrated.

Priming makes available interpretative constructs more accessible for use in an interpretation task. But these constructs or schemas may also be habitually more accessible for one individual versus another. Individuals may differ not only in the availability of relevant schemas but also in the extent to which they are "chronically" active in their interpretations of the environment. Prior social cognition and consumer research have generally found that chronicity and priming have additive or weak superadditive interaction effects (e.g. Ratneshwar *et al.* 1997). However, habitual modes of interpreting the environment tend to favor a positive concept of self. It was found, for example, that chronic "proselves" tend to interpret social dilemmas in terms of intelligence or good strategy (smart vs. dumb), whereas cooperators tend to interpret the same choice in moral terms (good vs. mean) (Sattler and Kerr 1991). It is possible therefore that "proselves" reduce cooperation even more when exposed to "dumb" cooperation primes.

Relevance, applicability, and use of primed constructs. Easily accessible constructs are not always used as a means to interpret ambiguous events. Their use is conditional upon judged applicability to the situation at hand. Earlier, it was often assumed that priming effects are only obtained when subjects are not aware of the priming event. Awareness of the prime would make salient that the source of accessibility of the prosocial construct is not internal but external. It is an empirical question whether this applies here. In a social marketing context, this would constitute a serious problem. Social marketers can "prime" consumers by presenting value-related messages on the recipients for garbage, or on the packaging of the products. It would be very hard to exclude awareness of the source. However, the studies finding such exclusion effects studied simpler and experientially isolated behaviors. Recycling is embedded in a complex sequence of household tasks and events, leaving little mental resources for further consideration. Several studies have shown that the crucial condition for behavioral assimilation to primes, is not the subject's unawareness of the prime, but his inability to allocate mental resources to the elaboration of its contents. For example, Martin, Seta, and Crelia (1990) found assimilation to primes, even when subjects were aware of the prime, when they were either not motivated or due to distraction not able to elaborate on its implications.

Selling brotherhood

Social marketing starts from a fairly pessimistic view of human nature. The motivational groundwork of marketing and economics does not include altruistic or cooperative motives. The motivated consumer is assumed to be a self-absorbed value maximizer. Recent social dilemma research suggests that this is not true: prosocial values are strong and dominant, strongly embedded in human socialization, and able to influence a variety of behaviors in real-life and laboratory social dilemma's (Van Lange *et al.* 1997). Then why would it be so hard to "sell" brotherhood? And why can it not be "sold like soap"? Our analysis, incomplete as it may be, suggests that there are different kinds of brotherhood, each with their analogies in traditional consumer marketing.

First, some forms of brotherhood are definitely not like soap. Buying an electrical car to help prevent inner-city air pollution (Harms and Truffer 1998), or giving up control over the functioning of the household air-conditioning unit (Osterhuis 1997) are not inconsequential. They carry high personal and economic risk, and consumers are likely to weigh their options carefully before making a choice. Here, the current social marketing paradigm, in which consumers are advised to reconsider the consequences of their choices, is most directly applicable. The social marketing task, however, is formidable, because most attempts to make consumers reconsider their options will strengthen not only the socially desirable beliefs and attitudes, but also the currently dominant attitudes.

Second, in some cases selling brotherhood is like selling a new brand of soap to "other-brand loyals" (Rossiter and Percy 1997). If consumers have developed stable individualistic or egoistic routine behavior, social marketing faces an excessively difficult task as well. Hoch and Deighton (1989) summarized the strategic advice for managing consumer learning in this group as "just struggle." Motivational approaches may not work, because any attempt to make them reconsider their beliefs will activate and strengthen the current beliefs, and their day-to-day routine behavior is driven by chronic – automatic – own-cost-minimizing goals. Behavior of this group may only be changed through structural changes in the dilemma pay-off structure. Current recycling programs change the pay-off structure by charging much higher prices for rest waste recipients than for recyclable waste recipients. This strategy only works, however, if the threat of control and penalization is believable, which is often a problem in practice.

We suggest that for the third and largest group of consumers, day-to-day recycling behavior is characterized by the absence of goal references of any kind. For this group, recycling is like the purchase of soap by an uncommitted consumer. Different brands of soap can be associated with different consequences and values, like hygiene and health or with bodily scent and social success. A brand may be positioned as a "means" to reach these valued ends, and these means-end chains may be well established in a consumer's mind. Similarly, the different behavioral alternatives involved in discarding waste can be linked with a number of more abstract consequences and values. Recycling may be associated with environmental values but also with values of social duty or morality. Not recycling may be considered smart (beating the system) or frugal. Every individual has experience with both alternatives, and the chains of associations may be as well established as the "means-ends" positioning of any consumer product. They only need to be activated by the appropriate cues in the decision environment.

Summary and conclusion

Sorting garbage during disposal is effortful for the individual and the household, but beneficial to society in the long run. This makes recycling a typical example of a social dilemma, and a prime target for social marketing interventions. Household disposal acts are relatively mindless routine behaviors embedded in daily housekeeping tasks of a well-managed household. Higher-order goals to support compliance with recycling guidelines are readily available for reflection, but so are justifications for defection.

Social marketing may therefore benefit from strategies that make values and higher-order goals accessible as a basis for decision-making without promoting further elaborative thought. Our current working hypothesis is that these values are available as a basis for choice in most individuals, that they will be considered relevant and applicable when activated, that they may be chronically accessible for some, but not for the majority of individuals in the flow of day-to-day housekeeping activities, and that they may be activated by direct "priming" in close temporal proximity to the actual behavior.

We believe that these observations are characteristic of the current recycling environment in many industrialized countries and regions of the world, and can be generalized to a relative large class of "brotherhood" behaviors, including tipping the waitress, courteous driving, or giving a coin to the Kosovar beggar. In each of these cases, defection from the prosocial alternative is rarely premeditated. It is due to inattention, negligence, and thoughtlessness. Thinking too much may activate justifications for defection, and interfere with the prosocial response. In each of these cases, social marketers may be better off by just "priming brotherhood."

References

Alba, J., Hutchinson, J.W., and Lynch, J. (1991) "Memory and decision making," in T.S. Robertson and H.H. Kassarjian (eds) *Handbook of Consumer Behavior*, Englewood Cliffs, NJ: Prentice-Hall.

Allen, J., Davis, D., and Soskin, M. (1993) "Using coupon incentives in recycling aluminum: a market approach to energy conservation policy," *Journal of Consumer Affairs* 27 (2): 300–18.

Allison, S.T. and Messick, D.M. (1990) "Social decision heuristics in the use of shared resources," *Journal of Behavioral Decision Making* 3: 195–204.

Andreasen, A.R. (1995) *Marketing Social Change: Changing Behavior to Promote Health, Social Development, and the Environment,* San Francisco: Jossey-Bass.

Bagozzi, R.P. and Dabholkar, P.A (1994) "Consumer recycling goals and their effect on decisions to recycle: a means-end chain analysis," *Psychology and Marketing* 11 (5): 313–40.

Bargh, J.A. (1990) "Auto-motives: preconscious determinants of thought and behavior," in E.T. Higgins and R.M. Sorrentino (eds) *Handbook of Motivation and Cognition,* vol. 2, New York: Guilford Press.

Bargh, J.A., Chen, M., and Burrows, L. (1996) "Automaticity of social behavior: direct effects of trait construct and stereotype activation on construct accessibility," *Journal of Personality and Social Psychology* 50: 869–78.

Barsalou, L.W. (1991) "Deriving categories to achieve goals," in G.H. Bower (ed.) *The Psychology of Learning and Motivation,* vol. 27, New York: Academic Press.

Baumeister, R.F., Bratslavsky, E., Muraven, M., and Tice, D.M. (1998) "Ego depletion: is the active self a limited resource?" *Journal of Personality and Social Psychology* 74: 1252–62.

Bettman, J. R., Luce, M.F., and Payne, J.W. (1998) "Constructive consumer choice processes," *Journal of Consumer Research* 25 (December): 187–217.

Bogaert, G. and Van Ootegem, L. (1997) *Inzamelmethoden voor papier en karton, glas, plastiek, metaal en drankkartons,* Mechelen, Belgium: OVAM.

Cialdini, R.B., Reno, R.R., and Kallgren, C.A. (1990) "A focus theory of normative conduct: recycling the concept of norms to reduce littering in public places," *Journal of Personality and Social Psychology* 58: 1015–26.

Clore, G.L. (1992) "Cognitive phenomenology: feelings and the construction of judgment," in L.L. Martin and A. Tesser (eds) *The Construction of Social Judgments,* Hillsdale, NJ: Lawrence Erlbaum.

Cohen, D., March, J.G., and Olsen, J.P. (1972) "A garbage can model of organizational choice," *Administrative Science Quarterly* 17: 1–25.

Cohen, J.B. and Warlop, L. (in press) "A motivational perspective on means-end chains," in T.J. Reynolds and J.C. Olson (eds) *Understanding Your Customers: Means-end Chain Theory and Practice,* Hillsdale, NJ: Lawrence Erlbaum.

Dijksterhuis, A. and van Knippenberg, A. (1998) "The relation between perception and behavior or how to win a game of Trivial Pursuit," *Journal of Personality and Social Psychology* 74 (4): 865–77.

Eagly, A.H. and Chaiken, S. (1993) *The Psychology of Attitudes,* Ft Worth, TX: Harcourt Brace Jovanovich.

Fishbein, M. and Ajzen, I. (1975) *Belief, Attitude, Intention and Behavior: An Introduction to Theory and Research,* Reading, Mass.: Addison-Wesley.

Frey, B.S. (1993) "Motivation as a limit to pricing," *Journal of Economic Psychology* 14: 635–64.

Goldenhar, L.M. and Connell, C.M. (1992–3) "Understanding and predicting recycling behavior: an application of the theory of reasoned action," *Journal of Environmental Systems* 22 (1): 91–103.

Grunert, K.G. and Grunert, S.C. (1995) "Measuring subjective meaning structures by the laddering technique method: theoretical considerations and methodological problems," *International Journal of Research in Marketing* 3 (October): 209–26.

Grunert, S. (1996) "Antecedents of source separation behavior: a comparison of two Danish municipalities," in J. Berecs, A. Bauer, and J. Simon (eds) *Marketing for an Expanding Europe*, proceedings of the 25th Annual Conference of the European Marketing Academy, vol. 1, Budapest: Budapest University of Economic Sciences: 525–38.

Gutman, J. (1982) "A means-end chain model based on consumer categorization processes," *Journal of Marketing* 46 (September): 60–72.

Harms, S. and Truffer, B. (1998) "Stimulating the market for lightweight electric vehicles: the experience of the Swiss Mendriso Project," *EAWAG Research Report*, Zurich: Technische Hochschule (www.jrc.es/snm)

Herr, P.M. (1986) "Consequences of priming: judgment and behavior," *Journal of Personality and Social Psychology* 51: 1106–15.

Hertel, G. and Fiedler, K. (1998) "Fair and dependent versus egoistic and free: effects of semantic and evaluative priming on the 'Ring Measure of Social Values,'" *European Journal of Social Psychology* 28: 49–70.

Higgins, E.T. (1997) "Knowledge activation: accessibility, applicability, and salience," in E.T. Higgins and A.W. Kruglanski (eds) *Social Psychology: Handbook of Basic Principles*, New York: Guilford Press.

Hoch, S.J. and Deighton, J. (1989) "Managing what consumers learn from experience," *Journal of Marketing* 53 (2): 1–20.

Hornik, J., Cherian, J., Madansky, M., and Narayana, C. (1995) "Determinants of recycling behavior: a synthesis of research results," *Journal of Socio-Economics* 24 (1): 105–27.

Komorita, S.S. and Parks, C.D. (1994) *Social Dilemmas*, Madison, WI: Brown and Benchmark Publishers.

Langer, E.J., Blank, A., and Chanowitz, B. (1978) "The mindlessness of ostensibly thoughtful action: the role of 'placebic' information in interpersonal interaction," *Journal of Personality and Social Psychology* 36: 635–42.

McCarty, J.A. and Shrum, L.J. (1994) "The recycling of solid wastes: personal values, value orientations, and attitudes about recycling as antecedents of recycling behavior," *Journal of Business Research* 20: 53–62.

McClintock, C.G. and Liebrand, W.B.G. (1988) "Role of interdependence structure, individual value orientation and another's strategy in social decision making: a transformational analysis," *Journal of Personality and Social Psychology* 55: 396–409.

Martin, L.L., Seta, J.J., and Crelia, R. (1990) "Assimilation and contrast as a function of people's willingness and ability to expend effort in forming an impression," *Journal of Personality and Social Psychology* 59: 27–37.

Messick, D.M. and McClintock, C.G. (1968) "Motivational bases of choice in experimental games," *Journal of Experimental Social Psychology* 4: 1–25.

Osterhuis, T.L. (1997) "Prosocial consumer influence strategies: when and how do they work?" *Journal of Marketing* 61 (October): 16–29.

Pelton, L.E., Strutton, D., Barnes, J.H., and True, S.L. (1993) "The relationship among referents, opportunity, rewards, and punishments in consumer attitudes towards recycling," *Journal of Macromarketing* 13 (1): 60–74.

Pieters, R.G.M. (1989) *Attitudes and Behavior in a Source Separation Program. A Garbology Approach*, Delft: Euburon.

Pieters, R.G.M., Bijmolt, T., van Raaij, F., and de Kruijk, M. (1998) "Consumers' attributions of pro-environmental behavior, motivation, and ability to self and others," *Journal of Public Policy and Marketing* 17 (fall): 215–25.

Ratneshwar, S., Warlop, L., Mick, D.G., and Seeger, G. (1997) "Benefit salience and consumers' selective attention to product features," *International Journal of Research in Marketing* 14 (3): 245–60.

Rossiter, J.R. and Percy, L. (1997) *Advertising, Communication, and Promotion Management*, New York: McGraw-Hill.

Rothschild, M.L. (1979) "Marketing communications in nonbusiness situations or why it's so hard to sell brotherhood like soap," *Journal of Marketing* 43 (spring): 11–20.

Sattler, D.N. and Kerr, N.L. (1991) "Might versus morality explored: motivational and cognitive bases for social motives," *Journal of Personality and Social Psychology* 60: 756–65.

Sedikides, C. and Skowronski, J.J. (1991) "The law of cognitive structure activation," *Psychological Inquiry* 2 (2): 169–81.

Smeesters, D., Warlop, L., Vanden Abeele, P., and Ratneshwar, S. (1999) "Exploring the recycling dilemma: consumer motivation and experiences in mandatory garbage recycling programs," research report no. 9924, Department of Applied Economics, Catholic University of Leuven, Belgium.

Stern, P.C. (1992) "Psychological dimensions of global environmental change," *Annual Review of Psychology* 43: 251–64.

Thøgersen, J. (1994) "A model of recycling behavior, with evidence from Danish source separation programs," *International Journal of Research in Marketing* 11: 145–63.

Van Lange, P.A.M., Otten, W., De Bruin, E.N.M., and Joireman, J.A. (1997) "Development of prosocial, individualistic, and competitive orientations: theory and preliminary evidence," *Journal of Personality and Social Psychology* 73: 733–46.

Van Vugt M., Meertens, R.M., and Van Lange, P.A.M. (1995) "Car versus public transportation: the role of social value orientations in a real-life social dilemma," *Journal of Applied Social Psychology* 25: 258–78.

Walker, B.A. and Olson, J.C. (1991) "Means-end chains: connecting products with self," *Journal of Business Research* 22 (March): 111–18.

Warlop, L. and Ratneshwar, S. (1993) "The role of usage context in consumer choice: a problem solving perspective," in L. McAlister and M.L. Solomon (eds) *Advances in Consumer Reseach*, vol. 20, Provo, UT: Association for Consumer Research: 377–82.

Wiener, J.L. and Doescher, T.A. (1991) "A framework for promoting cooperation," *Journal of Marketing* 55 (April): 38–47.

Wiener, J.L. and Doescher, T.A. (1994) "Cooperation and expectations of cooperation," *Journal of Public Policy and Marketing* 13 (fall): 259–70.

Wilson, T.D., Lisle, D.J., and Kraft, D. (1990) "Effects of self-reflection on attitudes and consumer decisions," in M. Goldberg, G. Gorn, and R. Polley (eds) *Advances in Consumer Research*, vol. 17, Provo, UT: Association for Consumer Research: 79–85.

12 Timestyle and consuming time

Why we do what we do with our time

June Cotte and S. Ratneshwar

Why do we do what we do with our time? We argue here that the answer depends, at least in part, on what we will call a person's timestyle. By timestyle, we refer to how an individual perceives, plans, and thinks about time. While one person might see a Saturday afternoon as a perfect time to socialize, someone else might perceive the same chunk of time as an ideal opportunity to be alone. One individual might think of this block of time as highly suited for many carefully planned activities, while another might prefer to let events unfold very spontaneously (Bergadaá 1990).

Prior consumer research on the topic of time's meaning for individuals has been quite insightful, but sporadic and fragmented (see, e.g., Feldman and Hornik 1981; Bergadaá 1990; Kaufman, Lane, and Lindquist 1991). Researchers have typically focused on single, isolated aspects of timestyle. Few efforts have been made to unify the emerging insights into a coherent framework (but see Golden *et al.* 1988; McDonald 1994; Kaufman *et al.* 1991). We build here on prior literature and offer a more comprehensive framework for timestyle (see also Cotte 1998; Cotte and Ratneshwar 1998; Cotte *et al.* 1999).

We suggest that timestyle is a dynamic, multidimensional construct – something that the individual creates even as he or she interacts purposefully with the sociocultural world. Timestyle, in turn, influences the individual's ongoing negotiations with the world around him or her, and it influences the individual's engagement in goals and activities involving time. We propose that an individual's timestyle has the following four dimensions: (1) social dimension (a person's preference for spending time with others versus being alone); (2) polychronic dimension (preference for spending time in parallel versus serial activities); (3) temporal orientation dimension (emphasis on the past, present, or future); and (4) planning dimension (emphasis on an analytic versus holistic approach to time management).

Several factors influence an individual's timestyle. Hence, after presenting the basic framework for timestyle, we use prior literature to discuss various antecedent influences. We examine seven sources of influence on timestyle: culture, family, work groups, age, gender, life themes and values, and life projects. In discussing these influences, we assume that the meaning of time will not be similar for everyone, but will vary in accordance with an individual's overall life experiences. Thus, individuals' unique perceptions of time arise from their attempts to interpret and integrate their cultural and social situations with their ongoing behaviors (see Lewis and Weigert 1981; Mick and Buhl 1992).

An examination of timestyle's antecedent influences is only one part of our story; we also examine how timestyle affects consumption goals and behaviors. The literature related to timestyle shows only occasional efforts at investigating relationships between different aspects of timestyle and individuals' goals and behaviors in specific domains. In this context, the consumption of leisure stands out as particularly worthy of investigation, since leisure consumption is, in fact, an active decision on how to consume specific blocks of time, and leisure consumption activities and related product consumption follow from the allocation of time to leisure. We therefore examine not only some of the major influences on timestyle, but also how timestyle, in turn, might influence leisure goals and behaviors. We illustrate some of our themes and conclusions with brief examples from a recent study.

Alternative approaches to time perception and consumption

A critical aspect of our approach is that we link the perception of time to the use of time (see McGrath and Kelly 1986). In contrast, the economic approach, characterized best by Becker (1976), treats time as a fixed resource and assumes consumers want to maximize use of money and minimize time expenditures on all activities. A somewhat related approach is that of Feldman and Hornik (1981), whose conception of time usage involves consumers choosing among desirable activities, and then making time and money trade-offs. Our approach is also different from the sociological time budget approach, which concentrates on collecting and analyzing time diary data (Robinson and Godbey 1997). Further, our approach differs in its emphasis from prior research that has dealt with time perception in at least two respects. First, we do not compare temporal perception to "real" or clock time (see, e.g., Cottle 1976). Second, since we assume that time does have some objective properties, we diverge from phenomenological research which views time as a mental construction having only subjective meaning (e.g. Bergadaá 1990; Gorman and Wessman 1977). Studying time in such a purely subjective manner does not allow study and prediction of what consumers might actually do with their time. Our approach to timestyle, its antecedent influences, and how it might influence consumption goals and behaviors is perhaps conceptually closest to research examining perception and use of time as dimensions of behavior at cultural, interpersonal, and individual levels (cf. McGrath and Kelley 1986).

Timestyle

We posit four key dimensions of timestyle: a social dimension, a polychronic dimension, a temporal orientation dimension, and a planning dimension. We offer here a summarized description of each of these dimensions. Space considerations preclude a detailed review of the relevant literature; however, a more complete discussion with supporting data is available in our other work (see Cotte 1998; Cotte and Ratneshwar 1999; Cotte *et al.* 1999).

Social dimension

People often approach units of time as either "time for me" or "time with/for others" (see also Hall 1976; Lewis and Weigert 1981). Accordingly, the social dimension of timestyle refers to the fact that individuals tend to vary in their preference for spending time alone versus with others, and this preference affects how they approach and categorize time. The motivation to categorize a unit of time as for (or with) others can be either voluntary (i.e. intrinsically preferring time with others to time alone) or obligatory (e.g. "this is time I should spend with my parents"). People can vary significantly in their allocation of time to being alone as opposed to being with others (Cotte *et al.* 1999). In identifying this dimension of timestyle, we recognize that an individual has a subjective perception of time (self-time) but must also interact with others: family, significant others, organizations, and cultural systems (Kaufman and Lane 1990).

Polychronic dimension

Prior research also suggests that people vary in whether they deal with time in a monochronic or polychronic manner (Graham 1981; Feldman and Hornik 1981; Kaufman *et al.* 1991). We call this the polychronic dimension. As Kaufman *et al.* (1991) demonstrated, some people prefer to approach time in a straightforward fashion by accomplishing one task at a time; they are unwilling or unable to juggle more than one thing in a given unit of time. Such people are primarily monochronic. For monochronic people, time is generally linear, separable, and divisible into units. These individuals prefer to engage in serial processing of tasks. Polychronic people, in contrast, often undertake multiple, concurrent tasks, perhaps interspersing small parts of activities with others. Their preferred mode of operation is parallel processing.

Temporal orientation dimension

Historically, researchers have been interested in a person's emphasis on the past, present or future (see Fraser 1981 for a review). This is our third dimension of timestyle, an individual's temporal orientation. Cottle (1976) provided evidence that temporal representations of experience help create an individual's unique personality, based in part on the emphasis he or she places on the past versus the future or present (see also Graham 1981; Kaufman and Lane 1990; Mowen 2000; Philipp 1992). This is not to say that, for example, future-oriented individuals will only consider the importance of the future in their lives. Still, the temporal orientation dimension helps differentiate individuals based on the relative importance they attach to the three temporal zones (Cottle 1976). Similarly, Holbrook (1993) suggests that even within a relatively homogeneous age group, there could be substantial individual differences in the temporal orientation dimension.

Planning dimension

Some prior researchers have also speculated that people vary considerably in the way in which they approach (or avoid) planning when it comes to time management (e.g. Bond and Feather 1988; Cotte *et al.* 1999; Macan 1994; Mowen 2000). We refer to this aspect of timestyle as the planning dimension: how an individual organizes and plans his or her time. The planning dimension involves a continuum from a highly analytical style, where time management occurs in terms of small, discrete time units and a preference for organization, to a more holistic orientation where temporal categories are loose and unstructured. (Indeed, at the latter extreme, there might be no planning at all.) For example, while some people might plan their workdays in 15- or 30-minute intervals using a day-planner, others might simply plan for "things to do this week."

If individuals have unique timestyles, as we have argued here, then an interesting question emerges: what are the major influences that might shape one's timestyle?

Potential influences on timestyle

In keeping with the spirit of this volume, we examine various levels of influences on an individual's timestyle. Beginning with a review of possible cultural influences, we progress through increasingly idiosyncratic categories, and end with the influence of life projects on timestyle. Table 12.1 provides a summary of these influences, along with a list of key literature cited in the discussion below.

Cultural influences

Culture is perhaps the most macro level of influence on timestyle. Hall (1976) suggests that a culture's orientation towards time permeates and influences the meaning of time for individuals within that culture. In a like vein, Graham (1981) argues that in contrast to the linear conception of time held by most "Anglo" cultures, other cultures (e.g. Latin American) often view time as cyclical or procedural (see also Jones 1988; Levine 1988). We do not

Table 12.1 Potential influences on timestyle

Potential influences	Representative research	
Culture	Cole and Scribner (1974) Cotte (1998) Cottle (1976) Graham (1981) Hall (1976)	Jones (1988) Manrai and Manrai (1995) Medin and Wattenmaker 　(1987) Rhee *et al.* (1995)
Family	Bergadaá (1990) Cotte (1998) Moore-Shay and Berchmans 　(1996)	Moore-Shay and Lutz (1988) Moschis (1987)
Work groups	Bluedorn and Denhardt (1988) Cotte and Ratneshwar (1999) McGrath and Kelly (1986)	Schriber and Gutek (1987) Slocombe and Bluedorn 　(in press)
Age	Bergadaá (1990) Gorman and Wessman (1977)	Havighurst (1973) Holbrook (1993)
Gender	Block, Saggau, and Nickol (1984) Feldman and Hornik (1981) Juster (1985)	Cottle (1976) Hall (1976) Manrai and Manrai (1995)
Life themes 　and values	Cotte (1998) Csikszentmihalyi and Beattie 　(1979)	Mick and Buhl (1992) Zirkel and Cantor (1990)
Life projects	Cantor (1990) Cantor *et al.* (1987) Cotte (1998)	Kleine *et al.* (1993) Mick and Buhl (1992) Zirkel and Cantor (1990)
Situational 　influences	Cotte (1998)	Graham (1981) Kleine *et al.* (1993)

believe that every individual within a culture will necessarily reflect the dominant timestyle of that culture (cf. Hall 1976). Cultural generalizations can easily sink in a morass of stereotypes. Still, several studies suggest that culture likely influences, though perhaps subtly, one's orientation to time.

Manrai and Manrai (1995) discuss how cultural context affects perceptions of time usage along the social dimension. Drawing on the work of Levine (1988) and Hall (1976), they distinguish different cultural contexts in terms of the importance accorded to social interactions. High context cultures (e.g. Asia, Latin America, and the Middle East) are supposed to strongly emphasize social interactions. These cultures typically are thought to value social time over time spent alone. Low context cultures (e.g. the US, Canada, and Western Europe) are presumed to treat time as a tangible asset and self-time is pre-eminent. Another source of cultural differences in the social dimension is due to individualistic (vs. collectivist) cultures typically placing less stress on the role of others in one's life (see Rhee *et al.* 1995).

Again, we reiterate our reservations about cultural stereotypes; nonetheless, to the extent that such generalizations arise from social norms actually prevalent in a particular society, they perhaps have some plausibility.

Prior literature also suggests that the polychronic dimension is likely to vary across cultures. As previously noted, monochronic people tend to perceive time as linear, separable, and composed of small intervals. Indeed, this is the traditional Western, Anglo cultural perception of time. In such cultures, serial processing is often encouraged and reinforced as a social norm (common phrases in the US include "Now is not the time for that" or "Do one thing at a time"). On the other hand, the representation of time tends to be polychronic in cultures (e.g. Latin American) that treat time as a system where the same events reoccur in natural cycles (Graham 1981). In these cultures, parallel processing presumably is common; hence, for example, a businessperson may conduct several meetings at once, elongating the time each meeting takes to complete.

Jones (1988) suggests that cultures also differ in the relative significance they attribute to the past, the present, or the future (see also Cottle 1976). In addition, Graham (1981) makes the case that the perception of time is an integral part of an individual's culture and it affects one's temporal orientation. As a perhaps extreme example, cultures with a belief in reincarnation will likely have completely different views of the past and the future than would a culture primarily focused on the "here and now."

Regarding the planning dimension, we are not aware of any strong evidence for cultural differences in basic cognitive processes such as perception and learning. Nevertheless, Cole and Scribner (1974) found cultural differences in when and how people use categorization. Cultures tend to share cognitive models and the categories used may vary cross-culturally (Medin and Wattenmaker 1987). It remains a question for future research whether cross-cultural variations in cognitive models and the relative prevalence of fine-grained temporal categories in a given culture are associated with corresponding differences in the planning dimension.

Note that we are not suggesting that timestyle mediates all cultural influences on time and leisure consumption. Culture can influence such consumption in several different ways without involving timestyle. For example, in Cotte's (1998) work she found that ethnicity directly influenced Latin immigrant women's leisure goals such as "maintaining cultural heritage and tradition." Therefore, although we suggest that culture – as well as the other influences discussed in this section – in many instances influences time and leisure consumption via timestyle, we recognize the fact that such factors can influence consumption more directly too.

Family socialization influences

Moschis (1987) argues that children learn to pattern their consumption behaviors after their parents and the latter often serve as role models. In a like vein, Bergadaá (1990) suggests that attitudes towards preferring time alone versus time with others can be learned through modeling or through direct communications between parents and children. A child raised to think that time is a valuable resource requiring careful planning will likely deal differently with time as an adult than will a child raised to value spontaneity. And when children constantly watch their parents juggle several tasks simultaneously instead of methodically proceeding through each task, they may be more inclined to adopt a polychronic orientation (see Timmer, Eccles, and O'Brien 1985).

Support – albeit indirect – for such speculations in a consumer behavior context is available in some recent research by Moore-Shay and her colleagues. Moore-Shay and Berchmans' (1996) work on intergenerational influence provides evidence that higher-level values (e.g. materialism) can be transmitted within a family from one generation to another. Moore-Shay and Berchmans' research also shows that children often react to a parent's perceived incompetence at some important task (e.g. living within one's means) by orienting themselves in the opposite direction (e.g. by becoming extraordinarily thrifty). However, when children perceive parents to be good at a task, they are quite likely to learn this skill. In a related study, Moore-Shay and Lutz (1988) found that children tend to adopt their parents' budgeting skills and buying decision rules.

More direct evidence of intergenerational influences on timestyle is available in the recent work of Cotte (1998). She assessed sibling similarity in the polychronic dimension among thirty dyads of sisters. She found a significant family influence on polychronicity even after controlling for age and income. Cotte also found evidence that the family factor significantly influences the temporal orientation dimension.

Work-group influences

Within a culture, one's work environment can also influence timestyle (Slocombe and Bluedorn, in press). For example, the dominant perception of time in an American multinational firm operating within a foreign culture will likely influence the timestyle of local employees. Typically, interaction in the workplace is a form of social interaction wherein two or more individuals communicate with each other in some meaningful way. When an individual begins working in a new group, meaningful communication will likely develop between the individual and others, thus meshing the individual's sense of self with the identity of the work group as a whole (McGrath and Kelly 1986; Mead 1977). And when it comes to attitudes towards time, to effectively interact with the group, the individual must either learn (i.e. accept) the group-created timestyle, or successfully communicate his or her own timestyle to others in the group (Cotte and Ratneshwar 1999; Macan 1994).

Consider a person with a holistic planning style and a preference for polychronic behavior who joins an organization whose culture encourages (or dictates) an analytic planning style and monochronic behavior. The new employee has a choice. The individual can adapt his or her timestyle to fit the group – even if only at work. Alternatively, the employee can try to convince the group to accept her or his timestyle. If the first alternative is not perceived as desirable, and the second option proves to be infeasible, the employee may have no choice but to leave the group.

The social construction view articulated above assumes that social (and work) life is constantly forming and changing due to complex interactions among individuals who face a common need to communicate and create meaning (see Blumer 1969). This view is quite consistent with prior ideas in the literature on time, especially the notion that work groups collectively construe their understanding of time and its boundaries (Schriber and Gutek 1987; Bluedorn and Denhardt 1988; Kaufman and Lane 1990).

The role of age

Based on prior research, it seems likely that age plays a role in shaping timestyle. Age likely influences the social dimension; Havighurst (1973) showed that as people age, they tend towards solitary rather than other-directed activities. Manrai and Manrai (1995) also suggest that there are individual differences in capabilities and preferences for polychronic behavior. Temporal orientation – whether people are past-, present-, or future-oriented – is also likely to be influenced by age (Bergadaá 1990; Holbrook 1993). Finally, we are not aware of any research that has explicitly examined the influence of age on the planning dimension.

The role of gender

Gender is also a likely influence on timestyle. Although the social dimension is not directly addressed by Manrai and Manrai (1995) or Feldman and Hornik (1981), their work suggests that gender differences likely exist on this dimension, with women likely more socially-oriented than men. Concerning temporal orientation, the results of both Cottle (1976) and Juster (1985) suggest that men are more future-oriented while women tended to be more present-oriented. Manrai and Manrai (1995) suggest women may be more polychronic. As with age, we do not know of research that explicitly addresses the link between gender and the planning dimension.

The role of life themes and values

Life themes and values refer to personal ideals of being (see Huffman *et al.*, this volume). They are overarching concerns that individuals address in their lives based on their own unique personal histories (Csikszentmihalyi and Beattie 1979). It is generally assumed that life themes and values are limited in number and do not vary much over an individual's lifespan (Huffman *et al.*, this volume; Mick and Buhl 1992). Examples of life themes include "aesthetics," "independence," and "congeniality."

We suggest that an individual's life themes and values, in their role as dominant and enduring forces in that person's life, should influence his or her outlook on time and use of time (see also Cotte 1998). For example, life themes such as congeniality are concerned with who a person is "trying to be" and will likely affect the relative preference for time spent alone versus time with others (i.e. the social dimension). Indeed, one might expect that a core aspect of one's self-conception is the relative emphasis on self over others. In addition, life themes are usefully conceived as "problems" which individuals constantly attempt to solve during their lives (e.g. "how to stay independent"). The means by which people attempt to solve these problems may have implications for timestyle – an individual with a life theme of "achievement and success," for example, may be a strong believer in creating time through multi-tasking. Thus, one's life themes and values, and the means by which one addresses these themes and values, are both likely to influence aspects of timestyle such as the social and polychronic dimensions.

Similarly, it is quite possible that life themes and values influence the temporal orientation dimension of timestyle. An individual's life themes and values will often reflect a definite emphasis on one of the three temporal zones. For example, a person with the life theme of maintaining tradition may be more likely to be past-oriented (Holbrook 1993). And in Mick and Buhl's (1992) research, an informant's theme of being true versus being false appeared to direct his temporal orientation to the "here and now" present rather than some far-off future. Finally, and somewhat speculatively, we suggest that life themes and values should influence the planning dimension. Whether one plans time meticulously, or simply lets things happen as they will, may be influenced by one's overall outlook on life in matters such as being organized and efficient or being impulsive.

The role of life projects

Life projects refer to the construction and maintenance of key life roles and identities (Kleine, Kleine, and Kernan 1993; Huffman *et al.*, this volume; Mick and Buhl 1992). Life projects are derived from and influenced by "trying to be" life themes and values (Huffman *et al.*, this volume). Examples of life projects include "become a partner in a law firm," "be a good mother," and "be great at chess." Although a person may have more than one current life project, and though projects usually change (perhaps slowly) over a life span, these projects are relatively long-term. Life projects help an individual selectively choose tasks, sub-goals, and activities that reflect their preferred life roles (Cantor *et al.* 1987; Cantor 1990; Huffman *et al.*, this volume).

As in the case of life themes and values, we propose that life projects may have an impact on all four dimensions of timestyle. Life projects (e.g. to be a good mother or a good boss) are often inherently concerned with the significant personal relationships in one's life. Consequently, the implementation of life projects will often involve actions and initiatives designed to build and preserve important relationships with others. This suggests that when it comes to timestyle, life projects should influence a person's social dimension. We also speculate that life projects will influence the polychronic dimension as a chosen life project may demand a greater multi-tasking orientation (see Kaufman *et al.* 1991; Manrai and Manrai 1995).

Further, Cantor and her colleagues posit that the nature and content of a life project will influence the cognitive strategies used in pursuing this project. An important dimension to these strategies is the relative emphasis on retrospection versus thinking ahead and future planning (see, e.g., Cantor *et al.* 1987). In the context of the temporal dimension of timestyle, a person with a life project such as succeeding in a particular career may primarily conceive time in terms of the future. Cantor *et al.* (1987) also suggest that a second critical aspect of these cognitive strategies is the stress placed by the individual on conscious and effortful planning. To the extent the achievement of a particular life project necessitates and prompts systematic time management by the individual, it should influence the planning dimension of timestyle.

Situational influences

An important question at this point concerns the stability of an individual's timestyle across situations. Some recent research suggests that timestyle can be domain-specific – for at least some individuals – and that it is possible that people oscillate on a situational basis between two very different timestyles (see Cotte 1998). For example, one might be very analytic and monochronic at work but, possibly in reaction to this style, deliberately holistic and polychronic in leisure. Graham (1981) also theorized that individuals might switch from one perception of time to another depending on the task being performed. Consistent with the present ideas, prior research has also shown that a person's sense of self-identity, and the various roles he or she mentally activates, are both significantly influenced by contexts such as office vs. home (Kleine *et al.* 1993).

Interestingly, some of Cotte's (1998) data suggest that timestyle oscillations are often related to highly premeditated patterns of rebellion on the part of some individuals against timestyles they see as somewhat imposed on them. It is not just that people simply select and activate a specific timestyle depending on situational domain. Rather, some people react against the style necessitated or imposed on them in one domain (e.g. work) by consciously reverting to a polar opposite style in another domain (e.g. leisure) where they have fewer constraints and more choice. Such patterns of reactive and mutinous swings in timestyles may reflect more fundamental dialectical tensions in the time domain – between being extremely planned versus being highly spontaneous, for example. In this sense, when individuals switch and swing between totally opposite timestyles, their phenomenological experience might well mirror the "teeter-totter" feelings described by Mick and Fournier (1998) in their recent work on consumer paradoxes. Indeed, Cotte (1998), in investigating how women cope with time, finds some of the same paradoxes and dialectical tensions that Mick and Fournier identify in regard to coping with technology – for example, freedom vs. enslavement, and efficiency vs. waste.

Relationships among the various influences on timestyle

In the preceding discussion, we outlined some of the important influences on timestyle. Some of these variables are obviously more under the individual's control than others. For example, one is of a certain age and gender and one is born into a certain family and culture. To the extent that such variables play a critical role, timestyle becomes a rather deterministic construct. Notwithstanding, other factors such as work groups, life themes and values, and life projects are far more idiosyncratic and individually determined. If future research shows that the latter group of variables is, in fact, more influential, the notion of timestyle becomes less deterministic and it takes on the nature of a true individual-difference variable.

Note that some variables may be "nested" or embedded within another; in other cases, there may be a natural correlation between variables (see also Lewis and Weigert 1981). Hence, it may be difficult to empirically disentangle and partial out the different influences on timestyle (see Mick and Buhl 1992 for a related discussion). For example, cultural and family influences often work together, but perhaps more so in some cultures than in others. Consider cultures where parental authority is far more absolute than it is in mainstream America. In these cultures, the family influence may be strong, causing family/culture interactions. Family may also influence one's overall life themes; for example, a child may choose a life centered on resisting authority, in part because of his or her experiences while growing up in a particular household. A final example of this interconnectedness would be the relationship between age and life projects. In general, the projects people undertake at age 21 are likely very different from projects they pursue at age 65. Thus, although we believe that each of the influences discussed in this section can potentially have a unique impact on timestyle, we do not suggest these influences are independent of one another.

Timestyle and leisure consumption

Consistent with the theme of this book, we assume most consumer behavior is goal-driven. To appreciate the close relationship between timestyle and consumer goals, consider the domain of leisure. Leisure consumption – whether it is browsing the Web, visiting one's family during the Christmas holidays, or taking a nap on a Saturday afternoon – implies the consumption of discretionary time. As we noted earlier, peoples' orientations toward time should have a pervasive influence on what they wish to do with their time (Bergadaá 1990; Feldman and Hornik 1981; Joncs 1998; Kaufman *et al.* 1991). This implies that one's view of time will likely influence the choice of leisure goals, and even the extent to which leisure goals are specific and well-defined. Timestyle, consequently, should also have an impact on leisure activities undertaken in the pursuit of leisure goals.

Take, for example, an individual who has a polychronic and "here and now" (present) orientation, a preference for holistic planning, and a preference for time with others. Leisure goals for this person might include the pursuit of multiple, spontaneous, hedonistic activities, many of which involve interactions with other people. Such a person might embark, for example, on a "pub-crawl" at the spur of the moment and with an impromptu gathering of friends. Conversely, if a person's timestyle is monochronic, future-oriented, analytic, and self-oriented, leisure goals might include the learning of new skills and a desire to excel in some chosen field. This individual might systematically set aside blocks of leisure time for reading self-help books or for taking lessons from a coach in a particular sport.

Two examples from recent research

Two brief examples from a recent phenomenological study illustrate some of the linkages between specific antecedent influences and timestyle, and between timestyle and leisure goals and behaviors. A full report of the study's findings is available in Cotte (1998). This study was designed to enrich our understanding of the timestyle construct, and to validate our emerging framework with qualitative data. In these examples, we first provide background information about two female informants and sketch their life themes and values as well as their life projects. We then suggest how these factors influence their timestyles and their ultimate leisure consumption behaviors.

Maria

Maria is a 24-year-old Peruvian woman who has been in the US for six months. She is future-oriented, a holistic planner with a polychronic bent, and has a strong social orientation. Maria's father, a very dominant influence in her life, owns a large construction firm in Peru and has sent

Maria to the US to study English language and then acquire an MBA degree, followed by a return to the family business in Peru. Beginning in high school, Maria's father chose her course of studies and her major. Now, Maria is having second thoughts about the MBA, preferring to study computer science for personal interest. She is quite afraid of confronting her father with her wishes, because of his likely disapproval and possible thwarting of her plans (e.g. by refusing to pay her tuition). Her father has also apparently interfered with Maria's past love relationships; Maria and her mother keep her current relationship with a non-Latino man a secret from her father. A dominant life theme for Maria is the resolution of the tension between pleasing her father versus pleasing self, or more simply, family versus independence. At this stage in her life, an important life project for Maria is to find and launch a career in which she will be successful and happy.

Maria's timestyle appears to reflect the aforementioned life theme and life project. She has a strong orientation to the future – she keeps looking ahead to the sort of career and life that she personally wants. Her life theme of independence is reflected in her preference for spur of the moment decisions when it comes to leisure time (i.e. holistic planning). She also takes a polychronic approach to leisure time and often finds herself engaged in multiple leisure activities simultaneously – notwithstanding the fact that this causes her considerable stress.

Further, the cherished life theme of becoming independent from family (especially her father) makes social relationships with others especially salient and important for Maria. Indeed, she approaches her leisure time with the primary goal of building a successful love relationship with her current, non-Latino boyfriend. And, consistent with her future orientation in timestyle, she takes a long-term perspective on her love relationship. Many of Maria's leisure activities reflect her principal leisure goal of gradually building her love relationship. These include not only dinners and movies with her boyfriend, but also teaching him Spanish and listening to Latin music with him.

Jane

Our next example is Jane, who, like Maria, is future-oriented. But concerning the other three dimensions, in contrast to Maria, Jane is an analytic planner with a monochronic style and a preference for spending time alone. Jane is a 28-year-old American woman who manages a fast-food franchise and is in the process of opening her own franchised store. She has been married for a year and she and her husband are looking to buy a home. Jane has been studying on a part-time basis for the last seven years to attain a college degree. For much of her adult life, Jane has been in a state of flux – nothing has quite been finished. Indeed, getting closure on some of her "projects" has become an important life theme for Jane, one that suggests an ongoing struggle between a desire for permanence and the reality of change. Jane's current life projects include a stable, happy marriage; a permanent home; completion of her college degree; and achieving career stability by becoming a successful entrepreneur and running her own business.

Jane's timestyle is consistent with her own life themes and projects. For example, Jane is very analytic in her planning and she has a strong monochronic orientation. Both of these aspects are obviously consistent with her goal of becoming a successful business owner. Further, given her desire to reach closure on multiple life projects, each of which requires a significant investment of her time, she treats time as a very precious commodity. Not surprisingly, Jane has adopted a rigorous planning style and a resolute "focus on one thing at a time" mentality; she believes these attributes are critical for her to make significant and visible progress on her life projects. In addition, Jane prefers to spend her spare time alone and is future-oriented. Spending her spare time by herself affords Jane the opportunity to plan and build towards a more permanent, stable future for herself and her husband. It might seem that Jane's preference for spending her leisure time alone is somewhat incongruent with her life project of having a happy marriage. However, the facts of her current life situation suggest an explanation. She works days and her husband works nights, so it is important (or perhaps even necessary) for her to be content spending her spare time alone in order to achieve a happy marriage.

Jane's timestyle, in conjunction with some aspects of her life themes and life projects, seem to influence her leisure goals and behaviors. Like Maria, Jane constantly looks ahead to the future and desires success both in her career and in a long-term personal relationship. Unlike Maria, however, when it comes to leisure time, Jane pursues these life projects through the learning and development of appropriate skills. As a consequence, at the "trying to do" level of goals, Jane wants to better her life situation and wishes to progress on her life projects through her leisure activities (cf. Cantor 1990; Huffman *et al.*, this volume). She does so by taking classes – one at a time – in subjects as diverse as golf, cooking, financial planning, and (interestingly) time management. These activities fulfill her learning goals, and because she takes a few of these classes with her husband, Jane's leisure activities help her also work on her life project of a happy marriage. In addition, Jane's monochronic orientation is consistent with her proclivity for pursuing one main leisure activity at a time.

Discussion and future research directions

Time is a central aspect of consumption. Consumers need time to consume most, if not all, products and services. And in explaining consumption activities – whether it is eating a meal alone in one's home, doing the laundry, visiting a museum, or vacationing at Club Med – we need to investigate how people perceive, think about, and deal with discretionary time. In this context, we have offered an integrative, four-dimensional framework for understanding individual differences in timestyle. Our framework includes a social dimension (preference for time alone vs. with others), a polychronic dimension (preference for serial vs. parallel activities), a temporal orientation dimension (to the past, present or future), and a planning dimension (analytic vs. holistic time management).

In addition to discussing the multiple facets of timestyle, we examined various factors that might influence an individual's timestyle. These factors ranged from "micro," individual-centered variables (e.g. life themes and values, life projects), to age, gender, family, and work groups, and finally to the broad, "macro" influence of culture. These influences – and there could be others – are diverse and yet they illustrate that timestyle is probably shaped by core aspects of a person's self-identity in conjunction with a set of sociocultural factors (see Brownstein *et al.*, this volume). These factors collectively determine how individuals perceive, interpret, and consume time.

Some of these antecedent influences can be extremely dynamic. Certainly, one's age is constantly changing, and influences such as work groups and life projects will likely vary over time (cf. Kaufman and Lane 1990; Holbrook 1993). In addition, situational influences are inherently dynamic. However, some of the influences we discussed are "hard-wired"; one is born into a culture and a family. One is also born a certain biological sex, although the term gender could be more dynamic. An individual's life themes and values change (if at all) very slowly (Mick and Buhl 1992). Therefore, our discussion of influences on timestyle includes both changing (and changeable) concepts, as well as influences that are more static. Overall, however, it does seem that individuals are quite capable of evolving and adapting their timestyles with the passage of time and in response to alterations in their circumstances and life endeavors.

Measurement issues

Our discussion here has been primarily theoretical, with brief illustrative data provided from a recent qualitative study. Future research could measure the four timestyle dimensions with appropriate scales and assess the impact of the various antecedent influences. Although researchers have done some psychometric work in this area, several of the dimensions currently lack reliable scales of measurement. Perhaps the most well-established work in this area concerns the measurement of polychronicity. Kaufman and her colleagues have created an impressive psychometric history for this dimension, which should easily lend itself to further quantitative research (see, e.g., Bluedorn *et al.* 1999; Kaufman *et al.* 1991). The temporal orientation dimension has proven more difficult to assess. Two main measurement methods are the "circles" approach (Cottle 1976) and more direct survey approaches (e.g. Bluedorn *et al.* 1999; Mowen 2000; Schriber and Gutek 1987). Cottle also suggests a more indirect measurement method, involving the temporal placement of the major events in a respondent's life (see also Philipp 1992). The differing approaches tend to produce varying results, and more work is needed for developing and validating appropriate scales for measuring temporal orientation. While some initial work has been done in the measurement of the planning dimension (see Bond and Feather 1988; Calabresi and Cohen 1968), work in the area of time perception often overlooks the planning dimension (but see Macan 1994). Our work theorizes that this planning dimension can have a major impact on leisure and other consumption behaviors; hence, valid scales for measurement and assessment of this dimension of timestyle should be a research priority. Finally, we note that virtually no scale development efforts have been made for the social dimension of timestyle.

Research on antecedent influences

When it comes to the various factors that potentially influence timestyle, it should be apparent to our reader that although there is considerable evidence to support many of our conjectures, we are being quite speculative in some areas. For example, based on Mick and Buhl's (1992) work on advertising meanings and Cotte's (1998) recent research in the time domain we suggested links between life themes and values and life projects and timestyle. However, the findings of the aforementioned investigations are only broadly suggestive of such links; more research is needed to establish the association between, for example, specific life themes and values and particular dimensions of timestyle. Similarly, future research might fruitfully examine the relationship between age and gender and each of the four dimensions of timestyle; very little data is available at present on this issue. In addition, researchers might further examine the relationships between personality traits and the individual dimensions of timestyle (see, e.g., Mowen 2000).

We noted that recent research suggests that work groups appear to influence timestyle by helping to shape the meaning of time for individuals within those work groups (see, e.g., Cotte and Ratneshwar 1999). Nevertheless, we do not know whether such work-group influences carry over to the individual's timestyle in non-work environments. For instance, it is conceivable that if an individual's work group demands and shapes a very analytic and monochronic timestyle, this person might eventually approach even leisure consumption decisions with a similar orientation. However, as previously discussed, there is some evidence that people might consciously rebel against their workplace styles by adopting diametrically opposite styles when it comes to leisure. We presume that some moderating variables could govern the relative likelihood of each of these outcomes. Future research could shed light on such moderating variables and whether, taken as a whole, individuals are more likely to assimilate or contrast their away-from-work timestyles to their workplace orientations.

We also discussed how the family environment could influence one's timestyle. The findings of Cotte (1998) and Moore-Shay and Lutz (1988) suggest that from a methodological perspective, the co-orientation approach offers considerable potential for future research in this area. Although their results are promising, much more empirical work is needed to verify the extent to which family socialization influences individual dimensions of timestyle. Researchers could also examine whether family influence on timestyle is mainly a result of vicarious observation and simple behavioral modeling on the part of children, or whether this influence is precipitated by "teaching" and exhortation on the part of parents. Many other interesting questions abound in this area. For example, are there situations where children rebel against their parents' views of time and deliberately adopt opposite timestyles? Do siblings influence each other's views of timestyle? If so, are the nature and direction of such sibling influences dependent on factors such as birth order, extent of age differences, and the gender of the siblings? And, perhaps even more fundamentally, is it even possible to separate out family influence from factors such as culture and ethnicity within which "family" is embedded?

Research on relationships between timestyle and consumer behaviors

The construct of timestyle seems relevant for consumer and consumption behaviors in many domains. First, as we pointed out earlier, timestyle is likely to affect consumers' decisions regarding leisure products, services, and activities. Consider a person, say Mrs A, who carefully sets aside every Friday evening in her calendar for playing in an organized Bingo game at her local club. Contrast her behavior with another individual of similar age and gender, Mrs B, who waits till Friday evening arrives before giving any thought whatsoever to the leisure time that is at her disposal that evening. Mrs B then spontaneously decides whether she should curl up with a book while watching TV, do her laundry while talking to her mother on a cordless phone, or perhaps go to a movie alone. We propose, in essence, that differences in leisure behaviors between people like A and B can be explained, at least in part, by differences in their timestyles.

Note that recent consumer research in the domain of leisure tends to focus on "extraordinary experiences" and experiential consumption in relation to activities such as river-rafting and skydiving (see, e.g., Arnould and Price 1993; Celsi *et al.* 1993). Such investigations typically attempt to uncover and describe a variety of motives (e.g. hedonic risk-seeking) that underlie such consumption decisions and behaviors. Our research complements this prior literature by suggesting that an individual's timestyle plays an important role in decisions regarding even the most mundane of leisure activities. Future research might explore whether and how the construct of timestyle can be combined with concepts such as utilitarian, hedonic, and symbolic motives to provide a more complete account of leisure consumption decisions (see Holbrook and Hirschman 1982).

The intricate ties between "being" or self-identity goals such as life themes and values and life projects (Huffman *et al.*, this volume) and timestyle seem important for explaining leisure activity choices and many other consumption behaviors as well. Huffman *et al.* emphasize the top-down impact of being-level goals on "doing" goals such as intended consumption actions (exercising at the gym, cooking, riding a bus to work, etc.). A crucial aspect of all "doing" goals is that they involve the appropriation (consciously or otherwise) of discretionary time, since doing anything fundamentally requires time. Hence, if the construct of timestyle is relevant at all for the consumption of time, it should be implicated in one way or the other in the relationship between being-level goals and consumption intentions. Future research may help us understand these relationships in regard to not only the consumption of leisure products and activities but also consumer motives for buying products as diverse as antiques, innovations that are "ahead of their time," time-saving technologies, time organizers, and time-consuming "do-it-yourself" home improvements.

The construct of timestyle also offers potential for researchers investigating shopping behaviors and styles, for example, in the retail domain (see also Kaufman and Lane 1996). The various dimensions of timestyle will likely have an impact on shopping behaviors such as how much pre-purchase planning is undertaken; whether people prefer browsing or "in-and-out" shopping; whether or not shopping lists are made; and whether people prefer to shop alone or with others. In a broader sense, timestyle might also influence a desire for convenience in shopping; it might also prove to be a good predictor of behaviors such as searching for product information and buying through the Web. Moreover, with timestyle as an intervening construct, one could examine how factors such as culture and one's family ultimately influence individuals' shopping patterns.

In terms of the practice of market segmentation, timestyle is a behavioral segmentation variable. Consequently, marketers will find it of value in targeting decisions only if the descriptive correlates of timestyle can be determined. Without such descriptive or identifying variables, marketers would have great difficulty in determining sizes of target market segments or selecting appropriate media for communications. Our previous discussion suggests that identifying variables such as age, gender, and ethnicity may prove to be correlated significantly with the various dimensions of timestyle. If so, it should be possible to build descriptive and managerially useful profiles of segments of individuals who have specific timestyles. Again, it is a topic for future research to ascertain the nature and extent of these correlations and thus the potential value of the timestyle construct to marketers.

Acknowledgments

We thank Robin Coulter, Carol Kaufman, John Mowen, and Priya Ratneshwar for their thorough and very helpful comments and suggestions.

References

Arnould, E.J. and Price, L.L. (1993) "River Magic: extraordinary experience and the extended service encounter," *Journal of Consumer Research* 20 (1): 24–45.

Becker, G.S. (1976) *The Economic Approach to Human Behavior*, Chicago: The University of Chicago Press.

Bergadaá, M. (1990) "The role of time in the action of the consumer," *Journal of Consumer Research* 17 (December): 289–302.

Block, R., Saggau, J.L., and Nickol, L.H. (1984) "Temporal inventory on meaning and experience: a structure of time," *Imagination, Cognition, and Personality* 3 (3): 203–25.

Bluedorn, A.C. and Denhardt, R.B. (1988) "Time and organizations," *Journal of Management* 14 (2): 299–320.

Blumer, H. (1969) *Symbolic Interactionism: Perspectives and Method*, Berkeley: University of California Press.

Bond, M.J. and Feather, N.T. (1988) "Some correlates of structure and purpose in the use of time," *Journal of Personality and Social Psychology* 55 (August): 321–9.

Calabresi, R. and Cohen, J. (1968) "Personality and time attitudes," *Journal of Abnormal Psychology* 73 (5): 431–9.

Cantor, N. (1990) "From thought to behavior: 'having' and 'doing' in the study of personality and cognition," *American Psychologist* 45 (6): 735–50.

Cantor, N., Norem, J.K., Niedenthal, P.M., Langston, C., and Brower, A.M. (1987) "Life tasks, self-concept ideals, and cognitive strategies in a life transition," *Journal of Personality and Social Psychology* 53 (December): 1178–91.

Celsi, R., Rose, R., and Leigh, T. (1993) "An exploration of high-risk leisure consumption through skydiving," *Journal of Consumer Research* 20 (June): 1–38.

Cole, M. and Scribner, S. (1974) *Culture and Thought: A Psychological Introduction*, New York: John Wiley and Sons.

Cotte, J. (1998) "Deciding what to do: a behavioral framework for leisure consumption decisions," unpublished doctoral dissertation, University of Connecticut.

Cotte, J. and Ratneshwar, S. (1999) "Juggling and hopping: the created meaning of working polychronically," *Journal of Managerial Psychology* 14 (3/4): 184–204.

—— (1998) "Consumer decisions on discretionary time: a sociocognitive perspective," in J.W. Alba and J.W. Hutchinson (eds) *Advances in Consumer Research*, vol. 25, Provo UT: Association for Consumer Research: 268–75.

Cotte, J., Ratneshwar, S., and Mick, D.G. (1999) "Timestyle: an integrated framework and application to leisure consumption decisions," working paper.

Cottle, T.J. (1976) *Perceiving Time: A Psychological Investigation with Men and Women*, New York: John Wiley and Sons.

Csikszentmihalyi, M. and Beattie, O.V. (1979) "Life themes: a theoretical and empirical exploration of their origins and effects," *Journal of Humanistic Psychology* 19 (1): 45–63.

Feldman, L.P. and Hornik, J. (1981) "The use of time: an integrated conceptual model," *Journal of Consumer Research* 7 (March): 407–19.

Fraser, J.T. (1981) *The Voices of Time*, 2nd edition, Amherst, MA: University of Massachusetts Press.

Golden, L.L., Mesh, U.N., Weeks, W.A., and Anderson, W.T., Jr. (1988) "Time styles: comparison of spouses complimentary and substituability of activities," in S. Shapiro and A.H. Walle (eds) *AMA Winter Educators Conference Proceedings*, San Diego: American Marketing Association: 400–3.

Gorman, B.S. and Wessman, A.E. (1977) "Images, values, and concepts of time in psychological research," in B.S. Gorman and A.E. Wessman (eds) *The Personal Experience of Time*, New York: Plenum Press: 218–64.

Graham, R.J. (1981) "The role of perception of time in consumer research," *Journal of Consumer Research* 7 (March): 335–42.

Hall, E.T. (1976) *The Hidden Dimension*, New York: Anchor-Press Doubleday.

Havighurst, R.J. (1973) "Social roles, work, leisure and education," in C. Eisdorfer *et al.* (eds) *The Psychology of Adult Development and Aging*, Washington, DC: American Psychological Association.

Holbrook, M.B. (1993) "Nostalgia and consumption preferences: some emerging patterns of consumer tastes," *Journal of Consumer Research* 20 (September): 245–56.

Holbrook, M.B. and Hirschman, E.C. (1982) "The experiential aspects of consumption," *Journal of Consumer Research* 9 (September): 132–40.

Jones, J.M. (1988) "Cultural differences in temporal perspectives," in J.E. McGrath (ed.) *The Social Psychology of Time: New Perspectives*, Newbury Park: Sage Publications: 21–38.

Juster, F.T. (1985) "Investments of time by men and women," in F.T. Juster and F.P. Stafford (eds) *Time, Goods, and Well-Being*, Ann Arbor, MI: Institute for Social Research, The University of Michigan: 177–204.

Kaufman, C.F. and Lane, P.M. (1990) "The intensions and extensions of the time concept: contributions from a sociological perspective," in M.E. Goldberg, G. Corn, and R.W. Pollay (eds) *Advances in Consumer Research*, vol. 17, Provo, UT: Association for Consumer Research: 895–901.

Kaufman, C.F. and Lane, P.M. (1996) "A new look at one-stop shopping: a TIMES approach to matching store hours and shopper schedules," *Journal of Consumer Marketing* 13 (1): 4–25.

Kaufman, C.F., Lane, P.M., and Lindquist, J.D. (1991) "Exploring more than 24 hours a day: a preliminary investigation of polychronic time use," *Journal of Consumer Research* 18 (December): 392–401.

Kleine, R.E., III, Kleine, S.S., and Kernan, J.B. (1993) "Mundane consumption and the self: a social-identity perspective," *Journal of Consumer Psychology* 2 (3): 209–35.

Levine, R.V. (1988) "The pace of life across cultures," in J.E. McGrath (ed.) *The Social Psychology of Time: New Perspectives*, Newbury Park: Sage Publications: 39–60.

Lewis, D. and Weigert, D.J. (1981) "The structures and meanings of social time," *Social Forces* 60 (2) (December): 432–57.

Macan, T.H. (1994) "Time management: test of a process model," *Journal of Applied Psychology* 79 (3): 381–91.

McDonald, W.J. (1994) "Time use in shopping: the role of personal characteristics," *Journal of Retailing* 70 (4): 345–65.

McGrath, J.E. and Kelly, J.R. (1986) *Time and Human Interaction: Toward a Social Psychology of Time*, New York: Guilford Press.

Manrai, L.A. and Manrai, A.K. (1995) "Effects of cultural-context, gender, and acculturation on perceptions of work versus social/leisure time usage," *Journal of Business Research* 32: 115–28.

Mead, G.H. (1977) *George Herbert Mead on Social Psychology*, ed. A. Strauss, Chicago: The University of Chicago Press.

Medin, D.L. and Wattenmaker, W.D. (1987) "Category cohesiveness, theories, and cognitive archeology," in U. Neisser (ed.) *Concepts and Conceptual Development: Ecological and Intellectual Factors in Categorization*, Cambridge: Cambridge University Press: 25–62.

Mick, D.G. and Buhl, C. (1992) "A meaning-based model of advertising experiences," *Journal of Consumer Research* 19 (December): 317–38.

Mick, D.G. and Fournier, S. (1998) "Paradoxes of technology: consumer cognizance, emotions, and coping strategies," *Journal of Consumer Research* 25 (September): 123–43.

Moore-Shay, E. and Berchmans, B.M. (1996) "The role of the family environment in the development of shared consumption values: an intergenerational study," in K.P. Corfman and J.G. Lynch Jr. (eds) *Advances in Consumer Research*, vol. 23, Provo, UT: Association for Consumer Research: 484–90.

Moore-Shay, E. and Lutz, R.J. (1988) "Intergenerational influences in the formation of consumer attitudes and beliefs about the marketplace: mothers and daughters," in M.J. Houston (ed.) *Advances in Consumer Research*, vol. 15, Provo, UT: Association for Consumer Research: 461–7.

Moschis, G.P. (1987) *Consumer Socialization: A Life-Cycle Perspective*, Lexington, MA: Lexington.

Mowen, J.C. (2000) *The 3M Model of Motivation and Personality: Theory and Empirical Applications to Consumer Behavior*, Boston, MA: Kluwer Academic Press.

Philipp, S.F. (1992) "Time orientation and participation in leisure activities," *Perceptual and Motor Skills* 75: 659–64.

Rhee, U., Uleman, J.C., Lee, H.K., and Roman, R.J. (1995) "Spontaneous self-descriptions and ethnic identities in individualistic and collectivistic cultures," *Journal of Personality and Social Psychology* 69 (1): 142–52.

Robinson, J.P. and Godbey, G. (1997) *Time for Life: The Surprising Ways Americans Use Their Time*, University Park, Pennsylvania: The Pennsylvania State University Press.

Slocombe, T.E. and Bluedorn, A.C. (in press) "Organizational behavior implications of the congruence between preferred polychronicity and experienced work-unit polychronicity," *Journal of Organizational Behavior*.

Schriber, J.B. and Gutek, B.A. (1987) "Some time dimensions of work: measurement of an underlying aspect of organizational culture," *Journal of Applied Psychology* 72 (4): 642–50.

Timmer, S.G., Eccles, J., and O'Brien, K. (1985) "How children use time," in F.T. Juster and F.P. Stafford (eds) *Time, Goods, and Well-Being*, Ann Arbor, MI: Institute for Social Research, The University of Michigan: 353–82.

Zirkel, S. and Cantor, N. (1990) "Personal construal of life tasks: those who struggle for independence," *Journal of Personality and Social Psychology* 58 (1): 172–85.

13 Using narratives to discern self-identity related consumer goals and motivations

Jennifer Edson Escalas and James R. Bettman

Introduction

People make sense of their lives by thinking about themselves and the events around them in story form (Bruner 1990). Narratives, considered here to be synonymous with stories, organize events into a framework that establishes causal relationships between the story's elements over time; hence, by their very structure, narratives focus on individuals' motivations and goals (Sanfey and Hastie 1998). In a narrative, a person's actions are evaluated in the context of achieving his/her goals (Pennington and Hastie 1986). Stories provide us with the reasons for why things happen and why people engage in particular behaviors. For example, I understand my father's love of 1941 automobiles through his boyhood stories about growing up during World War II, when cars stopped being manufactured and adolescents were allowed to drive.

Given our narrative understanding of the world, we also think of ourselves in terms of self-stories. Moments in time are not unrelated, rather there exist goal-directed, coherent sequences linking one's past, present, and future into a present identity (Gergen and Gergen 1988). Thus, my sense of self is guided by the story I create about who I am, what has happened to me, what I have done, and what I hope to become. This chapter examines the role of narratives in understanding human motivations and goals. We focus on the relationship between consumption and creating a sense of self because we believe that to be an important and central motivation for consumers.

Much consumer research, influenced by the information processing paradigm of the 1970s and 1980s, conceptualizes people as "naïve scientists." In this chapter, we make the case for thinking of consumers as story-builders. A major focus of the stories created by consumers is to make sense of who they are and what they consume. We begin by offering a definition of narrative, including a review of narrative structure, quality, and processing. Then we examine the function of narratives, particularly their ability to provide structure for our higher-order goals, such as defining and constructing the self (see Huffman *et al.*, this volume). Next, we examine how research on narrative thought can be used to uncover motives and goals, with a series of propositions for how structural narrative analysis can complement content focused interpretation of consumer stories. By understanding the function and structure of narratives, we will be better able to determine how people engage in consumption activities to create a sense of self.

Narratives

Although a great deal of research in cognitive psychology has examined how people process information, form mental categories, and encode and retrieve information, there has only recently been an interest in narrative thought. Many scholars now assert that people naturally tend to think about and interpret the world around them through narratives (Bruner 1986; Kerby 1991). Narrative thought creates stories that are coherent accounts of particular experiences, temporally structured, and context sensitive (Baumeister and Newman 1994). The narrative mode of thought does not necessitate that individuals form elaborate, complex novels in their minds. Rather, under conditions of narrative processing, people think about incoming information as if they were trying to create a story. In day-to-day living, individuals continuously attempt to impose narrative structure on occurrences in order to understand them. For example, if I buy stale candy from my favorite brand, I may think of a narrative explanation: when the candy was being shipped out to Arizona, the truck broke down. Stuck in the heat, the candy melted, leaving it stale when it cooled again.

Thus, narrative is the mode of thought that best captures the experiential aspect of human intention, action, and consequences; it involves reasons and goals (Reissman 1993). Meaning is created by establishing relationships to other events rather than by determining category membership (Somers 1994). The narrative process is so pervasive that people spontaneously create stories to explain the random movement of colored rectangles, attributing causality to the movement (Michotte 1963 in Hermans 1996). Bruner (1986) even suggests a genetic proclivity for narrative. He proposes that the reason people have no early infancy memories is that they are unable to organize events in narrative form at that stage of development.

The structure of narratives

What makes a story a story? An important aspect of narrative thought is its structure. This structure consists of two important elements: chronology and causality. First, narrative thought organizes events in terms of a temporal dimension; things occur over time. Time is configured in narratives as episodes, whereas time in reality is an undifferentiated, continuous flow.

The human perception of events imposes a beginning, middle, and end. Polkinghorne (1991) theorizes that temporality is the primary dimension of human existence, and Kerby (1991) asserts that the general narrative objective of achieving closure (by framing the story with a beginning, middle, and end) is a fundamental way in which human events are understood.

Second, narrative thought structures elements into an organized framework that establishes relationships between the story's elements and allows for causal inferencing. Narrative story organization incorporates general knowledge about human goal-oriented action sequences that consist of a goal, action, and outcome (Stein and Albro 1997). Events are organized according to the causal and intentional relations among them. Plot transforms a listing of events into a schematic whole by establishing the contribution certain events make to the development and outcome of a story (Polkinghorne 1988).

Episode schemas, which represent a standard sequence of events in both the real world and in stories, are one way to characterize narrative structure (Pennington and Hastie 1986). In an episode schema, an event, or series of events, initiates a psychological reaction and activates goals in a main character. The goals may be formulated on the spot in response to the initial event or may be pre-existing goals that are activated by the initial event. The protagonist's psychological state and goals provide reasons for his/her subsequent actions, and these actions lead to an outcome or result. Because these narrative elements are organized through time, causal inferences can be made. What happens in time one (for example, the protagonist's car breaks down) causes what happens in time two (he buys a new car).

There is no universal agreement on narrative structure, however, particularly across differing academic fields. In psychology, Bruner (1990) contends that there are four necessary dimensions of narrative structure. First, narratives must contain agents engaged in actions undertaken to achieve goals. Second, sequential order must be established and maintained. Events and states are linearized in a standard way; there is a causal sequence of events. Third, Bruner contends that narratives must be canonical; they organize events following normative rules. When rules are broken within a story, the narrative focuses on the unusual events, with the goal of explaining such events in a way that conforms to accepted standards. Finally, narrative is never voiceless; it always comes from a narrator's perspective.

Alternatively, in the field of rhetoric, Burke (1969) defines a "pentad" of five essential elements of narrative. He asserts that any complete statement about motives will answer the following five questions, which correspond to his five elements of narrative. First, what was done? (the action). Second, when or where was it done? (the scene). Next, who did it? (the actor). Fourth, how did the actor do it? (the instrument or agency). And finally, why? (the purpose or intention). The drama, or emotional impact, of narrative emerges from an imbalance between the elements of Burke's pentad. For example, actions may not achieve the actor's goals, scenes and agents may not match, etc. Narratives strive to understand and explain these imbalances.

In linguistics, Labov (1982 in Reissman 1993) asserts that narratives have six formal properties, each with its own function. These six properties are: an abstract, which summarizes the substance of the narrative; the orientation, which is the time, place, situation, and participants; the complicating action, which is the sequence of events; the evaluation, which is the significance and meaning of the action, as well as the attitude of the narrator; the resolution, which is what finally happened; and the coda, which returns the perspective to the present. This definition goes beyond the episode schema of Pennington and Hastie and incorporates the narrator perspective of Bruner (the evaluation) as well as the interactive aspect of storytelling (the abstract, orientation, and coda situate the listener/reader).

Story grammarians, such as Mandler (1984), assert that stories have an underlying structure that remains relatively invariant in spite of differences in content from story to story. Stories consist of a setting and a series of episodes, with a final ending event. Episodes are further decomposed into smaller units, consisting of a beginning, development, and ending. The development, in turn, consists of reactions and goals. Essentially, story grammars postulate a set of categories that must be included in a story and provide rules that specify the relations between categories (Brewer and Lichtenstein 1981).

To summarize, while these theories about the necessary elements of narrative structure vary as to the fine points of what constitutes a narrative, they consistently agree on the necessity of a temporal dimension (chronology) and the presence and critical role of goals and defined relationships between story elements (causality).

Narrative quality

Beyond the basic structure of narrative, other theories have identified story characteristics that contribute to a narrative's quality, i.e. what makes a *good* story. In one such theory, Bruner (1986) proposes two dimensions to narrative: the landscape of action and the landscape of consciousness. The landscape of action is the causal sequence of events and consists of events that are visible to the casual observer: the initiating event, resulting action(s), and outcome(s). The landscape of consciousness makes the reader/listener aware of the psychological state(s) of the story's character(s) – what the character is thinking and feeling. There is an emphasis on attitudes, motivations, goals, and personal development. Whereas a landscape of action is necessary for any narrative, a landscape of consciousness has been shown to make a narrative more compelling. Readers make more inferences and exert a greater effort to construct an interpretation when a story has a well-developed landscape of consciousness (Feldman *et al.* 1990).

In addition to Bruner's landscape of consciousness, other aspects of narrative have been identified as contributors to a story's quality. Gergen and Gergen (1988) theorize that the dramatic engagement of a narrative depends on the evaluative slope of the story where the events in a story are evaluated over time (as it occurs in the narrative) for the degree to which they improve or worsen the state of the protagonist. Stories that have a steep incline or decline in evaluative slope and those that alternate in sign (e.g. rising, falling, then rising again) evoke the most emotion. The classical tragedy, *Oedipus Rex*, is an example of a narrative with rapidly deteriorating events, from the perspective of the protagonist. Gergen and Gergen would contend that this steep downward evaluative slope creates drama and generates emotion.

Stein and Albro (1997) contend that a good story is a story that is highly complex and also coherent. Complexity is an increasing function based on the inclusion of four progressively more complex dimensions: (1) an animate protagonist capable of intentional action; (2) explicit reference to the desires and goals of the protagonist; (3) actions taken by the protagonist to achieve goals; and (4) outcomes relating to the achievement or non-achievement of these goals. The most complex stories consist of multiple goal-oriented action episodes, often beginning with an initial event that is a state of loss or "lack state" which creates trauma or stress for the protagonist. The first episode ends with the protagonist facing an obstacle in the way of achieving his/her goals and subsequent episodes lead to goal achievement. Coherence depends on causal connections (versus only temporal sequencing). Coherence improves when the story contains goal-directed action episodes.

While we have only touched on a few theories about story quality, one can see that there are many ways to evaluate a story. However, the ideas presented above do not contradict each other. In general, high quality narratives evoke emotion and elaboration in listeners/readers. Bruner proposes this happens when the story includes insights into what the characters are thinking and feeling; Gergen and Gergen, when the story has a rising and falling series of events; and Stein and Albro, when the story presents a series of complex and coherent goal-directed action sequences. We would like to point out that our approach to narrative is based on the social sciences rather than literary criticism. We focus on consumer narratives reflecting their lived experiences, rather than on literary narratives composed by writers.

Narratives as a constructive organizing process

Narratives are similar to the general concepts of schemas or scripts in that they are organizing mental structures or frameworks. However, schema are defined as the general knowledge a person possesses about a particular domain (Alba and Hasher 1983). Narratives are distinct from schema in that narratives have a more narrowly defined form and function. Narratives are also different from scripts; a category that may be considered a subset of schema. Scripts are mental representations of commonly experienced events as abstractions (Abelson 1981). (A common example is the script for restaurant behavior: when you enter a restaurant, you are seated by a host, select a meal from a menu, and place an order with a wait-person. A chef prepares the food, you eat it, then a server removes the plates and you pay the bill, typically with an accompanying tip.) Narratives, however, often vary significantly from scripts, paying attention to specific details and unusual events (such as the wait-person spilling food on the customer). In fact, stories conforming strictly to scripts have been given low story ratings by subjects (Brewer and Lichtenstein 1981). Therefore, narratives are a unique concept, used by individuals to make meaning of the world at an intermediate level of abstraction. Narratives are not a camera-recorded view of reality, but they are also not as abstract as scripted behavior.

In this chapter we focus on the narrative mode of thought as a process, not a mental representation. Narratives are constructive. The typical story consists of interrelated episodes describing human action sequences; people are willing to make inferences and even delete (or forget) information in order to make their stories coherent and complete (Baumeister and Newman 1994). Narrative thinking does not lead people to ignore contradictions, but it provides a way for the inevitable inconsistencies that people observe in human behavior to be interpreted and remembered more easily (Baumeister and Newman 1994). In the narrative mode of thought, meaning is fluid and contextual (Reissman 1993). Building stories is an ongoing process; people fit characters and episodes together in a narrative form to render the world and their lives meaningful.

Thus, as story-builders, people do not record the world but rather create it, mixing in cultural and individual expectations, and combining sensory input and schematic knowledge (Chafe 1990). As a construction, narratives require creativity (Olson 1990). Stories are also greatly influenced by the social setting in which a person exists (Kerby 1991). The stories that people tell each other and themselves are determined in part both by shared language and the genre of storytelling inherited from traditions.

The function of narratives

We have argued that people naturally think about things, people, and events in the form of narratives in order to make sense of what goes on in the world. By constructing stories, individuals organize their experiences, create order, explain unusual events, and gain perspective (Bruner 1990). Narratives place events into framing contexts so that the parts can be understood in relation to the whole. The meaning of an event is the result of its being a part of a plot (Polkinghorne 1988). As a result of this emplot-ment, people can make meaningful evaluations (Pennington and Hastie 1986), form judgments (Gergen and Gergen 1988), and inform action (Olson 1990). This format for experienced events also makes them memor-able and sharable (Olson 1990). Stories allow individuals to differentiate and reintegrate action, affect, and cognition (Bruner and Lucariello 1989).

In this section, we will examine one function of narratives that is particularly relevant to understanding consumer motives and goals: creating a coherent sense of self. To build on the ideas of Huffman *et al.* (this volume), the higher-level goals of "being" (life themes and values and life projects) motivate consumer narratives. People use narratives to define who they are; only then can they act and consume (see Arnould and Price, this volume). Narratives tangibilize and structure motives and goals.

Self-narratives

People think of themselves in terms of self-stories. When asked "Who are you?" many people give a narrative account of the past, a chronologically organized, mini-history of sorts. The self is given content through narrative constructions; who one is is embedded in an ongoing, narrative history (Kerby 1991). With a more complex view of the self, where an individual has multiple aspects of self, consisting of roles and personality traits (e.g. the professor self or the independent self), self-stories can be used to define each aspect and to integrate multiple aspects into a coherent whole. For example, different aspects of the self may be illustrated with different stories about the past.

People construct identities, which can be multiple and changing, by locating themselves in stories (Somers 1994). The term self-narrative has been employed to refer to the individual's account of the relationship among self-relevant events across time (Gergen and Gergen 1988). Individuals use self-narratives for various goals: to establish a stable self, to develop an improving self, to express how difficulties are overcome, or, if depressed, to relate how events are taking a turn for the worse. Polkinghorne (1991) asserts that a major role of psychoanalysis is to assist in the reconstruction of personal stories, which under stress may decompose. In this volume, Arnould and Price examine how self-narratives are created and sustained through consumption acts and performances, in the face of a modern and changing world.

Some scholars argue that life stories are constructed around emotional reactions and evaluations, making individuals' lives more meaningful and important (Hardcastle 1999). Emotional responses tell people when things are important because they signal the relevance of a situation to their concerns and goals (Frijda 1994). A person feels emotion when he/she has a personal stake in an event or situation (Lazarus 1991), with more important personal goals leading to more intense emotions. People create stories in order to understand and cope with emotion. Narratives are able to give meaning to one's emotions, likes and dislikes, and affective ties by interpreting these feelings in light of past life events and future life goals (Averill 1994). Meaning and emotion motivate individuals to create their self-concepts using narratives. Through stories individuals are able to understand their affective responses and the significance of important events.

Some evidence for this view comes from children's self-stories, which begin with affective ties and likes and dislikes (Hardcastle 1999). Children's self-stories tend to focus on emotional affiliation and likes and dislikes, the fundamental building blocks to children's sense of self. Additional support for the emotion-centered self comes from research on autobiographical memories (Brewer 1986): because emotionally involving incidents are those that people remember best, over time the majority of autobiographical memories have strong affect associated with them.

There are also social dimensions to self-narratives. Relationships with others are lived out in narrative form (Gergen and Gergen 1988). Self-narratives also involve important relationships, because individuals often include important others in their extended self-concept (Belk 1988). Furthermore, self-stories are framed by the society in which one lives. Individuals construct themselves by adapting the plots they have learned from the cultural stock of stories and myths (Polkinghorne 1991). Narratives serve as a critical means by which people make themselves intelligible within the social world (Gergen and Gergen 1988). When we tell stories about ourselves, we select certain aspects of ourselves to communicate, projecting an image to others and reinforcing our own self-conceptualization. When I tell my students the story of how I bought my last car via the Internet, I construct my narrative to include rational, intelligent aspects of my self in order to manage the students' impression of me. This also serves to reinforce these self-dimensions in my own mind.

Autobiographical memories for particular events often take the form of narratives as well (Baumeister and Newman 1994; Fiske 1993). Autobiographical memories tend to be episodic in nature, structured as goal-oriented action sequences, where goals lead to actions with resulting outcomes (Stein and Albro 1997). Autobiographical narratives are interpretive, driven by one's goals and desires. Autobiographical stories reconstruct memories to achieve self-identity and self-presentation goals. This reconstruction helps one discover identities and deepens the understanding of significant life events and poignant emotional experiences (Woike *et al.* 1999; Polkinghorne 1991). Woike *et al.* (1999) show that personality motives, which are recurrent preferences that orient, select, and direct behavior, affect both the content and structure of autobiographical memories.

In sum, people use narratives to create a sense of self. Self-stories link the events in one's life to build a coherent self-concept, motivated by one's higher-order identity, value, and role goals. Self-stories may consist of multiple stories to account for different aspects of one's self-concept (e.g. the parent self, the professional self, the sports enthusiast self, etc.) and self-stories often include other people who are central to one's definition of self. Self-stories are often built around emotion evoking experiences, as these are the generally the most important and significant events in our lives. Overall, narratives allow people to construct their self-concepts in a temporally organized, social world (Nelson 1989).

Using narratives to gain insight into consumers' goals and motives

As argued above, narratives function by enabling individuals to create their sense of self. The structure of narratives allows stories to be used in this capacity: emotion is understood in the context of an initial event affecting an actor, unusual events are explained through canonical storylines, and self-goals are situated in relation to actors and outcomes. Hence, by examining consumer narratives, we can gain insight into how consumers understand their consumption patterns and how consumption plays a role in self-creation.

There are two aspects of narrative that may be studied: structure and content. Much of the current qualitative research done in consumer behavior, some of which is briefly highlighted below, examines the content of consumer narratives. Despite the fact that many scholars argue that form is as revealing as substance (Bruner 1990), structural narrative analysis is seldom done (for notable exceptions see Stern 1995; Stern, Thompson, and Arnould 1998). Following the brief overview of current research on narrative content, we outline a series of propositions as to how research on narrative structure could complement the current focus in consumer research on narrative content.

Qualitative research on consumer narratives

Traditional marketing interpretation of qualitative data analysis aims to uncover common patterns or themes that transcend individual experiences, as well as those aspects that vary from one individual to another (Schouten 1991). The analysis procedure is an iterative system of coding, categorizing, and abstracting the data (McCracken 1988) in order to integrate the themes found. Often these data are referred to as "consumer narratives," and since we think of ourselves in storied form, these in-depth interview protocols may indeed be relatively narrative in form. However, most of these verbal protocols have not been examined from a structural perspective, so it is difficult to know if the data adhere to Pennington and Hastie's episode schema or any other definition of narrative structure.

In most, if not all, these studies, the relationship between consumption and the self emerges through the narratives presented by informants, primarily because these individuals are sharing their personal life stories. For example, Thompson *et al.* (1990) examine self-narratives focusing on the shopping experiences of contemporary married women with children, uncovering shared goals of being in control, deliberate, and free from restrictions. Schouten (1991) looks at the consumption of aesthetic plastic surgery through life stories, focusing on self-concept dynamics during liminal periods. More recently, Kleine *et al.* (1995) take the view that possessions are artifacts of the self and are used in consumers' personal stories of self. These authors develop distinct types of possession attachments depending on the portion of the life story that the attachment reflects. Thus, all three papers uncover higher order self-identity goals by analyzing the content of consumer narratives.

However, such studies do not examine individual self-narratives (i.e. they do not analyze a story as a single unit that provides insight into the development of a single individual). In nearly all cases, the consumer narratives are gathered to compare and contrast themes across individuals to arrive at content-based categories. While this approach has been very useful, we believe it can be enhanced through the use of structural narrative analysis.

Not all research in consumer behavior focuses exclusively on content over structure, nor are we the first to make the argument that studying the structure of qualitative data, such as narratives, is useful. Advertising structure, for example, has been examined by Mick and colleagues (e.g. Mick 1987; McQuarrie and Mick 1996). In the realm of consumer narratives, Stern (1995) has analyzed the same in-depth interview data Wallendorf and Arnould (1991) gathered in their Thanksgiving article. Using Frye's genre taxonomy (i.e. comedy, romance, tragedy, and irony), she finds that the structure of the consumer stories reveals values and beliefs about what consumption events should be like in our culture. In another article, Stern *et al.* (1998) analyze a single shopping encounter narrative. Conclusions are drawn not only from what is said, but also from *how* it is said. In particular, the authors focus on departures from linear chronology, which indicate importance. The story's "flashbacks" reveal critical aspects of the protagonist's self-identity.

Stern's research is the strongest example of the additional insights a structural approach can contribute to the content-based approach currently popular in qualitative consumer research (for another example of the importance of studying both content and structure, this time in the realm of metaphors, see Coulter and Zaltman, this volume). In the next section, we propose that examining narrative structure, including overall structural quality, story genre, and individual story elements (such as the role of goals), will provide a richer interpretation than examining content alone.

Structural narrative analysis

While there are many different methods of structural narrative analysis, the main differentiating factor between it and content-based research is that in structural analysis, the qualitative data are analyzed as one narrative unit, rather than being decomposed into themes and exemplars. Thus, the first step in the analysis process is to examine the qualitative data for narratives that will be analyzed as story units. This requires detailed transcription and evaluation prior to the actual analysis. The researcher also has to decide a priori what structural definition of narrative will be used to identify the story units.

Next, the narrative units are analyzed via any one of a variety of techniques. As an example of one structural narrative analysis method, Reissman (1993) recommends core narrative reduction where stories are decomposed into a "skeleton plot" which is then compared to the skeleton plots of other subjects' stories. Typically, this analysis is done at the level of individual clauses, but with the important caveat that the entire story is treated as one larger unit per subject, rather than being dissected and fractured into smaller subparts. This is not to say that the analysis cannot be performed at a very detailed level (e.g. the use of particular words), but the comparisons are made in relation to their role in the overall story (e.g. words that indicate the identification of goals).

Comparisons are made according to any one of a variety of taxonomies that lend themselves to analyzing narratives. Examples include Bruner's four narrative elements, Bruner's landscape of action versus landscape of consciousness, Labov's six functional properties, Mandler's story grammars, Gergen and Gergen's evaluative slope, Frye's genre taxonomy, or Stein and Alba's complexity dimensions. After coding stories into these structural components, comparisons are made between plotlines and story elements within and across subjects for differences in the research areas of interest. For example, consumer stories can be analyzed for the type of goals that are mentioned and the role brands or possessions play in the achievement (or lack of achievement) of these goals.

Structural narrative analysis, whether the main methodology used to analyze qualitative data or as a complement to content-based analysis, can provide insight into consumers' goals and motivations. The following three propositions highlight some of the ways structural analysis can elucidate what's important to consumers in their consumption activities. We focus on the relationship between consumption and creating a sense of self because we believe that to be an important and central motivation for consumers. This section is organized as follows: we state each proposition, discuss it in detail, describe relevant methodological issues, then present empirical support.

> P1: Consumption behaviors that are central to consumers' goals and motivations will be described with narratives that are of higher quality than stories about consumption behaviors that are less important.

We have argued that individuals use stories to understand themselves and what they and others do. An longstanding question in consumer research is how products, brands, and possessions achieve meaning, including how consumers interpret this meaning and apply it to their lives. McCracken (1988) proposes a theory of meaning transfer where the meaning in products is transferred to the consumer through consumption rituals. We would like to suggest that people use stories to make sense of product and consumption activity meanings. (In those cases where rituals create meaning, narrative processing may be used to understand the rituals.) Narratives, motivated by consumers' goals, help people understand their experiences with products, creating meaning through emplotment. Although Keller (1993) and others assert that brand associations in a consumer's mind are what a brand means, they do not examine in detail how associations are formed. Narrative structure organizes events into a framework that establishes relationships between the story's elements, creating meaning for consumers.

Consumer's ongoing self-stories should contain the possessions, brands, and consumption behaviors that are critical in defining who consumers are and who they want to be. These stories will have undergone extensive elaboration, leading to better quality narrative structures. We follow the theoretical stance of Stein and Albro (1997) that more complex stories are better quality narratives. (Mandler (1984) and others have argued that the relationship between complexity and quality is an inverted U; at some point stories become too complex and quality suffers. However, in the context of consumer stories elicited in an interview or experimental setting, we believe that such a high level of complexity is unlikely.) While content-based analysis of consumer stories may indicate that a consumption behavior is important to a subject's sense of self, structural narrative quality analysis will reveal the underlying level of elaboration, unknown (and therefore less likely to be manipulated in response to social norms) by the consumer.

Methodological issues

There are many different ways a researcher can assess narrative quality. For example, Bruner and Lucariello (1989) identify textual markings for each of Bruner's four narrative dimensions. Their analysis compares the percentage of episodes across stories that correspond to each dimension. Stein and Albro (1997) equate quality with complexity. They evaluate stories using a taxonomy based on the degree to which a story incorporates goal-based action. This methodology uses counts of critical indicators of each level (e.g. number of embedded episodes, percentage of success and failure outcomes, etc.) to determine complexity. In story grammar research, complexity can be evaluated based on the number of episodes, the number of base structures, or the number of transformations made to the base structures (see Mick 1987). Regardless of how quality is operationalized, we assert that story quality and importance to one's self-concept will be positively related.

Empirical support

A recent study examining narrative structural quality lends some support for the first proposition. In this study, Escalas (1996) examined consumer narratives about brands, based on the idea that individuals use narratives to understand the role of brands in their lives. To extend the "life is a stage" metaphor of Goffman (1959), brands can be considered to be props used by actors for character development in consumer narratives. Undergraduate college student subjects wrote stories (i.e. autobiographical memories of their past experiences with a brand, recounted as a narrative) about two of six brands: three athletic shoe brands (Adidas, Nike, and Reebok) and three brands of clothing (the GAP, Levi's, and Polo).

Based on brand attitude data provided by each subject, the experimenter had each subject write personal experience stories about the two brands with the highest and lowest individual brand attitude scores, regardless of product category. In all, 122 brand stories were written by 61 subjects (two each). Forty-two of these stories were eliminated because they were self-described by the writer to be "untrue" or because the "stories" were not narratives (i.e. not well-developed stories, such as an explanation of why the brand is important to the writer in non-narrative terms). This left 80 stories (66 percent of the original 122) included in the data set.

Narrative structural quality was evaluated using the ten-item narrative structure scale in Table 13.1. The items draw primarily on Pennington and Hastie's episode schemas and Bruner's landscapes of action and consciousness. Stories are higher quality when they contain more of the narrative elements defined by episode schemas and landscapes of action and when they provide insight into what the protagonist is thinking and feeling (landscape of consciousness). These ten items were evaluated by an independent coder, who referred to each subject's story as one complete unit, rather than breaking the stories down sentence by sentence or categorizing themes. The items were rated on a five-point scale, anchored by not at all and very much so, and were averaged to form one narrative structural quality measure (Chronbach $\alpha=0.91$).

The independent variable in this study was self-brand connections. Self-brand connections are intended to measure the extent to which individuals have incorporated brands into their self-concept (Escalas 1996). To achieve their identity goals (life themes and values and life projects) people use products and brands to create and represent desired self-images and to present these images to others or to themselves. As a result of this process, a link bridges the brand and the self. Krugman (1965) was one of the first marketing researchers to theorize about connections to self. Csikszentmihalyi

Table 13.1 Narrative structure coding scale items

1	To what extent do these thoughts begin with an initial event that leads to a psychological state in a character? (This character can be the subject him/herself.)
2	To what extent do these thoughts begin with an initial event that leads to a course of action by a character? (Again, this character can be the subject him/herself.)
3	To what extent do these thoughts explain how a psychological state in a character leads to a course of action? (Again, this character can be the subject him/herself.)
4	To what extent do these thoughts explain how a course of action results in a particular outcome?
5	To what extent do these thoughts have some sort of ending, resolution, or conclusion?
6	To what extent are these thoughts organized in a temporal sequence, that is, organized as occurring over time?
7	To what extent do these thoughts focus on and explain particular events rather than developing general generalizations, categorizations, and/or abstractions?
8	To what extent do these thoughts give you insight into what a character is feeling sort thinking? (Again, this character can be the subject him/herself.)
9	To what extent do these thoughts give you insight into the intentions and/or goals of a character?
10	To what extent do these thoughts provide reasons for the actions that occur (if any actions do occur)?

and Rochberg-Halton (1981) view goods as helping in the individual cultivation process, allowing a person to achieve direction and purpose. Studies on attachment to products have defined it as the extent to which an individual uses an object to develop and maintain a cognitive structure of self (Ball and Tasaki 1992). McCracken (1989) contends that consumers use product meanings to construct, sustain, or reconstruct their notion of self. Belk's (1988) extended self paradigm builds on a multiple levels of self theory with possessions becoming who one is, not just what one owns. Possession and brands can also be used to achieve one's communal goals (Wallendorf and Arnould 1988).

To assess the degree to which the subject had developed a self-brand connection, a ten-item scale was used, on a seven-point scale ranging from −3 to +3 (see Table 13.2 for a list of the ten items, Chronbach $\alpha=0.95$). The scale items span the different manners through which the brand is connected to the self (Q1, 2, 3, 7, 8, 10), is used to communicate the self (Q6), is a relationship partner (Q5), and evokes emotion (signifying importance to one's self) (Q4, 9).

The relationship between story quality and self-brand connections was analyzed in a GLM model, where the structural narrative quality dependent variable was considered a function of subject, brand (nested in category), category, product category expertise, and the self-brand connection score (story genre was also included as a covariate, see proposition 2 below). The author found a significant, positive relationship between subjects' self-brand

Table 13.2 Self-brand connection scale items

1	Brand X reflects who I am.
2	I can identify with Brand X.
3	I feel a personal connection to Brand X.
4	I feel affection towards Brand X.
5	I have a relationship with Brand X.
6	I use Brand X to communicate who I am to other people.
7	I think Brand X helps me become the type of person I want to be.
8	I consider Brand X to be "me" (it reflects who I consider myself to be or how I want to present myself to others).
9	I have strong, positive feelings about Brand X.
10	Brand X suits me well.

connections and the narrative quality of the consumer brand stories ($\beta=0.17$, $F_{1,18}=4.55$, $p<0.05$). Since narrative processing is used to interpret consumer experiences with brands (leading to the formation or enhancement of self-brand connections), it follows that consumers with these thoughts and feelings should be able to write "good" stories about themselves and the brand. If narratively structured thought has been used to develop these connections, then subsequent narrative thought should be facilitated. Furthermore, in conducting structural narrative analysis on autobiographical depth-interview data, Bruner (1990) defines an important theme for an individual (or group of individuals) as one where resolution of imbalances in Burke's pentad occurs in the story. Such an imbalance resolution produces a story of high structural quality. In the stories where negative self-brand connections exist, such an imbalance would typically not be resolved in the story, leading to lower structural quality scores (thus lower self-brand connections result in lower quality stories).

> P2: The narrative genre of consumer stories will differ depending on the consumer goals, motivations, and creation of self described by the story.

This proposition recommends categorizing narrative structures into different genres and comparing the use of these genres within and between consumers. Stern (1995) has conducted this type of analysis, examining the genre of consumer Thanksgiving narratives, where she found different genres correspond to different issues for consumers. Comedies, for example, were used to describe the evolution of new social units, often a redefined family, with the happy ending of a festive gathering for the holiday. Tragedies, which end badly, on the other hand, were used to describe protagonists that were doomed by a fatal flaw. Thus, consumers use different genres to reveal their values and beliefs.

Gergen and Gergen (1988) have developed a genre taxonomy based on their model of dramatic engagement where narratives with changing evaluative slopes (i.e. the slope alternates in sign) lead to more emotion than those that have a constant, improving, or declining slope. Thus an evaluative slope that rises and declines over the timeline of the story will evoke more emotion than one that does not. The emotional impact of different genres is of interest because, as discussed above, emotion can be thought of as an indicator of importance or centrality to one's self-concept, goals, and motivations. Emotional responses tell us when things are important because they signal the relevance of a situation to our concerns and goals (Frijda 1994). We feel emotion when we have a personal stake in an event or situation (Lazarus 1991). Therefore, genres that evoke more emotion should reveal goals and motivations that are important to consumers.

Methodological issues

There are many different ways of evaluating a narrative's genre. For example, Stern (1995) uses Frye's taxonomy, where stories are categorized as comedy, romance, tragedy, and irony. As mentioned above, Gergen and Gergen's (1988) narrative slope genre taxonomy is based on the evaluative dimension of a story over time. The five basic categories are progressive, regressive, stability, comedy-romance, and tragedy narratives. In progressive narratives, events continuously improve for the protagonist over time, while in regressive narratives, events decline over time. In stability narratives, events neither improve nor decline significantly over the time frame of the story. The final two genres involve evaluative slopes that alternate in sign – that is, evaluative slopes that rise and decline (or decline and then rise) over the timeline of the story. In the case of comedies and romantic sagas, the series of events start out favorable, deteriorate, then end on a positive note (see also Stern 1995). Thus it is a regressive narrative, followed by a progressive narrative. In this genre, the hero eventually does attain his goal. The opposite of this form is the tragedy, which is a progressive narrative, followed by a regressive narrative (ending on a down note). For example, when a hero has almost attained his goal, then is brought low, drama is created, emotion is often evoked in the listener, and the genre is considered to be tragedy.

Empirical support

In addition to the story quality analysis discussed above, Escalas (1996) also applied Reissman's (1993) core narrative reduction techniques to decompose consumer stories into "skeleton plots" organized around Labov's six functional properties (abstract, orientation, complicating actions, evaluation, resolution, and coda). She then examined the relationship between genres and self-brand connections, using Gergen and Gergen's (1988) evaluative slope-based taxonomy, to see if genre based structural narrative analysis provided any insights into the role played by consumers' connections to brands in meeting self-identity related goals.

Most of the autobiographical brand stories were regressive in their evaluative slope (41 percent). Thirty-one percent of the stories were progressive, 15 percent were comedy-romance, 8 percent were stable, and 5 percent were tragedies. There was a significant relationship between genre and self-brand connections (mean$_{progressive}$=1.01, mean$_{comedy-romance}$=0.45, mean$_{regressive}$=-1.76, $F_{2,19}$ =8.01, $p<0.01$; there were very few stories that were tragedy or stability narratives, four and five, respectively, so they will not be discussed further.) Progressive narratives had the most positive relationship with self-brand connections followed by comedy-romance narratives. This is a logical finding in that both these genres have happy endings. It appears that within the context of brands, when things continually improve over time (as in progressive narratives), connections to the self are enhanced. Enduring a rocky history (as in comedy-romance narratives) also has a positive effect on self-brand relationships, but the effect is smaller than an entirely positive history with the brand. The negative effect of regressive narratives was as expected: when brand experiences decline and deteriorate, so do self-brand connections.

> P3: Consumption behaviors that are central to consumers' goals and motivations can be better understood by conducting structural analysis of the role of narrative elements in consumption stories.

By analyzing specific narrative elements and their role in the structure of the story, insights into consumers' goals and motivations can be gained. For example, in the realm of brand research, a brand can be evaluated as to how central it is to the plot. Is the brand merely part of the setting? Is it an instrument used to achieve a goal? Or is it embued with human qualities, becoming an active relationship partner (see Fournier 1998)? These structural aspects of narrative elements can indicate the role of the brand in the consumer's mind. Structural analysis of narrative elements extends to consumption behavior beyond brand research. For example, in analyzing consumer narratives about favorite movies, the researcher can ask whether a particular movie is important to a single narrative episode (e.g. by meeting a need for entertainment) or whether it is a central element in an ongoing sequence of embedded episodes (e.g. does the movie lead to an evolution in the consumer?) Another issue might be whether the movie-going experience creates a narrative imbalance or becomes an important aspect of imbalance resolution.

Methodological issues

Many individual narrative elements can be examined in this type of structural analysis. Some examples include Bruner's four dimensions of narrative or the elements of Pennington and Hastie's episode schema. Structural narrative analysis can also examine the imbalances among Burke's pentad, which create drama in narratives. The development, attempt, and achievement (or lack of achievement) of goals is also an important element of narrative (Stein and Albro 1997). Given the many structural definitions of narrative, a large number of individual elements potentially can be analyzed.

Empirical support

Again, Escalas' (1996) brand story study lends support for this proposition. After coding stories into skeleton plots, the author made comparisons across plotlines for differences in whether or not goals were mentioned and the role the brand played in the achievement (or lack of achievement) of these goals. This analysis included whether the goals were agency motivations (self-needs such as differentiation, achievement, or power) or communion motivations (needs of intimacy and relationship formation) (Woike *et al.* 1999).

Seventy percent of the brand stories did not have brand-related goals. Of the 30 per cent that did have brand-related goals, 22 percent were communal goals, including connecting to family and friends, while 8 percent were self-related agency goals, including differentiation or achievement. The presence or absence of goals did not have a significant effect on self-brand connections. However, whether or not the goal discussed in the story was achieved or not was marginally related to self-brand connections (mean $_{goal\ achieved}$=0.64, mean $_{goal\ not\ achieved}$=−0.80, $F_{1,16}$=3.98, p=0.06). It is logical that using a brand to achieve one's goals, whether they be self-related goals or communal goals, should improve the connection one feels between the brand and one's sense of self. The effect of self-brand connections on goal type (communal vs. self-related) was not significant. This supports the notion that our self-concepts include significant others because stories that had goals of personal achievement and self-differentiation had the same effect as having goals of connecting to important others (family members, classmates).

Summary of propositions

These three propositions illustrate just some of the ways that structural analyses can complement content-based analyses of consumer narratives. Structural narrative quality provides insight into the importance of the story to the consumer's self-identity goals and motivations (P1). The brand story study empirically demonstrates the positive relationship between story quality and self-brand connections, which indicate the degree to which the brand has been used to meet consumer self-identity goals. Genre analysis also provides insight into consumer goals and motivations (P2). The brand story study found progressive narratives to have a more positive relationship with self-brand connections than comedy-romance narratives, despite the fact that both have happy endings. While it may be intuitive that in interpersonal relationships surviving a hardship strengthens a relationship, structural narrative analysis indicates that for brands this is not the case. Brands are more likely to be used to meet self-identity goals when all goes well over time. Finally, there are many structural narrative elements that can be evaluated to provide insight into consumers' goals and motivations (P3). Consumers had stronger self-brand connections with brands that had helped them achieve their goals (this effect was marginally significant). This effect was not dependent on whether the goal was self-related, such as differentiation or achievement, or communal, such as building connections to family or friends.

Conclusion

Narratives are used to create one's sense of self. A reciprocal relationship exists: self-identity goals motivate narratives and narratives provide the structure necessary to understand goals. Narratives provide people with the cognitive vehicle to achieve a sense of self both by structuring events in time and space and delineating the relationships between individual actors acting within a socially constituted world. Narratives allow people to represent themselves as individuals within a social nexus, existing in a world where events unfold through time and space (Nelson 1989).

From this foundation, this chapter has extended the role of narratives to the realm of consumer behavior, focusing on consumption experiences that help individuals create their sense of self. We have encouraged the use of structural narrative analysis on consumer stories by developing a series of propositions about how structural analysis can complement the content-based analysis currently favored by our field. We hope that our empirical examples illustrate some of the gains that can be made in understanding consumers by augmenting the methodological tools used by consumer researchers.

Acknowledgments

We would like to thank Cynthia Huffman, Barbara Stern, and Eric Arnould for their thoughtful comments and suggestions.

References

Abelson, R.P. (1981) "The psychological status of the script concept," *American Psychologist* 36: 715–29.

Alba, J.W. and Hasher, L. (1983) "Is memory schematic?" *Psychological Bulletin* 93 (2): 203–31.

Averill, J.R. (1994) "I feel, therefore I am – I think," in P. Ekman and R.J. Davidson (eds) *The Nature of Emotion: Fundamental Questions*, New York, NY: Oxford University Press: 379–85.

Ball, A.D. and Tasaki, L.H. (1992) "The role and measurement of attachment in consumer behavior," *Journal of Consumer Psychology* 2: 155–72.

Baumeister, R.F. and Newman, L.S. (1994) "How stories make sense of personal experiences: motives that shape autobiographical narratives," *Personality and Social Psychology Bulletin* 20 (6): 676–90.

Belk, R.W. (1988) "Possessions and the extended self," *Journal of Consumer Research* 15: 139–68.

Brewer, W.F. (1986) "What is autobiographical memory?" in *Autobiographical Memory*, Cambridge: Cambridge University Press: 25–49.

Brewer, W.F. and Lichtenstein, E.H. (1981) "Event schemas, story schemas, and story grammars," in J. Long and A. Baddeley (eds) *Attention and Performance IX*, Hillsdale, NJ: Lawrence Erlbaum Associates: 363–79.

Bruner, J. (1986) *Actual Minds, Possible Worlds*, Cambridge, MA: Harvard University Press.

—— (1990) *Acts of Meaning*, Cambridge, MA: Harvard University Press.

Bruner J. and Lucariello, J. (1989) "Monologue as narrative recreation of the world," in K. Nelson (ed.) *Narratives from the Crib*, Cambridge, MA: Harvard University Press: 2: 73–97.

Burke, K. (1969) *A Grammar of Motives*, Berkeley, CA: University of California Press.

Chafe, W. (1990) "Some things that narratives tell us about the mind," in B.K. Britton and A.D. Pelligrini (eds) *Narrative Thought and Narrative Language*, Hillsdale, NJ: Lawrence Erlbaum Associates: 79–98.

Csikszentmihalyi, M. and Rochberg-Halton, E. (1981) *The Meaning of Things: Domestic Symbols and the Self,* Cambridge: Cambridge University Press.

Escalas, J.E. (1996) "Narrative processing: building connections between brands and the self," unpublished dissertation, Duke University.

Feldman, C.F., Bruner, J., Renderer, B., and Spitzer S. (1990) "Narrative comprehension," in B.K. Britton and A.D. Pelligrini (eds) *Narrative Thought and Narrative Language*, Hillsdale, NJ: Lawrence Erlbaum Associates: 1–78.

Fiske, Susan T. (1993) "Social cognition and social perception," *Annual Review of Psychology* 44: 155–94.

Fournier, S. (1998) "Consumers and their brands: developing relationship theory in consumer research," *Journal of Consumer Research* 24 (4): 343–73.

Frijda, N.H. (1994) "Emotions are functional, most of the time," in Paul Ekman and Richard J. Davidson (eds) *The Nature of Emotion: Fundamental Questions*, New York: Oxford University Press: 112–22.

Frye, Northrup (1973) *Anatomy of Criticism: Four Essays*, Princeton, NJ: Princeton University Press.

Gergen, K.J. and Gergen, M.M. (1988) "Narrative and the self as relationship," *Advances in Experimental Social Psychology* 21: 17–56.

Goffman, E. (1959) *The Presentation of Self in Everyday Life*, Garden City, NY: Doubleday & Company, Inc.

Hardcastle, V. (1999) "The development of self," paper presented at the Cognitive Science Seminar Series, University of Arizona, 12 March, 1999.

Hermans, H.M. (1996) "Voicing the self: from information processing to dialogical interchange," *Journal of Personality and Social Psychology* 119 (1): 31–50.

Keller, K.L. (1993) "Conceptualizing, measuring, and managing customer-based brand equity," *Journal of Marketing* 57 (1): 1–22.

Kerby, A.P. (1991) *Narrative and the Self*, Bloomington, IN: Indiana University Press.

Kleine, S.S., Kleine III, R.E., and Allen C.T. (1995) "How is a possession 'me' or 'not me'? Characterizing types and the antecedents of material possession attachment," *Journal of Consumer Research* 22 (3): 327–43.

Krugman, H.E. (1965) "The impact of television advertising: learning without involvement," *Public Opinion Quarterly* 30: 349–56.

Labov, W. (1982) "Speech actions and reactions in personal narrative," in D. Tannen (ed.) *Analyzing Discourse: Text and Talk*, Washington, DC: Georgetown University Press: 219–47.

Lazarus, R.S. (1991) "Progress on a cognitive-motivational-relational theory of emotion," *American Psychologist* 46: 819–34.

McCracken, G. (1988) *Culture and Consumption*, Bloomington, IN: Indiana Uniersity Press.

—— (1989) "Who is the celebrity endorser? Cultural foundations of the endorsement process," *Journal of Consumer Research* 16: 310–21.

McQuarrie, E.F. and Mick, D.G. (1996) "Figures of rhetoric in advertising language," *Journal of Consumer Research* 22 (4): 424–38.

Mandler, J.M. (1984) *Stories, Scripts, and Scenes: Aspects of Schema Theory*, Hillsdale, NJ: Lawrence Erlbaum Associates.

Mick, D.G. (1987) "Toward a semiotic of advertising story grammars," in J. Umiker-Sebeok (ed.) *Marketing and Semiotics: New Directions in the Study of Signs for Sale*, Berlin: Walter de Gruyter & Co.: 249–78.

Nelson, K. (1989) "Monologue as the linguistic construction of self in time," in K. Nelson (ed.) *Narratives from the Crib*, Cambridge, MA: Harvard University Press: 284–308.

Olson, D.R. (1990) "Thinking about narrative," in B.K. Britton and A.D. Pelligrini (eds) *Narrative Thought and Narrative Language*, Hillsdale, NJ: Lawrence Erlbaum Associates: 99–112.

Pennington, N. and Hastie, R. (1986) "Evidence evaluation in complex decision making," *Journal of Personality and Social Psychology* 51 (2): 242–58.

Polkinghorne, D.E. (1988) *Narrative Knowing and the Human Sciences*, Albany, NY: State University of New York.

—— (1991) "Narrative and self-concept," *Journal of Narrative and Life History* 1 (2 & 3): 135–53.

Riessman, C.K. (1993) *Narrative Analysis* (Qualitative Research Methods 30), Newbury Park, CA: Sage.

Sanfey, A. and Hastie, R. (1998) "Does evidence presentation format affect judgment? An experimental evaluation of displays of data for judgments," *Psychological Science* 9 (1): 99–103.

Schouten, J.W. (1991) "Selves in transition: symbolic consumption in personality rites of passage and identity reconstruction," *Journal of Consumer Research* 17 (2): 412–30.

Somers, M.R. (1994) "The narrative constitution of identity: a relational and network approach," *Theory and Society* 23: 605–49.

Stein, N.L. and Albro, E.R. (1997) "Building complexity and coherence: children's use of goal-structured knowledge in telling stories," in M. Bamberg (ed.) *Narrative Development: Six Approaches*, Mahwah NJ: Lawrence Erlbaum Associates 1: 5–44.

Stern, B.B. (1995) "Consumer myths: Frye's taxonomy and the structural analysis of consumption text," *Journal of Consumer Research* 22: 165–85.

Stern, B.B., Thompson C.J., and Arnould E.J. (1998) "Narrative analysis of a marketing relationship: the consumer's perspective," *Psychology and Marketing* 15 (3): 195–214.

Thompson, C.J., Locander, W.B., and Pollio, H.R. (1990) "The lived meaning of free choice: an existential–phenomenological description of everyday consumer experiences of contemporary married women," *Journal of Consumer Research* 17 (2): 346–61.

Wallendorf, M. and Arnould, E.J. (1988) "'My favorite things': a cross-cultural inquiry into object attachment, possessiveness, and social linkage," *Journal of Consumer Research* 14: 531–47.

Wallendorf, M. and Arnould, E.J. (1991) "'We gather together': consumption rituals of Thanksgiving Day," *Journal of Consumer Research* 18: 13–31.

Woike, B., Gershkovich, I., Piorkowski, R., and Polo, M. (1999) "The role of motives in the content and structure of autobiographical memory," *Journal of Personality and Social Psychology* 76 (4): 600–12.

14 The power of metaphor

Robin Coulter and Gerald Zaltman

"I survived the wedding!" "When I grow up." "Let's go for it." The ideas of surviving or lasting, growth or journey, and movement in these quotes are metaphors relating to goals. So, too, are metaphors such as "When my ship comes in," "Let's shoot for that date," and "My life's mission," which involve notions of vessel and arrival, choosing targets and triggering actions, and a deep sense of purpose. In fact, so fundamental are metaphors to the expression of goals that it is very hard to describe the metaphoric content of these ideas without using still other metaphors. What is a goal after all, if not a metaphor? A goal is a proxy, a representation of one thing such as reaching a finish line, scoring, graduating, finding inner peace, and achieving other physical and emotional states. Consider football, for instance, which involves literal goal lines to be crossed or defended. The process of literally achieving a goal in this business called a game involves *clutch* first downs, *big plays, time out, dead ball fouls, beating another player, and a Hail Mary.* It may also involve being on cloud nine and spiking. At the same time, there are other metaphoric statements about what the defending team does to prevent a goal from being achieved. Viewed from the larger systems perspective of an action on a playing field by two teams and officials, we see conflicting purposes and objectives being experienced all at once and necessarily described with the use of metaphor. This shouldn't be surprising since it is estimated that people use an average of 5.7 metaphors per minute of speech (Gibbs 1994). The topic of conflicting goals will be addressed later in this chapter.

As other chapters note, most definitions of a *goal* incorporate the terms, "desired end-states," acknowledging that goals occur over time, and often involve a series of interrelated phenomena essential to the achievement of a goal. In consumer, psychological, and social psychological research, the predominant conceptualizaton of the structure of goals is hierarchical (Gutman 1982; Huffman *et al.*, this volume; Reynolds and Gutman 1988). This perspective argues that the highest order of goals or values, for example, freedom (Rokeach 1973) or self-concept (Sirgy 1986), serve as guides for our lower-level goals or sub goals, such as personal projects (Little 1989), life tasks (Cantor *et al.* 1987), and current concerns and product purposes (Huffman *et al.*, this volume). Alternative ways of structuring goals including networks, graphs, and lattices (Hebb 1995; Ortony, Clore, and Collins 1988) have also received some attention. To elicit and examine individuals' goals and their importance, researchers have employed multiple methods which we discuss in more detail later in the chapter.

The majority of this research has contemplated the conscious aspects of goal setting and goal striving (Bagozzi and Dholakia 1999). Recent research (Austin and Vancouver 1996; Bargh and Barndollar 1996) however, suggests that many goals and the processes encompassing goal attainment are unconscious. Thus, while methodological pluralism has aided in understanding conscious goals, their structure and content, there continues to be a need for methods that will help to tap the unconscious goals and related processes, and deal with their idiographic nature, interrelatedness, and evolution over time (Austin and Vancouver 1996).

Our purpose is to examine goals as desired states or experiences and discuss how goals, both conscious and unconscious, are represented and/or expressed in terms of metaphors. Specifically, we consider how consumers express goals through metaphoric expressions, conceptual metaphors, complex metaphors, and deep metaphors. Second, we contemplate the ability to use metaphor and a metaphor-based method to better understand goals, and their idiographic, interrelated, and evolutionary nature. After arguing the power of metaphor for realizing and understanding goals, we provide an empirical illustration using a metaphor-based method to examine consumers' goals with regard to visiting a dentist. We conclude with some suggestions and questions for going forward with goal-related research.

Cognition and metaphor

In making the case that metaphor can be a powerful tool for understanding goals, we draw upon literature with regard to cognition and metaphor. Two recent findings, (1) thought is mostly unconscious, and (2) thought is largely metaphorical and imaginative, have challenged our understanding of reason and metaphor while providing grounding for our argument that metaphor can help us to understand goals. In this section, we briefly discuss these two findings.

Thought is mostly unconscious

With regard to the first point, "thought is mostly unconscious," there is consensus in cognitive science and neuroscience that most cognition occurs in the cognitive unconscious. Lakoff and Johnson (1999) suggest that unconscious thought accounts for 95 percent or more of all cognition. Others (Damasio 1994; LeDoux, 1996; Hoffman 1998) support this perspective. For example, while we are aware of experiencing memories, we are not aware of the far more complex processes whereby these memories are formed and forgotten. Nor are we aware of the reconstructive processes involved in their recall. We may be keenly aware in our mind's eye of a novelist's description of a flower soaking up sun but not have any awareness of the many other events required of our mind to produce that picture, to give it meaning and to provide us with the experience of having produced it. In fact, most of our creation of what we see, smell, touch, taste, and hear is the product of a large number of unconscious but highly intelligent, creative rules whose operation generally escape our attention (Hoffman 1998; Bornstein and Pittman 1992). Imagine, too, trying to teach someone else to paint, catch a ball, ride a bicycle, blow a bubble with bubble gum, stifle a sneeze, or fly a kite relying only on your ability to share knowledge that is consciously available. Or try explaining how ideas occur to you, what it is like to feel joy or claustrophobia, know you have found your mate for life, or why a movie brought tears such that someone else can share that experience with you. We simply don't have sufficient access to all that goes on in our minds to be able to report accurately. We may do many things at once, but are capable of only maintaining awareness of one thing at a time (Dowling 1998).

This is not to suggest that conscious thought is unimportant. To the contrary, it is very important. Among many other things, it is what allows us to examine matters with care and to learn from experience. In all likelihood, for something to reside in the unconscious mind, it should be capable in theory of being brought into the conscious mind (Searle 1994). Emotions are an example. They are generally thought to exist as biological systems outside conscious awareness (LeDoux 1996). Under some circumstances they are occasionally experienced consciously as feelings. Some emotions like pride, guilt, embarrassment, and shame seem to be experienced as feelings more readily than others such as fear, anticipation, surprise, or joy (Tangney and Fischer 1995). The hard wiring involved in all emotions is to some degree influenced by or adaptive to changes in the social environment. Moreover, important variations occur across cultures and across unique individual experiences. These variations account for differences in what triggers an emotion, whether it emerges as a conscious feeling, and how the feeling is managed (Bagozzi *et al.* 1999). This brings us to the important possibility that emotions are the birthplace of conscious (as well as unconscious) goals. For some consumers financial security as a goal may have been born in fear and for others with a somewhat different personal history, it may have been born in embarrassment. It is easy to imagine self-fulfillment having pride or joy or even guilt as a birthplace.

To the extent that conscious goals are given life and salience by emotions (unconscious events), and that other unconscious processes such as those involved in memory, learning, and socialization shape the ways goals are pursued, frustrations and disappointments dealt with, and judgments made about whether or not goals have been adequately fulfilled, then we need to find ways of exploring and surfacing unconscious cognitive processes. This is especially the case when these processes are malleable to begin with and used as a kind of play dough by social and cultural processes. This brings us to the second important point, that thought is largely metaphorical. The import of this idea is that metaphors and idiomatic expression serve as vehicles for transporting less than conscious thoughts into the realm of consciousness where they can be examined and understood more fully. Beyond serving as vehicles, metaphors and particularly systems of metaphors signal unconscious evaluations of things and processes.

Thought is largely metaphorical

The second point, which acknowledges that thought is not purely literal, but is indeed largely metaphorical and imaginative, provides us with some basis for suggesting that we should listen to metaphor and other figurative speech, as well as see how people use images to express one thing in terms of another. This section offers a discussion of metaphor (i.e. metaphorical expressions, conceptual metaphors, complex metaphors, and deep metaphors), but the interested readers may also see, for example, Lakoff and Johnson (1980, 1999) and Ortony (1993).

A metaphor is often thought of grammatically as "A is B." Lakoff and Johnson (1980) define *conceptual metaphors* as mappings across conceptual domains that structure our reasoning, our experience, and our everyday language. These conceptual metaphors are articulated in our everyday conversations through *metaphorical expressions,* the words, phrases, or sentences that are the surface realization of the cross-domain mappings (Lakoff 1993). Continuing in the football domain, one might use the metaphorical expression, "that defensive back is a well-oiled machine," to mean that he is an outstanding performer.

Research indicates that conceptual metaphors occur as a consequence of repeated pairings of two domains (Johnson 1997), and "we acquire them automatically and unconsciously as part of the normal process of neural learning, and may be unaware that we have them" (Lakoff and Johnson 1999). "Conceptual metaphor is pervasive in both thought and language" (Lakoff and Johnson 1999: 45), and arise from us conceptualizing an idea, a subjective experience, in terms of grasping an object, a sensorimotor experience. So, observing that well-oiled machines continue to perform, whereas those not oiled break down would lead one to make the connection between being well-oiled and good performance, and the consequent metaphor that a well-performing athlete is a well-oiled machine. In the goal context, two conceptual metaphors – *goals are destinations* and *goals are desired objects* – embody the definition of goal. Returning to our football example, the metaphorical expression "Fourth and goal" illustrates that the destination is near, while the metaphorical expression "playing their hearts out" or "they are all pumped up" conveys the desirous nature of the goal.

In both cases, scoring a touchdown involves subjective and sensorimotor experiences.

Importantly, *conceptual metaphors* serve as building blocks for *complex metaphors* which are represented as metaphorical maps. In other words, the linkages between and among conceptual metaphors construct mental models (Lakoff and Johnson 1999; Grady 1997, 1998). These mental models, by definition of metaphor, are culturally shared. Consider our conceptual metaphors – *goals are destinations* and *goals are desired objects*. Collectively, they can be thought of as a complex metaphor, *"goals are journeys."* For instance, "the road to the Super Bowl," which taken metaphorically speaks to the process, the journey, that one must travel to reach that desired goal: playing in the Super Bowl. For that matter, the expressions, "It's not whether you win, but how you play the game" and "It's not how you play the game, but whether you win" are complex metaphors, used in and out of athletics, juxtaposing two important aspects of goals: *how* they are achieved or lost and *whether* they are achieved or lost. This juxtaposition conveys an important position with respect to certain values one associates with goals and how they are pursued.

Metaphorical expressions, conceptual metaphors, and complex metaphors serve as the basis for identifying *deep metaphors*. Deep metaphors serve as a means to organize a whole system of concepts. They provide a higher level of abstraction to the phenomena than do the previously discussed conceptual and complex metaphors. Because of their abstractness, deep metaphors both reflect and guide people's thinking. In essence, they are fundamental orienting concepts or "viewing lenses" that predispose people to perceive and interpret information in particular ways. Lakoff (1993) discusses deep metaphors, such as "orientation" (references to spatial orientation; e.g. up/down), "container" (references to being in/out of something), "time" (references to the passage of time), and "journey" (references to taking a trip, to following a path). An extended but not exhaustive listing of deep metaphors and their respective references are presented in Table 14.1.

To illustrate the relationship among metaphorical expressions and conceptual, complex and deep metaphors, in Table 14.2, we present metaphorical expressions consistent with the conceptual metaphors, "goals are destinations," and "goals are desired objects," and the complex metaphor, "goals are journeys." With regard to the conceptual metaphor, "goals are destinations," we offer metaphorical expressions that relate to reaching a goal, making/not making progress toward a goal and the process of reaching a goal. As noted in Table 14.2, the metaphorical expressions related to "reaching a goal" are associated with the deep metaphor, motion. The other three aspects of "goals are destinations" (i.e. making progress, not making progress, and the process of reaching a goal) involve a variety of deep metaphors, including motion, force, orientation, and physicality. With regard to the conceptual metaphor, "goals are desired objects," the

Table 14.1 Deep metaphors and metaphorical expressions

Deep metaphors	Metaphorical expressions
Physicality	Body references such as taste it; feel it; pick up, ingest, see my point; hurts me.
Balance	References to equilibrium, balance, equalize or compensate; including both sides; images of scales, teeter-totter, balance beam.
Motion or movement	References to moving (flowing, traveling, running or walking); references to action (doing something, getting going); keep moving; keep it going.
Nature	References to nature, outdoors, natural world, wildness; chaotic, untamed; specific images of nature – rain forest, desert, woods; references to breeding, evolving, growing.
Force	References to power, a powerful presence, or a source of energy; references to the consequences of force (getting hit; slammed, impact).
Fight vs. flight	References to war; fights, battles; choose your battles; avoid a fight; don't get involved; running away or hide from something.
The ideal	Reference to the ideal object, situation, feeling; statements about one's ideal self; references to perfection, the perfect one.

metaphorical expressions are tied to the deep metaphors, ideal, physicality, and nature. Finally, the complex metaphor, "goals are journeys" reflects the deep metaphors of motion, journey, and ideal.

Contemplating goal assessment and the power of metaphor

While the previous section illustrates that we do indeed use metaphors to discuss goals, questions remain about the value of metaphor in helping to elicit goals, both conscious and unconscious. Austin and Vancouver's (1996) review of goal constructs, and their consideration of methods to assess goals, underscores the power of metaphor in understanding goals. Additionally, Bagozzi and Dholakia (1999) suggest that metaphor-based methods have merit in eliciting and understanding goals and goal processes. These ideas, augmented by other research, are noted below.

Latent versus phenomenological perspectives on goals

Austin and Vancouver (1996: 339) draw a conceptual distinction between latent and phenomenological perspectives on goals. The former holds that "goals define the pursuits of individuals, regardless of awareness or

Table 14.2 Metaphoric expressions and conceptual, complex, and deep metaphors

	Metaphoric expressions	Deep metaphors
Conceptual metaphor:		
Goals are destinations		
Reaching the goal	He's coming down the home stretch	Motion
	He's crossed the finish line	Motion
	His ship has come in	Motion
Making progress toward the goal	He's off and running	Motion
	He's seen the light at the end of the tunnel	Physicality, Motion
	He's covered a lot of ground	Journey
Not making progress toward goal	His hands are tied	Physicality
	He's hit a brick wall	Force
	He's behind the eight ball	Orientation, Force
The process	He's on a roller coaster ride	Journey, Orientation, Motion
	There are hills and valleys along the way	Journey, Motion, Orientation, Balance
	He's fighting an uphill battle	Journey, Fight vs. Flight, Orientation
Conceptual metaphor:		
Goals are desired objects		
	It's the cat's meow	Ideal
	My heart skipped a beat	Ideal, Physicality
	It's the cream of the crop	Ideal, Nature
Complex metaphor:		
Goals are journeys		
	He's reaching for the brass ring	Motion, Journey, Ideal
	He's going for the gold	Motion, Journey, Ideal
	He's reaching for the stars	Motion, Journey, Ideal

volition," whereas the latter holds that "an individual's goals may be a simple rationalization." While these two perspectives can seemingly co-exist, research indicates that most emotions and cognitive functions that guide thought and behavior occur without our awareness (Plutchik 1993; Shimamura 1994). And as noted previously, Lakoff and Johnson (1999) state that cognitive operations are largely unconscious, and that unconscious thought accounts for 95 percent of all cognition. With this in mind, we take the latent perspective, arguing that goals may be either conscious or unconscious. In fact, a given goal may shift between these two states, acknowledged by expressions such as "losing sight of our goals," "getting side-tracked," or "being excessively driven." The first two expressions involving losing sight and being side-tracked reflect having a goal that slips from awareness, whereas the third expression reflects the over prominence of a goal. At any one time, most goals lie below awareness even when we are fully aware of doing things to attain them (e.g. driving to work, and performing work).

Metaphors have a long history of use in clinical contexts ranging from projective tests to clinically driven content analyses of ordinary discourse. Of relevance here is their value as vehicles for transporting ideas from the unconscious mind to the conscious mind where they can be examined more readily by clients and therapists or consumers and researchers. Metaphors are expressed non-verbally as well as verbally and often both are used simultaneously. Even when expressed verbally, they may involve various physical senses ("Let's put them in touch"), as well as more abstract references ("They need to partner" or "How do we bridge that rift?").

An important and often under-appreciated quality of metaphor is that they hide as well as reveal thoughts and feelings (Glucksberg 1995). This is another reason why metaphor is often more revealing than conventional verbal and behavioral protocol analysis (LeDoux 1996). This quality of metaphor becomes particularly evident when analyzing systems of metaphors. For instance, when people use competitive metaphors involving, say, sports or war, they may be hiding notions of cooperation and mutual gain which are present but may be judged ideologically unacceptable in a social context (e.g. board-room meeting, consumer activist planning, developing lobbying strategy). Or, the use of a system of metaphor that stresses cooperation and mutual gain may be sufficiently threatening to the person using zero-sum systems that they need to actively avoid them – the unconscious equivalent to letting sleeping dogs lie. When a system of metaphor becomes evident, it is almost always productive to try to understand what system it is being used in lieu of and why. Revealing unsurfaced thoughts and feelings to consumers may make tacit assumptions and knowledge more explicit thereby helping consumers and researchers to better understand motives and desires (Belk *et al.*, this volume).

Idiographic goals lacking in shared meaning

Researchers have approached goal assessment in a number of ways. One popular method is the use of self-reports using scales of goal items (Houston and Walker 1996). These methods have respondents identify their goals using a list of predetermined goal items, or have respondents help to develop the list and then indicate salience, relevance, or priority (Little 1989). Qualitative methods, including: projective techniques (Kingten and Holland 1984), laddering (Reynolds and Gutman 1988; Valette-Florence and Rapacchi 1991), and phenomenological depth interviews (Mick and Buhl 1992) also have been employed. Additionally, see Escalas and Bettman (this volume) for a discussion of using narratives to discern self-identity related to consumer goals and motivation. While "more" quantitative methods allow us to *know* about the existence of specific goals, "more" qualitative methods allow for a better understanding of these goals' *meanings*.

Austin and Vancouver (1996) express concern about assessing goals in any manner because of their *uniqueness*, and their *lack of shared meaning*. Other perspectives (Geertz 1973) suggest that goals are not unique and can have shared meanings even across different people. The critical underlying issue in this range of perspectives seems to be the depth or level at which a goal is being examined, as well as the context. With rare exceptions, everyone seeks success, although they may define success in very different ways depending on their chronological age, physical endowments, geography, fiscal and other resources, and what a particular culture encourages or values. Even those who experience anomie share a common goal state.

These countervailing perspectives with regard to the idiosyncratic nature of goals and their content suggest the need for a method that through some common vocabulary could find commonalities across idiosyncrasies. Because metaphors are necessarily culturally shared, a metaphor-based method could serve as a basis for not only eliciting goals that are shared, but also in bridging the idiographic nature of goals.

Goal interrelatedness

Still, whether (or even when) goals are idiosyncratic or widely shared at any level of analysis, assessing their structure and content can be difficult. One reason for this difficulty is that goals are interrelated. Some, who view goal interrelatedness from a hierarchical perspective (Gutman 1982), suggest that goal interrelatedness occurs because a lower-level goal (e.g. controlling a child's sugar consumption) is linked to a higher-order, typically more abstract, goal (e.g. teaching children proper nutrition) which may be related to still another goal (e.g. enhancing the quality of the mother–child relationship). The difficulty this poses for understanding goals is basically one of categorization. When does one goal begin and the other leave off? How does one establish a boundary around a particular goal so that its structure and content can be understood adequately?

Another perspective which is essentially a more complex version of that noted above, is the heterarchical perspective (Broadbent 1985). This view holds that a goal at one level may be attached to multiple higher-order goals. So, for example, controlling a child's sugar consumption could be linked to teaching the child good nutritional habits, *and* it could be linked to a desire to maintain or improve the child's physical appearance. Both of these goals may be linked to multiple higher-order goals which include not only enhancing the quality of the mother–child relationship, but also the quality of the relationship the mother has with her peers. The heterarchical view also allows for interrelatedness between or among goals that appear to co-exist at the same level.

The co-existence of multiple goals begs the question of their compatibility. While in some cases goals are compatible (e.g. moderating a child's sugar intake and teaching sound nutritional practices), in other cases they have the potential to conflict (e.g. over-control of sugar intake does not allow children to learn about balance and moderation when making food choices). Note the complication introduced with this last example. The manner in which a goal is pursued (controlling sugar intake and teaching sound nutritional practices) determines whether the goal is achieved and hence experienced in a beneficial or dysfunctional way. Moreover, who experiences the benefit and/or the dysfunction, the child and/or the mother, illustrates yet another important quality of goals complicating their study: goals are ultimately rooted in social relationships. More specifically, their origins, the manner in which they are pursued, and the experience of their consequences are not an individual affair.

Several conceptualizations of metaphor underscore their ability to tap into the linkages among goals and goal-related processes. First, Narayanan's (1997) neural theory of metaphor holds that in the course of learning, the repeated co-occurrences or conflation (Johnson 1997), are realized neurally, and result in permanent neural connections which serve as the basis for metaphorical associations. Second, Fauconnier and Turner's (1998) theory of conceptual blending suggests that distinct conceptual domains can be co-activated and under certain conditions connections across domains can be formed, leading to new inferences (Lakoff and Johnson 1999). Thus, the connections of metaphors across domains enables, perhaps even requires, one to contemplate the hierarchical and heterarchical nature of goals. Thus, a metaphor-based method appears to be a viable approach to assessing goal structure, content, strength or impact with an ability to both disentangle interrelated goals and/or to treat them in their more natural interconnected states.

Goal development and change

The *dynamic* nature of goals also contributes to the difficulty of assessing their structure, content, and functioning. While higher-order goals, e.g. life themes and values and life projects are relatively invariant over time, lower level goals, e.g. personal projects (Little 1989), life tasks (Cantor *et al.* 1987), and current concerns, and product purposes (Huffman *et al.*, this volume) tend to be more changeable. Various self-report methods using longitudinal designs may be efficient ways to track changes in goal intensity and purposes being served for lower- and, perhaps, higher-order goals.

For understanding more abstract goals or the deeper meanings of lower-level goals, metaphor-based methods used in clinical practice in mental health settings, and marketing, organizational, and cultural studies, for instance, are likely to be more appropriate. Metaphor-based methods, because of their ability to surface unsurfaced or hidden knowledge, are better able to tap consumers' meaning with respect to recent and historical knowledge. For example, changes in the specific metaphors and in the metaphor systems that patients use provide immediate and meaningful clues about how a patient's goals are changing at all levels of a goal hierarchy (Kopp 1995; Weiser 1993). Whether traditional self-report methods, metaphor-based methods, or some combination are preferred, it is desirable to track goal dynamics longitudinally. Insights about how goals change in dynamic ways are central to a deep understanding of their structure, functioning, and even content.

Being carried to the dentist: an illustration

We have argued that using a metaphor-based method would help us to surface unsurfaced knowledge, identify hidden goals and have a deeper understanding of the meaning of goals. We draw upon research using a metaphor-based method, the Zaltman Metaphor Elicitation Technique (ZMET)[1] to illustrate the types of metaphors and the insights they might provide into consumer goals. The study was conducted by Futuredontics, a company interested in understanding consumers' thoughts and feelings related to good oral hygiene. Details of ZMET and its theoretical underpinnings can be found in Zaltman and Coulter (1995) and Zaltman (1997).

Based on Futuredontics' screening criteria, eight women and four men between the ages of 24 and 39 with an annual income of at least $40,000, and who had no dental insurance and had not been to the dentist within the past two years, were selected to participate. Prior to participating in a one-on-one depth interview, each participant was asked to collect 8 to 10 images (e.g. photographs, pictures in books or magazines) that expressed their thoughts and feelings about going to the dentist. The two-hour interview primarily focused on the images that the participant brings. The interview is relatively unstructured but typically involves a seven step process: (1) storytelling, (2) missed images, (3) construct elicitation, (4) metaphor elaboration, (5) sensory images, (6) the vignette, and (7) the summary image.

Our discussion here reports on selected findings from our analysis with a focus on participants' perspectives with regard to good oral hygiene. To briefly summarize, our analyses clearly illustrate the co-existence of conflicting goals. On the one hand, individuals have goals related to *going* to the dentist to practice good oral hygiene, to get clean, white teeth, to feel good about one's appearance, be more self-confident, and to be at peace. On the other hand, they have goals related to *avoiding* the uncertainty and anxiousness about going to the dentist, the wait for the dentist, the pain of the exam, the smells and sounds in the office, and the related costs of dental care. The visit to the dentist's office is at best an approach-avoidance dance.

In the following discussion, we offer illustrations of identified metaphorical expressions, and conceptual, complex and deep metaphors as they relate to lower- and higher-level goals, and the subtleties of the dentist–patient relationship.

The conceptual metaphors: necessary evil and the knight in shining armor

Our analyses revealed that participants in the study saw the dentist and his work as a *necessary evil* and as a *knight in shining armor*. The former of these two conceptual metaphors is evidenced in the following metaphorical expressions:

> This is a picture of two women hugging each other. That represents that I usually go to the dentist with someone else . . . I don't like going to the dentist . . . always in the back of my mind, I feel that something is going to go wrong. Maybe they might cut my gums, and I might swallow a filling.
>
> (Female, 37)

> [Deciding to go to the dentist] is like a battle with myself . . . a macho thing. I feel I don't need to go unless my teeth really hurt . . . I can hold out from going to the dentist because my teeth don't hurt that bad. I'm strong, I can make it without the dentist. It's a macho thing, like the running of the bulls.
>
> (Male, 27)

> [The drill] is the most feared item in the dentist's repertoire of tools: that bzzz, that little bzzz. When I was a kid I used to worry about the thing spinning off and into my cheek or onto my tongue. [I also feared] the vibrations on the teeth. It's just [a part of] going to the dentist.
>
> (Male, 32)

The other side of the picture, so to speak, is that the dentist was perceived in a very positive light, as if he was a knight in shining armor.

> [It's a picture of] a guardian angel, and it's how I feel safe with the dentist that I have gone to for a long time, Dr Schwartz . . . I've just gone to him for years and I really didn't have to think of anything, just sat in the chair and he did his thing . . . Dr Schwartz, he was a protecting, loving force.
>
> (Female, 38)

> Once you get to know how [the dentist] works, you can talk about different things. It is more relaxed. My dentist, he grew up with us . . . we have a lot in common . . . He tells me exactly what he is doing. You've got to trust the dentist to feel easier . . . When you are all done with [what is] going to be done, [you feel] confident about yourself.
>
> (Male, 35)

The complex metaphor: good vs. evil

The complex metaphor, *good vs. evil*, seems to capture the conceptual metaphors, *dentist as necessary evil* and *dentist as knight in shining armor*, as well as the meanings communicated by participants' summary images and the consensus map. Both participants' summary images and the consensus map serve as complex metaphors; the former is each participant's network of meaning related to good oral hygiene, and the latter is an aggregation across study participants that represents the socially shared network of meaning. To exemplify the value of examining these metaphors, we present one participant's summary image and the consensus map (and related metaphorical expressions) to illustrate the *good vs. evil* complex metaphor.

The summary image

During Step 7 of the ZMET interview each participant works with a computer graphics technician to create a composite image from the pictures that they brought to the interview. As the name suggests, this image serves as a summary of the participant's thoughts and feelings about going to the dentist. Figure 14.1 is one participant's (Male, 27) summary image, and Figure 14.2 is the participant's description of the meanings related to the various components of the summary image. Upon reading the description, the co-existence of conflicting goals becomes evident. There are certainly positive physical and emotional outcomes associated with the dentist, e.g. having clean, white teeth, feeling good about one's appearance, and becoming more self-confident. Alternatively, the participant also has goals related to *avoiding* the wait for the dentist, the pain of the exam, and the smells and sounds in the office.

The consensus map

Metaphorical expressions are a key mechanism through which participants in a ZMET study express ideas. Thus, we review transcripts of all interviews and code them for the main ideas (i.e. constructs) that were elicited. Constructs, therefore, represent basic ideas mentioned by participants when discussing their thoughts and feelings about going to the dentist. The aggregation of participants' constructs and their interrelationships form a complex metaphor, a mental model which illustrates the linkages between goal-related actions and behaviors. (For more details on construction of the consensus map, please see Zaltman and Coulter 1995, Zaltman 1997.)

Figure 14.3 illustrates the consensus map for our study about dental hygiene; the map represents connections between constructs made by at least one quarter of the participants. The *good vs. evil* complex metaphor is apparent, with two central constructs being *Go to the Dentist* and *Don't Go to the Dentist*. On the *good (Go)* side of the consensus map, participants relate *positive childhood experiences, a favorable ambiance in the dentist's office, a trusting*

Figure 14.1 Participant's (male, 27) summary image.

and positive rapport with the dentist as factors that encourage them to schedule dental visits. Moreover, the participants relate their lower-order (relatively speaking) goal of dental hygiene to higher-order goals of self-esteem, personal worth, and peace. The following metaphorical expressions illustrate the positive aspects of visiting the dentist.

> When I go to the dentist I feel confident, not just for that day . . . but for months after and you just feel better and have a better attitude, a better outlook, a healthier attitude. You're confident, you know everything's okay.
>
> (Female, 35)

> When I think about going to the dentist, I think about getting my teeth white again, clean . . . I feel better about myself. If I look good, I feel good, self-confident, and professional.
>
> (Male, 39)

[In the center of the image is] a person with sort of a large head with different ideas floating around it. The main body is shrugging to indicate my "oh well" feeling towards everything, and my very strong belief in my ideas about why I go or don't go to the dentist.

The bottom of my body is represented by a tiger, or actually I think it is a leopard's body, being pulled by the tail, by a man. This represents my feeling that the dental industry is pulling my tail as far as telling me that I have to go to the dentist every six months.

Off my right arm is an image of children, swinging on a swing. This represents me feeling like a child when I go to the dentist, and having very little control over the environment, and being treated like a child. It represents having very little control in being placed in this chair and being told that this is for my own good and digging around in my mouth.

In the upper left corner of the picture there is an image of this woman, who is anxious. She is on the phone and she has two phones up to each ear and she has a pencil in her mouth. It looks like she has a lot of sources of information around her. She seems confused, an overflow of info. That's how I feel about having to find a dentist, and then schedule an appointment, and make sure that it is all ok with my insurance, and that I can squeeze it into my schedule. There is this anxiety over the logistics of going to the dentist.

On the opposite side of the head, swerving around, there is an image of a person being carried by one of the people. This is my feeling. I would need to be carried to the dentist in the sense that either it would have to be because of a physical pain, my teeth really hurt, in excruciating pain, or some other reason that someone would make me go. But literally, they almost have to carry me to the dentist, because I won't go there on my own free will.

The background is cloudy, dark on top around my head where it is filled with all this anxiety. This is different from the normal color, the light color below which represents a day to day existence.

[*You talked about this image in the upper right-hand corner being carried to the dentist, what is it that deters you?*] Well, I don't like being at the dentist, the sharp objects, very obtrusive and painful and unpleasant. Sitting in the chair and having them dig with these sharp little scrapers in my teeth. [*What would make it more pleasant?*] No sharp objects in my mouth. It's funny the dentists tell you, "Don't every put anything sharp and obtrusive in your mouth," and then they go and scrape you with these things. Geez, you think they could figure out new ways to clean your teeth without having to scrape you with metal, like a medieval torturing device.

The head itself has these really weird images floating around that represent this deeper anxiety of going to the dentist. People telling me that I need to go, and me not wanting to go. It's that whole conflict between the two that creates anxiety and these weird images, I don't even know what they are. The expression of myself in this is, my hands outstretched saying, 'Well, this is me and this is how I am and I am not going to change.' I don't know whether the shrugging is actually conveyed in the picture, but that is my attitude, 'Oh well, this is how I am, and this is how I plan to stay. Don't pull my tail.'

[*If you were to put a title on this image what would that be?*) 'Doctor, please don't pull my tail or don't yank my tail,' playing on the pun of having your teeth yanked.

Figure 14.2 Verbatim for participant's (male, 27) summary image.

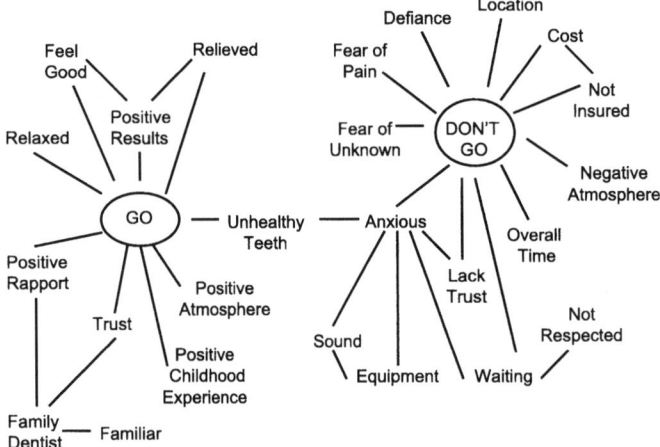

Figure 14.3 Consensus map for thoughts and feelings about good dental care.

On the *evil* (*Don't Go*) side of the consensus map, participants comment on a variety of negative factors, including *cost-related issues, time- and location-related concerns,* as well as *the fears and anxieties related to pain, the unknown, and the dreaded office-related equipment and sounds.* Our participants' metaphorical expressions vividly convey their negativity toward going to the dentist.

> [Going to a dentist] could be inclement weather. It looks like it is getting dark. It could be like a major thunderstorm about to happen and there is no real place to go undercover immediately. So I am vulnerable to the elements.
>
> (Female, 38)

> I just don't feel right about having someone dig into my mouth with metal tools. They feel like sharp, little bullhorns going into my teeth. They poke you. It feels like flesh in a chair being ripped around with their little pointy metal things . . . I feel like I am being interrogated in the dentist's chair.
>
> (Male, 27)

> It is the whole waiting room process. You rush to get there on time to be a good patient, you are waiting in the waiting room with bad magazines. It is not fun . . . You probably have to be at work. [T]he waiting room causes a lot of anxiety. I want to go home . . . You pay them all this money and they can't keep their appointment.
>
> (Female, 32)

> To me, the dental office smells like flesh or burning flesh or some kind of a smell that you can't even put your finger on . . . I would hold my stomach if there weren't other people in the waiting room. I want to . . . stop the butterflies and try to make my stomach feel better.
>
> (Female, 34)

The deep metaphor: balance

The deep metaphor, *balance*, refers to equilibrium, to equalize or compensate, to viewing both sides of a matter. Balance aptly captures the essence of the conceptual metaphors, *dentist as necessary evil* and *dentist as knight in shining armor*, and the complex metaphor of *good vs. evil*. A closer look at participants' metaphorical expressions reveals three themes regarding balance. The first concerns participants' balancing the positive outcomes of the dental visit against the negatives associated with a visit to the dentist's office, the second refers to participants' need to achieve a more "favorable balance" during their office visit, and the third refers to discussing the "imbalance" in power between the dentist and the patient.

A dominant theme with regard to *balance* and the dental visit involves consumers trading off the negative aspects of the dental visit and its preparation against the physical and emotional good that can come from following through with a dental visit. With regard to the former, consumers deal with the pre-visit anxieties such as the anticipation of the unknown, the impending pain, the financial concerns, and the waiting game in the office. These negatives coupled with the physical unpleasantries of having a dentist work on their teeth, and listening to the nerve-wracking dental equipment unnerve dental patients. Alternatively, the positive outcomes, including white, healthy teeth, being self-confident, and feeling relaxed help to counter, or at least give a somewhat favorable light, to the gloomy visit to the dentist's office. Several participants' comments illustrate the trade-off between the dental visit occurrences and their more abstract goals, e.g. post-visit emotional comfort.

> I hate the smell of the dental office. I get kind of nervous . . . I don't like waiting. If I hear the drills going on, it makes me think more. Once I'm there, I want to get it over with . . . [and when it's over] I'm more relieved . . . more relaxed.
>
> (Male, 35)

> This picture is three guys with machine guns and they are all firing at the same time. It's the same song [that you hear] in the dentist's office – when [my mouth] is open and they are drilling . . . I would rather have a baby than a toothache, and that's a lot of pain. When there is pain in your mouth, it hurts everywhere . . . and you can't function . . . I can't wait to finish [my dental appointment]. Peace.
>
> (Female, 37)

A second theme with regard to *balance* deals specifically with the patient's time in the office. Participants, after harping on bothersome aspects of the dental visit, seemed compelled to offer suggestions that they believed would make a dental visit a more palatable experience, to bring it more into balance with their expectations of a more favorable service encounter.

As evidenced in the following, participants use vivid metaphors to communicate the perceptions of the dental visit and provide advice for the dentist to improve the experience.

> When the dentist is scraping my teeth, it reminds me of someone dragging their nails across a chalkboard. It's very unpleasant . . . If the next time I went to the dentist and had a really positive experience, I'd say, "I could do this again." If the dentist was really nice and had fresh breath, and the chair was comfortable, and they gave me gas, so I wouldn't feel the pain, and there was music, I might even like it.
>
> (Male, 27)

> With the insurance hassle, getting bills . . . I feel like I should just be banging my head against the wall . . . And, another problem I had with dentists, I just felt that they weren't gentle enough and my teeth are really sensitive . . . I can tolerate a lot of pain, and when I say "I'm in pain," I'm in pain . . . Going to the dentist should almost be like a field trip. It should be nice and soft and recreational and not sporty, but fun . . . You look forward to going and seeing everyone, and you know you're going to have a good experience.
>
> (Female, 30)

A final theme on *balance* concerns the imbalance of power between doctors and patients, with the dentist in control, and the patient relatively helpless and vulnerable. The participants talk about their vulnerability, their feelings of no power, and perceptions of being treated like a child. Participants' feelings are evoked by dentists who keep them waiting, who don't listen to their cries of pain, and who aren't conciliatory.

> [This is] a picture of a shark. Fear, like if someone had a knife at my throat. Just a fear that seems like it is out of my control. Large, ravenous teeth, sharp that can take a bite out of you . . . [When I am at the dentist's office] I feel like a homeless person . . . feeling vulnerable and feeling open and exposed . . .
>
> (Female, 38)

> [Dentists] have control of you. You are the patient and the doctor has control . . . you are downright helpless . . . [the dentist] is the dominant one, and [the patient] is the helpless one.
>
> (Male, 35)

> [The dentist] is not respectful of my time . . . The last couple of times I've been to the dentist, it is just a matter of waiting and confusion . . . I may not be a doctor, but my time is valuable, and I just get mad that people don't respect it.
>
> (Female, 27)

To summarize, our analyses revealed the paradoxical nature of participants' goals and good oral hygiene. Participants' metaphorical expressions, e.g. the picture of the shark; the smells of burning flesh, the little bullhorns going into teeth, and the sound of fingernails on chalkboards, more clearly articulate participants' issues related good dental hygiene than would be the case using more typical self-report methods. In discussing their goals to avoid pains and anxieties, and desires for peace and self-confidence, as related to their goal of good dental care, participants tried to balance the good of going to the dentist, against the bad of being there, against the good of leaving. And, while acknowledging that going to the dentist is the "right thing to do," some participants resolved their goal conflict by going to the dentist, others resolved it by staying home. The meanings behind the metaphors elicited in the study provide valuable insights into the customer's perspective of the doctor–patient relationship and about their goals and interrelationships. Moreover, though not the focus of this chapter, our findings have significant strategic and managerial implications.

Summary

Goals are everywhere. Goals litter stadiums, are prominent on the lawns of non-profit groups during fund raising, are evident in the migration of various animal species, surface in sales force training programs, appear in the personal classified sections of magazines, and are the raison d'être of commencement speeches. Durkheim's classic work on anomie and suicide reminds us of the centrality of goals in giving life meaning. Goals even endow people with the ability to delay death for short periods of time until after a major cultural, religious, or family event. It is not surprising given their ubiquity that, in one way or another, goals are the foundation on which consumers base their acquisition, consumption, and disposal of goods and services. Goals are not only the foundation on which consumer behavior is built, they are also the energy source or fuel for constructing these activities.

We have noted as others have, that studying consumer goals is challenging for a number of reasons. First, goals are often contiguous with one being a means of achieving another and in the contiguity they may appear nearly seamless. This introduces the challenge of separating contiguous goals from one another. It also raises the issue of whether the appropriate unit of analysis is an individual goal (assuming it can be readily isolated) or a goal cluster. Second, a given goal or goal cluster is part of a system and may be related to multiple other goals of both a higher and lower order if one takes a heterarchical perspective in viewing goals. This raises the following methodological challenge: if the meaning of a goal is found in its association with other goals, how do we understand a given goal without taking into account multiple other goals? Third, the context of a goal has an important impact on how it is structured, its exact content, the benefit it may provide. This context is frequently, maybe unavoidably, social in nature. This presents us with the challenge of understanding goals using the convenience of individuals while knowing goals are not individual affairs.

These and other challenges prompt us to encourage the use of more diverse methods for understanding goals. The most commonly employed methods for studying goals in consumer behavior contexts have proven quite productive and will continue to be so. They are helpful and efficient in making comparisons across multiple groups about the presence and relative importance of particular goals. They are also helpful in tracking changes in goals and goal sequences within a population. This, in turn, provides insight into the dynamic ways in which goals do and do not operate, especially as changes in life circumstance occur.

This chapter has encouraged more frequent use of metaphor-based approaches to studying goals as a way of augmenting the insights offered by other methods. Metaphor-based approaches such as those used in a variety of mental health counseling settings, and now increasing in business settings, provide a special opportunity to learn about the deeper qualities of goals. These deeper qualities include the hidden emotional character of goals, the manner in which goals interact to produce paradox and conflict, and the socially negotiated character of goals which individuals ultimately accept. Metaphor studies make this possible by digging deeper into the unconscious mind of the consumer, helping them, in effect, to open windows into their own mind and look in and then share their observations with a researcher. In the process, hidden knowledge about goals, including what a person doesn't know they know about the presence of goals, and how those goals operate, is frequently surfaced. Metaphor-based methods better enable individuals to understand and share goals that they simply had not had the occasion or ability to explore. Importantly, they enable consumer and other researchers to tap into varying levels of goals, to elicit deeper meanings of goals, better know the linkages among goals and their potentially paradoxical nature. Continued investigation of methods used to explore goal setting and goal processes will enable us to more fully understand consumers' mental models for goal attainment.

Acknowledgments

The authors greatly appreciated the comments and suggestions from Susan Fournier, Beth Hirschman, and George Zinkhan on an earlier draft of this chapter.

Note

1 ZMET is available for use without restriction for academic research purposes. Training materials are available and we are pleased to provide additional guidance to academics. The technique is patented, and non-academic use

requires prior authorization. Further information for academic purposes can be obtained by contacting the Director, Mind of the Market Laboratory, Harvard Business School, Boston, MA 02163. ZMET is also widely used in proprietary commercial studies in markets worldwide.

References

Austin, J.T. and Vancouver, J.B. (1996) "Goal constructs in psychology: structure, process, and content," *Psychological Bulletin* 20 (3): 338–75.

Bagozzi, R.P. and Dholakia, U. (1999) "Goal setting and goal striving in consumer behavior," *Journal of Marketing* 63 (special issue): 19–32.

Bagozzi R.P., Wong, N., and Youjae, Y. (1999) "The role of culture and gender in the relationship between positive and negative affect," *Cognition and Emotion* 13 (6): 641–72.

Bargh, J.A. and Barndollar, K. (1996) "Automaticity in action: the unconscious as repository of chronic goals and motives," in P.M. Gollwitzer and J.A. Bragh (eds) *The Psychology of Action: Linking Cognition and Motivation to Behavior,* New York: Guilford Press: 457–81.

Bornstein, R.F. and Pittman, T.S. (1992) (eds) *Perception Without Awareness*, New York: Guilford Press.

Broadbent, D.B. (1985) "Multiple goals and flexible procedures in design of work," in M. Frese and J. Sabini (eds) *Goal Directed Behavior: The Concept of Action in Psychology*, Hillsdale, NJ: Erlbaum: 285–94.

Cantor, N., Norem, J.K., Niedenthal, P.M., Langston, C.A., and Brower, A.M. (1987) "Life tasks, self-concept ideals, and cognitive strategies in a life transition," *Journal of Personality and Social Psychology* 53 (6): 1178–91.

Damasio, A.R. (1994) *Descartes' Error: Emotion, Reason, and the Human Brain*, New York: G.P. Putnam's Sons.

Dowling, J.E. (1998) *Creating Mind: How the Brain Works*, New York: W.W. Norton Company.

Fauconnier, G. and Turner, M. (1998) "Principles of conceptual integration," in J.P. Koenig (ed.) *Discourse and Cognition: Bridging the Gap*, Stanford, CA: CSLI/ Cambridge.

Geertz, C. (1973) *The Interpretation of Cultures*, New York: Basic Books.

Gibbs, R.W. Jr. (1994) *The Poetics of Mind: Figurative Thought, Language, and Understanding*, New York: Cambridge University Press.

Glucksberg, S. (1995) "Commentary on nonliteral language: processing and use," *Metaphor and Symbolic Activity* 10 (1): 47–57.

Grady, J. (1997) "Foundations of meaning: primary metaphors and primary scenes," PhD dissertation, University of California, Berkeley.

—— (1998) "The conduit metaphor revisited: a reassessment of metaphors for communication," in J.P. Koenig (ed.) *Discourse and Cognition: Bridging the Gap*, Stanford, CA: CSLI/Cambridge.

Gutman, J. (1982) "A means-end chain model based on consumer categorization processes," *Journal of Marketing* 46: 60–72.

Hebb, D.O. (1955) "Drives and the CNS (Conceptual Nervous System)," *Psychological Review* 62: 243–54.

Hoffman, D.D. (1998) *Visual Intelligence: How We Create What We See*, New York: W.W. Norton & Company.

Houston, M.B. and Walker, B.A. (1996) "Self-relevance and purchase goals: mapping a consumer decision," *Journal of the Academy of Marketing Science* 24 (3): 232–45.

Johnson, C. (1997) "Metaphor vs. conflation in the acquisition of polysemy: the case of SEE," in M.K. Hiraga, C. Sinha, and S. Wilcox (eds) *Cultural, Typological and Psychological Issues in Cognitive Linguistics,* Current Issues in Linguistics Theory 152, Amsterdam: John Benjamins.

Kingten, E.R. and Holland, N.N. (1984) "Carlos reads a poem," *College English* 46 (5): 478–91.

Kopp, R.R. (1995) *Metaphor Therapy: Using Client-Generated Metaphors in Psychotherapy,* New York: Brunner/Mazel Publishers.

Lakoff, G. (1993) "The contemporary theory of metaphor," in A. Ortony (ed.) *Metaphor and Thought,* 2nd edition, Cambridge: Cambridge University Press: 202–51.

Lakoff, G. and Johnson, M. (1980) *Metaphors We Live By,* Chicago: University of Chicago Press.

—— (1999) *Philosophy in the Flesh: The Embodied Mind and Its Challenge to Western Thought,* New York: Basic Books.

LeDoux, J.E. (1996) *The Emotional Brain: The Mysterious Underpinnings of Emotional Life,* New York: Simon and Schuster.

Little, B.R. (1989) "Personal project analysis: trivial pursuits, magnificent obsessions, and the search for coherence," in A.R. Buss and N. Cantor (eds) *Personality Psychology: Recent Trends and Emerging Directions,* New York: Springer-Verlag: 15–31.

Mick, D.G. and Buhl, C. (1992) "A meaning-based model of advertising experiences," *Journal of Consumer Research* 19 (December): 317–38.

Narayanan, S. (1997) "Embodiment in language understanding: sensory-motor representations for metaphoric reasoning about event descriptions," PhD dissertation, Department of Computer Science, University of California, Berkeley.

Ortony, A. (ed.) (1993) *Metaphor and Thought,* 2nd edition, Cambridge: Cambridge University Press.

Ortony, A., Clore, G., and Collins, A. (1988) *The Cognitive Structure of Emotions,* Cambridge: Cambridge University Press.

Plutchik, R. (1993) "Emotions and the vicissitudes: emotion and psychopathology," in M. Lewis and J.M. Haviland (eds) *The Handbook of Emotions,* New York: Guilford Press: 53–66.

Reynolds, T.J. and Gutman, J. (1988) "Laddering theory, method, analysis, and interpretation," *Journal of Advertising Research* 28 (1): 11–31.

Rokeach, M. (1973) *The Nature of Human Values,* New York: Free Press.

Searle, J.R. (1994) *The Rediscovery of the Mind,* Cambridge, MA: M.I.T. Press.

Shimamura, A.P. (1994) "The neuropsychology of metacognition," in J. Metcalfe and A.P. Shimamura (eds) *Metacognition: Knowing About Knowing,* Cambridge, MA: MIT Press: 253–76.

Sirgy, M.J. (1986) *Self-Congruity: Toward a Theory of Personality and Cybernetics,* New York: Praeger.

Tangney, J.P. and Fischer, K.W. (1995) (eds) *Self-Conscious Emotions: The Psychology of Shame, Guilt, Embarrassment, and Pride,* New York: Guilford Press.

Valette-Florence, P. and Rapacchi, B. (1991) "Improvements in the means-end chain analysis using graph theory and correspondence analysis," *Journal of Advertising Research* 31 (1): 30–45.

Weiser, J. (1993) *Phototheraphy Techniques: Exploring the Secrets of Personal Snapshots and Family Albums*, San Francisco: Jossey-Bass.

Zaltman, G. (1997) "Rethinking market research: putting people back in," *Journal of Marketing Research* 34: 424–37.

Zaltman, G. and Coulter, R. (1995) "Seeing the voice of the customer: metaphor-based advertising research," *Journal of Advertising* 35 (4): 35–51.

15 Lattice analysis in the study of motivation

Steven Brownstein, Ajay Sirsi, James C. Ward, and Peter H. Reingen

Introduction

The motive to buy appears to spring from the individual, but its sources run deep into the social and cultural environment. Too often, studies of the why of consumption focus on cognitive, social, or cultural forces, as though one source might be "the" source of motivation. For example, on the one hand, consumer researchers have sought the why of consumption by examining consumer cognitive structures through means-end analysis and related methods (Gengler and Reynolds 1995). But these approaches usually do not relate the structure of motivating beliefs to the structure of the social and cultural environments in which they are produced, shared, and enacted. On the other hand, consumer researchers have striven to reveal the social and cultural motives for consumption through ethnographic inquiry. However, such studies have often not systematically explored how motives of sociocultural origin are represented in the minds of participants (e.g. O'Guinn and Belk 1989). While focus on a particular source of motivation is of value, it is also limiting. Motivation in the daily lives of consumers springs not from cognitive, social, or cultural forces in isolation, but from the swirl of their interaction. It is in understanding this interaction that significant potential for advance in motivation research may lie.

We thus prefer a broad view of the origins of motivation, but one that entails a methodological challenge. We view an individual's consumption decisions as events occurring in social and cultural space that reflect a socioculturally shared reality (Hardin and Higgins 1986) and socioculturally shared motives. Therefore, motivation should be studied as it occurs within the minds of individuals participating in the groups and subcultures that play a role in forming and validating their motives. In any actual sociocultural environment, the influences of individual cognition, group, and culture contain one another. The methodological challenge is in understanding how the structure of these containments influences one another in motivating behavior. Progress in meeting this challenge has the potential to answer theoretical questions of keen interest to motivation researchers in consumer researcher and other disciplines. These issues include how motives are learned socially, how position in a social structure relates to individual goal structure, and how social structure and goal structure relate to the distribution of motivating forces within a social group. Such across levels issues have been neglected in motivation research, but their theoretical importance is clear along with their potential to enlighten practice.

The challenge of understanding these interfaces is the more daunting because of the complex internal structure of each of the forces producing motivation. Like their interrelations, the internal structure of cognitive, social, and cultural forces is often overlooked. Consider cognition as a motivational force. Rather than a list of independent salient beliefs or goals (Ajzen and Fishbein 1980), the beliefs motivating consumption are likely to be interrelated. For example, if a consumer believed that "animal products are unethical to eat," a moral motivation for the "why not" of consumption, he or she can very likely cite a variety of reasons for this belief. These reasons are likely to conform to an "if-then" structure, perhaps reflecting the complex implicational structure of a network of reasoning, an ideology, extant in the broader culture. These reasons exercise their motivating force on behavior as a structure, and thus should be studied accordingly.

For consumption decisions made outside the laboratory, cognitive networks of beliefs are often intertwined with social networks. The consumption motives of an individual are often influenced by the beliefs of those surrounding the individual in his or her social environment. Like the relations of beliefs, the relations of individuals are structured in networks. The position of the individual in these social structures, and the structure of the networks themselves, can influence the motives of their members. The methodological challenge that emerges from the foregoing is to understand not only how cognitive structure and social structure influence consumption in isolation, but to understand how these structures interact in influencing consumption.

The lack of work on how across-levels forces influence motivation may reflect a lack of appropriate tools for systematically relating structures at one level to structures at another. For example, the tools of network analysis have often been used to understand how either cognitive or social structure influence consumption behavior, but these tools have an important limitation. Network analysis in consumer behavior·has usually been confined to the study of one-mode data. Consumer researchers (e.g. Ward and Reingen 1990) have used network analysis to study n × n networks of the relations of phenomena of like kind (e.g. the n × n social ties of actors in a matrix or the n × n relations of beliefs in a matrix), but they have not usually utilized a method for analyzing the structural relations of two different phenomena at once.

To "break out of the box" of traditional network analysis, and better understand the intricate relations of across-levels phenomena, we need a rigorous method of analyzing two-mode data. Two-mode data record the relations of two different phenomena – for example, the relations between motivating beliefs and actors – and not just actor-to-actor or belief-to-belief relations.

The analysis of dual-mode data bears the potential to reveal not only the structural properties of each mode of data individually, but the structural properties of their relations.

This chapter will introduce an approach to the representation of dual-mode data, but our contribution will be more than merely methodological. We will use this method to explore the motivating power of ideology on consumption behavior using data from a study of animal rights activists. Ideologies are systems of interrelated beliefs that prescribe how people should behave. They are cultural belief systems that organize both the cognitions and social structure of participants to achieve moral ends, often focused on consumption. Understanding their motivating power requires understanding the relations of different orders of phenomena (people, beliefs, and behaviors) to one another. Our analysis will thus illustrate not only the utility of dual-mode analysis for understanding motivational phenomena that are inherently multiplex in nature, but will result in theoretical insights about how ideology motivates consumption behavior through its simultaneous influence on cognitive and social phenomena.

Representing two-mode network data

Analytical techniques which have been applied to categorical two-mode data in the field of consumer behavior include *correspondence analysis* and *means-end chain analysis* (Hoffman and Franke 1986; Gengler and Reynolds 1995). However, there is also a set-theoretical methodology known as *Galois lattice analysis*, which has proven useful in the analysis of dual, highly inseparable phenomena occurring in such areas as database theory (Wille 1982) and social network theory (Freeman and White 1993), that possesses distinctive advantages for the researcher wishing to understand the interrelations of different spheres of inquiry (e.g. the cognitive and social or cultural). These advantages can best be seen in the light of a review of more familiar methods of dual-mode analysis.

Means-end analysis posits a specific cognitive model in which elements of one dimension (an amalgam of product features, possible consequences of those features, and possible values derived from those consequences) are ordered into chains directed specifically from attributes to consequences to values by the individuals who constitute the other dimension of the data. In order to obtain a group-level perspective and to limit the role of idiosyncrasies in the data, the links derived at the individual level are aggregated by frequency, and a cutoff is established above which an aggregate relation is declared to exist. In cases where such data aggregation is desirable, and where the cognitive model posited by this technique can be theoretically supported, such analyses may be highly informative. However, the specificity and richness may be obscured by multiple levels of aggregation, because one mode of the input data (people as separate data points) is lost.

Both correspondence analysis and Galois lattice analysis are more general techniques for analyzing two-mode categorical data. Neither technique presupposes any specific cognitive model, although both can be useful in uncovering cognitive patterns that may exist in the data. Both the Galois lattice technique and correspondence analysis utilize each dimension, or continuum, of a categorical two-mode dataset to place an order on the other dimension. However, in correspondence analysis, the induced order has the structure of a set of metric or pseudometric relations, while in the Galois lattice technique, the induced order has the structure of a series of dually-ordered set containments. Each approach has particular strengths and weaknesses.

In correspondence analysis, the fact that each row and column of a contingency table becomes representable by a point in a derived metric space in which deviations from independence between the row and column dimensions are proportional to products of these derived coordinates (Greenacre 1984) yields certain desirable analytical properties. For instance, one can obtain a chi-square statistic for row – column association, broken down to each derived dimension of the metric representation. Furthermore, one obtains the canonical correlations between the optimally scaled categories as a product of this analysis. However, the most often used feature of this technique is the interpretive power provided by the graphical display of the data in the derived metric space. This allows one to judge the relative similarities of stimuli in terms of these derived dimensions. However, the number of dimensions to derive is open to the judgment of the analyst, and often this number is far less than the maximum obtainable from the data. In other words, data reduction is performed. Furthermore, there is widespread debate as to whether the points in the derived space which stem from one mode of the data should be compared to those which derive from the other mode of the data (Greenacre 1989). Lastly, although one can ascertain a sense of the relative similarities of stimuli to each other through an analysis of the graphical display, one cannot see the specifics of how one stimulus relates to another in terms of the elements of both dimensions that they share or do not share. Therefore, if one wishes to recover a detailed description of exactly how the elements of one mode of a dataset are both hierarchically related to one another and to the hierarchical 'containment' pattern in the other mode of the dataset (in all its link-by-link complexity), he or she must abandon some of the niceties of a metrical technique such as correspondence analysis, and turn instead, or in combination, to a set-theoretical technique specifically designed to fully elucidate these precise relationships. The Galois lattice technique is well formulated for such an analytical role.

In the Galois lattice technique, one utilizes a dichotomous data table to formulate a correspondence, or mapping, between two component continua within a dually-structured phenomenon. Assuming without loss of generality that a "1" in the cell located at row i and column j of a data table signifies that the ith element of one dimension (say p_i, the ith member of a group of people) possesses the jth element of the other dimension (say b_j, the jth belief in a set of beliefs), and conversely assuming that a '0' in that location signifies a lack of said attribute, we say that $(p_i, b_j) \in R$ if and only if the entry in the $(i, j)^{th}$ cell of the data table is "1," and that $(p_i, b_j) \notin R$ if the entry in the $(i, j)^{th}$ cell of the data table is "0." In this manner, we establish R as a *correspondence* between the subsets of one dimension (say the subsets of people) and those of the other dimension (say the subsets of beliefs). In situations where such an assignment is clear, we term the elements of one dimension (say, the *people*) as *objects*, and the elements of the other dimension (say, the *beliefs* characterizing these persons) as *attributes*. To summarize, then, the statement $(p_i, b_j) \in R$ is equivalent to stating both that the $(i, j)^{th}$ entry in the data table is "1," and that the ith object possesses the jth attribute present in the dataset.

A small illustrative example will help clarify and extend these notions. Table 15.1 shows the data matrix for a hypothetical group considering visiting a theme park together. The group consists of *Mom, Dad, Grandma*, a teenage daughter *Mary*, a 10-year-old son *Bobby*, and a teenage cousin *Billy*. Furthermore, we suppose that each group member cites some of the following reasons for attending a theme park: "*Good Clean Fun*," "*Plenty To Do*," "*Meet Girls/Guys*," and "*Good Snacks*," as detailed in the Table.

Denoting the correspondence represented by this data table as R_{park}, note, for example, that (*Mom, Good Clean Fun*) $\in R_{park}$, while (*Mom, Good Snacks*) $\notin R_{park}$. The Galois lattice technique uses an induced correspondence such as R_{park} to retrieve the maximal sets of elements in the "object" dimension A (in this case, the *people*) that correspond to a given element or set of elements in the "attribute" dimension B (in this case, the *reasons* for attending the theme park), and vice-versa, as follows. Given a subset $A = \{a_1, a_2, \ldots, a_n\}$ of *objects* (all belonging to dimension A), we define $A\uparrow$ to be the set of all *attributes* (elements of dimension B) which

Table 15.1 Group members and their reasons for attending a theme park

Group member	Good clean fun	Plenty to do	Meet girls/guys	Good snacks
Mom	1	1	0	0
Dad	1	1	0	1
Grandma	1	0	0	0
Mary	0	0	1	0
Bobby	0	1	0	1
Cousin Billy	1	1	1	0

correspond, under R, to *each* object in A . Formally, then, we have that A↑ := {b ∈ **B** | $(a_i, b) ∈ R ∀ a_i ∈ A$ }. Dually, given a subset B = {$b_1, b_2, . . ., b_n$} of *attributes* belonging to dimension **B**, we define B↓ := {a ∈ **A** | $(a, b_j) ∈ R ∀ b_j ∈ B$}, which is simply the set of all *objects* which possess each *attribute* in B (i.e. which correspond, under R, to *each* element in B).

Examining the data in Table 15.1, one can verify, for instance, that {*Good Clean Fun, Meet Girls/Guys*}↓ equals {*Cousin Billy*}. The dual statement is not true, however, as one can verify that {*Cousin Billy*}↑ equals {*Good Clean Fun, Meet Girls/Guys, Plenty To Do*}. However, one can also verify that applying the ↓ operation to this larger set of reasons; i.e. computing {*Good Clean Fun, Meet Girls/Guys, Plenty To Do*}↓, still results in just {*Cousin Billy*}. Adding the reason "*Plenty To Do*" to the reasons "*Good Clean Fun*" and "*Meet Girls/Guys*" has *not* changed the results we get when we apply the ↓ operation. Furthermore, by including this extra reason, we have the dual correspondence:

{*Cousin Billy*}↑ = {*Good Clean Fun, Meet Girls/Guys, Plenty To Do*}

{*Good Clean Fun, Meet Girls/Guys, Plenty To Do*}↓ = {*Cousin Billy*}

Such "special" pairs of subsets which "map" into each other via ↑ and ↓ are termed *formal concepts* (Wille 1982), and are the building blocks of the Galois lattice representation of the data. The *pair* of subsets { {*Cousin Billy*}, {*Good Clean Fun, Meet Girls/Guys, Plenty To Do*} } is *one* formal concept contained in the data of the table.

A Galois lattice is formed by uncovering *all* formal concepts inherent in the data, and placing an ordinal relation on them via the condition that concept [A_1, B_1] is less than or equal to concept [A_2, B_2] if and only if A_1 is a subset of A_2 (i.e. $A_1 ⊆ A_2$). It can be shown (Birkhoff 1967; Wille 1982) that this condition is equivalent to the 'reverse' containment relationship $B_2 ⊆ B_1$ in the other dimension. The elements of the Galois lattice, namely the formal concepts inherent to the data, are placed at the nodes of a labeled line diagram in which the node representing one formal concept, say [A_1, B_1], is connected by an *ascending* line segment to another formal concept, say [A_2, B_2], if it is *less than* [A_2, B_2] in this induced ordinal relation. Note that since [A_1, B_1] ≤ [A_2, B_2] is equivalent to both $A_1 ⊆ A_2$ *and* $B_2 ⊆ B_1$, this implies that when one moves *up* the ascending line segments of a Galois lattice, the size of the sets in the first position of each formal concept (the set of *objects* to which the concept applies) *increase* in size (i.e. $A_1 ⊆ A_2$), while those in the second position (the set of *attributes* possessed by these objects) *decrease* in size (i.e. $B_2 ⊆ B_1$). The Galois lattice representing the data in Table 15.1 is shown in Figure 15.1. By tradition, one places the names of the *objects* of each formal concept immediately *below* the node of the concept to which they correspond, and dually the names of the *attributes* of the concept immediately *above* that node.

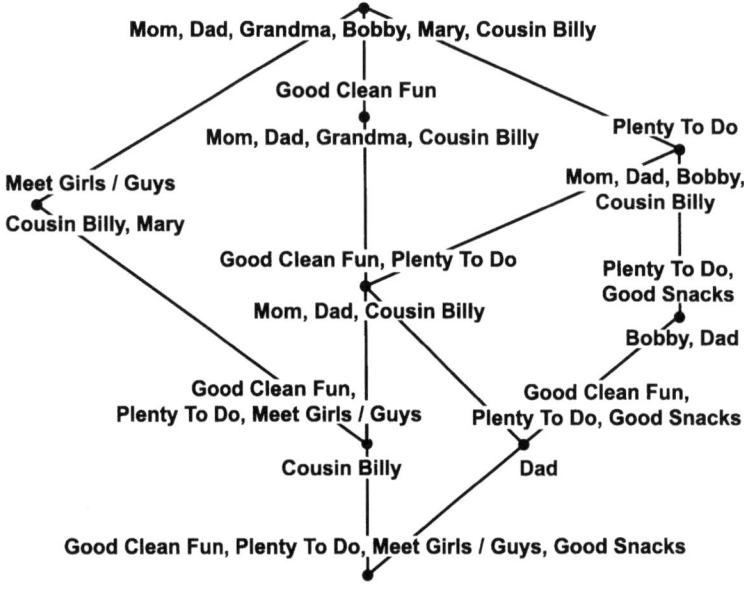

Figure 15.1 Galois lattice of family members and their reasons for attending a theme park.

In order to reduce the complexity of labeling within a Galois lattice, one typically employs a technique known as *reduced labeling*, in which the *objects* of each formal concept are explicitly labeled in the Galois lattice only at the *lowest* node at which they are present, and are assumed to be present at all nodes connected to this node by *ascending* paths. Thus, for instance, since "*Mom*" is present at the top node and the two nodes directly below it, we need only exhibit the label "*Mom*" at the bottommost of these three nodes. Dually, we only explicitly label the *attributes* of each formal concept at the *highest* node at which they are present, and assume that they are present at all nodes connected to this node by *descending* paths. Thus, for instance, since the attribute "*Good Snacks*" is present at the bottom node and the two nodes above it along the rightmost ascending path, we need only exhibit the label "*Good Snacks*" at the topmost of these three nodes. Employing this simplifying methodology to all objects and attributes results in the *reduced labeling* for this lattice, which is shown in Figure 15.2.

Note that no information is "lost" when transitioning to the reduced labeling of a Galois lattice. The full labeling is completely recoverable merely by employing the rule that objects (in this case "persons") continue to accumulate as one moves "up" the ascending paths of the Galois lattice, whereas attributes (in this case "reasons") continue to accumulate as one moves "down" the descending paths of the Galois lattice. Thus, for example, the node labeled "*Mom*" in Figure 15.2 contains the attributes above it,

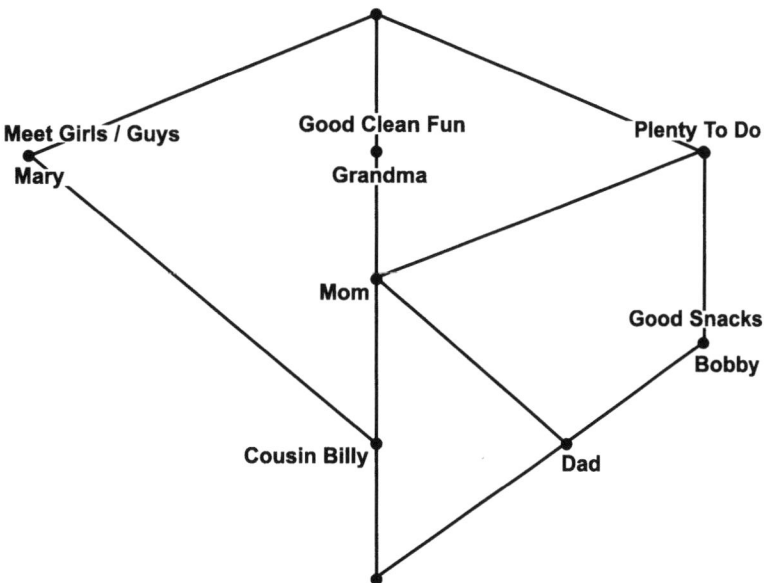

Figure 15.2 Reduced labeling for the Galois lattice of Figure 15.1.

namely "*Good Clean Fun*" and "*Plenty To Do*," as well as containing the persons located at or below it, namely *Mom*, *Dad*, and *Cousin Billy*. Note that by this convention, the topmost node in the lattice will "automatically" contain *all objects* (i.e. persons), but since the reduced labeling procedure only explicitly labels persons at the lowest node at which they are present, no persons' names will be labeled at the topmost node unless this is the only node at which they are present. Despite this, it is helpful to remember that the topmost node does, indeed, contain all individuals. Dually, of course, the bottommost node of the lattice will "automatically" contain all attributes (i.e. reasons), but only those attributes not present at any node above the bottommost node will be explicitly labeled there. Nevertheless, it is helpful to remember that the bottommost node does always contain all attributes.

The following facts concerning this dataset are evident from an examination of the associated reduced-labeled Galois lattice of Figure 15.2:

1 The fact that no *attributes* are present at the top node of the lattice (which automatically contains all *persons*) indicates that none of the reasons for attending the theme park were held by all individuals simultaneously. Dually, the observation that no *objects* are present at the bottom node of the lattice (which automatically contains all *beliefs*) indicates that none of these family members hold all the reasons simultaneously.

2   *Persons* "lower down" along the paths of the lattice are more central, in the sense of having more reasons for attending the theme park. Dually, *beliefs* that are "higher up" along the paths of the lattice are more central than are those lower down, in the sense of being held by more of the participants. Thus, in Figure 15.2, we can see that *Dad* and *Cousin Billy* are the most central *individuals* with regard to reasons for attending the theme park, while "*Meet Girls/Guys,*" "*Good Clean Fun,*" and "*Plenty To Do*" are the most central *reasons* for this family.

3   Persons labeled at a particular node of the reduced-labeled Galois lattice "imply" all those persons labeled at nodes located along those paths *descending* from that particular node, in the sense that any attribute associated with this particular "higher" person will necessarily be associated with any of these "lower" persons. For instance, Figure 15.2 shows that *Mom* "implies" *Dad* and *Cousin Billy*, which corresponds to the fact that any *reasons* held by *Mom* are also held by both *Dad* and *Cousin Billy*. Furthermore, this lattice admits the following additional person implications: *Bobby* → *Dad*; *Mary* → *Cousin Billy;* and *Grandma* → *Mom, Cousin Billy, Dad*. One can rephrase this fact by stating that those persons lower down along a path in the reduced labeled Galois lattice "contain" all those persons located higher up along these paths, in the sense that they account for all the attributes (beliefs) held by these upper persons. This is termed the *upward containment structure of actors* in the Galois lattice. One can therefore state an implication, such as *Bobby* → *Dad* , as a containment relation, *Dad* ↑ ⊃ *Bobby* ↑, since the set of attributes possessed by *Bobby* (i.e. *Bobby* ↑).

4   A dual description of implication holds for the *attributes* of a lattice. An attribute will imply all other attributes located at nodes along paths ascending from that node. As an example, "*Good Snacks*" → "*Plenty To Do,*" in the sense that any persons holding the reason "*Good Snacks*" will necessarily hold the reason "*Plenty To Do.*" Again, we can rephrase this fact by stating that attributes located higher up along paths in the reduced labeled Galois lattice "contain" all those attributes located lower down along these paths, in the sense that they account for all the objects (persons) which hold these lower beliefs. This is termed the *downward containment structure of beliefs* in the Galois lattice. For example, the belief implication "*Good Snacks*" → "*Plenty To Do*" becomes the belief containment relation (*Plenty To Do*) ↓ ⊃ (*Good Snacks*) ↓ .

Galois lattices may be computed algorithmically. The basic notions behind such a task are explained in Ganter (1987) and Wille (1989). The Galois lattices utilized in this chapter were initially determined using the DIAGRAM program (Version 2.12), created by Vogt, Bliesener, and Viehmann (1985).

Study background

The data to be used in the present chapter are from a group of animal rights activists operating in a major Southwestern city. The overarching goal of the ideology motivating this group is to reduce the incidence of cruelty to animals. The first phase of the study involved extensive ethnography which yielded the following general insights.

First, the consumption of (or rather avoidance of) animal products was driven by participants' understanding of ideological beliefs. Second, participants varied in their understanding of these beliefs. And third, more expert participants appeared to take the role of leaders and teachers.

To arrive at a more complete and systematic understanding of the motivational forces at work in the activist subculture, we drew upon structured data that we collected after the ethnographic phase of our inquiry. The structured data included: (a) cognitive maps of participants' ideologically-influenced reasoning about their consumption behavior toward a set of foods, including beef, chicken, fish, milk, sugar, and honey; (b) measures of participants' expertise in the ideology; and (c) measures of the strength of participants' social ties to the other participants (see Sirsi, Ward, and Reingen 1996 for methodological details). For our present purposes, these measures yielded: (a) a list of the beliefs each participant held about why he or she avoided consuming certain products; (b) a classification of each participant as an expert, intermediate, or novice in the belief system; and (c) a list of each participant's strong social ties that were used to analyze the social structure of the activist group.

Lattice analyses

The capability of Galois lattice analysis to reveal the relations between participation in an ideological movement and motivation to avoid consuming animal products will be illustrated with three types of lattices. Each lattice will reveal a "gestalt" visualization of the relations between two phenomena related to behavior, but each will also allow the viewer to trace the intricate patterns of relationship between the two phenomena under examination. The three lattices to be presented will be participants-by-beliefs lattices for food avoidance, beliefs-by-food avoidance lattices for individual participants varying in expertise, and a participant-by-clique membership lattice.

Participants-by-beliefs lattices

Participants indicated which foods they avoided consuming, and then selected beliefs that explained why they did not consume a food. The participant-by-beliefs lattices were constructed from a binary matrix of participants (the "objects" in the lattices) by their beliefs (the "attributes" possessed by these people) concerning the avoidance of a particular food.

Honey

Figure 15.3 shows the participants-by-beliefs lattice for the avoidance of honey. The numbers in the lattice represent the animal rights activists. Numbers surrounded by square boxes with thick lines correspond to experts in the belief system. Numbers surrounded by ovals with thin lines correspond to novices in their expertise. Numbers without lines correspond to intermediate-expertise individuals. The beliefs are spelled out in the figure. The lattice, which is displayed in its reduced-label form, reveals several kinds of patterning.

We can see the dual containment structure of individuals and beliefs. Each actor holds the beliefs on lines ascending from his or her labeled node in the line diagram, and each belief contains the actors on lines descending from its labeled point. The diagram provides an immediate "gestalt" impression of the relation between actors and beliefs. At the top of the lattice we see the set of activists who hold no beliefs about avoiding honey and toward the bottom we see the activists who hold the most beliefs (i.e. all those beliefs on paths ascending from them). By placing most participants above most of the beliefs about honey, the lattice conveys the highly skewed distribution of motivation to avoid honey in the subculture. Honey is a product that only a few tend to view as ideologically relevant, and almost all who do hold this view are experts (square boxes with thick lines). They are motivated to avoid honey. Note that only five of the 34 participants (#15, 21, 26, 27, 29) view honey as an animal product, and the lattice reveals that all five of them necessarily also hold the belief "*humans should not use animals as resources.*" This serves to link their view of honey as an animal product to a dictum about subculturally relevant behavior.

From this Galois lattice, we can see further details about the downward containment structure of beliefs. The uppermost beliefs are most central in the ideology as they are shared for honey among the activists. If a belief (e.g. "*humans should not use animals as resources*") is present, then all the beliefs along the paths descending from it are implied. The lattices thus show the implicational structure of the belief system, not as it exists in theory, but as it is actually instantiated in the minds of participants in the ideology.

From the Galois lattice, we can also see the upward containment structure of participants. Participants 21, 26, 27, and 29 are the most cognitively central participants. Specifically, any of these four individuals contains all participants except for #32. Other participants are contained within subsets of these participants' belief systems. For example, participant 29 (as well as participants 21, 26, and 27) holds the beliefs that honey "*is an animal product*" and "*humans should not use animals as resources*" along with participant 15, and holds the belief that "*animals are like living beings like us,*" "*unethical to eat,*" and "*humans should not use animals as resources*" along with participant 24. Thus we have that $29\uparrow \supset 15\uparrow$ and $29\uparrow \supset 24\uparrow$.

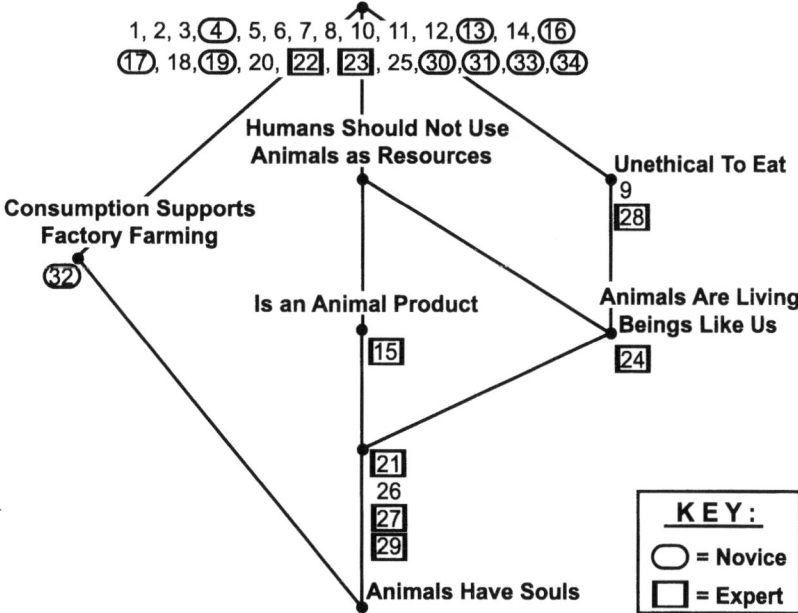

Figure 15.3 Participant-by-belief lattice for the avoidance of honey.

However, participants 15 and 24 do not share these beliefs together. Thus, participant 29's cognitive structure unites those of participants 15 and 24, placing participant 29 in a more cognitively central position, and also laying a cognitive foundation for participant 29 to be socially more central in the teaching of elements of the belief system that are not evoked by participants 15 and 24. Of course, the least cognitively central participants with respect to honey are those at the top of the lattice who hold no beliefs about the product.

In a single picture, a lattice conveys the essence of an ideologically motivated social movement – the dual containment structure of participants and ideological beliefs. The dual containment structure of the lattice suggests the structure of the ideology (the if-then implications of the beliefs as they are differentially and hierarchically applied across the participants) and hints at the potential relation between embeddedness in this structure and embeddedness in the social power structure of the movement. Only experts tend to know the range of implications of the ideology about honey. Their sharing of many of these implications is one aspect of their expertise, a cognitive characteristic that places them in a social position of prestige, conveying the right to teach others, create norms, and enforce norms through social pressure.

Beef

Turning to Figure 15.4, we see the participants-by-beliefs lattice for the behavior of avoiding beef. We can once again see the overall containment structures of beliefs and participants – the downward containment structure of beliefs, and the upward containment structure of participants. The lattice for beef appears different than that for honey, but the patterns will buttress our interpretations of the honey lattice while revealing unique aspects of the relations among beliefs, participants, and the motivation to avoid beef.

Looking at the overall containment structure of individuals and beliefs conveys a different impression than that for honey. Beef avoidance appears to be more central to the animal rights ideology than honey avoidance. In contrast to honey, we see immediately that most participants appear toward the bottom of the lattice instead of toward the top, meaning that they viewed the ideology as highly relevant to beef.

The dual containment structure of individuals-by-beliefs reveals the symbiosis among participants, ideological implications, and motivation. For example, if we look to the right of the diagram, we see that both "*animals are living beings like us*" and "*unethical to eat*" are motives for avoiding beef shared by all experts. Lines can be traced from these beliefs down to all experts shown in the lattice. Under both of these beliefs we see the belief "*animals have souls.*" Tracing down the lattice from this belief, we see that participants 30, 5, 6, 7, 14, 25, 3, 12, 15, 18, and 27 held this belief while all others did not. Thus we can see from the lattice that the set of participants who believe, for instance, that "*animals are living beings like us*" can be partitioned into those who also believe that "*animals have souls*" (#5, 6, 7, 14, 25, 3, 12, 15, 18, 27, and 30) and those that do not (# 16, 17, 33, 31, 24, 2, 8, 10, 21, 26, 32, 1, 9, 20, 22, 23, 28, and 29). While all participants except #13, 34, 19, 4 and 11 avoided beef because they viewed animals as living beings like us, only a subset also believed that animals have souls. When viewed in terms of the downward containment structure of beliefs, this insight reveals that all participants holding the belief "*animals have souls*" also necessarily believe that "*animals are living beings like us,*" hence (*animals are living beings like us*) $\downarrow$ $\supset$ (*animals have souls*) $\downarrow$.

This conclusion is just one example of how the downward containment structure of beliefs provides insight into how the structure of the beliefs motivates participants to avoid beef. Higher beliefs in the lattice "contain" those on lines below them. As we just saw, (*animals are living beings like us*) $\downarrow$ $\supset$ (*animals have souls*) $\downarrow$. Tracing upwards from "*animals have souls*" also leads to "*unethical to eat,*" thus one can also be certain that all those participants who are motivated by "*animals have souls*" are also motivated by "*unethical to eat,*" or stated as a belief containment relationship, (*unethical to eat*) $\downarrow$ $\supset$ (*animals have souls*) $\downarrow$. In other words, there is an "if-then" relationship between these beliefs – if a participant believed that "*animals*

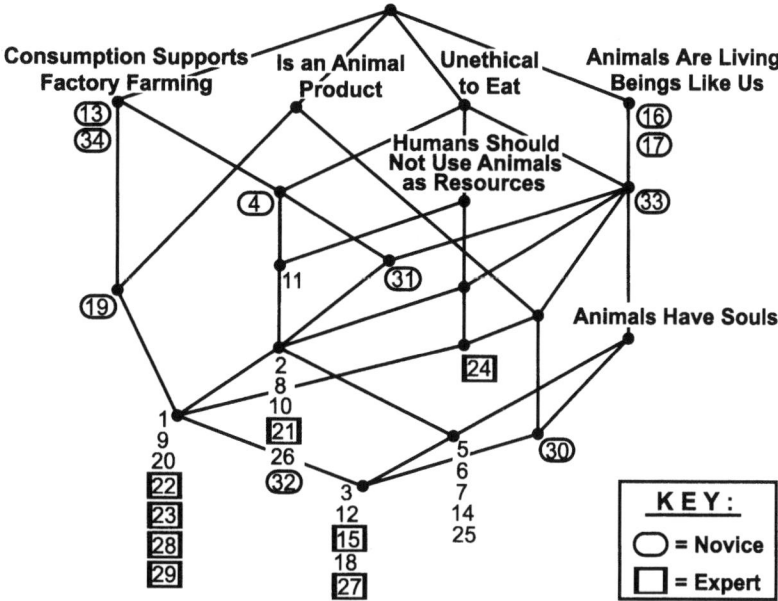

Figure 15.4 Participant-by-belief lattice for the avoidance of beef.

have souls" the participant certainly believed beef is "*unethical to eat.*" It can be easily seen from the lattice that such an "if-then" relationship does *not* exist between "*animals have souls*" and any of the beliefs "*consumption supports factory farming,*" "*is an animal product,*" or "*humans should not use animals as resources,*" since *no* line can be traced upwards from "*animals have souls*" to any of these three other beliefs. From this lattice, one can also see that "*humans should not use animals as resources*" uniquely implies "*unethical to eat*" – all persons believing the former also believe the latter. However, the relationship is not symmetric. Persons #4, 31, 33, and 30 can be seen to believe "*unethical to eat*" without believing "*humans should not use animals as resources.*" Thus, stated as a belief containment relationship, (*unethical to eat*) ↓ ⊃ (*humans should not use animals as resources*) ↓, but not vice-versa.

The lattice thus reveals the different logical paths in the ideology, as it is instantiated with an actual group, that lead to conclusions motivating the behavior of avoiding beef. The relations revealed are not statistically derived; rather, they are set-theoretical "if-then" relations that match the logic of ideological belief systems. Furthermore, the logic revealed is attributable through the lattice to the exact participants who hold that logic, and no others.

Looking at the upward containment structure of participants, we see a pattern recalling the lattice for honey. The lowest labeled participants are primary. Their cognitive structures contain the beliefs of the participants on the nodes above them. Experts appear almost exclusively at the lower levels of the lattice. No experts appear toward the upper levels. As in the lattice for honey, experts are deeply embedded in the lattice for beef. However, they are not alone. The lattice for beef shows a large number of intermediates holding almost as many beliefs about motivating beef avoidance as experts. In contrast to honey, ideological beliefs about beef have diffused more widely, suggesting that beef is an ideologically central example of the evil of animal product consumption. In addition, the lattice for reasoning about beef contains far more links crossing from one formal concept (i.e. node) to another than does the lattice for reasoning about honey. This demonstrates that participants held not just more beliefs about beef consumption, but more complex belief interactions as well. The lattice hints that experts focus their teaching of the ideology on the example of beef, and as a result, experts do not have expert power because of what they know about beef, which most in the culture might regard as widely shared or obvious knowledge. These last suggestions reach beyond the data contained in the lattice, but suggest the power of lattice analysis to prompt insight and spur investigation.

Beliefs-by-foods avoidance lattices for expert and novice participants

What is missing in the honey and beef lattices is a third dimension – the across-products dimension. A sense of the distribution of belief sharing across products can be gained by dropping one dimension of analysis (e.g. sharing across people) and adding another, products.

The resulting figures show beliefs-by-product lattices for respondents individually. Figures 15.5 and 15.6 show an expert's and a novice's beliefs, respectively, as they apply to a set of products that vary in relevance to the animal rights ideology. These individual lattices may be viewed as the mathematical equivalent of vignettes – short case studies in naturalistic inquiry that exemplify more general points. As quantitative vignettes, the lattices summarize a great deal of data (beliefs across six products) in a readily discernible form that facilitates interpretation of the relationships between two phenomena of different orders. The lattice for expert 27 (Figure 15.5) shows at the bottom the products to which this expert applied the greatest number of beliefs (beef, chicken, fish, and milk). Each belief at nodes located above a particular product was applied to that product by this participant. At the top of the lattice are the most central beliefs (*"animals are living beings like us," "animals should not be used as resources,"* and *"unethical to eat"*). Since these are located above the nodes containing each of the products, they apply to all six products studied. Notable from this lattice is the fact that expert 27 applied the same reasoning to the three animal "flesh" products (beef, chicken, fish), while applying differentiated reasoning to the three "non-flesh" products (sugar, milk, honey). Specific-

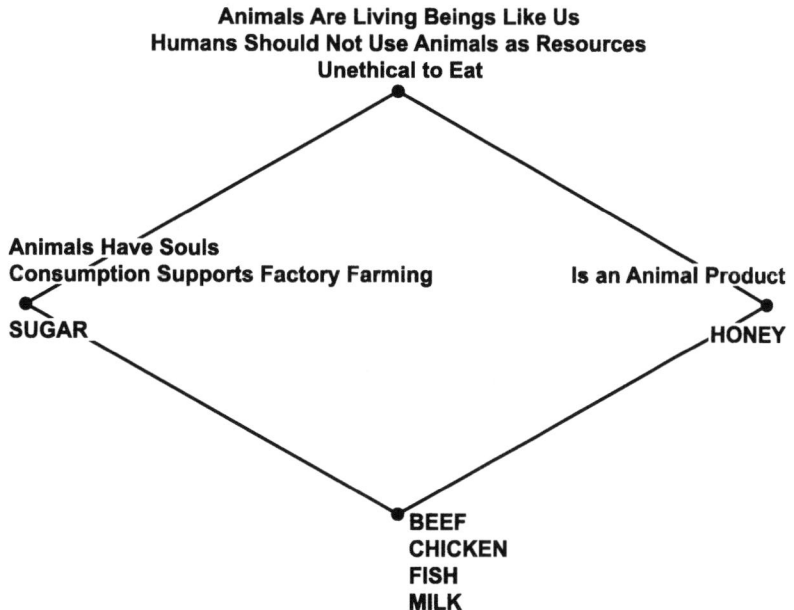

Figure 15.5 Belief-by-food avoidance lattice for expert #27.

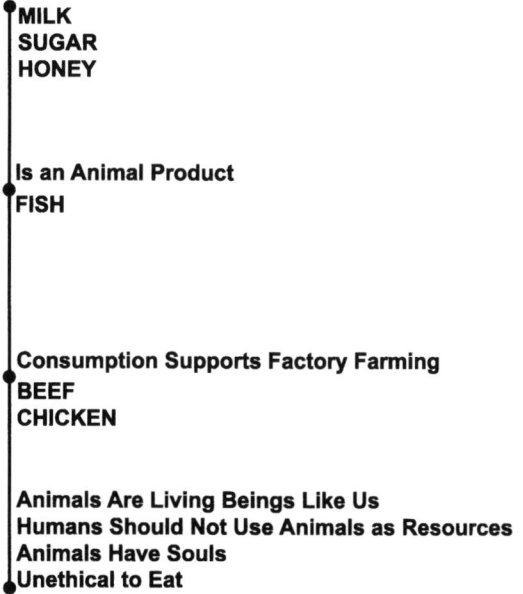

Figure 15.6 Belief-by-food avoidance lattice for novice #19.

ally, we can see that with respect to these elements of the animal rights belief system, milk was regarded as an equivalent of beef, chicken, and fish, while sugar and honey received patterns of reasoning that differed from the other products and from each other.

The lattice for novice 19 (Figure 15.6) tells a very different story. The most central products still appear toward the bottom of the lattice and the most central beliefs still appear toward the top. But in this case, these sets are almost empty. The novice applies no ideological beliefs to milk, sugar, and honey. Furthermore, at the bottom, four beliefs appear that the novice applies to no products. The most central products to which beliefs are applied are beef and chicken while the least central is fish. The novice only applies two beliefs to any of the products studied. The most central belief for this participant is "*is an animal product*," which is a highly obvious distinction to make among products. Furthermore, this novice only identifies beef, chicken, and fish as animal products (as contrasted with the expert who also placed milk and honey on this list), and only believes that beef and chicken support factory farming (as contrasted with the expert who also applied this belief to fish, milk, and sugar).

These two lattices provide insights into the motive power of ideological beliefs, how ideological beliefs are learned, and how the ideology organizes the world-views of its members. The expert found the logic of the belief system relevant to all of the products that were the subject of our inquiry, even products representing non-obvious cases of animal abuse such as honey. Perhaps as a result, the expert consumed none of these products. A glance at the participants-by-beliefs lattices for honey (Figure 15.3) and beef (Figure 15.4) suggests the generality of this expert's case. The novice applied relatively few ideological concepts to few products, and then only to the most obvious cases of animal abuse (beef, chicken, and fish). The novice viewed the ideology as irrelevant to milk, sugar, and honey. Perhaps as a result, the novice consumed all of the latter products. A glance at the honey lattice (Figure 15.3) and beef lattice (Figure 15.4) suggests that novices apply few beliefs to any but the more obvious exemplars. These lattices clearly suggest the motivating power of ideological beliefs on consumption behavior in the activist subculture.

The two vignettes also suggest insights into the social transmission of motives. Experts know the ideology. The ideology links consumption of animal products with cruelty and exploitation of animals, and thus motivates the experts to teach others about these links. The data suggest that experts may teach novices about the ideology's moral reasoning by first invoking the most prototypical cases. We would speculate that if activists were asked to rate the prototypicality of foods as examples of animal abuse, beef would emerge as the most prototypical example, followed by chicken and then fish. The lattices clearly suggest the ideological centrality of these products. They appear toward the base of the lattices, providing a grounding point for the greatest number of core beliefs, especially for experts. In fact, experts often indoctrinated novices using beef as the first example. Once novices applied the ideology to beef, a cognitive beachhead was established and they were taught the application of the same principles to other products, along with additional logic linking these products to animal abuse.

Participants-by-cliques membership lattice

Lattice analysis can also be used to understand the relations of individuals to social structure.

The data collected on social ties was used to perform a clique analysis. The analysis found that the activists' social structure consisted of many overlapping cliques. However, a social structure characterized by many overlapping cliques is often difficult to comprehend without the aid of lattice analysis. Figure 15.7 provides an easily grasped representation of the activists-by-cliques membership matrix based on lattice analysis. The cliques are labeled by capital letters A through H, and each person is a member of all cliques connected to his or her node via an ascending path. At the top, we see the activists involved in no cliques. At the bottom, we see the activists involved in the most cliques. These activists were virtually all experts (15, 27, 28) with the exception of activist 6, an intermediate. The downward containment structure of cliques and the upward containment structure of the participants revealed by this lattice are highly informative of the centrality of the bottommost actors in the social structure of the group. For example, cliques F and G can be seen to intersect in persons 32 and 15, cliques E and F in persons 30 and 15, but all three cliques only intersect in person 15. Thus, person 15, by lying "deep" within the participants-by-cliques lattice, provides a "link" among the members of three cliques. Furthermore, one can see from the lattice that persons 32 and 30 are not present in a clique unless person 15 is also present, but not the reverse. Similar conclusions hold for all four persons at the deepest level of the lattice, three of whom are experts. Recalling the persons-by-beliefs lattices for honey and beef, experts also tended to be at the bottom of these lattices because they viewed more of the beliefs in the ideology as relevant to their avoidance of honey and beef.

Combining insights from these two types of lattices, we can see the apparent power of ideology to create not only cognitive structure but to motivate social structure. In this subculture, the ideological structure motivates a hierarchical social structure because the ideology is (a) complex enough to be better learned by some than others, (b) places those who understand more in a position of moral superiority to those who understand less, and (c) requires those who know more to lead and teach those who know less. This hierarchical social structure, in turn, motivates transmission of the ideology to individual participants in a self-perpetuating social-cognitive cycle.

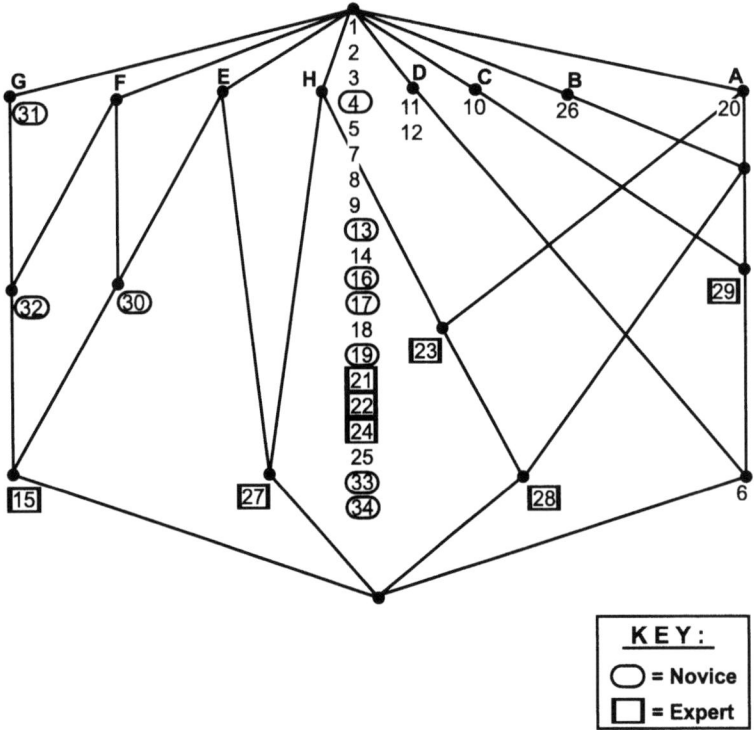

Figure 15.7 Participant-by-clique membership lattice.

Discussion

Lattice analysis seems a promising means of demystifying the relations of different kinds and levels of phenomena in the motivation of behavior. What could easily seem an impossible tangle of relations to the ethnographer or the quantitative analyst is, once captured in a lattice, apparently obvious. The three types of lattices produced for this chapter (the participants-by-beliefs lattices, the beliefs-by-products lattices, and the participants-by-cliques lattices) each summarized the complex relations between two different orders of phenomena into a simple and readily comprehensible diagram. In each case, the diagrams were productive of insights into how ideologies create and relate to the cognitive structures and social structures that motivated movement participants to avoid eating animal products. In combination, the lattices provided a comprehensive picture of the distribution of motivational forces at work in the subculture and how their workings interrelated.

The lattices provided deeper insight into the dual containment structures of our data than we might have gained by means-end analysis, correspondence analysis or traditional one-mode network analysis. The lattice diagrams of beliefs by participants for honey and beef provided, at a single glance, pictures of the distribution of motivating beliefs across participants, their implicational structure, and the cognitive containment structure of the individuals. These diagrams produced immediate insight into which beliefs were more structurally central in the subculture for motivating product avoidance, and which individuals were likely to supply the cognitive motives for avoidance to others through their deep embedding in the belief system. The participants-by-cliques lattice provided additional insight into how these expert participants bound together the many cliques within the group through their embeddedness in the social structure, and, thus, how they were in positions of both cognitive and social dominance. Finally, the food avoidances-by-beliefs lattices provided insight into the degree to which foods were central to or perhaps good exemplars of the belief system, prompting speculation about the role of ideologies in categorization processes.

Earlier, we suggested that our work would provide theoretical insight into how ideology motivates consumption. Theoretical advances in many disciplines often depend upon advances in the scholar's ability to visualize the phenomena under study. For example, the advance of early theory in biology depended on improvements in the microscope (Wilson 1995). In the present case, lattice analysis provided clear pictures of the relations among ideologically inspired reasoning, social structure, and behavior. These diagrams support our views of how ideologies organize both the cognitive structures of believers and the social structure of their group in ways that propagate the ideology itself. The expert participants in the activist subculture were deeply embedded in the social structure because (1) their cognitive containment of other participants gave them social power, and (2) they were more involved in the movement than others in part because of their greater knowledge of the ideology. Thus, cognitive and social embedding both occurred as a function of and in the service of ideology.

Lattice analysis can deepen insight into the relations among a broader range of phenomena than studied in this chapter. The n × m dimensions of input data to a lattice analysis might be possessions by consumption goals, emotions by consumption goals, or personality traits by consumption goals. Indeed, lattice analysis might produce insights into any circumstance where the consumer researcher is interested in the patterning of two phenomena, and in particular the patterning of their interrelations. As the analyses in this chapter demonstrated, lattice analysis is capable of revealing structural relations between two phenomena that might otherwise escape observation. Such discoveries can be potent motives themselves for further naturalistic or traditional inquiry, and also have important implications for the practice of marketing.

Consider, as an applied example, a marketer attempting to segment a database including information on consumers, their goals, and their purchases. As we saw with the participants-by-beliefs examples, lattice analysis is capable of revealing the relations between the containment structures of beliefs and the containment structure of subsets of people that could be important information to a marketer attempting to segment a market into subgroups with different motives. The lattice reveals the most commonly shared beliefs across the market, the specific beliefs that separate subsegments, and the implicational structure of these beliefs in a single diagram.

Gordon Allport (1955) suggests that "when we set out to study a person's motives, we are seeking to find out what that person is trying to do in this life, including what he is trying to avoid, and what he is trying to be" (p. 112). This quote reflects a broad perspective on the origins of motivation, a perspective that in spirit should take us beyond the behavioral laboratory and beyond the embrace of any one discipline. We may contrast the broad perspective many of the early scholars in psychology took on human behavior with the schism that arose not long ago between cognitive social psychologists and social psychologists with a motivational research orientation. Instead of studying the interaction of cognition and motivation, these two camps battled to explain which of these concepts better predicts human behavior (Sorrentino and Higgins 1986). In contrast to this divisive and atomistic dispute, we hope consumer researchers will take an integrative approach to the study of consumer motivation. Recognizing that conceptual advances in a field are often limited by the available methods of inquiry, we offer lattice analysis as a tool we hope will encourage an interdisciplinary perspective on motivation without sacrificing either mathematical rigor or summarizing away the intricate relations within and between phenomena that produce the lived motives of consumers.

References

Ajzen, I. and Fishbein, M. (1980) *Understanding Attitudes and Predicting Social Behavior*, Englewood Cliffs, NJ: Prentice-Hall.

Allport, G. (1955) *Becoming: Basic Condsiderations for a Psychology of Personality*, New Haven, CT: Yale University Press.

Birkhoff, G. (1967) *Lattice Theory*, 3rd edition, Providence, RI: American Mathematical Society Publications.

Freeman, L. and White, D. (1993) "Using Galois lattices to represent network data," in P. Mardsen (ed.) *Sociological Methodology*, Cambridge, MA: Blackwell: 127–46.

Ganter, B. (1987) "Algorithmen zur Formalen Begriffsanalyse," in Bernhard Ganter and Rudolf Wille (eds) *Beitraege zur Begriffsanalyse*, Zurich: Bibliographisches Instuit & F.A. Brockhaus AG Wissenschaftsverlag.

Gengler, C. and Reynolds, T. (1995) "Consumer understanding and advertising strategy: analysis and strategic translation of laddering data," *Journal of Advertising Research* 35 (4): 19–32.

Greenacre, M.J. (1989) "The Carroll–Green–Schaffer scaling in correspondence analysis: a theoretical and empirical appraisal," *Journal of Marketing Research* 26: 358–65.

Greenacre, M.J. (1984) *Theory and Applications of Correspondence Analysis*, London: Academic Press.

Hardin, C. and Higgins, E. (1986) "Shared reality: how social verification makes the subjective objective," in R. Sorrentino and E. Higgins (eds) *Handbook of Motivation and Cognition*, vol. 3, New York: Guilford Press: 28–67.

Hoffman, D. and Franke, G. (1986) "Correspondence analysis: graphical representation of categorical data in marketing research," *Journal of Marketing Research* 23 (August): 213–27.

O'Guinn, T. and Belk, R. (1989) "Heaven on earth: consumption at Heritage Village, USA," *Journal of Consumer Research* 16 (2): 227–38.

Sirsi, A., Ward, J.C., and Reingen, P.H. (1996) "Microcultural analysis of variation in sharing of causal reasoning about behavior," *Journal of Consumer Research* 22 (4): 345–72.

Sorrentino, R. and Higgins, E. (1986) *Handbook of Motivation and Cognition: Foundations of Social Behavior*, vol. I, New York: Guilford Press.

Vogt, F., Bliesener, J., and Viehmann, V. (1985) *DIAGRAM*, a DOS program for determining Galois lattices, Darmstadt, Germany: Arbeitsgruppe Begriffsanalyse, Technische Hochschule Darnstadt.

Ward, J.C. and Reingen, P.H. (1990) "Sociocognitive analysis of group decision making among consumers," *Journal of Consumer Research* 17 (3): 245–62.

Wille, R. (1982) "Restructuring lattice theory: an approach based on hierarchies of concepts," in I. Rival (ed.) *Ordered Sets*, Dordrecht, The Netherlands: D. Reidel.

Wille, R. (1989) "Lattices in data analysis: how to draw them with a computer," in Ivan Rival (ed.) *Algorithms and Order*, Dordrecht, The Netherlands: D. Reidel.

Wilson, C. (1995) *The Invisible World: Early Modern Philosophy and the Invention of the Microscope*, Princeton, NJ: Princeton University Press.

16 More than a rat, less than God, staying alive

Jerome B. Kernan

It is hardly necessary to justify a book about "why," a term that frustrates most everyone, from the callow child ("how come?") to the seasoned philosopher bent on understanding. And it is doubly unnecessary to apologize when the question pertains to consumption, given the consumer society in which we live, the sheer dominance of material culture at the dawn of the twenty-first century. "Why" is a complex term, implicating many others – as the editors of this volume note, it implies who, what, where, when, and how.

Once while traveling with my 4-year-old son we became stalled in traffic. When he asked me why we weren't moving, I retorted in frustration: "Because we're standing still." Accurate, perhaps, but not the explanation sought. My son expected me to tell him the cause of our delay and when it might be over; it was only his literal mindedness that justified my tautological response. But this book is not likely to be read by literal-minded people (much less 4 year olds), so it must offer more than truisms if its title is to be anything more than a come-on. I think that test has been passed. The chapters – focusing on perspective, domain, and method – contain much that is non-obvious and the editors summarize this material in their introductory chapter, where they tell us what the book says. My job as a commentator is to tell us what it means.

Be all that you can be

Over the centuries, personhood has been construed in a variety of ways by the behavioral sciences and humanities and by medicine, philosophy and religion. Metaphors have been used to portray abstruse phenomena such as the nature of being (Weiner 1992). These do not constitute explanations, but they afford us insight into the workings of unfamiliar phenomena (e.g. human motivation), based on our understanding of familiar ones (a self-regulating machine). So long as we do not take the comparisons literally (life is *not* a bowl of cherries, no matter how often the lyric is repeated), metaphors enable us to talk about very abstract things as though we understood them.

Metaphors give perspective, in the sense that they frame our perception of a phenomenon. For instance, we distinguish among *Homo sapiens, Homo faber,* and *Homo ludens* (Hirschman and Holbrook 1992 offer many more distinctions), and their varying implications about human nature and the character of our species. Similarly, to say that people are consumers or decision-makers or semioticians is to tell us not only what they are, but also how we should think about them. Metaphors provide points of view – right or wrong, agreeable or not – useful for portraying and "understanding" phenomena. So I interpret this volume's chapters through metaphors (those commonly engaged to account for consumption), in the hope that this trope gets us beyond the accumulation of empirical findings to their meaning.

With apologies to Procrustes, we can consider consumption according to three metaphors – people as machines, people as God, and people as *flaneurs*. The first two of these are well developed by Weiner (1992) and the third reflects my attempt to capture the postmodern mentality. Although these perspectives developed historically in the order listed (think of an instinctual–modernist–postmodernist progression), each remains vibrant and useful and no one of them accounts satisfactorily for everything about consumption. Generally, the machine metaphor (the "rat" in the chapter's title) refers to the physiological and genetic underpinnings of our behavior, parts of which are shared with animals. The God (more accurately, god-like) metaphor, a modernist conception, implicates knowledge and judgment and mind over matter, attributes which elevate humans above animals, but not to the level of a Supreme Being. And the *flaneur* (one of those strolling Parisian dilettantes bent on seeing and being seen) is used to suggest the communicative symbolism so prevalent in contemporary society's cosmo-politan eclecticism, where self-identity markers run rampant. John Travolta disco-danced to this metaphor in the 1977 hit film *Saturday Night Fever*, the soundtrack for which ("Staying Alive") made the Bee Gees famous.

The human condition is reflected in *each* of these metaphors. Consider: we claim superiority over animals, yet recognize that some of our hard-wired attributes are shared with them. Few humans claim to *be* God, yet most people are happy to assume they have been "created in that image." And it would be difficult to scare up even a small crowd of disco dancers (let alone a *flaneur*), yet everyone understands that "staying alive" impli-cates not morbidity, but the pulsing vitality and excitement of living. Thus, most of us regard ourselves as some amalgam of hard wiring (including our "dealt hand" of genetics), of reasoning and feeling (ideally, one hopes to be sensible and just, perhaps even temperate), and of *flanerie* (authenticating ourselves to ourselves and to others by means of complex signaling behaviors). Moreover, we work at developing all these facets of our being – in our natural ambition and over the course of maturation (Baltes, Staudinger, and Lindenberger 1999) we try to be all we can be. Explaining consumer behavior is anything but easy (Kernan 1995), so if only in the interest of dialectical thinking (Kahle, Liu, Rose, and Kim 2000) all three metaphoric perspectives should be consulted for insights. Indeed, it might be argued that the "why" of consumption represents not one, but three very different kinds of questions, depending on the metaphoric model assumed. Such an argument has profound implications.

More than a rat

The machine metaphor and its organic counterpart, the automaton, imply behavior that is based on bounded reflexes (responses to internal or external stimuli), rather than on consciously aware volition. This model fixes behavior as an instrumental act, a process that accomplishes a predetermined purpose in a predetermined way, such as relieving stress by slowing pace. Much human physiology is subsumed under this metaphor, as when we remark that the kidney is a wonderful machine, but the focus is hardly restricted to raw biology. Indeed, Weiner (1992) places Freudian theory, ethology (Lorenz), drive theory (Hull, Spence, Festinger), Lewin's field theory, Heider's balance theory, and Wilson's sociobiology under this rubric, since each of these is rooted in some machine-like property. All these theories posit that behavior is pre-determined by evolution and genetics, in some cases (e.g. reinforcement) abetted by learning. Yet few people cherish a construal of themselves as mindless machines (even efficient ones), so it is common to assert that we are more than "just a rat." We like to think we can effect what sociologists call *agency* (choice or options in our social actions), and this does not seem consistent with a hard-wired, stimulus–response model. Indeed, we like to think we can *think*, even though some of our behaviors appear to occur beyond consciousness, beyond our effective control.

Faber's chapter is the only one in this volume that reflects the machine metaphor (and at that, not totally). This is curious, given the broad scope of consumer behaviors over which this metaphor ranges. Considering the focus of the book (see the Huffman, Ratneshwar and Mick chapter), however, such skewness is understandable – emphasizing goals privileges cognition and one finds little of that in machine models. Moreover, we have come to expect imbalance among research foci (see Lehmann 1999) and everyone knows this is not the high season for mechanistic accounts of behavior.

The Faber essay on compulsive buying "belongs" as a machine model because, even though it is organized around uses-and-gratifications and is supported by qualitative interview data, its thrust in my opinion is psychoanalytic. That's what sets it apart from the other chapters in this volume – the notion of self-energizing, involuntary instrumental behavior, that people buy because they can't help themselves. Never mind that some of the causes are sociological and circumstantial, truly compulsive consumption is out-of-control behavior, not driven by reason (even by play), but by a "spectrum of psychiatric disorders." This is not an inconsequential conclusion in today's consumer society and we would do well to learn more about such maladies.

Less than God

If Darwin is to blame for affiliating us with the animal kingdom (although Leonardo is reputed to have remarked that man is a marvelously constructed machine), Descartes – with an unlikely assist from the Roman Church – should be credited with dissociating us from lower species. His famous "I think, therefore I am" punctuated the mood of the Enlightenment and set the stage for the mind/body problem that, even today, we call Cartesian dualism.

Since its early days, the Christian Church had a metaphysical problem concerning the distinction between the mortal human body and the immortal soul. The corporal flesh was seen as the site of weakness and transgression, while the soul shared supernatural properties with the Creator. Well enough, so long as the soul mediated the body. But if this arrangement did not hold, *all* earthly bodies were implicated and the Church would slip into the untenable position of holding even animals responsible for their behavior. So for very practical reasons (to say nothing of hegemony) animals could not have a soul. (Do not reveal this verity to young children when they inquire about their pets going to heaven.) The soul was used to distinguish humans from animals and this separation continues to reside at the root of asceticism.

But people are naturally curious (madding, in the extreme) and they began "looking" for the soul, in spite of early clerical pedantry (the soul is not corporal). Then the eighteenth-century Enlightenment served up the *mind*, which was purported to have properties remarkably well suited to the mediating function of the soul. "Close enough," we might imagine the Church's conclusion, "let's co-mingle the soul with the mind. And we can toss in this other troublesome thing, conscience." Descartes' forerunning notions of thinking and judging, of mastery, and of tolerance and beauty were well received. And why not, since this new construal lifted humankind from a brute to the master of all s/he surveyed? Similarly, it is not surprising that in the nineteenth century when Darwin reminded us of our commonalities with animals, he was widely dismissed as an agent of the devil. We have been clinging for a long time to the idea that we are mature, rational beings. Indeed, a contemporary Scopes trial would surprise no one, even were it to occur in one of the more populous states in the USA.

A large part of this book's contents reflects a god-like metaphor of consumption behavior. Goals are set by (emotional) people who think. Decision-makers choose, based on how they reason and feel. Beliefs are a matter of the mind. The litany goes on, one interesting chapter after another. There is no fault to find with them, only an observation to make. These papers – Huffman, Ratneshwar, and Mick on goals, Bagozzi, Baumgartner, Pieters, and Zeelenberg on emotions, Luce, Bettman, and Payne on emotional trade-offs, and Kardes and Cronley on belief change – are so *rational*. Of course they are supposed to be rational, given their metaphoric stance, but their models are so tidy, so rigid. For example, Huffman *et al.* proffer some profound ideas, yet their model (admittedly) excludes some of the more interesting forms of consumer behavior. Bagozzi *et al.* (also see Bagozzi and Dholakia 1999) summarize a plethora of literature, but we are left with the bewildering imperative that emotions (general or specific) might be experienced as a result of goal attainment or they might energize, which is to say precede, goal-directed behavior. Apparently, people set goals in order to achieve a feeling or because of how they feel already. (Now I understand why interviews of athletes always follow the same pop-psych script.) Luce *et al.* demonstrate how anticipated negative emotions complicate decision-making, as well as the importance of distinguishing how people respond to trade-off possibilities. (I could have saved them some time – always choose the car with the fastest 0–60 speed, so no high-school kid in a Mustang can embarrass you.) Kardes and Cronley, in a clever twist of the venerable Katz model, argue that beliefs implicate particular end-states and that these, in turn, implicate certain approach/avoidance tendencies. A nice, if somewhat mechanical, take on persuasion. (I wonder whether it applies to all those low-involvement cases where attitude change follows behavior change?)

The book's domain chapters (excepting Faber, treated above) also provoke a restrictive reaction. Warlop, Smeesters, and Vanden Abeele provide an elaborate architecture through which the motivation to recycle waste might be traced; yet they conclude that simple priming may be just as effective an inducement. (One can't resist referring them to the stunning methods chapter by Brownstein, Sirsi, Ward, and Reingen, where the origin of ethical imperatives might be seen to run deep in people's social and cultural structures. Perhaps a rotten lattice awaits cultivation – no genetic alteration necessary.) Cotte and Ratneshwar's chapter on timestyle is intriguing, but it has little to do with time, per se, except in the sense that anything we do takes time. I think these authors are too modest – self vs. others, past vs. present, one thing vs. many, and analytic vs. holistic are universal dichotomies which might be applied to most any facet of thought or action.

The two remaining methods chapters – Escalas and Bettman on narratives and Coulter and Zaltman on metaphors – treat topics that are philosophically neutral, but their presentations point them in a cognitive direction. For example, Escalas and Bettman (in a very comprehensive paper) focus on the *structural* properties of narratives in order to deduce how people organize themselves in a social world and represent personal events in time and space. From these "data" they infer informants' goals and motives. That is certainly interesting and useful, but isn't the content (the cant, the argot, the emic voice) of the narrative the high-assay part? Similarly, Coulter and Zaltman illustrate a very potent methodology, but only to the limited purpose of raising motives to the level of consciousness. (My dentist would love their chapter, but the ZMET procedure could reveal so much more about quotidian life for the rest of us.)

None of my remarks about these chapters should be taken as fault-finding. They are merely to highlight the overwhelmingly cognitive bent of the papers and their thinking, god-like, perspective. My comments reflect the state of consumer research at this juncture, and if lab smocks and video cameras ever become *de rigueur* in the halls of the world's management schools perhaps academic scholarship will feature a different silhouette. In the meantime, I wish we would attend more carefully to a couple of assumptions that seem implicit in cognitively oriented research. One of these is the notion that choice is (as Martha Stewart might put it) "a good thing." This truism likely derives from people's love of liberty, but some work by Iyengar and Lepper (1999) suggests that this may be a peculiarly Western preference. The other assumption relates to the primacy of self in thought and action. Following Gaertner, Sedikides, and Graetz (1999), we might be more particular about *which* sense of self is motivationally primary. Both these assumptions are important in the rational, god-like perspective of humankind, so it would be comforting to know that we have them right.

Staying alive

Those who have a philosophical quarrel with personhood depicted as rational, mind-centered, knowledgeable, and good (all god-like qualities), might be induced to consider the postmodern perspective, which pretty much rejects these attributes. The postmodern person, often depicted as a product of the information age, carries little of the modernist's angst baggage. S/he lives in a global, wired world, which has no past (once there was no TV?) and little future (life is beyond control), just constant change. Hierarchical markers (Oxbridge vs. redbrick schools) have given way to egalitarianism (anybody can go to any school, get any job, earn lots of money) and the traditional moral influences – religion, community, society – have been neutralized by skepticism and relativism (abetted, some argue, by media conglomerates). The postmodern person does not fret over mastery or success, yet knowledge of products is important. Morality isn't a matter of good and evil, it's just about responsibility (who made this mess?). Living, very much a present-tense concern, has to do with establishing and preserving one's identity in a fragmented world. There are two parts to this latter. First, each of us tries to individuate ourselves – to be different from everybody else. Second, we try to affiliate with certain groups or ideas (ethnic, cause-related, etc.; sometimes called "tribes" in postmodern writing). And the way we effect these self-serving things often-as-not is through consumer behaviors. That is the case because consumption is the privileged activity in a postmodern world – what a person has determines what s/he can do, and these two combine to define what the person "is." "Being" (establishing, maintaining, changing one's self) is the paramount enterprise for the postmodern person (Cassam 1999; Harre 1998), and it is to that end that much of our behavior is directed. Actions might serve utilitarian purposes, but it is their communicative potential to mark or symbolize us that accounts for their engagement (e.g. Gottdiener 1995).

All this seems a bit heathen (at a minimum, secular) to god-like modernists. Any perspective of human nature that allows for "celebration" (postmodernists love to celebrate), fun, even visceral pleasures is likely to strike puritanical modernists as suspicious, and there is little chance that they would mistake the book's four *flaneur*-like postmodern chapters for gospel readings. Beginning with Belk, Ger, and Askegaard's paper on desire ("a taboo word in consumer research"), each of these chapters speaks to a topic beyond the traditional pale. In a bit of irony, Belk *et al.* remind us that we have censored desire from the lexicon of our models, even though "to desire is to live, to hope, to enjoy life and its promises." Not to be outdone, Thompson observes that irony is just one of the things we should expect from postmodern consumption – look for paradox, parody, and playfulness, too. And the unexpected, since postmodern consumers are not predictable, even in the limited sense that modernist consumers are.

Arnould and Price show us how postmodern consumers create communal identity through "authoritative performances" and agency (self-identity) through "authenticating acts," in either case to locate themselves in today's fragmented world. Both these processes reflect acts of communicating, of signaling, and this in turn implies a focus, which usually is apparent (e.g. individuating via a unique hairstyle or community-oriented, perhaps by donning the garb of the hometown team), but which sometimes must be discovered. Identity enhancement requires an ideal, an aspiration, to guide one's behavior and such a focus is not always palpable. An example of this latter case is offered by Hirschman and Stern's chapter, which suggests that the mass media over the years have portrayed women in a mixed, dynamic fashion, such that audiences have had to discern which "message" (or combination of them, via *bricolage*) to read in order to select an appropriate focus for their ideal selves (also see Griswold 1993). One must choose carefully, lest an uncongenial identity be pursued. The only thing worse is being regarded as unsophisticated.

Tell me why (not)

Emerging from this tripartite classification, we recognize that consumers might be thought to behave like machines, like gods, even like *flaneurs*. So *why* they behave is really a mediated query – we must specify the language before asking how to spell a word. And we require many such spell checks because we need to speak several languages. At this writing cognition is the lingua franca of consumer research, but that will change. One day we may find ourselves uttering a metaphysical Esperanto, but in the meantime we should have the good sense to tap all the linguistic sources of understanding. We may not agree with some of postmodernism's politics, but the perspective should not be dismissed as irrelevant. Pomo language (admittedly dense to the uninitiated) is worth our best efforts to comprehend. At the other extreme, mechanistic models may seem primitive, even brutish, something our species has outgrown and therefore not relevant to present-day concerns. We should reconsider – there is nothing simplistic about things like genetic engineering and gene therapy. Perhaps most of all we should resist the complacency lurking in cognitive models because, in spite of their current dominance, these too will lose favor and we shall need a place to turn.

A theory of why seems as likely to emerge as physicists' proverbial theory of everything. It's not a burning issue, but in trying to critique, reconcile, even balance the chapters in this volume, I have wondered whether Morris Holbrook's construal of "value" might not contain most of the elements such a grand theory would require. He regards value as "an interactive relativistic preference experience," which means that our relationships with consumption experiences vary among people and change according to circumstance (Holbrook 1999: 9). The idea, of course, is that we consume in order to acquire value and one wonders whether that's not the same as explaining why we consume.

Holbrook gets beyond tautologies by arguing that value resides simultaneously in three dimensions – intrinsic/extrinsic, self-oriented/other-oriented, and active/reactive. These dimensions, in turn, are used to illustrate eight types or manifestations of value (e.g. efficiency, esteem, play), which look suspiciously like drivers of behavior. They apply almost without modification to (indeed, they virtually blanket) the three metaphoric construals discussed here. So in passing we might speculate whether Brother Holbrook's fecund imagination has opened yet another vein of understanding.

Let me conclude with a redundant point. The sensible way to regard the metaphoric construals presented here is as complements. We need to control our appetites, instincts, and obsessions and that begins by recognizing their origins as hard-wired. We need to develop our potential as humans, our ability to think straight, and our capacity to judge others fairly, and that takes a nurtured mind. Finally, even when it's done in a spirit of high cynicism, we need to realize ourselves, to find our place in the sun and to accord others their place, and those occasions require that we wear a hedonistic mask. If there can be a triune God, why not a tripartite consumer?

Acknowledgments

I thank the flu bug for relenting after felling me the second time, the weather god for dispatching the Y2K storms out to sea before they wrought even more devastation, and Dean Teresa Domzal for pretending this commentary was my only professional responsibility.

References

Bagozzi, R.P. and Dholakia, U. (1999) "Goal setting and goal striving in consumer behavior," *Journal of Marketing* 63: 19–32.

Baltes, P. B., Staudinger, U.M., and Lindenberger, U. (1999) "Lifespan psychology: theory and application to intellectual functioning," *Annual Review of Psychology* 50: 471–507.

Cassam, Q. (1999) *Self and World*, New York: Oxford University Press.

Gaertner, L., Sedikides, C., and Graetz, K. (1999) "In search of self-definition: motivational primacy of the individual self, motivational primacy of the collective self, or contextual primacy?" *Journal of Personality and Social Psychology* 76: 5–18.

Gottdiener, M. (1995) *Postmodern Semiotics*, Oxford: Blackwell.

Griswold, W. (1993) "Recent moves in the sociology of literature," *Annual Review of Sociology* 19: 455–67.

Harre, R. (1998) *The Singular Self*, London: Sage.

Hirschman, E.C. and Holbrook, M.B. (1992) *Postmodern Consumer Research*, Newbury Park, CA: Sage.

Holbrook, M.B. (1999) *Consumer Value: A Framework for Analysis and Research*, London: Routledge.

Iyengar, S.S. and Lepper, M.R. (1999) "Rethinking the value of choice: a cultural perspective on intrinsic motivation," *Journal of Personality and Social Psychology* 76: 349–66.

Kahle, L.R., Liu, R.R., Rose, G.M., and Kim, W. (2000). "Dialectical thinking in consumer decision making," *Journal of Consumer Psychology* 9: 53–8.

Kernan, J.B. (1995) "The interface of consumer cognition and motivation: desperately seeking Susan (or *anyone* who can organize this stuff)," in Frank R. Kardes and Mita Sujan (eds) *Advances in Consumer Research*, vol. 22, Provo, UT: Association for Consumer Research: 273–4.

Lehmann, D.R. (1999) "Consumer behavior and Y2K," *Journal of Marketing* 63: 14–18.

Weiner, B. (1992) *Human Motivation: Metaphors, Theories, and Research*, Newbury Park, CA: Sage.

17 Four questions about consumer motivation research

Dennis W. Rook

Early in my doctoral studies, I found myself strongly attracted to the work of Ernest Dichter, Burleigh Gardner, William Henry, Sidney Levy, and other consumer motivation researchers. Their deep, provocative, and sometimes controversial insights about why consumers think, feel, and behave in various ways struck me then as profoundly interesting and basic. Today, in my Consumer Behavior classes I explain on Day 1 the centrality of "why" questions in managerial research and decision-making, while simultaneously acknowledging how difficult such questions often are. The subsequent coursework leads students through activities that emphasize analytic diversity and creativity. My hope is that the class experience will encourage some young managers to approach marketing behavior "why" issues in more nuanced, original, and less drone-like ways. And I am frequently looking for new materials that will support this objective. Consequently, it has been a pleasure to read and comment on a volume that focuses so directly on consumption "whys." The chapters provide a rich yield of new and productively-recycled concepts that promise to reinvigorate our field's analyses of why consumers do what they do. Also, several chapters extensively detail innovative techniques and data sources for investigating goals, motivations and desires.

I have been asked to provide some commentary about this book, and advised by Ratti, Cindy and David to do "whatever I want." I just read an amusing critique of Powerpoint in Fortune, which made me think that I should conform to the contemporary corporate norm of getting your point across in three slides. Well, I'll pass, but I will keep it short. The authors included in this volume are prominent and influential scholars, and this should provide some momentum to the current resurgence of research interest in consumer motivation. Overall, the book is an excellent resource for researchers who seek to explore what I think is the mother lode of consumer behavior. Many chapters are intellectually grounded in quite particular theoretical and/or methodological paradigms. Rather than comment directly on each, I would like to provide a few more general comments on theory and method in motivation research, and suggest how the various chapters relate to the issues raised.

Where's the sex?

At the mid-point in my reading of these sixteen chapters, I noted the almost complete absence of any reference to libidinal, specifically sexual motivation. And I had self-selected chapters that I though might get my motor runnin'! The trend continued, and I'm forced to ask, "Where's the sex?" Human sexual behavior is prominent in the earliest theories of motivation; it also plays a huge and continuing role in most consumers' lives. One study reports the frequency with which adult males think about sex at six times per hour. Sexual thoughts, perhaps, encourage behavior, as the marketplace domain of sexually-motivated consumption is staggering in size, scope, reach, and growth.

The articles in this book are certainly not unique in their slight consideration of sexual dimensions in consumption behavior. As a field, academic consumer research demonstrates a general timidity about sexual topics, despite its proximity to "sex-and-marketing" sirens. A recent exception is Levy's (1996) *JCR* essay that elaborates a consumer "sensorium" in lyrical graphic detail. This sexual shyness is somewhat puzzling, as many consumer researchers today are marketing professors, and all are consumers! And it takes very little in either capacity to observe the daily, pervasive presence of sexual themes, promises, products, and services that are for sale 24–7. Presumably, the marketers of sexual lubricants, for example, need to get beyond individual managers' reluctance about sexual frankness, and get down to the real nitty-gritty. Fascinating case studies would emerge from investigating how such companies conceptualize and investigate the motivational lives of their consumers.

It seems to me that in numerous marketing situations, consumer research that explicitly includes sexual and sexually-related motivational factors would add a lot to the general field and, also, likely increase the interest-factor of published research. After all, sex in universally interesting and involving. The Belk, Ger, and Askegaard article's focus on desire comes closest to such an approach, and demonstrates persuasively the cross-cultural importance of consumer passion for products, particularly in comparison to more conventional attitudinal measures of motivation. Also, some research topics represented in this book seem ideal candidates for extensions that include sexual behavior and motivation variables. For example, Ron Faber's work on compulsive buying notes the fascinating phenomena of co-morbidity. This suggests to me that much might be learned by studying the buying behavior of sexual compulsives or, conversely, the sexual motivations and goals of compulsive buyers. One common characteristic of the articles in this book is some basic, guiding theoretical framework; throwing a little sex into the conceptual mix couldn't hurt.

How high the theory?

As a behavioral scientist, I understand and value the role of theory in both basic and applied research. That notwithstanding, over the past several years I've observed a tendency in published consumer research of increasing, often obfuscatory theoretical verbiage. At this year's ACR conference, I raised this concern with a few colleagues, one of whom responded, "Oh, you're talking about all the high theory." That struck a chord, and got me thinking. Ironically, much of the highest theory today comes from scholars who profess preferences for "grounded" theory. Not that these orientations are mutually exclusive; rather, it seems a question of balance, something which the Arnould and Price article achieves rather well. They use the higher-order constructs of "authenticating acts" and "authoritative performances" to discover a silver lining in the generally gloomy depictions of postmodern consumption. Still, I wonder if such a grand sounding concept as an "authenticating experience" leads subtly to a focus on extraordinary rather than everyday events. And, revisiting my earlier point, isn't sexual consumption behavior replete with authenticating and authoritative elements?

The Huffman, Ratneshwar, and Mick article included here actually deals with this issue directly by offering a conceptual model that incorporates six different levels of abstraction of consumer goals. Such a model helps link mundane product feature preferences to higher-order themes and values. I'm certainly not arguing for the theoretical dumbing down of consumer research. On the other hand, I fully agree with Bill Wells' (1993) viewpoint about the discovery-potential of research that relies on small "t" theory, and which "starts small" and "stays real." Also, I've read and reviewed too many articles that involve creative investigations of novel, interesting topics, but which are weighed down literally and intellectually by immense theoretical superstructures that obscure as much as they illuminate. Regrettably, I don't have any easy answers here, although I think the concept of "grounded" theory is ripe for reconsideration and unbundling. More generally, the level of abstraction that a particular research employs has non-trivial audience and communication implications. On the other hand, maybe we're dealing to some extent with aesthetic preferences. In religion, consumers' orientations range from Zen-like simplicity to High Catholic elaboration. Consumer researchers have aesthetic preferences, too, and I guess I've expressed mine for mid-century modern: simple and functional.

What's important?

The foregoing ambivalent grumbling aside, the articles in this book share and reflect Luce, Bettman, and Payne's notion that consumer research should focus on "more consequential decision contexts." The chapters cluster into several topic domains that are intellectually and substantively important. A number help extend work in the recently revived area of emotional consumption. The Belk *et al.* article introduces the construct of "desire" as a vehicle for deeper understanding of consumption motivation and fantasy. Luce *et al.* report from a research program investigating how emotional factors affect consumers' decision behavior. Somewhat more broadly, Bagozzi *et al.* propose a general framework for conceptualizing the role of emotions in goal-directed consumer behavior. Finally, Faber's work on compulsive buying provides a compelling context for studying emotional factors in consumption.

A second important topic involves a fresh look at approach/avoidance theory, offered by Kardes and Cronley. They provide an intriguing framework that links variation in the functional aspects of mental beliefs to actual behavioral response differences. A newer topic, consumers' "time-styles," is addressed by Cotte and Ratneshwar. Temporal orientation strikes me as under-researched area with much potential for understanding how consumers make time usage decisions, and how numerous factors influence their approach and choice proclivities.

I doubt that I'm alone in expressing some uncertainty regarding what all the fuss about "postmodernism" is really all about, and I'm grateful that two chapters in this book have helped lift my veil of ignorance. Early on, much discussion of postmodern consumers and consumption struck me as too negative in interpretation. In their discussion of "authenticating acts" and "authoritative performances," Arnould and Price depict more positive, constructive, and dynamic aspects of postmodern consumers' ontological angst. Thompson's review of postmodern principles provides more than a "postmodernism for dummies" summary. It is wickedly amusing, wonderfully detailed, kind of hip hop, bitchy, and very Stephen Brown in spirit. Finally, the vast majority of consumer research assumes that consumers know why they do what they do, more or less. I think less, and the Coulter and Zaltman article shares my bias. They take on the historically controversial topic of unconscious motivation, and explain how metaphor elicitation provides access to more primary thinking involving images, archetypes, impulses, and fantasy.

What's "in depth?"

This may be the hardest question of all. Motivation, historically, is conceptualized as multidimensional, sensitive, and only partially conscious. This has sobering implications for how researchers study it. Although I am methodologically catholic, some research approaches are inherently, or at least out-of-the-gate, better suited for capturing the breadth and depth of consumption motivation. And I am skeptical about the capabilities of poorly designed surveys and focus groups to deliver the goods. Gathering fixed-format responses to lists of motives and goals, in serious, unnaturally sterile settings raises similar validity and effectiveness concerns. Several chapters in this book offer innovative and more promising approaches.

The Coulter and Zaltman article builds on the use of in-depth interviews and projective techniques. Significantly, the authors argue explicitly for the need to explore unconscious aspects of motivation, and they illustrate the use of elicited metaphors in providing access to consumers' underlying ideation. Hirschman and Stern approach the issue of depth from a different perspective, relying on cultural products, in this case motion pictures, as a data source that reveals the evolving roles and images of American women. An advantage of this technique is its unobtrusiveness, which is particularly valuable in research contexts where consumers may be both unwilling and unable to explain their motivation and behavior. Simplicity and depth are not mutually exclusive, and the lattice output of Brownstein *et al.* provides an integrative visual model of the cognitive and social structures that motivate particular behaviors. Their analytic framework evokes the old notion that sometimes a picture is worth a thousand words. Escales and Bettman demonstrate a similar interest in structural analysis, and argue that deconstruction of consumer narratives will enhance research that typically rely on analyses of narrative content alone.

Arguably, more depth in consumer research is a trend, but what exactly "depth" means remains relatively fuzzy. Certainly, it is not simply related to the length of an interview or the depth of field note transcripts. Rather, I think the issue centers around the depth of interpretation and understanding a particular study achieves. As a field, we tend to have strong views about mapping linkages between data, findings, and conclusions. Such views generally conform to hypothetic-deductive paradigms, but this perspective typically fails to accommodate the reality of researchers' subjective analytic illuminations that go "beyond the data." To hardcore empiricists, this is a mortal sin; to others, it represents "getting it," and crossing the border into a new place. I think we should be less anxious and angry about how individual researchers get there. No matter how much data we have, how long the interviews, how extensive the transcripts, analytic depth won't jump out of the "thick" cake. Close encounters with consumers don't necessarily require extensive engagement; sometimes, it just takes a wink.

In conclusion, a reading of this book makes it clear that consumer motivation remains a rich domain for theory development and research, just as it was fifty years ago at the height of the so-called "motivation research" era. The individual contributions included here provide many different directions that should assist current and prospective researchers. Also, I hope that researchers might conceptualize motivation issues and topics with more attention to their sexual dimensions, construct simpler and less abstract theoretical models, stay focused on things that are important to consumers, and approach their research with more methodological creativity and tolerance. Finally, let me egocentrically recommend theoretical and methodological source material (1999) that has guided my thinking on these matters.

References

Levy, S.J. (1999) *Brands, Consumers, Symbols, and Research: Sidney J. Levy on Marketing*, ed. Dennis W. Rook, Thousand Oaks, CA: Sage.

—— (1996) "Stalking the Amphisbena," *Journal of Consumer Research* 23 (3) (December): 163–7.

Wells, W.D. (1993) "Discovery-oriented consumer research," *Journal of Consumer Research* 19 (l) (March): 489–502.

Index

Printed in Great Britain
by Amazon